Unearthing the Family of Alexander the Great

Unearthing the Family of Alexander the Great

The Remarkable Discovery of the Royal Tombs of Macedon

David Grant

First published in Great Britain in 2019 by
Pen & Sword History
An imprint of
Pen & Sword Books Ltd
Yorkshire – Philadelphia

Copyright © David Grant 2019

ISBN 978 1 52676 343 3

The right of David Grant to be identified as Author
of this work has been asserted by him in accordance
with the Copyright, Designs and Patents Act 1988.

A CIP catalogue record for this book is
available from the British Library.

All rights reserved. No part of this book may be reproduced or transmitted in
any form or by any means, electronic or mechanical including photocopying,
recording or by any information storage and retrieval system, without
permission from the Publisher in writing.

Typeset in 10.5/13 Ehrhardt by Vman Infotech Pvt. Ltd.
Printed and bound in the UK by TJ International Ltd, Padstow, Cornwall.

Pen & Sword Books Limited incorporates the imprints of Atlas, Archaeology,
Aviation, Discovery, Family History, Fiction, History, Maritime, Military,
Military Classics, Politics, Select, Transport, True Crime, Air World,
Frontline Publishing, Leo Cooper, Remember When, Seaforth Publishing,
The Praetorian Press, Wharncliffe Local History, Wharncliffe Transport,
Wharncliffe True Crime and White Owl.

For a complete list of Pen & Sword titles please contact

PEN & SWORD BOOKS LIMITED
47 Church Street, Barnsley, South Yorkshire, S70 2AS, England
E-mail: enquiries@pen-and-sword.co.uk
Website: www.pen-and-sword.co.uk

Or

PEN AND SWORD BOOKS
1950 Lawrence Rd, Havertown, PA 19083, USA
E-mail: Uspen-and-sword@casematepublishers.com
Website: www.penandswordbooks.com

Contents

Foreword vii

Chapter 1:   The Day of Archangels 1
Chapter 2:   A Meeting of Controversies 5
Chapter 3:   How a Kingdom May Rise and Fall and Vanish 11
Chapter 4:   A Phoenix Rises from the Ashes 37
Chapter 5:   The Scientist's Elation and the Desecrator's Guilt 43
Chapter 6:   Of Scythians and Amazons 63
Chapter 7:   The First War of Women 77
Chapter 8:   The Battle of the Bones 93
Chapter 9:   Bones Don't Lie! 123
Chapter 10:   Orphic Masks and Burial Rituals 143
Chapter 11:   Entering the Chthonic Debate 161
Chapter 12:   Finding Material Witnesses 173
Chapter 13:   Afterlife in Amphipolis 193
Chapter 14:   The Queen's Gold and the King's Craftsmen 205
Chapter 15:   Warrior Father, Warrior Daughter and the Bactrian 221
Chapter 16:   Preparing to Gene-Tag the Royals 245
Chapter 17:   The Little Summer of Saint Demetrius 263

Postscript 277
Notes 279
Bibliography 321
Index 333

Foreword

> When a nation forgets where it came from,
> it no longer knows where it is going.
> —Author

On an undisclosed autumn day in October 336 BC, King Philip II of Macedon was assassinated at the city of Aegae, the nation's ancient capital and the burial ground of its kings. It was a world-shaking event that heralded in the reign of his son, Alexander the Great, whose decade-long campaign in Persia changed the course of history. Although Alexander died in Babylon at the tender age of 32, the complex intermarriages between the dynasties established by the brilliant generals he campaigned with ensured Macedonian successors dominated the Graeco-Persian world for generations. But following its defeat by Rome, Macedon's legacy and its cities were gradually forgotten in the rolling hills and valleys of what is now northern Greece.

This is a unique account of rediscovery which unearthed the very heart of the ancient kingdom that rose to unparalleled heights and then sank to anonymous depths. It is a story of a royal family that indelibly stamped its identity on history's pages, recalling their lives, deaths, toils, triumphs and tragedies; the adage, 'archaeologists are digging up, not *things*, but *people*', was never so relevantly spoken as here.

This is equally a testament to the forensic work being undertaken to bring the Macedonian royalty back to life by a dedicated team of anthropologists, archaeologists, geneticists, material scientists and historians, who together, like stonemasons chiselling rough-hewn evidence into a statuesque form, are bringing this remarkable investigation to life.

The excavations at the modern town of Vergina, now identified with ancient Aegae, presented as many questions as they once yielded answers, when only faint whispers from the inhabitants of the tombs could be heard from intriguing clues found inside. Fortunately, advances in forensic sciences and a greater scrutiny in employing them are finally enabling the gold and silver, the paintings and papyrus, and the ancient bones to speak.

This book is dedicated to Professor Theodore Antikas, Laura Wynn-Antikas and the team about them, who, following the decades of work by earlier archaeologists, are attempting to identify and reunite the 'lost' family of Alexander the Great with the nation's first city and its royal tombs.

Chapter 1

The Day of Archangels

Patience is bitter, but its fruit is sweet.
—Aristotle

It was 8 November 1977, Archangels Day in Greece. Professor Manolis Andronikos, head of the archaeological excavations at the town of Vergina, looked about him at the dignitaries, police, priests and a gathering tribe of archaeologists descending upon the burial ground of the ancient city of still-debated identity he had been slowly unearthing for years. It was late in the excavation season and Andronikos had been planning to wrap up the year's dig, with funds only available for a few more days of work.[1] But now television cameras were arriving, tensions were high, and the weather was unseasonably mild and, thankfully, dry. He wondered what the day would reveal as he anxiously lit another cigarette.

The determined excavator was standing in what was left of the 'Great Tumulus', as the conspicuous man-made hill overlooking the town had been lately named. It was a mound that had defied him since 1962 when the first exploratory trenches were dug into the 100-metre-wide perimeter of soil and stone that has been compacted 12-metres high.[2] But not until the spring of 1977 had sufficient funding and political support become available for a full-scale investigation of the tumulus, which was by now covered in 20-year-old pines.

Andronikos had logically assumed that its major secret lay under the hill's hardest-to-excavate apex, where a hollow crater suggested the collapse of a significant structure below, when he and his colleagues, Professors Stella Drougou and Chrysoula Paliadeli, had begun probing the soil there in the late-August heat. Early exploratory trenches penetrated 8 metres down but still without results; the shallow crater at the summit turned out to be a time-consuming red herring and the disappointment of finding nothing more than virgin soil and scattered broken gravestones weighed heavy on the team. With no sign of construction or human activity below, they were beginning to wonder if the tumulus was a barren folly, and if it *did* hold subterranean secrets from antiquity, whoever buried them was outwitting modern archaeology.

Five new trial trenches were carved out, and over the next thirty-five days 18,000 cubic metres of earth were removed until a different soil texture told the excavators they had reached ancient ground level. But no structures were found; any tombs hidden by the tumulus must lie *below* the original terrain.

Manolis Andronikos was in the process of preparing an access ramp for the following season's dig when he noted yet another change in the colour of the earth. The distribution of this redder soil, similar to that in the smaller mounds running across the adjacent cemetery, suggested an older and smaller tumulus originally stood under what was now the south-west perimeter of the great hill, so all efforts were concentrated there. Professor Drougou was studying the unearthed pottery and she immediately dated the sherds and bowls that lay about in hollows to the last quarter of the fourth century BC;[3] here the charred remains of small animals suggested some form of burial ritual had been performed. A crudely constructed wall of unfired bricks was next encountered, but still it did not appear to be part of a recognizable structure.

On 11 October, the team finally revealed the foundations of a once free-standing building which appeared to have been destroyed and looted in antiquity. A second oblong box-like tomb lay beside it, below ancient ground level, with a stone slab missing from its roof; the soil heaped inside made it clear that it had also been opened and pillaged. Further into the mound, they slowly unearthed a stone facade which stood proud of a larger and more ornate building, and the importance of what lay below was betrayed by a remarkable hunting-scene painting above the entrance. The presence of protective limestone slabs holding back the weight of soil suggested that the sturdy marble doors beyond were still sealed. Andronikos' pulse started racing.[4]

Greece was in the grip of election fever, the second democratic ballot to be held in seven years following an earlier dictatorship, but the nation was about to have its attention divided between politics and tombs. Manolis Andronikos had been excavating at Vergina for over twenty-five years on never-sufficient funds and with dwindling hope of finding an intact grave, work sobered by the fact that fifty of the fifty-one tombs already discovered in ancient Macedon had been robbed.[5] But on that day the Olympian Gods smiled down. Each year on 8 November, the Greek Orthodox Church recognizes the feast of the Archangels Michael and Gabriel in a celebration of the sobriety and unity of the angelic powers; this was the day chosen for the first opening of the structure labelled 'Tomb II'.

The heavy marble entrance doors were wedged closed under a warped stone lintel, and not trusting the ancient hinges, Andronikos adopted the method of the tomb robbers of old: he had the keystone from the rear of the vaulted roof removed, on this occasion by technicians from the Restoration Service of the Museum of Thessalonica.[6] Andronikos was carefully lowered into a 5-metre-deep gloom cut by the first shafts of light in 2,300 years. Suspended on an ungrounded ladder, he slowly peered around him and then up with disappointment at the roughly plastered and undecorated walls of a square chamber measuring some 4.5 metres on each side.

A conservator was roped down and a clearing was found where the ladder could be grounded; they finally stepped onto the tomb floor. With security in mind and wishing to keep whatever the tomb contained undisclosed for the time being, Andronikos and the conservator, along with a member of the archaeological team, had the keystone replaced above them; the three were immersed in a black, sepulchral silence.[7] Andronikos shone his torch about the chamber until the beam fell upon an ancient object standing in one corner. And then his breathing stopped.

It was convention to conduct a thorough analysis of a site and its artefacts before a discovery as momentous as this was made public. Although Andronikos had tried to remain 'cool, calm and collected in order to live up to the responsibilities of the situation' as he emerged from the tomb, following the tenets of his mentor, the archaeologist Konstantine Rhomaios, he felt the discovery demanded more than 'a single, solemn announcement' to the world.[8] He called for a press conference in Thessalonica, but he first informed the President of the Republic and the newly re-elected Prime Minister of Greece, Konstantine Karamanlis.[9] Dignitaries, politicians, historians, archaeologists and those sufficiently aware of the gravitas of the find were soon descending upon the hillside village of Vergina.

Ancient Macedon was finally yielding up its secrets to a world no less fractured by politics and war than the nation Philip and his son Alexander had left behind them. And for a brief moment, when standing apart from his colleagues after they ascended from the crypt, Manolis Andronikos inhaled the very essence of the day of the ancient burials, without revealing to anyone else what he had just witnessed inside.

Chapter 2

A Meeting of Controversies

> The life of the dead is set in the memory of the living.
> —Cicero

30 January 2017

Moments before the plane descended into the low cloud that shrouded Thessalonica, I was dazzled by the rugged snow-capped peaks that separated north-western Greece from Albania, or, in another age, divided the cantons of ancient Macedon from the neighbouring kingdom of Epirus. It was the last sun I was to see on this journey, but not the last snow on a day when heaven and earth seemed to converge on the windscreen of my car. I drove through the unfinished network of concrete overpasses and new ring roads that catapult you out of the city and headed south-west towards the Thermaic Gulf, whose marshes were malaria-ridden until the last century. On the fog-bound horizon, I could just make out the hills at the foot of the Pierian mountains that still cradle ancient secrets in the modern village of Vergina.

I had unknowingly landed in the middle of a nationwide strike which had become a regular calendar event; the day was witness to the chaotic closing of highways by a legion of farmers' tractors in protest at pension reforms and other austerity measures to prop up the beleaguered economy. Mandatory detours confounded my GPS and sent me towards the inland ranges that back-dropped Veria, a settlement first mentioned by the Greek historian Thucydides in his history of the Peloponnesian War.[1] With the navigation system barking in one ear like a frustrated Balkan dictator, and the traffic police bellowing diversions in the other, I swung south over the once gold-rich Haliacmon River and its new hydroelectric dam, a torrent that in centuries past cut off entire communities when its waters were swollen.

Mist still shrouded the adjacent hills and snow clung precariously to sunless slopes; what should have been a one-hour journey had taken almost three-and-a-half hours. A piercing wind was rolling off the mountains as I parked, and it was now 3.35 pm. I knew the Vergina museum was due to close at 5.00 pm, so I pulled my jacket tight around my shoulders, purchased a ticket and quickly headed to the entrance and down into the bowels of the earth.

Although this was my first visit to the archaeological site, I was familiar with the museum's layout, contents and exhibits, as well as their history and provenance, because the reign of Alexander the Great and his family started and ended rather tragically here at the ancient royal necropolis. But I had little time to let my thoughts drift through the gloom of the eerie catacomb, made more otherworldly by the fact that I was the last remaining visitor on this short winter day. I darted between the tombs to better gauge their relative positions, because this had been difficult to fathom from the few research papers and pictorials that had been published; each structure, I knew, still guarded a particular secret and a deep historical conundrum.

A security guard became suspicious and tracked me all the while to make sure flashes were not going off, because photography is strictly forbidden. I made mental notes, I listed questions in my head and vowed to come back in better weather to tramp the aboveground ruins of the cemetery, the palace with its close-by theatre and the city walls that sprawl towards the neighbouring town of Palatitsia, a reminder of the vastness of the former capital of Macedon.

When I emerged into the late-January twilight, heavy iron doors were swung closed and bolted behind me; I had lingered rather longer than the museum staff had hoped. Then I realized I would be late for my meeting with Professor Theodore Antikas and Laura Wynn-Antikas, the anthropologists who, for the past eight years, had been analyzing the bones from Tomb II, now dubbed the 'Tomb of Philip II'. I had many questions for them; a few of them obscure, some more fundamental and others that might prove uncomfortable, but I judged my first had to be: 'how does it feel to be holding the remains of the family of Alexander the Great?'

On Theo's advice, I took the inland route from Vergina through the Pierian hills and its scattered villages to meet up with the southbound highway. The road was almost deserted as I wound my way past Palatitsia, Meliki and southeast through the white houses and orange-tiled roofs of Neokastro, Livadi and Paliampela. I arrived in Makrygialos at 6.45 pm and made my way to one of the only two open tavernas on the grey, windswept seafront, and after dialling the number I had been given, I heard the warm familiar voice of Theo in tones of comfortably ageing leather.

'*Kalispera* David, you were supposed to be here yesterday, no?'

'No Theo, I was stuck in Berlin yesterday and rescheduled for today.'

'No matter, welcome to ancient Pydna; why they stupidly renamed it "Makrygialos" I have no idea. Laura will drive down to collect you. You can't miss her: she is a redhead amongst Greeks.'

Apparently, in 1923, the bishop of the nearby new town of Kitros suggested the new name for its neighbour: 'Makrygialos', meaning 'long beach', though Theo is raising support to have the decision reversed. That might prove tricky, because Kitros has since staked its own claim to be the site of the ancient city of Pydna where famed sieges and the final battle between Macedon and Rome took place.

I had not yet met Laura, a Californian by birth but of clearly Celtic descent, and I had only spoken to Theo once in person when he was visiting his son in England the previous Christmas. I quickly downed the small aperitif I believed I deserved for getting there at all in the face of the strike, sleet, roadblocks and a petulant GPS, and I tried to settle up with the taverna owner, who politely refused payment; he and Theo, it transpired, watch their favourite football team there.

Laura arrived like a highly charged battery of anthropological discovery and osteoarchaeological frustration. By her own admission, she doesn't like ruins, tombs or bones that refuse to give up their secrets. She greeted me warmly, but with more than a glance of forensic curiosity and suspicion as we jumped in her compact four-by-four.

'Hammond used to stay there,' she told me, pointing at the modest and now-empty hotel at the southern end of the harbour. I looked across the bay where flamingos were stealing themselves against the breeze and the whitecaps, and to the faded pink building beyond, whose walls appeared void of their former romance. I knew, as did any historian of the era of Alexander the Great, that it was the British scholar, Professor Nicholas Hammond, the Professor Emeritus of Greek at Bristol and later the University of Cambridge, who voiced the 'heretical' idea that Vergina *was*, in fact, the ancient city of Aegae, the long-lost first capital of Macedon.[2] That was at the First International Symposium of Ancient Macedonia held in 1968, and time proved Hammond correct.

The evening commenced besides a blazing hearth at the home of Theo and Laura, with thick slabs of semi-soft cheese from the Peloponnese and a rapid fire of questions. I handed her one of the first off-the-press copies of my technical treatise on Alexander, which opened and closed, not by coincidence, with the Vergina excavations. She began to read, while Theo and I took a more meandering path through the subject that first drew us together by correspondence nine years before. I noted Laura's enthusiastic head nodding and some occasional questioning stares as yellow marker tabs began entering my pages.

I settled besides the crackling logs and grazed on olives harvested from their own grove until Theo announced they were taking me back down to the seafront for a more formal dinner. The restaurant appeared closed to the unknowing eye, but we managed to nestle besides the warmth of an even larger open fireplace. As I roamed through the menu, Theo informed me that Makrygialos is the mussel capital of Greece, and sure enough, '*mydia yiachni*', Macedonian mussel stew, appeared with an assortment of regional dishes reverently set down by the restaurant owner, Athena.

This was not a meeting without risk; I was an Englishman appropriating Macedonian history from under their noses by proposing an alternative identity for the cremated bones found in the antechamber of the tomb Andronikos first entered in 1977. By doing so, I was aware that I was undermining the opinion of Theo and Laura, and one that was widely upheld by other scholars, with Nicholas Hammond and Manolis Andronikos among them.

Theo had published over 240 research articles and twenty-one books on aspects of Greek and Roman history, the ancient and modern Olympics, as well as papers on anatomy, archaeozoology and unique insights into the equine world. I, on the other hand, had just completed one, and it was an imbalance I was acutely aware of. But as far as the Vergina tombs were concerned, we shared an overriding goal: the search for the truth amidst decades of misleading identity claims. 'Bones don't lie,' Theo assured me earnestly when describing the scrutiny with which they had analyzed the skeletal remains from the unlooted Tomb II.

That evening the atmosphere was uplifting and Theo's favourite day of the year was just a sunrise away. In the Balkans, 1 February is the day of Saint Tryphon, the patron of wine growers, when pruning starts and estate owners sprinkle their vineyards with the yield from their own grapes; more than a little of the propitious offering is left over for immediate consumption.

In reverence to Tryphon, we emptied the carafe of local young wine from the cellar of Adamos in nearby Kitros, while discussing the trials, tribulations and frustrations of their past eight years of research. We pondered improbable possibilities and equally vexatious just-possible improbabilities from every angle when mentally re-excavating the tombs. And it was by the fragrant olivewood glow of the candlelit taverna, and not in the archaeological museum of ancient Aegae or the academic papers I had waded through during the previous decade, that we truly began the journey of re-enacting the lives and deaths and names of the occupants of the tombs.

When departing Vergina earlier in the day, I had been deeply affected by what I encountered beneath the reconstructed tumulus that covers the archaeological museum, and as I headed through the countryside I found myself pondering the mighty upheavals in the history of Macedon that made these grave relics such poignant echoes of its past. The overriding emotion was frustration at their continued anonymity and silence, and at how a mighty nation vanished into the ground for over two millennia. I was also shocked at how sparsely inhabited and little developed the inland region appeared when driving south-east from Vergina through the Pierian hills; this was once the dynamic heartland of ancient Macedon, where Philip II and Alexander had conscripted and drilled their infantry brigades and cavalry regiments to conquer Greece and the Persian Empire.

Laura must have read my mind. She painted a picture of the once-vibrant ancient city of Pydna, with the ships coming to the port, and the hustle and bustle of a province whose population was thought to be in the hundreds of thousands then; now there are only 1,200 residents in Makrygialos, she told me. I found it counter-intuitive to imagine that some 2,200 years ago, before the Romans marched on the city, it was such a populous metropolis eclipsing its importance today.

But then I recalled the earlier cataclysmic period in the history of the region: around 1200 BC, the mysterious 'Sea Peoples', as historians refer to a still-unidentified confederation of invaders, swept through the Eastern Mediterranean and left great cities in ruins. This marked the collapse of the Bronze Age, and with it Mycenaean civilization in Greece. Somewhere in the 'magnificent obscurity' which fuels the imagination of historians who have largely pieced the story together by diagnosing pottery and the signs of destruction, there were great population upheavals, leaving us semi-mythical accounts of migrations, invasions and exoduses by tribes of Dorians, Achaeans, Aeolians and Ionians, whose date, origin and purpose remain the stuff of speculation.[3]

Whether famine and civil strife stemming from a plague – as Homer's *Iliad* might suggest – or the result of the invaders from overseas, there followed a Greek 'Dark Age', during which the population of the Peloponnese is thought to have declined by 75 per cent.[4] What finally emerged from the illiterate darkness, which symbolically ended with the first documented Olympic Games in 776 BC, was a very different archaic society that gradually coalesced into the Greek city-states. There followed the triumphs of the Classical Age and the evolution of democracy, which was terminated by the reigns of Philip II and Alexander the Great.[5]

Alexander's death in Babylon in 323 BC heralded a new world order that marked the beginning of the 'Hellenistic era', when Greek culture was fused to Macedonian military might, spreading its customs, trade, settlers and a 'common' form of the Greek language through the Eastern Mediterranean and former provinces of the Persian Empire. But the story of Alexander's successors could equally be considered as one extended tragedy, leading to the eventual break-up of the Graeco-Macedonian world, through civil war, dynastic war, by Rome's ever-lengthening shadow in the West and Eurasian invasions from the East. In the chaos, libraries burned, city walls fell and citadels were stormed. When Rome marched on the state capital of Macedon and its burials grounds, the nation fell into a 2,000-year-long silence.

One of the tragic outcomes was the wholesale loss of literature from the period. The accounts we read today were compiled by non-contemporary writers centuries removed from the long-lost memoirs of generals and philosophers who fought and campaigned with Philip and Alexander. More often than not, they were the output of philosophers, antiquarians, poets, politicians and propaganda pamphleteers whose agendas give us conflicting testimony dipped in rumour and hearsay. 'Truth is, after all, the first casualty of war,' the Athenian tragedian Aeschylus sagely warned.

As a result, the history of ancient Macedon is one painted in *sfumato*: blurred, faint and uncertain at the edges, leaving scholars to join the scattered dots of evidence in the hope that images will appear. This is why making the Vergina tombs speak of their past seemed such an important quest.

Chapter 3

How a Kingdom May Rise and Fall and Vanish

Now sit in the hall and feast, and take pleasure in ancient stories.
—Homer, *Odyssey*[1]

808 BC

In a late-Roman-era text that drew from an even older Latin manuscript of a once-voluminous history now lost to time, an otherwise unknown writer named Justin narrated one of the founding tales of Macedon.[2] He claimed that in the shrouds and folds of a more languid and malleable time when myth and men coexisted, Caranus, the son of King Temenus of Argos, migrated north from the Peloponnese, planning to establish a new kingdom and avoid further bloodshed with brothers vying for the Argive throne.[3]

On his journey, Caranus visited the ancient oracle at Delphi and in time-honoured fashion solicited advice from the entranced priestess perched high upon an iron tripod. The Pythia was gifted with visions of the future through her connection with Apollo, but her oracular replies were notoriously ambiguous and often given in verse, so obliging priests were on hand to interpret them for a not-unsubstantial fee. The hallucinogenic vapours rising from the chasm below the inner sanctum at Delphi are said to have added to the prophetic intrigue of the accompanying indecipherable gibberish she uttered, but on this occasion some clear direction was provided to the Argive prince.[4] Caranus was handed an uplifting prophesy about the charmed land to the north known as 'Emathia': 'You should find your kingdom there and it will be teeming with game and other domestic animals.'[5]

Caranus departed Argos with a mobile city of men, women, slaves, children and chattels in wagons pulled by ponderous beasts of burden. They threaded their way north through the valleys, mountains and precipitously deep gorges that made the interior so impenetrable. His warriors would have been outfitted in boar-tusk helmets and iron bell-corsets that recall legends of Mycenae and Troy, the armour handed down through the generations if not buried in fathers' graves. Others carried forerunners of the classical hoplite panoply: a heavy round Argive shield, a menacing Corinthian-type helmet and a sturdy 8ft spear of light but stout ash, with short swords and slashing scythes on hide belts suspended from lean hips that knew famine years. This was the 'bloody age of the iron blade', in the words of the ancient poet Hesiod, not the older Bronze-Age weapons of Troy, and iron ore was the currency of war in the land some were beginning to refer to as 'Hellas'.[6]

The Argive prince and his nobles would have gleaned information and local lore from traders and seafarers plying the Aegean in their linen-sailed ships: the Phrygian tribes who once occupied Emathia had marched east through Thrace and crossed the sea-narrows of the Hellespont to Anatolia a century or more ago, where they settled on the interior plateau once dominated by an even more mysterious people, the Hittites.[7] Caranus and his men surely knew of the presence of King Midas, who accrued his wealth from mining in Emathia where rose gardens below Mount Bermion bore his name, while reports of the vast forests of the interior and the gold deposits of the Haliacmon and Echedorus rivers that watered fertile plains, beckoned the Argives north.[8]

On one nameless day, in the heavy rain and thick fog that cloaked their arrival, Caranus and his tribe descended on Aegae, 'the city of goats', following an oracle that predicted a gleaming-horned snowy white flock would be grazing on the spot.[9] Following sacrifices to the gods in the foothills above the coastal plains overlooked by Mount Olympus in what would in time become the heartland of ancient Macedon, tribes were slowly expelled or subdued and Caranus established a dynasty referred to as 'Temenid' after his Argive father.[10]

479 BC

In the last quarter of the sixth century BC, the Achaemenid Great King of Persia began extending his influence into Europe; both Thrace and Macedon were annexed by Darius I under the unified title of 'Skudra' as vassal states of the vast Persian Empire.[11] By now, seven generations of Temenids had reigned in Macedon, and the next, King Amyntas I, proffered earth and water to Darius as a sign of the subjugation of the nation which, as far as the Greeks were concerned, remained an uncivilized and barbaric-tongued backwater to the north.[12]

Greek settlements on the western shores of Anatolia refused Darius homage and their Ionian League of cities commenced a full-scale revolt. The uprising was eventually crushed, but in 498 BC, the Persian administrative capital at Sardis was impetuously burned by supporting troops from Athens. Darius was slow to forgive and symbolically loosed an arrow with the cry: 'Grant, O God, that I may punish these Athenians.' Mainland Greece knew it was only a matter of time before the Persians landed on its soil.[13]

In 492 BC, Darius' expedition force under the command of his son-in-law, Mardonius, poured into Europe to establish a foothold for the planned invasion of the unyielding Hellenes. Once Thrace had been conquered, the Persian fleet island-hopped across the Aegean from Rhodes to Samos and then Naxos, while annexing or torching each harbour in its wake and sending captured youths back to Persia as slaves. Darius' army finally reached the Greek mainland at Eretria just north of Marathon in late summer 490 BC; the Persians set the land ablaze and received submission from all Greek cities except Athens and Sparta. But while the Athenians prepared for war, the sullen and aloof Spartans observed the religious festival in progress and declined to mobilize its army until the next full moon, despite Athens sending its now-legendary day runner, Pheidippides, some 225km in twenty-four hours with a request for the city to mobilize.[14]

The Athenian infantry and a small force from its Boeotian ally, Plataea, stood alone on the plain at Marathon in a face-off that lasted days.[15] Then a sudden, unexpected Greek charge in full armour across the battlefield, a feat unprecedented in hoplite warfare, followed by a disciplined wheeling manoeuvre, saw the Persians retreat in panic towards their ships. In the words of the poet Simonides: 'Fighting at the forefront of the Greeks, the Athenians at Marathon laid low the army of the gilded Medes.'[16] Darius died in Asia in the process of raising a new army, and it was left to his son, Xerxes I, to march on Hellas ten years later in search of revenge.

Xerxes mustered troops from the further regions of the Persian Empire, and with vastly increased numbers he ordered his engineers to bridge the narrow straights of the Dardanelles. The invading flotilla was a magnificent sight: 674 oared-ships were roped and chained together and transformed into two pontoon bridges across which his army could march. The hemp and papyrus warps were tensioned for the crossing by a Macedonian engineer, and the Persian Great King finally linked Europe and Asia together in defiance of Themistocles' warning on such sacrilegious hubris: 'the gods forbid a king should rule Asia and Hellas too.'[17]

King Alexander I of Macedon, Amyntas' son, faced the prospect of Xerxes' army of 180,000 men marching through the lower seaboard provinces of his supplicant state, a force so vast that it drunk the Echedorus River dry.[18] Macedon had benefited from Persian occupation, during which its client-kings saw their borders broaden four-fold in return for ongoing obeisance; Alexander even sealed the peace by offering his sister and a handsome dowry to a prominent Persian general whose envoys he had allegedly slaughtered at a banquet when he was a young crown prince, probably to avoid retribution.[19] The Macedonian king was playing a dangerous double game: superficially Xerxes' ally as the clouds of war thundered over Thrace, Alexander provided supplies of timber to the Greeks and strategic advice on Persian positions.

A hand-picked force of 300 Spartans led a 4,500-man blockade of the narrow pass at Thermopylae, where their self-sacrificing defence held out for three full days until the Greeks were flanked by a hidden path. The desperate action was designed to galvanize Greece into war, while 250 allied Greek ships formed a 'wooden wall' at sea and met the Great King's fleet off the coast of Artemisium with heavy losses to both sides. The Persian advance was slowed, and though this provided time to complete the evacuation of Athens, once the priests and the infirm left to defend the Acropolis were impaled, the city was burned to the ground by Persian fire.

Greece could have capitulated, but a newly strengthened Athenian fleet, recently fitted out at the now-fortified harbour of Piraeus, broke the back of the Persian flotilla blockading the island of Salamis where the Athenians had taken refuge. Without a naval supply chain, the vast Persian land army could not be provisioned. Xerxes' cousin, the reinstated Mardonius who had vigorously called for the second invasion, was left in Greece with a core of 30,000 men and tasked with increasing his numbers over the winter from local recruits.

Mardonius attempted to 'divide and rule' the already-fractious Greek city-states and enrolled King Alexander I of Macedon as his envoy. Athens was offered supremacy in return for Persian allegiance, but the artful politicking only brought Spartan 'patriotism' back to the negotiating table. In a rare oath of solidarity, the Greeks agreed to fight the invading host together, though the decision to resist Xerxes was far from unanimous.

Come summer, Mardonius' 50,000-strong army, which now included 20,000 Hellenic 'collaborators', including levies from Macedon, had to face a united force of 38,700 infantrymen from thirty-six Greek city-states led by Athens and Sparta at Plataea.[20] In a devious nocturnal double-dealing on the eve of the land battle in late August 479 BC, a lone horseman rode into the Greek camp under the cover of darkness and announced himself as King Alexander I. When his loyalty was questioned by a suspicious Greek officer, Alexander reminded him of the pedigree of what was now referred to as the royal 'Argead' clan of Macedon, descended, as they were, from the ancient kings of Argos.[21] Alexander revealed the Persian battle plan which was due to be implemented the very next morning so that the Greeks could adapt their phalanx formation as the sun rose over the plain.[22]

The more lightly armed, felt-capped, wicker-shielded and scythe-wielding ranks amassed from across the Persian Empire, driven forward by the lash of their officers, were once again no match for the Greek hoplites advancing in tight order behind their overlapping shields which absorbed the myriad arrows from the Persian archers which are said to have blocked out the sun. The exceptions were the 'Medised' Theban, Thracian, Thessalian and Macedonian levies who, despite Alexander's alleged Hellenic loyalty, were arrayed in Xerxes' ranks on that day.

The Persian Great Kings had always put their faith in their overwhelming numbers and their feared crack brigade of 10,000 'Immortals'. But after much confusion within the city-state ranks and quarrels between their officers, the Hellenes managed to employ more flexible battlefield tactics. Backboned by the defence of native soil, they were victorious at Plataea, but it was a close-run outcome that was hard fought all the way. 'No prisoners!' cried the Greeks; after Mardonius fell, the retreating Persians were trapped inside the barricaded walls of their camp, where 10,000 barbarians were allegedly slaughtered.[23]

What remained of the Persian army was depleted by the defection of its local levies and faced the prospect of a northward retreat through the coastal lowlands of Macedon. The opportunistic Alexander I saw his chance, and according to one much-debated ancient text, he fell upon the remnants of the once-mighty invasion force at the estuary of the Strymon River and cut it to pieces.[24]

'The bold scheming son of Amyntas', as the Greek poet Pindar termed Alexander I, was not slow to dedicate golden statues of himself at Delphi and Olympia, where the Pan-Hellenic games had been held for the previous three centuries. It was a propitious moment for him to propagate his new foundation myth more widely: the kings of Macedon *were* of Greek Argive descent, dating back to the sons of Temenus whose line stretched back to the mighty hero Heracles, just like the royal families of Sparta. Greece confirmed Alexander's heritage at Olympia and he was awarded the epithets 'friend' and 'benefactor of the Greeks', while his new prestige saw him minting new currency in his own name.[25]

Macedon was independent once more, and over the next century, Alexander's descendants gradually consolidated the state's uncertain borders with new roads, bridges and hill forts, while to the south the Greeks continued to war incessantly despite the moments of unity at Artemisium and Plataea. Hellas eventually tore itself apart in the thirty-year Peloponnesian War, which was fuelled in no small part by the frequent switches of allegiance between Athens and Sparta by the new Macedonian king, Perdiccas II. The war rested on a complex and unstable state of affairs witnessed by Thucydides, who was exiled for twenty years by the Athenian council for a failed military intervention in the thick of it; it was an exile that led him to craft one of the most influential histories the ancient world would ever see.

359 BC

King Amyntas III of Macedon came to the throne in 393 BC after assassinating his predecessor who reigned for less than a year. He would have been raised on stories of his great-grandfather, Alexander I, who not only liberated the state but convinced the ruling judges from Ellis of his Argive lineage so that he could compete in the Olympic Games; non-Hellenes were branded 'barbarians' and barred from participating in any competitive way.

Amyntas would have been equally impressed with the stories of the most effective of Alexander's five sons, reform-minded political chameleon Perdiccas II, and his offspring Archelaus I, who, according to Thucydides, did more to strengthen

16 *Unearthing the Family of Alexander the Great*

Ancient Macedon and its occupied territories in 359 BC.

Macedon with roads and fortifications than all the previous monarchs. The great doctors, poets and playwrights of Greece had all been invited to Archelaus' new political capital at Pella to 'civilize' the nation in an enlightened reign that had ended with assassination in 399 BC, the common fate of the late Argead kings.[26]

Greece had become increasingly aware of the rising power to its north, and diplomats were dispatched to Macedon to ensure the continuance of timber contracts for felling its great deciduous and evergreen forests. The Athenian navy needed pitch and wood, and so did its merchant fleet for indispensable grain imports from Egypt and the Black Sea route to the Kingdom of Bosporus.[27]

But King Amyntas III was beset on all sides by would-be usurpers, and his twenty-four-year reign was at times interrupted. Macedon's borders were pressed and his sons by the more prominent of his two wives had to assume the throne when hardly out of their teens. The eldest was Alexander II, who was assassinated by a pretender who, according to one ancient source, was the lover of his politically ambitious mother, Eurydice.[28] Next on the throne was Perdiccas III, who was slaughtered along with an army of 4,000 men in battle against the fearsome Illyrians to Macedon's north-west. Finally, Philip II, the youngest of Eurydice's sons, took up the reins of power.

Philip was aged 23 in 359 BC when he became the twenty-fourth recorded king of the royal line of Macedon, more recently promoted as 'Argead', whose lineage had already been exploited to good political effect. His father had stamped currency with the symbols of the family ancestor Heracles, with his legendary club and lion skins appearing on state coinage. But no fewer than eight predecessors had sat on the throne in the last forty years, a testament to the ongoing turmoil, and Philip had himself been a hostage twice as a youth in a period when Persian gold and rival factions installed puppet regimes on Macedon's borders.[29]

Philip was immediately forced to deal with five rival claimants to the throne, including three half-brothers; the polygamy of the Argead house led to a constant oversupply of kings from rival branches of a clan not governed by strict rules of primogeniture, 'power to the firstborn'.[30] Thessaly had thrown out its Macedonian garrisons, and the Greek city-states in an anti-Macedonian league still dominated the coastal regions of the strategically important Chalcidice peninsula forming Macedon's eastern seaboard.

Weighing up his limited options, Philip resorted to 'consorting for survival' and there began the first of seven strategic marriages, said to be 'in connection with war', to daughters of neighbouring kings and warlords he neutralized through the wedlock.[31]

Philip next oversaw a series of military reforms that modernized the rigid structure of warfare Greece had waged for centuries, and he soon commanded the first professional year-round army in the Hellenic world.[32] The war cry of his unstoppable pikemen was terrifying when saluting Ares, the god of war, while his lance-carrying heavy cavalry rode in flying wedges that could cut through enemy ranks. Athens and its allies were crushed at the Battle of Chaeronea in August 338 BC, where Philip rolled out his secret weapons in a set-piece confrontation for the very first time.[33]

Over the previous twenty years on the throne, during which Philip survived against all odds and manipulated himself to the forefront of Hellenic politics, he achieved what Persia had failed to do and brought Hellas to its knees. His dominance effectively made Philip 'commander-in-chief' of Greek forces in a confederation of states termed the 'League of Corinth'. Despite his lenient treatment of the captured Athenians following the battle at Chaeronea – a necessary precursor to gaining their support for his planned invasion of Persia – Greek democracy, which was far from a unifying political system since its introduction in 507 BC and now more of an aristocratic clique in Athens itself, would never recover.

Philip trebled the size of both the Macedonian army and the territories under its control into the first land empire Europe had ever seen, but his most important legacy would be his equally ambitious son, Alexander III, whose birth propitiously coincided with Philip's equestrian triumph at Olympia in 356 BC, a victory over the Illyrians and the successful conclusion to a city siege.[34] By the age of 16, as acting regent, the precocious youth had already founded a city in Thrace in his own name, and the world would come to know him as 'Alexander the Great'.

October 336 BC

The entrails were carefully scrutinized by the court seer and deemed favourable for the day. Philip was celebrating the marriage of his own daughter Cleopatra to the king of the dominant Molossian tribe of the neighbouring state of Epirus; the groom was Cleopatra's own uncle. The resulting alliance would expand Philip's influence further and stave off the scheming of the groom's sister, Olympias, his now-estranged wife whose own Epirote lineage was said to be traceable back to Achilles and the kings of Troy. Olympias was the mother of both Cleopatra and the 20-year-old Alexander, who had already demonstrated an appetite for sitting on the throne.[35]

Philip's ambitions had not been confined to Greece and the Balkans. At Corinth the previous year he declared war on the new Persian Great King, Artaxerxes III, for across the narrows that separated Europe from Asia lay the riches of the empire's western provinces; an expedition force of 10,000 men had already established a bridgehead in north-western Anatolia. But conscious of the scrutiny of the ever-mercurial gods, Philip sought divine approval before his campaign and visited Delphi to ask the priestess for a divination on success. 'Wreathed is the bull. All is done. There is also one who will smite him,' came the hopeful but cryptic reply, which Philip interpreted as a prediction that Persia would fall like a sacrificial beast.[36]

By now, Macedon enjoyed income from war indemnities, captured gold and silver mines, and from the sale of slaves and booty, enabling Philip to enlarge the royal palace at Aegae. He even minted gold 'Philippics' to imitate Darius' Persian coined 'Darics'.[37] Games had been held the previous days and visitors had been banqueted in rowdy Macedonian style. Every room in the city was full as dignitaries arrived from across Greece and supplicant kingdoms to the north for the royal wedding, where they were monitored by the king's garrisons and resident city oligarchs.

Philip's court was demonstrating its wealth as his canny generals surely slapped shoulders, poured unmixed wine and listened for words of dissent or hostile coalitions in the making on the palace reclining couches. Guest friends and potentially useful foreigners had been encouraged to attend and crowns were presented to Philip from each city, even from Athens, the unreliable 'captive ally' still smarting from its wounds. A Macedonian garrison now occupied the pass of Thermopylae, enabling Philip's formidable army to march on Greece at will. The Athenian assembly had recently passed a politically expedient decree declaring that Philip should be worshipped, though the city's politicians were rapidly becoming obsolete, just as he had planned.[38]

At dawn on this autumn morning, Philip would have watched on from the shade of the palace's Doric colonnade as the procession made its way down the wide, shallow steps that led to the theatre nestled in the fold of a natural hillside below. The view from its stone and upper wooden seats was spectacular, ranging out across the fertile plains where land reclamation projects were underway, and then east to the Aegean and the promise beyond.[39]

The day of festivities was organized with the same precision with which the king drilled his standing army. Ignoring the warning from a herald and the sinister lines embedded in a poem by the tragic actor Neoptolemus, which seem to describe a dangerous plot in the making, Philip watched on as statues of the twelve Olympian Gods were carried into the theatre and paraded before the crowd. Each had been elaborately worked in the likeness of a deity, and following them was a thirteenth, a statue of Philip himself, as if he sat among them; the implication was clear, it was unprecedented, and the excitement and unease would have been palpable in equal measures.[40]

Sporting a fine white cloak and with a wreath on his head, Philip walked at the rear of the royal entourage and insisted that his bodyguards, as well as his son and the groom, file ahead so that he could enter the theatre alone, unprotected and confident in his new godlike status in Hellas. An assassin then darted out, headed straight for the king and plunged a Celtic dagger through Philip's ribs. Pausanias, the disgruntled captain of the king's bodyguard who bore a grudge of ignored sexual abuse, made off westwards to the nearest city gate, where his two accomplices held getaway horses. He didn't make it far; several more of the king's personal guard gave chase and impaled the tripped assassin with javelins before he could be interrogated.[41]

Philip died in a pool of blood at the entrance to the theatre at Aegae. Alexander, possibly with Olympias already beside him, demanded immediate fealty from his father's generals and set about executing anyone related to the assassin and his accomplices. It was an accession of blood, of revenge and the additional culling of lines of nobility that might challenge for the throne. Olympias' son was now the king of Macedon and her daughter was a queen in Epirus, though that formal title for women was a generation away.[42]

When the immediate crisis was under control, the newly crowned King Alexander III oversaw his father's funeral. Following the traditional two days of mourning, a lavish pyre was constructed, and Philip's body was dedicated to the flames and the Underworld gods. In archaic custom, his ceremonial armour, weapons and the finer accessories of court life were interred inside the tomb alongside his cremated bones, and the massive marble doors of its main chamber were bolted from inside and wedged closed for all time.

Alexander would not have contemplated anywhere else but the nation's first capital for his father's burial. Generations before, King Perdiccas I had prophesied the importance of the necropolis at Aegae:

> He made it known to his son, Argaeus, the place he wished to be buried and directed that not only his own bones, but those of the kings that should succeed him, should be deposited in the same spot; signifying that, as long as the relics of his posterity should be buried there, the crown would remain in his family.[43]

Philip's tomb was covered with an earthen tumulus like the graves of the heroes of old, following the rites of Homer's *Iliad* and the protocols set down more recently in Plato's *Laws*. Alexander, who, some whispered, played a silent part in his father's assassination in league with Olympias, planned his own odyssey to Asia to reap the glory of defeating Darius III, the new Persian Great King who was already amassing his forces in Anatolia, surely with an eye on reoccupying Thrace.[44]

323 BC

Philip's death led to widespread unrest, from the Balkan tribes in the north to the cities of southern Greece. Alexander immediately recalled friends whom his father had exiled and drafted trusted companions into key administrative posts. Oaths from his father's old-guard generals were redirected to the untested son, and the superbly drilled army Alexander inherited was put into action when Greece refused to recognize him as head of the League of Corinth. With lightning speed incomprehensible to the hoplite armies being mustered by the city-states to the south, Alexander force-marched his men into Thessaly and the shell-shocked Greeks sued for peace.

Renewed trouble in the north saw Alexander reach the southern banks of the Danube, where he drove the hostile tribes across the river, and in a series of

How a Kingdom May Rise and Fall and Vanish   21

The expanded state of Macedon in 336 BC at the end of Philip II's reign.

lightning campaigns in Thrace and Illyria, Alexander displayed the depth of his cunning and tactical genius. But in his protracted absence, and funded by the purse of Darius in his bid to stall the planned invasion of Persia, false rumours were spread throughout Greece of Alexander's death, and Thebes and Athens combined in a new bid to shake off the Macedonian yoke.[45]

With a new turn of astonishing speed, Alexander trekked his men south to blockade the northern route out of Athens and his army appeared before the walls of an incredulous Thebes. The defences were breached, with thousands of the inhabitants slaughtered or sold into slavery, and the city was razed to the ground, save for temples and the house of the poet Pindar, whose verses Alexander much admired. Athens immediately capitulated and grudgingly returned to the oath sworn by the League of Corinth members, requiring the city to supply ships for the Macedonian-led invasion of Persia.[46]

Like Philip before him, Alexander remained observant to the gods. He visited Delphi, only to find it was not a day for oracles; when the priestess refused to prophesize, Alexander dragged her into the temple, where she uttered, 'you are invincible, my son.'[47] In the spring of 334 BC, before the crossing into Asia, he mustered the invasion army at Dium on the slopes of Mount Olympus and held purification rituals in a farewell festival that lasted nine days.[48]

The bulk of the allied flotilla of 100 ships finally crossed the Hellespont and headed to the coast of north-west Anatolia carrying a total of some 35,000 Macedonian soldiers and Greek auxiliaries, both infantry and cavalry. As the fleet prepared to land, Alexander hurled his weapon from the prow of the leading ship to signify his claim to eastern lands 'by the spear' in a symbolic gesture that relived the moment Agamemnon's Greeks had first landed to take Troy.[49]

The invasion force forged south, and accounts recall the various sieges and agile diplomacies Alexander employed to win over the cities on the Mediterranean seaboard, while his victories in the two great set-piece battles at Granicus and Issus pushed Darius back into the heart of the Persian Empire.[50] Although the Macedonians were vastly outnumbered and faced disciplined Greek mercenaries in Darius' employ, the superior tactics and training of Alexander's army sent the Persian ranks into flight with relatively few Macedonian losses. The Phoenician city of Tyre was stormed after a seven-month siege, and Egypt lay open and welcomed the conqueror as a liberator from Persian oppression.[51]

Oracles invested Alexander with a god-like status, and early plots against him were fortuitously revealed. Darius even offered to share power in Asia, divided at the Euphrates, with the hand of his daughter in marriage.[52] Alexander spurned the advances by declaring that he would legitimately take anything he wanted, and in the wake of the mighty battle at Gaugamela in northern Mesopotamia in late 331 BC, he became the de-facto Great King of the Persian Empire at the age of 25.[53] The aftermath saw remnants of the Persian army streaming into the mountains of the upper satrapies, and the conqueror entered Babylon without opposition.

The Macedonians marched east to the Achaemenid winter capital of Susa and the ceremonial capital of Persepolis, both of which were stripped of their enormous treasuries, and whether a calculated message to the still-at-large Darius or a veiled warning to further sedition in Greece, the palace complex at Persepolis was burned to the ground.[54]

Alexander became the most powerful man alive, with the vast wealth of the Great Kings, and yet he yearned for an elusive completion to a destiny incomprehensible to his troops: the conquest of *all* lands under Persian control and beyond to the ends of the Earth. His was a bid to better the fabled feats of the hero Heracles and the god Dionysus, the conqueror of the East. Although the Macedonians expected the torching of Persepolis to signify the end of the Persian invasion, they faced years of further campaigning.

New plots against the king, subsequent executions of the plotters – including popular veteran generals – unconscionable atrocities against native tribes and costly guerrilla warfare in the mountains of the remote eastern provinces each took their toll, as did the final great set-piece clash with the Indian raja Porus and his 'city of war elephants' at the Battle of the Hydaspes. Macedonian troops were ravaged by poisonous snakes, frost bite, thirst, malaria and dysentery as they crossed the Hindu Kush and descended into India, while the wounded had been garrisoned in mud-brick forts in territories hardly pacified, never to see Greece or Macedon again. Weapons rusted in monsoon rains, morale was low and after eight years of campaigning, the Macedonians had marched a river too far. They mutinied when ordered to venture further east towards the Ganges, where Alexander and prevailing doctrine believed the boundary of the eastern world lay.

Alexander gave one of his rousing signature speeches, but it failed to turn the tide of disaffection. By now, many soldiers had wives, concubines and children in a 'moving city' of allegedly 120,000 infantrymen who had lost their appetite for war.[55] In emulation of Achilles at Troy, Alexander sulked in his campaign tent for two days. When he finally emerged, he threw games and built twelve giant altars to reassuringly familiar gods to mark the limit of his conquest, and then resentfully led his grand army with a 1,800-boat flotilla south to the Indus delta and into the bloodiest campaigning of all. Alexander was retreading the footsteps of Darius the Great, who took control of the Indus Valley in 515 BC, but he was almost killed storming one of many walled cities that refused to submit on the orders of their Brahmin priests, and new rumours of his death caused far-reaching garrison mutinies.[56]

The fleet finally reached the Indian Ocean, where Alexander made the worst decision of the campaign: the disastrous crossing of the Makran desert, where soldiers were 'lost in the sand like sailors lost overboard at sea', while his admiral embarked on a sea voyage which was just as uncertain and perilous.[57] When the stragglers of each venture finally reunited, the despondent king executed misgoverning officials who must have doubted he would return. 'In short, the whole empire was in turmoil, and an atmosphere of instability prevailed everywhere,' claimed one Greek historian of events before the return to Babylon.[58]

Having occupied vast provinces, stormed mountain-top cities and slaughtered any tribe that resisted, the Persian Empire had finally, fragilely, been tamed, but at a huge price to Alexander and his men, and to the collapsed Persian administration. Superficially, Macedon's new empire stretched from the shores of the Adriatic to the Indus in the East, and from the lands bordering the Caspian Sea down to southern Ethiopia. But storm clouds had been steadily gathering: Alexander's adoption of Persian dress, his demand that his men prostrate themselves before him, his sacrifices to foreign gods and marriages into the Asiatic lines of the defeated nobles, alongside his never-ending quest for the ends of the earth, had led to plots and mutinies by his infantrymen, whose former Macedonian-only ranks were now permeated by Asiatic recruits.

What remained of the original homebred 24,000 infantry and 1,800 cavalry who crossed to Asia with Alexander had marched or ridden well over 20,000 miles by the time they returned to Babylon, the 'gateway of the gods', in 323 BC, eleven years after departing Macedon. All the while, the influence of his top generals and bodyguards had been rising – more so after Alexander had strategically married them to Persian nobility at Susa – and they were now awaiting the opportunity to govern in their own right.[59]

Babylon had become the campaign headquarters and the staging point for pending expeditions to Arabia and along the southern shores of the Mediterranean. But as the army neared the ancient bitumen-walled city, reports of Alexander's growing tyranny and paranoia emerged, along with warnings of disaster from the Chaldean Magi who recognized portents of his predicted death.[60] Inside the fortified palace on the east bank of the Euphrates, ambassadors and envoys were arriving from nations across the known world, those already occupied and those expecting to be, carrying pledges of fealty to the first Macedonian 'Great King'.

In mid-June, the new succession crisis finally came to a head. Alexander, whose scarred body had sustained a number of life-threatening wounds through the campaign years, lay weak and feverish in the summer palace of Nebuchadnezzar. It was a scene of confusion, suspicion, fear and the veiled hopes of some as the king's condition worsened. Alexander finally descended into a coma, and any succession instructions he provided were soon silenced with him.[61]

The 'terrible meteor' who flashed across the sky for a generation had claimed descent from the Greek hero Heracles and even Perseus, the founder of the Persian race. Although Alexander had performed superhuman deeds in his almost-thirteen-year reign, he was mortal after all and he was publicly pronounced dead at the age of 32 years and 11 months.[62] Immediately cancelled were Alexander's 'last plans' for the invasion of Arabia and the West, the construction of temples, roads and dockyards and great population transfers into hybrid settlements where Hellenes and Persians would live side by side. A world that had been governed by just one king, now had to accustom itself to none.

There followed days of mutual suspicions and infighting as his command argued the succession issue, until a fragile compromise was reached at the gathering of infantry and cavalry at the traditional assembly of Macedonians which convened on such occasions. Two kings would be crowned: the potential unborn son of Rhoxane,

How a Kingdom May Rise and Fall and Vanish 25

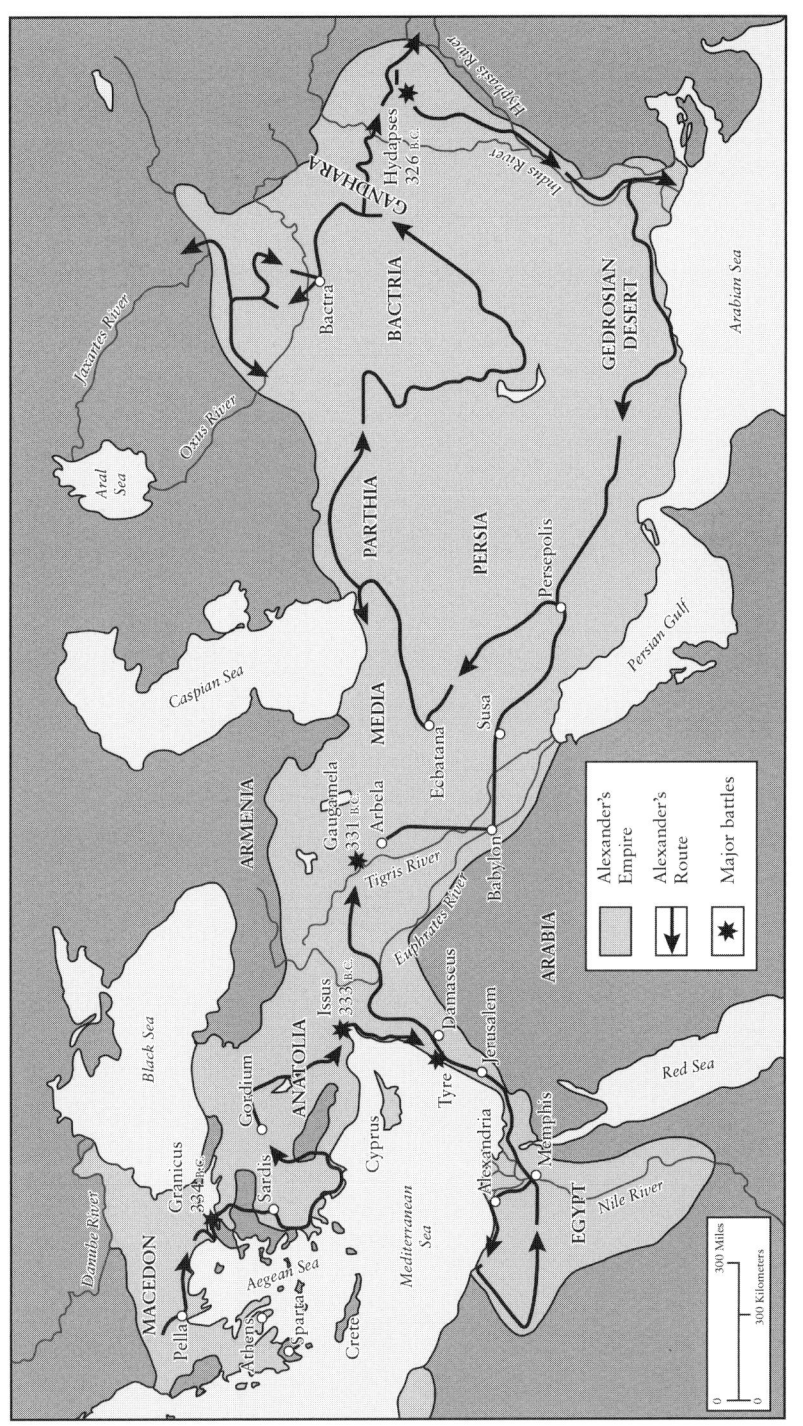

The empire of Macedon at Alexander's death.

Alexander's pregnant Asiatic wife, alongside Alexander's mentally impaired half-brother, Arrhidaeus, a *Macedone* at least. Later propaganda claimed Alexander had left his kingdom 'to the strongest' of his generals, but this was simply a contrived declaration which invited the most powerful of his men to slug it out for supremacy. Which is exactly what they did.

It required two years to construct an elaborate funeral hearse. Once completed, Alexander's body was wheeled out of Babylon, only to be intercepted in Syria by Ptolemy, one of his bodyguards, and ferried to Egypt as a talisman for the coveted province he inherited. Ptolemy interred the corpse first in the more defensible ancient city of Memphis above the Nile Delta, and a generation later it was transferred to 'Alexandria-by-Egypt', the city that would become the great *entrepôt* of the Eastern Mediterranean.[63]

Various other factions and coalitions emerged from the succession crisis with plans of their own, some loyal and some hostile to Alexander's two sons born of Persian and Bactrian brides of noble blood. One was led by Perdiccas, Alexander's former second-in-command, who considered Ptolemy's hijacking of the body a direct challenge to his authority in the post-Alexander world. Perdiccas led an ill-fated invasion of Egypt and was stabbed to death in his campaign tent by his own ambitious officers, an event that marked the true beginning of a protracted Macedonian civil war.

Like hapless pawns in a dynastic chess game stretching across the empire, Alexander's sons were used as rallying points for those who through self-interest called for the continuation of Argead rule, but who secretly planned their own bid for the throne. Once the 'royalists' had been defeated, the boys were executed on the orders of Cassander, the son of Alexander's former state regent, who then seeded his own part-Argead royal line through one of Alexander's captured half-sisters. Several years later, the appointed governors of the Asian provinces declared themselves independent 'kings'.

Over the next forty years, the empire fragmented into the kingdoms founded by the very generals who had campaigned with Alexander. Initially, five superpowers dominated and occasionally they combined in self-serving alliances: the dynasties of Seleucus in the East, Antigonus the One-Eyed in Syria and Anatolia, Lysimachus in Thrace, Ptolemy in Egypt, and in Macedon itself Cassander, who murdered his way to the throne.

Following the great 'Battle of the Kings' at Ipsus in 301 BC, when the empire was redistributed by the factions who conspired in the downfall of the biggest mutual threat in the form of Antigonus, the nation of Macedon was itself divided at times. Sons, wives and daughters were each murdered by jealous parents, manipulated into dynastic marriages or committed patricide in their impatience to govern. In the words of the ancient Greek historian Plutarch, who hailed from Chaeronea, where the tree known as 'Alexander's oak' still stood in his day: 'Many

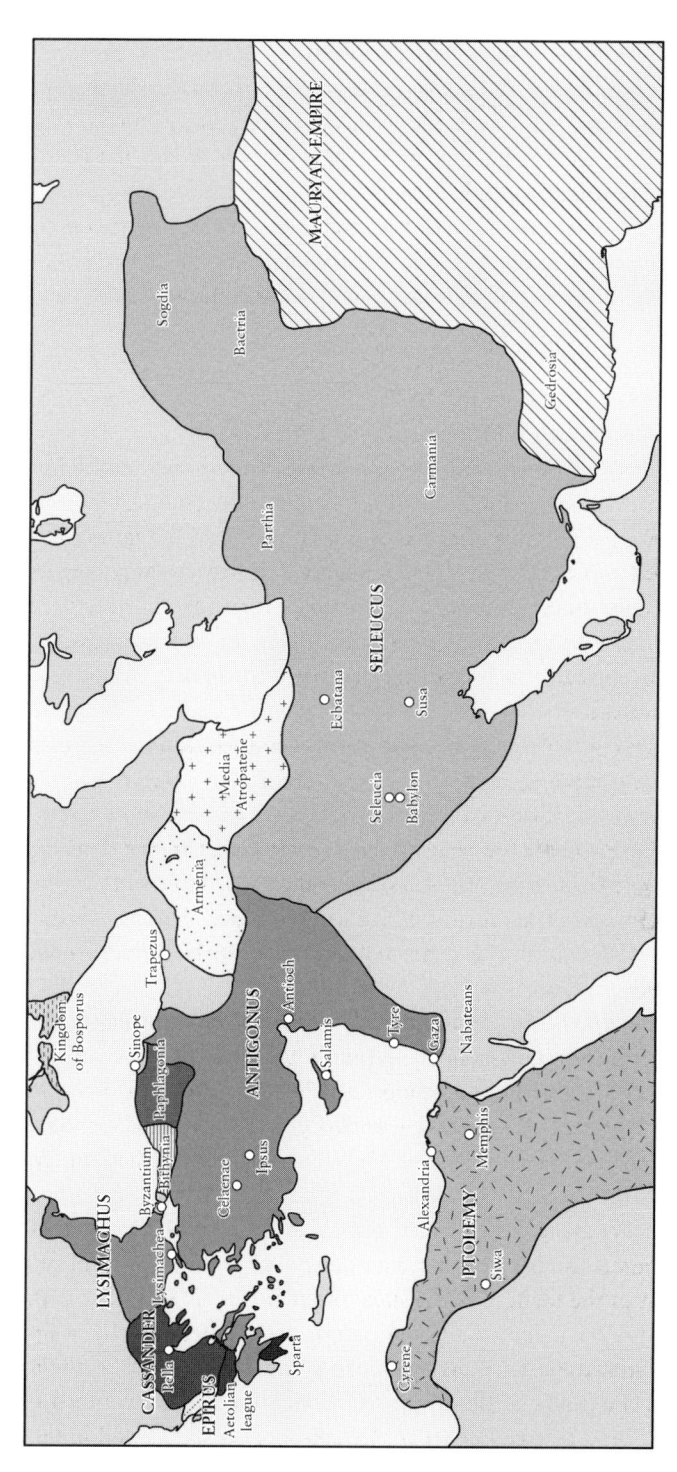

The kingdoms of Alexander's successors before the Battle of Ipsus in 301 BC.

killed their mothers and wives ... as for the killing of brothers, like a postulation in geometry, it was considered as indisputably necessary to the safety of the reigning prince.'[64]

Veterans of the campaigns had returned with wealth and the status of having fought with Philip and Alexander, but the price Macedon paid was commodity-price inflation, continued depopulation and perennial war as the next generation of dynasts, bred through a series of 'labyrinthine' intermarriages, vied for domination in the Macedonian-controlled Graeco-Persian world.[65]

280 BC

Throughout the Successor Wars that raged in the decades after Alexander's death, Greece remained in the grip of the garrisons, tyrants and compliant politicians installed by the Macedonian kings, who controlled or occupied Athens and its ports for much of the time. In Asia, the first generation of conflict burnt itself out when Seleucus and Lysimachus, the last of Alexander's great campaign generals and who survived into their 80s, engaged in battle in Anatolia in 281 BC. Lysimachus' defeat left a power vacuum in the kingdom of Thrace and weakened the northern borders of Macedon itself.

In the summer of 280 BC, the previously unthinkable happened: 160,000 treasure-hungry Celts, reputed to be the 'tallest people in the world', amassed under three generals of the Galatae, as the Celtic Gauls were known.[66] The Greeks, who had already employed contingents of Celtic mercenaries, knew their value as fighters; Alexander had himself once been visited by their hardly submissive ambassadors on the Danube fifty-five years before.

'What do you fear the most?' he had quizzed them, perhaps expecting to hear his own name. 'We fear only that the sky will fall on us and crush us one day or the earth open and swallow us or the sea rise and overwhelm us,' came the unexpected reply.[67] The men Aristotle once described as 'excessively fearless', here reciting elements of an ancient Celtic ritual, certainly did not fear the name of 'Macedon' a generation after Alexander's death.

The Galatae divided into three armies in a loose tribal confederation and poured out of the Balkan hills. They slew the army of King Ptolemy 'the Thunderbolt', who arrogantly declined diplomacy. Ptolemy, a son of the Egyptian dynast who had bloodily manipulated his way to Macedon's throne, was summarily decapitated, his head paraded on a javelin, and prisoners were sacrificed in a gruesome pagan rite.[68] The Celts marched south, plundered neighbouring Thessaly and reached the 'hot gates' of Thermopylae, leaving tales of atrocities behind. The renowned Celtic cavalry and their chariots were neutralized by the valley's narrow terrain, and it was their infantry, protected by their distinctive long oval shields, who confronted the Greek coalition holding the defile. It turned into a bloody stalemate and the pass could not be breached.

The Galatae moved west, slaughtering every male in their path, and 'drank the blood and ate the flesh of the slaughtered babies who were fattest with milk', grimly reported Pausanias, a Greek travelographer and antiquarian who wrote in Roman times. Greek contingents followed, and Thermopylae was left relatively undefended. The invaders doubled back and discovered the very mountain path that Xerxes' Immortals had used to flank the Spartans of Leonidas two centuries before; hidden by early morning mist, the Celts descended behind what remained of the Greek lines. Hellas, already worn down by Philip, Alexander, their long-serving regent Antipater and by his ambitious son Cassander, lay wide open with no united army for its defence.[69]

The treasure-hungry marauders targeted Delphi and its famed shrine of Apollo, laden with the amassed wealth of centuries of tribute and votive offerings. Snow and frost decimated the Galatae ranks, but not before they had pillaged the sacred grove, killed the priestess Pythia and made off with the temple riches. Home-grown propaganda claimed a Greek victory, but this likely referred to the ongoing skirmishing that saw 16,000 Celts fall as they headed north towards Macedon through the inhospitable mountain passes.[70]

In the winter of 278 BC, Antigonus II Gonatas of Macedon, the grandson of Alexander's charismatic one-eyed general who died at Ipsus twenty-three years before, arrived in the city of Lysimachea in eastern Thrace. Antigonus requested a meeting with the Galatae to discuss the terms of a peace, but coveting his rumoured wealth, the Celts formulated their own plan: they would overwhelm his army in a surprise attack and raid the state treasury. Raised on the tactics of his wily father, Demetrius the Besieger, and on stories of his grandfather's role in Alexander's fight for supremacy in Persia, Antigonus II Gonatas anticipated the deceit, leaving his own camp deserted and attacking the Galatae in the rear. His victory, in the spring of 277 BC, signalled deliverance from the Celts, though Macedon was not completely devoid of the invaders from the north.

Antigonus was recognized as the king of a newly united nation. Hearing of the atrocities in southern Greece and seeing firsthand the destruction when the Celts first marched through Macedon, he knew it was only a matter of time until bands of brigands descended on the grave-strewn necropolis of Aegae, where mound upon mound broadcast the presence of burial pits and chambers filled with precious funerary artefacts below. Antigonus directed his engineers to throw up a huge tumulus over the still-unplundered graves of the former Argead kings, but he cunningly positioned the tombs close to the southern periphery and not under the apex of the hill, where broken gravestones from the already-plundered cemetery were piled instead.

274 BC

Four years on, with bands of the still-at-large Celts marauding the country and Macedon still reeling from their earlier incursions, it was Pyrrhus, the king of the neighbouring state of Epirus, who made a new bid for the throne.[71] Dynastic intrigues further afield meant Pyrrhus, who could trace his ancestry twenty generations to the hero Achilles, had already served a term as a hostage in Egypt at the court of Ptolemy I, but with remarkable results: he married Ptolemy's stepdaughter and was restored to the Epirote throne. With Ptolemy's support, Pyrrhus launched campaigns in Italy with a corps of war elephants. But his costly successes against Rome and his sea battles off Sicily against the fleet of the temporary Latin ally Carthage were so high in casualties that in time men would refer to them as 'Pyrrhic'; 'another victory against Rome,' he famously said, 'and we will be undone.'[72]

Pyrrhus had watched from Italy as the Celts ransacked Greece. By 274 BC, he had abandoned his local allies and cast his eye to Macedon, where he had briefly held the western cantons in the reign of Antigonus' father. Pyrrhus had a depleted army of just 8,500 men and no immediate funds to pay them, but the intervening years gave him one distinct advantage: he had fought alongside Celts in northern Italy against the common Roman enemy, so he hired the bands of roving Galatae as mercenaries on the promise of loot. Local Macedonians, especially those from the upper provinces, soon joined the charismatic Epirote who knew each commander by name in the style of the great Alexander, and Antigonus was left with no choice but to retreat with his cavalry to a coastal fortress city and prepare for a siege.

Pyrrhus marched with his elephants on the new state capital at Pella and the rich burial grounds of Aegae, where he directed his Celtic contingent to garrison the old capital; with no coined money at hand, he listened with indifference to reports of their desecrating the necropolis. The graves of Aegae were overturned once more, the headstones were smashed, tombs were opened and, once inside, 'the treasure they plundered, and the bones they insolently cast to the winds', in the words of Plutarch.[73] But this time a great hill stared back at them, one far greater than the modest mound they had seen when passing through Aegae on their way south.

Excavating the immense man-made tumulus would be a near-impossible task, but local residents may have informed them of the location of the tombs within, as the Celts commenced strategic digging at the southern edge. Their tools struck the foundation stones of a box-like shrine made from huge porous stones covered in fine marble. Once standing above ground, its walls had already been pulled down, and any gold and silver votive offerings had long-since departed.

The Galatae knew more riches lay beyond and pushed an exploratory tunnel further northward; within a matter of feet they were at the wall of a deeper tomb.

They hammered out a section of the most accessible blocks, and once a torso-sized hole had been punched through the lower wall, one of the looters tried to crawl into the chamber but found a sturdy internal shelf barring his way.[74] It was equally clear that to extract valuables from the tomb a larger opening was needed without the risk of collapsing tunnels, so the Celts removed sufficient soil from the edge of the tumulus until the thick stones slabs of the roof were exposed, and with much effort they managed to lever away a section.

The Celts were in; by lamplight, the raiders must have grudgingly marvelled at fine wall paintings whose depictions they failed to comprehend and at the riches that were still stacked and carefully arranged about the single chamber. They quickly bagged every valuable they could carry, as the tomb floor was rapidly being covered by soil infill slipping through the opened roof. The bones of the former royalty were also tipped out of their ossuaries and scattered across the darkening floor.

The Galatae knew more tombs lay beneath the towering hill, along with rumours that they held the legendary wealth of Philip II and Alexander. But days of digging new tunnels into the depths of the mound revealed nothing and the increasing weight of soil threatened the new shafts; continued looting was perilous, threatened also by the prospect of Antigonus' return. Pyrrhus was becoming impatient and was being lured south in the hope of increased power in southern Greece, so he rallied his Celts on promises of riches in the Peloponnese and departed Aegae, leaving the tumulus part-raped and scarred.

Pyrrhus finally came face to face with Antigonus' rebuilt army at Argos. The once-neutral population of the city spied his Celts, recalled their reputation and turned against him. Pyrrhus was wounded in a side street and reportedly collapsed on the grave of a Homeric hero. With victory secured, Antigonus headed north in haste to reclaim the Macedonian throne. On his journey to Pella he saw the wounded tumulus at Aegae and used what materials were at hand to repair the gaps in the roof of the exposed tomb and cover the scar in the western wall before filling in the looters' trenches and covering the monuments with soil and stone. The Great Tumulus was whole once again and hid the still-unplundered subterranean tombs.

Antigonus II Gonatas, grandson of the one-eyed general of imposing physique and booming voice who had almost claimed Alexander's Asian empire for his own, sat on the throne of Macedon for a further thirty-five years, producing sons and heirs who would govern for the next four generations. 'No man ever set up such absolute rulers in Greece,' commented the historian Polybius on his continued stranglehold through his network of tyrants.[75] Antigonus made short work of an Athenian-Spartan alliance formed in 267 BC, stirred up by the Ptolemaic regime in Egypt, which was itself attacked by the Seleucids, and both overseas dynasties meddled where and when they could in Greece and Macedon.[76]

Throughout his turbulent reign, Antigonus' court remained an environment which welcomed Greek performers, philosophers and poets, as in the time of Archelaus and Philip II. It was in this violent and bewildered world, dominated by warring kings and tyrants, and in the absence of true political freedoms, that Stoicism emerged to help the common man rationalize the world against overwhelming odds.[77]

The Celts never left Hellas and Macedon for good; they were integrated into future armies and even infiltrated the Illyrian royal tribes, while the remnants of the once great Galatae army crossed to Asia and founded a kingdom in the highlands of Anatolia named 'Galatia'.

168 BC

The Roman general Aemilius Paullus surveyed the terrain at Pydna and didn't like what he saw. A river ran squarely through the centre of the battlefield, where skirmishing had already broken out along its banks, and foothills back-dropped his position, while the ranks of Macedonians under King Perseus had their backs to the sea.[78] Entrails were not sufficiently propitious for him to commence the fight – so the diviners warned him – and his men had the morning sun in their eyes, disadvantaging a head-on attack.

Over the previous sixty years, Rome had used any justifiable means to establish a foothold on the Greek mainland as the Senate navigated its way through a mix of paranoia and naked aggression; the Adriatic saw naval actions, Illyria was invaded and 'protectorates' were established to 'safeguard' Greek interests against a possible Illyrian-Macedonian alliance. A generation earlier, in the so-called 'Second Macedonian War', the charismatic King Philip V, the grandson of Antigonus II Gonatas and father of King Perseus, had managed to extend Macedon's borders; after witnessing Hannibal's successes in Italy, he allied with the Carthaginians and attacked Roman interests in the Mediterranean.[79] Rome's response was to bring war to Greece itself. Its experienced legions had massed in Thessaly in 197 BC for the Battle of Cynoscephalae on a new pretext of 'liberating Greeks', whose Aetolian ranks joined Rome for the battle.

Cynoscephalae had been a tough-fought battle in hill terrain and dense fog that saw the Roman legions master the Macedonian phalanx. Although Philip V was allowed to escape, he had to pay 1,000 talents of silver to the victors: some 26,000kg in weight and equivalent to 6 million drachmas. Macedon's state army and navy were largely disbanded, and Philip's son was shipped to Rome as a hostage.

Twenty-nine years later, at Pydna on 22 June 168 BC, almost two centuries after King Philip II had first rolled out his phalanx at Chaeronea, the Macedonian 6-metre-long two-handed pike in the hands of 16,000 phalangites at the centre of the infantry ranks, the tight formation remained 'awe-inspiringly intimidating' when Aemilius Paulus watched it deploy to face his men. Packed in close order in which five or more of the leaf-shaped blades protruded through their front ranks, the '*sarissa*' pike could pierce both Roman shields and armour, claimed Polybius, who was deported to Italy in the political outfall of the battle.[80] More troubling still was a recent lunar eclipse that saw Paulus' superstitious Romans clashing bronze utensils and waving firebrands at the heavens to avert disaster.

Having recently conquered Carthage and the Near East, the Romans had a corps of war elephants, the 'tanks' of the ancient battlefield. They knew Alexander had faced a significant wall of them in India, and they had seen first-hand the devastation they could cause under the command of Hannibal at Zama and in battles against Pyrrhus and Seleucid Syria. Not only could elephants trample through tight infantry formation, they were an effective screen against cavalry charges as horses detested their smell.

The clash of arms at Pydna finally commenced in the afternoon. Aemilius Paullus knew the Macedonian phalanx could not be penetrated or even engaged head-on without huge losses, so the Romans skilfully withdrew in good order until the terrain became uneven to loosen the enemy formation. By now fewer home-grown citizen soldiers comprised Perseus' ranks, with Gallic, Thracian and Illyrian mercenaries to be found in greater proportions. As at Cynoscephalae, the more versatile Roman maniples began pouring into the gaps in the Macedonian ranks to stab and slash the pike bearers, who lacked sufficient flank protection from more mobile hoplites. When the outcome looked hopeless, King Perseus and his cavalry ignominiously fled the field.

Some 20,000 of his Macedonians were killed on that day, with 11,000 more captured alive. The Romans then marched on Aegae and Pella, where they tore down the outer walls and partly destroyed the royal cities. Courtiers were exiled, along with the king's generals and garrison commanders, while the state's nobles and their children over age 15 were shipped to Italy, along with the chained King Perseus who had been captured in Thrace. The Third Macedonian War was over.

Macedon was divided into four civic zones, population movements were halted and interregional marriages were forbidden. The state's mines were closed before it formally became a Roman province a few decades on after pretenders claiming to be Perseus' sons briefly steered the nation to war, whereupon Macedon was finally occupied and the monarchy abolished. Cicero later claimed the wealth arriving in 250 wagons full of the spoils of war did away with taxes 'for all time to come', and Livy stated in his account of the rise of Rome that the triumphant procession displaying the booty lasted ninety days.[81]

Yet Macedon's strategic position between Europe and Asia meant it remained a vital communications hub, and soon the Roman-built highway, the *Via Egnatia*, stretched from the Adriatic coast through the former capital Pella and onto the Dardanelles, along which Rome's legions marched on their way to conquer the

Near East. For a while, the strategically important river and coastal cities flourished under occupation.

Foreshadowing Macedon's fall, the dynasties of Alexander's successors in Asia – both the Seleucids in Syria and to the East, and the Ptolemies in Egypt – were humbled when Roman legions under the brothers Scipio marched through Anatolia to battle at Magnesia, and when Rome's fleet was invited to sail into Alexandria to 'protect' Egyptian affairs. The prophetic verse of the Sibyl, who predicted the empire's downfall, entered the history books:

> Macedon whose kings are from Argos,
> Your good and your bad both come in the reign of Philip,
> One shall create lords for cities and for people:
> The other shall utterly destroy your glory
> Beaten down by eastern and western men.[82]

Macedon's capital cities began to crumble under the march of seasons as the expanding Roman Empire shifted the focus of power to new battlefields and emerging centres of wealth. Aegae stagnated until a landslide buried much of the old city in the first century AD, after which it became uninhabited.

The Huns migrated from Central Europe in the fourth century, pushing the Gothic tribes south into Roman-occupied provinces, and the boundaries of the greater 'Macedonia' waxed and waned to the bordering provinces of Epirus 'Nova', Moesia, Dardania, Dacia, Thessalia and what became known as the Praetorian Prefecture of Illyricum.[83] Eastern Roman power survived the collapse of its western provinces in the form of the Byzantine Empire, and although the *Via Egnatia* was fortified as a vital communications line, power gravitated to the city of Byzantium on the Bosphorus, now renamed Constantinople. Eventually, the name 'Aegae' ceased to be used; only in oral legend did the former Macedonian city of kings survive. Its history was grazed over by goats once more and the only witness to its forgotten location was an early Christian basilica built with the stones from the fallen ruins.

Recurring bubonic plagues hit the Byzantine Empire in the sixth century AD, decimating the local population and leaving many provinces abandoned, while the threat of the invading Avaroslavs, who penetrated the coastal plains beside the Strymon River and settled in northern Macedonia, led to further evacuations in the seventh century when a major earthquake hit.[84] A new Dark Age descended on the Eastern Mediterranean.

Although a so-called 'Macedonian Renaissance' took place through the ninth to eleventh centuries, it was established by an allegedly Thracian-born peasant of Armenian stock and imperial power remained in Constantinople. New efforts to regain former 'Roman' territory focused on campaigns against Arabs in the

Adriatic, Asia Minor and the Near East. The hinterland of ancient Macedon slept as crusaders marched past to regain the Holy Land and establish outposts in the Seljuk Sultanate that would in time become Turkey.

Below a huge grass-covered mound, tombs lay silent under the weight of earth and time. At some point, an earthquake must have toppled silver wine pourers and double-handled drinking cups like those poetised in the *Iliad*; an internal marble door to a tomb collapsed on burial objects, which clattered and bounced off the stone floors of the humid porous chambers and settled into ink-black corners.[85] Still more centuries passed; wooden tables and couches with ivory inlays crumbed to dust and spear shafts turned to ash, leaving iron blades lodged in walls. In the adjacent antechamber of the most sumptuous tomb of all, rotted arrow shafts filled a gold-faced bow-and-arrow quiver with ash, leaving bronze arrowheads behind as their evidence. Five gold bands tumbled to the floor as one of the vexatious epitaphs of its owner.

Sometime in the generations that followed, a stone pile at the centre of the conspicuous hill collapsed under its own weight, so that the apex became a concave bowl from which shepherds might survey the plains below. Seasons were born and died in droughts and snow, while the winter wash from the mountain streams hurled down the Pierian hills that backed the ancient abandoned cemetery the tumulus overlooked.

Vibrant wall paintings slowly faded to haunting pastel hues, but the careful hand of the artist never departed. Wine pourers fashioned in silver, the metal of the Moon Goddess, sat hauntingly ready for new use, while the gold boxes containing the bones of Macedon's royalty retained their ageless youth. Still the tombs held their breath and never gave away the location of the bone-burned dead below. The first capital of the kingdom, which once forged a mighty empire, was slowly subsumed by the pastoral hills, and so was a sullen population that knew nothing but occupation armies ever since.

Chapter 4

A Phoenix Rises from the Ashes

>Every new beginning comes from some other beginning's end.
>—Seneca the Younger[1]

Spring 1855

In the late spring of 1855, as the Ottoman Empire was embroiled in the Crimean War, a young French archaeologist named Léon Heuzey arrived in recently liberated Greece. He began searching for clues of ancient habitation in the now partially accessible north, a region still named 'Selanik' and under waning Turkish occupation.

The Byzantine Empire had been overrun by the Ottoman Turks in the fifteenth century; Greece, the Balkans and Central Europe as far west as Vienna faced the advance of the Sultan's regiments threatening the 'infidels' and their Christian god. In 1821, Greek nationalists began a series of uprisings, and though the Acropolis in Athens was finally occupied by the Turks in 1827, a growing tide of philhellenic sentiment across Europe, mixed with veiled political aspirations in the fallout of the Napoleonic Wars, resulted in the call for an armistice; Greece would be autonomous in return for an annual tribute to the Sultan.

The truce was an artful call to armed intervention by allied western powers and led to a decisive naval action in October of that year. British, French and Russian gunships sailed into Navarino Bay in the southern Peloponnese and sunk the joint Turkish-Egyptian fleet, a victory so overwhelming that it marked the beginning of the end of Ottoman occupation. The Kingdom of Greece was officially declared independent in 1832, but the newly liberated nation only extended north as far as lower Thessaly.

By now, the written records of Greece and Macedon's classical past resided in dilapidated manuscripts in Western European scriptoriums, where they had been ferried to safety by late-Medieval and Renaissance scholars in the face of the Ottoman threat. Guided by the clues he had found in these contradictory ancient sources, Léon Heuzey saw intriguing mounds of unknown origin and fallen stones in patterns and geometric lines that appeared far from random in the sparsely populated rolling countryside that overlooked the Thermaic Gulf.

After questioning an educated priest, Heuzey learned he had walked blindly past masonry that was almost underfoot amidst the winding tracks used by buffalo and bullock-carts. He had been within a few leagues of the city ruins 'without ever learning so much as its name'.[2] Local peasants led him to the remains of a sprawling building complex that suggested a substantial settlement, now hidden by the dense green shade of elms, had been 'sanctified by ancient religious customs'.[3] The tantalizing name of the nearby villages – Palatitsia, 'little palaces' – hinted that somewhere in the foothills of the Pierian mountains, Macedon's ancient capitals lay waiting to be unearthed.

Apart from stumbling on a flooded vaulted tomb of 'Macedonian design' which had been looted in antiquity, and surveying a curiously isolated hill with suspiciously symmetrical proportions, Heuzey's next expedition six years later in 1861, supported by architect Pierre Daumet and financed by the French emperor Napoleon III, failed to find its prize in the still-sparsely inhabited rolling countryside which was blighted by the ever-present risk of malaria. Heuzey believed the sprawling ruins, which incorporated what was left of a post-Byzantine chapel with a curious inscription housing an archaic Greek architectural term, were part of the ancient city of Valla; it was a misidentification perpetuated by Justin's claim that it was the ancient town of Edessa some 40km to the north that had been renamed 'Aegae' by Caranus in dim prehistory.[4]

A still-vexed Heuzey transported promising masonry from the ruins to the Louvre in Paris, but he nevertheless left us a vivid description of the region, 'Roumlouki' as the Ottomans termed it, and its people, the 'Romioi': 'of Greek villages in which the only cohesive remnant of the ancient Macedonian population is concentrated. The residents retain under their sheepskins and the tight Bulgarian turban a type which is entirely Hellenic: the long oval face with the straight nose, the deep-set almond eyes, rather close to one another, the expressive and intelligent features.'[5] Heuzey added the prophetic prediction:

> If indeed there is a chance to solve the mystery which envelops the history, institutions and even the topography of Macedonia, if there is still some hope of rescuing from deep oblivion the antiquities of a people who played a significant role in the world, we are convinced that the answer to these difficulties is concealed in the hills of Palatitsia.

No excavations followed.

In August 1913, after the Balkan Wars, the Province of Macedonia was formally ceded to Greece by the Ottoman Empire under the terms of the Treaty of Bucharest. Yet the region remained politically explosive: previously ruled by Turkish, Greek and Albanian overlords, it was now administered by an Athens-dominated government far to the south, while its northern borders were being disputed by Serbia and Bulgaria, who were seeking an Aegean seaboard.[6] Although British and French infantry units created an allied zone here in the First World War, a clear recognition of its strategic importance, the 1920 British Admiralty *Handbook of Macedonia* described it as 'a region which has been for the last forty years less traversed by Western Europeans than any other parts of Europe south of the Arctic regions'.

The defeat of the Greek army in Turkey a decade later led to a forced population exchange and over a million refugees traversed the Dardanelles. Many of them were settled in the Macedonian principality of Emathia, where hundreds of thousands of immigrants were soon decimated by malaria.[7] In the early 1920s, the Greek refugees from the Euxine Pontus region of Turkish Anatolia established a village on higher ground above the malarial marshlands between the two small poverty-stricken settlements of Koutles and Barbes, naming it 'Vergina' after the legendary queen who was believed to have occupied the nameless ruins nearby.

With no historic affiliation to the site and scant knowledge of its past, the fallen stones from the site were used as sturdy masonry in new houses they constructed beside a prominent mound. In time, the barren and depressed hillsides and the vast plains below were transformed into horticulturally rich terrains and drained of the malarial pest. Fruit trees, tobacco, cotton and corn were cultivated, replacing the herds and flocks of cows and goats which gradually disappeared from sight.

The late 1920s and 1930s saw brief and intermittent British expeditions to the region, including a series of walks through the Haliacmon gorge by the classicist Nicholas Hammond, but little was discovered except pottery when topographical surveys were being made. The walls and graves of Homer's 'golden, wide-wayed Mycenae' excavated by Heinrich Schliemann in the 1870s, and southern Greece's better-documented classical past, still lured excavation budgets to tomb-rich Boeotia, Attica and the ruins of the Peloponnese.

In 1938, after almost eighty years of archaeological neglect, during which the interior of northern Greece was still largely inaccessible to foreign civilians, Konstantine Rhomaios, a professor and folklorist at the newly founded Aristotle University of Thessaloniki, recommenced excavations at Vergina, where he slowly unveiled the shape of what conformed to a vast royal palace. A second Macedonian-styled chamber tomb with an intact marble throne was discovered, though it too had been looted and half-filled with soil; shepherds, it appeared, had taken refuge inside for centuries. Intermittent work continued, though it was hindered by foreign war, domestic conflict and chronic underfunding.

Work ceased with general mobilization of the country in 1940. The Second World War was calamitous for the Balkans and northern Greece; to suit his shifting foreign policy, Adolf Hitler offered eastern Macedonia and the city of Thessalonica to Bulgaria and Yugoslavia to provide them an Aegean port. In 1946, during the Greek Civil War, a military brigade camped in the hollow of the great mound at

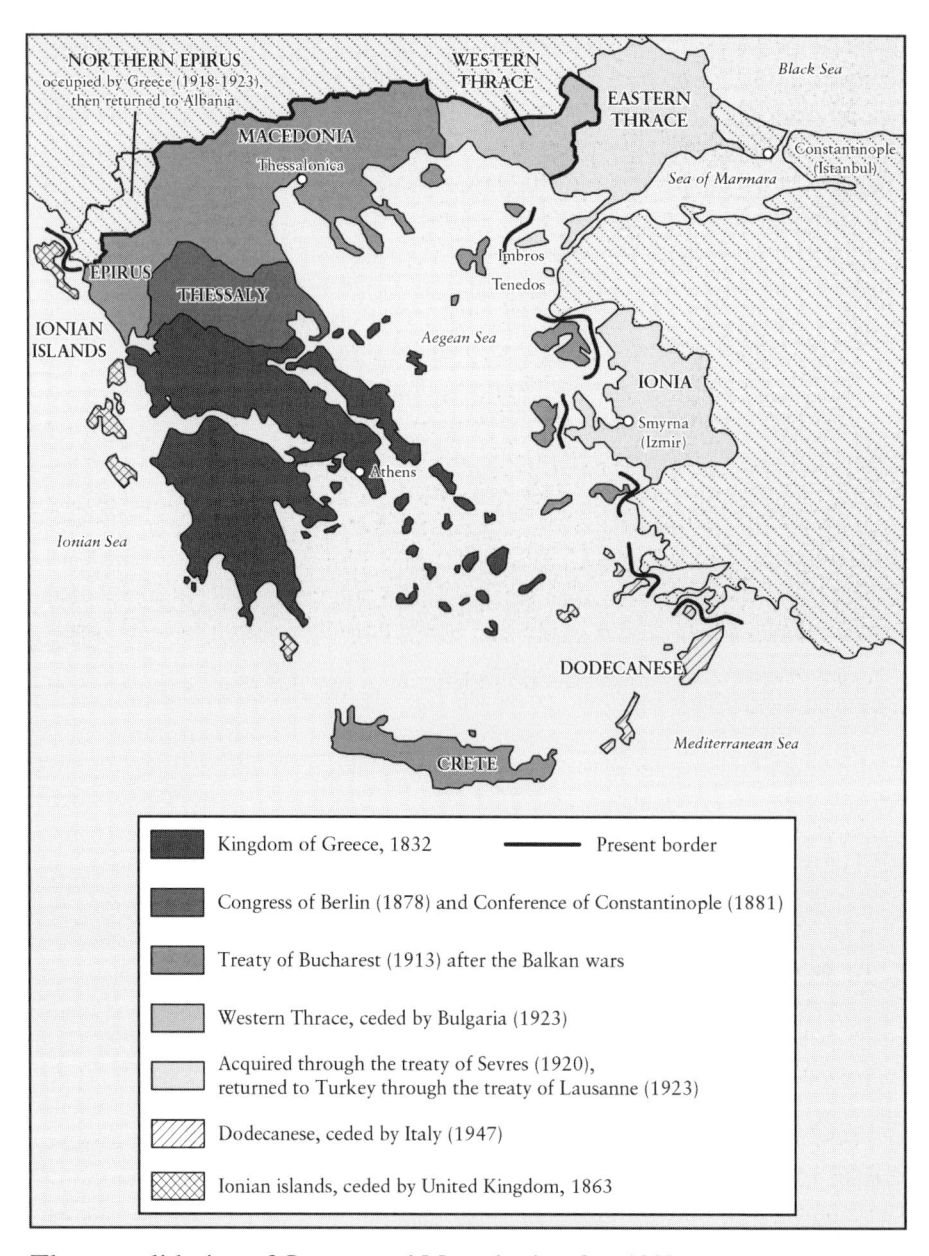

The consolidation of Greece and Macedonia after 1832.

Vergina and dug defensive trenches into its entire upper surface, leaving mysterious marble shards and inscribed stones strewn about the site. Ten of eleven unearthed fragments even joined at the edges to form a four-line epigram, but the clues to what lay below were once more abandoned.[8]

Professor Rhomaios and pupils including a young Manolis Andronikos at Vergina in 1938.

As recently as 1948, in his *History of the Persian Empire*, in which Macedon had played a major part, Albert Ten Eyck Olmstead stated of the still-misidentified capital city:

> The Macedonia of Alexander has disappeared, almost without a trace. Its older capital Aegae is a malaria-ridden site and nothing more ... The tombs of the Macedonian rulers, where Alexander had thought to be gathered to his fathers, have never been found; his own capital, Pella, is a mass of shapeless ruins.

From 1957 onwards, excavations in the area were carried out by Professors Georgios Bakalakis and then by Photius Petsas, former Curator of Antiquities in Macedonia for excavations at Pella.[9] But the name 'Aegae' would not be spoken of at Vergina for another twenty years.

Chapter 5

The Scientist's Elation and the Desecrator's Guilt

> If you do not expect the unexpected,
> you will not recognise it when it arrives.
> —Heraclitus

Any twentieth-century classicist was nurtured on the archaeological triumphs of the century past: the unravelling of the mystique of the Egyptian *Book of the Dead* which guided the path for the mummified pharaohs, and the recent rising from the dust of the ruins of ancient Nineveh and Babylon. The discovery of the forgotten cities of the Hittite Empire, mentioned in the Old Testament more than fifty times but not unearthed until the end of the 1880s, along with the deciphering of both Egyptian hieroglyphics and cuneiform tablets from the Near East, had each helped to unlock doors to the once dim and unfathomable civilizations.

Above all, scholars were inspired to pick up shovels by what Heinrich Schliemann uncovered at Troy and Mycenae through the 1860s and 1870s, and by Howard Carter's 1920s excavations in the Valley of the Kings, where Tutankhamun lay buried for 3,200 years. But unearthing treasure troves is as rare as fishermen catching coelacanths, and many archaeologists spent their careers digging up nothing except pot sherds. Schliemann, however, had a powerful divining rod when searching for Priam's treasure: an unwavering belief in the historicity of the verses of Homer.

The *Iliad* was nothing short of a *Bible* to the ancient Greeks, even though it only captured detail of the final two months of the ten-year epic struggle at Troy. But in Schliemann's day, the epic poet Homer was generally thought of as a re-teller of unfounded ancient sagas and Priam's city was still relegated by scholars to the shadowland of myth.

Schliemann was not deterred; he was a staunch 'euhemerist' who saw in the hills and tumuli scattered across the plain that he targeted indisputable proofs of the siege that took place in the Late Bronze Age of the twelfth century BC. The site he was excavating lay close to the ancient Hellespont in north-western Anatolia, today's Dardanelles, a geographically sound location when cross-referenced with

Homeric texts, despite the receded coastline. The nine cities since discovered in the once-prominent hill at Hissarlik have not yielded definitive proof of Troy, though modern excavations are turning up new evidence of defensive ditches and an expansive city in the shadow of the always-troublingly small citadel, which assist the excavator's claim.[1]

There are many parallels between Schliemann's quest for Troy and Andronikos' excavations at Vergina, where graves dating back to the Homeric Age exist. The first was a major geographic misidentification: archaeologists of the 1860s believed the remote Turkish village of Bunarbashi, some three hours inland from the Aegean coast, was the true site of Priam's citadel, as it had natural springs consistent with Homer's description of the Trojan mound. Similarly, in the early days of Greek archaeology, Edessa in northern Greece was associated with ancient Aegae, thanks to Justin's faulty statement concerning Caranus' founding city.

Both Heinrich Schliemann and Manolis Andronikos were digging in malarial regions and in the shadow of a great mountain upon which sat the gods: Mount Ida in Anatolia, where Zeus looked down on Troy, and Mount Olympus on Macedon's southern border, from where the immortal aristocrats spied upon its kings. Moreover, each archaeologist was excavating a hill described as a 'tremendous onion' due to layer upon layer of debris,[2] and both were about to terminate the season's work when shovels hit the treasure troves that had them spellbound in gold; on 14 June 1873 in Schliemann's case, while Andronikos' work paid off on 8 November 1977.[3] But unlike his German counterpart, Andronikos was working in native soil, so he felt an overriding obligation to display his artefacts at their home, whereas Schliemann hid the Trojan treasure from Turkish officials and spirited his gold away.

Like all excavators before him, Andronikos had to take his archaeological bearings from conflicting ancient texts and uncertainties therein: the disappearance of the first-hand eyewitness accounts, the poor condition of those that survived, determining how faithfully the manuscripts represented the author's original wording and intent, and separating genuine from frauds. Close scrutiny of the rare paraphrases we have from the era of Philip and Alexander suggest even the eyewitnesses to events were involved in double-dealing; they elevated their own contributions to the kings' campaigns, incriminated their rivals and airbrushed out unsavoury episodes best swept under the mat. All this made listening to exactly what ancient ruins of Macedon had to say something of a challenge.

Andronikos had been a student of Konstantine Rhomaios at Vergina in the pre-Second World War years. Upon his return from the Middle East in 1945, he seized an opportunity to visit the site, which still appeared as he remembered it, but 'the people had suffered much'.[4] He remained doggedly determined after he was appointed to the Archaeological Service at the city of Veria in 1949. It was a post that fortuitously included responsibility for the still-nameless mounds and stone walls at Vergina some 12km away, and he commenced his excavating there in 1951.[5]

In the 1920s, Andronikos' family had been amongst the refugees leaving Turkish territory under the forced resettlement plan. A professor of classical archaeology since 1961, with a spell at Oxford University, he began digging new exploratory trenches in the Great Tumulus in 1962/63 when it became clear from the soil that the mound *was* man-made. But it was not until 1976 that he claimed his first significant breakthrough at Vergina: hundreds of broken marble tombstones were unearthed from the mounds scattered across the rolling hillside to the west of the town. Some of them, from the poorer tombs of ordinary city residents 'whose name was the most important thing they possessed', had mysteriously ended up in the upper soil of the Great Tumulus itself.[6]

Up until this point, the 'palace' ruins that Heuzey had misidentified a century before, covering a rectangle measuring an impressive 104.5 × 88.5 metres, were still tentatively referred to as part of an unknown 'summer resort' for the ancient nobility, though clearly fortified with walls. 'Towards the north, Mount Paikon rises in a steep cone and it spreads eastwards in a long chain of descending hills at the end of which the observer in antiquity would have been able to decry the high gables of Pella,' Heuzey poetically wrote of the majestic position of the royal building, in which almost all rooms opened onto an internal courtyard.[7] But it had also become clear from the excavations carried out by the Aristotle University under Rhomaios since 1938, as well as from the 'robber trenches' still visible at Vergina, that the Greek refugees who fled the Pontus had removed a great deal of the stonework to build new homes, especially from the ancient acropolis above the palace.[8]

Nevertheless, excavations of the cemetery in 1976 turned up corroborating evidence for Plutarch's description of the sack of Aegae by the Gallic Celts. This marked the 'jumping-off point' at which Andronikos took Hammond's 'heretical' theory seriously: Vergina may, indeed, lie on the site of Macedon's ancient capital Aegae. And yet Andronikos was still left with 'a feeling of both hope and dread': the promise of tombs was intoxicating, but the fear of finding them looted remained ever present.[9]

The shattered tombstones adjacent to the Great Tumulus were clearly part of a necropolis which lay outside the city walls where over 100 burial mounds averaging 15–20 metres in diameter were still visible over its one square kilometre spread, despite the repeated ploughing of the undulating terrain in recent years. Many mounds covered multiple clan graves dating to the Early Iron Age, suggesting the site had been continuously occupied for 700 years *before* the reigns of Philip II and Alexander, earlier even than the founding myths of the royal line, when Phrygians of debated origin are said to have inhabited the land.[10]

The engravings on the tombstones of ancient Aegae made it clear that by the fifth century BC, the root-names of the occupants were Greek, although some

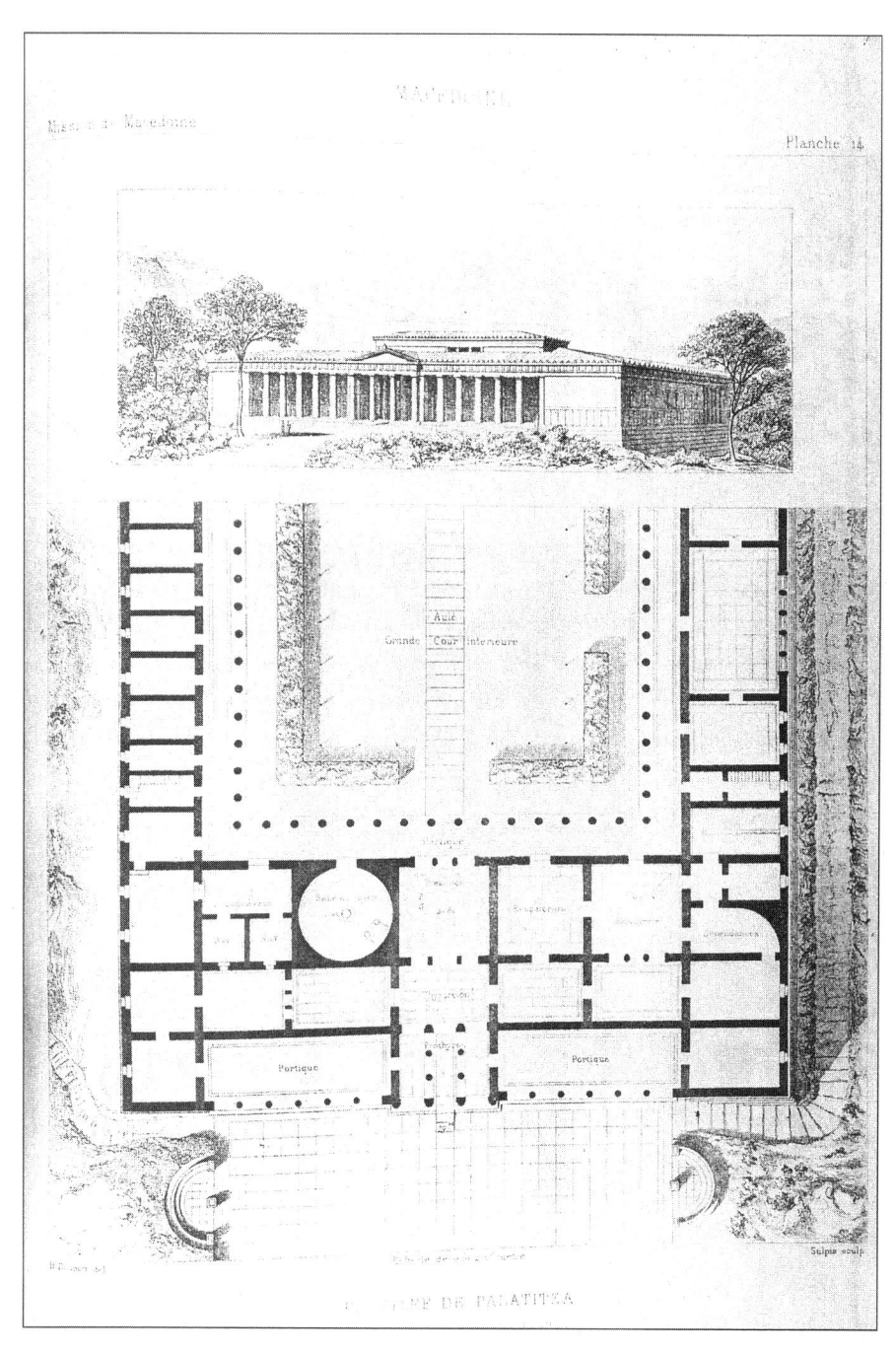

H. Daumet's 1861 hypothetical reconstruction of the elevation of the palace based on the ruins he believed to be part of the ancient city of Valla.

The ancient cemetery of the tumuli adjacent to modern Vergina.

indigenous titles that are unknown to Attica suggested that the population once had a naming convention characteristically Macedonian. The ruins were becoming key witnesses in an ongoing philological debate: did the Macedonians originally have a distinct language, which would suggest they were of a different race, or were their idioms from a different branch of early proto-Greek?

As one scholar has pointed out, unlike the Israelites, the Greeks preserved no legends recalling their entry into the peninsula sometime in the second millennium BC, and tribal migrations we read of remain the stuff of legend.[11] Moreover, unlike Latin, which spawned the offshoot vernacular languages in the regions of Europe once governed by Rome, the archaic dialect or regional tongue of Macedon became extinct. Nevertheless, Andronikos felt the linguistic archaeology at Vergina pointed to the Macedonians and Greeks being kindred, as King Alexander I had claimed, and neither of Thracian or Illyrian origin.[12]

A year on, in 1977, Andronikos began the main assault of the 60,000 cubic metres of earth in the Great Tumulus itself, where sixty-seven broken grave markers were soon uncovered.[13] After finding evidence of a modest sacrificial fire in the soil and a section of a free-standing wall of unbaked bricks, the first recognizable structure unearthed by his team appeared to have been a shrine or place of hero

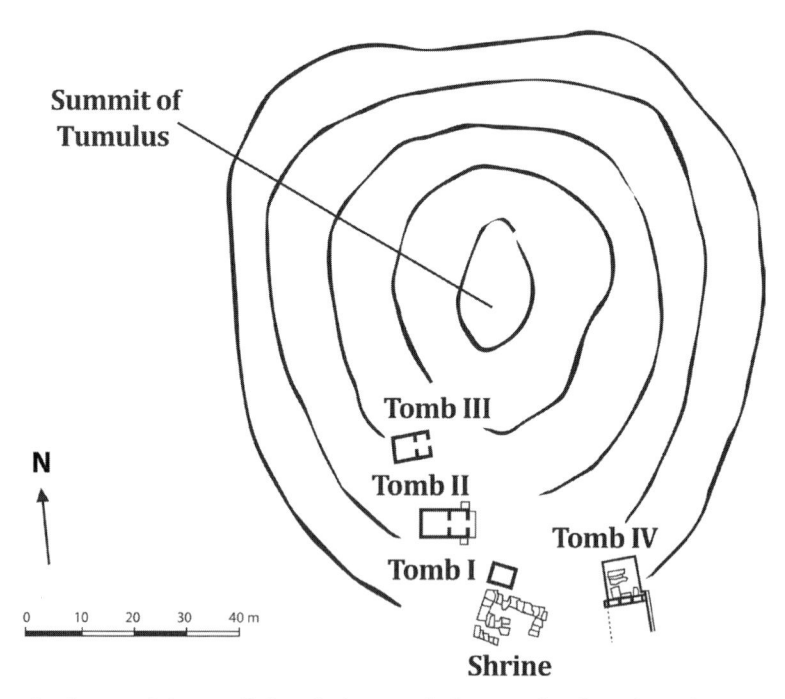

48   Unearthing the Family of Alexander the Great

The relative positions of the shrine and the tombs forming the so-called 'cluster of Philip' found under the Great Tumulus at Vergina.

worship, a '*heroon*' to the Greeks.[14] Andronikos based the identification on its construction *above* ancient ground level, in contrast to graves and tombs which were generally buried *below* the ancient terrain. If it had functioned as a cenotaph, ceremonial fires and libations no doubt took place on the spot in remembrance of the dead, and it must have been erected to honour the occupant of a close-by tomb.[15]

The shrine had been completely destroyed and only its foundation stones remained. They told of sturdy, thick stone walls measuring some 9.6 × 8 metres, and scattered marble fragments suggested it once had a superstructure of extremely fine workmanship. Andronikos believed it had most likely been erected posthumously to honour a king or his royal line, and no doubt it was once full of valuable votive offerings. Its foundations lay *outside* the southernmost edge of the smaller inner tumulus, which was betrayed by reddish soil, some 4 metres high and 20 metres wide, and which originally covered what would soon be labelled Tombs I and II.[16] Only two kings of this period are known to have been worshipped with such hero shrines or cenotaphs this way: Philip II and his father Amyntas III, whose shrine at Pydna was known as the 'Amyntaeum'.[17]

Unearthed next was Tomb I, which lay less than 2 metres from the shrine and a little further north into the rising depth of the Great Tumulus. It had no entrance

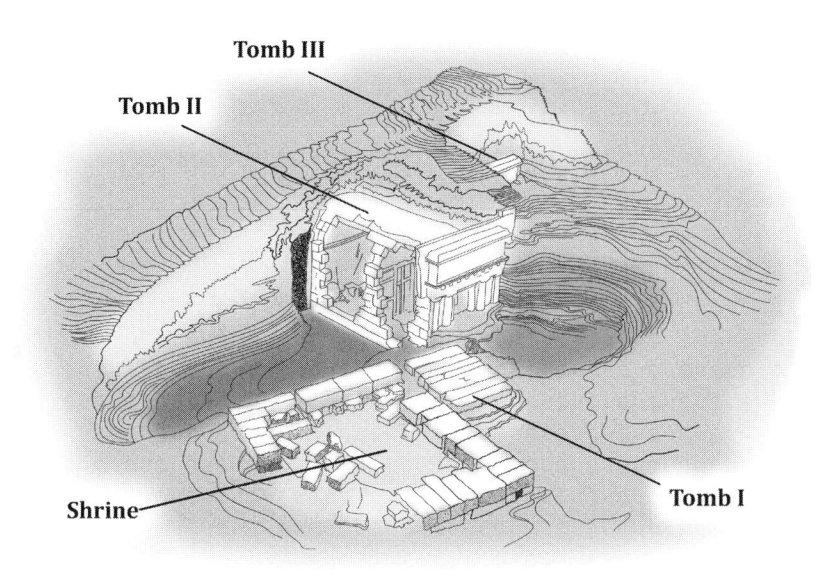

A model of the shrine in the foreground, the roof of the underground Tomb I immediately beside it, Tomb II standing in the background, with the entrance to Tomb III just visible beyond, deeper into the rising tumulus.

door and was a simple 'cist tomb', an oblong stone-lined box in the ground, measuring 3.5 × 2.09 metres, roofed by thick, dressed limestone slabs. It had been looted in antiquity, and a hole had also been punched through its southern wall. Internal edging inside Tomb I suggested that wooden planking had once formed a ceiling immediately below the stone roof. Made from the same porous dressed limestone as the shrine, any planking must have rotted away or been removed in the process of pillaging.

Andronikos reasoned that because Tomb I was positioned so close to the above-ground shrine, it must have been built first, or it would have undermined and destabilized the above-ground temple, a theory supported by the fact that the northern wall of the shrine appeared to rest on soil excavated from the pit of Tomb I. Some chronology of the building seemed to be emerging.

Tomb I was the scene of a 'violent disaster', as Andronikos put it, with bones scattered about from their original positions. As excavators removed the deep soil, they found human and animal remains at various levels; bones closest to the stone floor *might* logically belong to the original occupants. The only remaining artefacts were sherds of black glazed pottery dating 'to around the middle of the 4th century BC', along with a rare marble shell and an ivory comb, possibly from a woman's toiletry. The gender theory was supported by the lack of iron weapons, as these were usually left behind by looters who were searching for more valuable gold and silver.[18]

Yet skilful plastering still clung to the inside walls of Tomb I, which were covered with beautiful frescos, despite the marks left by tomb robbers' chipping tools.[19] The most striking was a depiction of the mythical theme of the Abduction of Persephone by Hades on the north side. This was the most accomplished art in any of the tombs, despite its quick impressionistic style in which the artist's preliminary sketches remain visible in the style of Leonardo da Vinci's later sketches. Hermes is depicted running in front of a four-horsed chariot in which Hades, 'the conductor of the souls' with a sceptre in one hand, has his arm around the waist of a frantic Persephone, who strains to look back at her despairing friend, Kyane. The orange lines of Zeus' thunderbolt hang above.[20] The Three Fates and what appears a grieving Demeter adorn the walls.

The occupant was clearly someone of great status deserving such an artist, who, Andronikos proposed, may have been Nicomachus of Thebes, a 'quick painter' according to the Roman naturalist Pliny the Elder. Nicomachus was broadly contemporary with the proposed tomb dating and is said to have painted this very theme.[21] Thanks to this 'other-worldly' art, Tomb I also became known as the 'Tomb of Persephone'.[22]

The Archangel's Deliverance

Discovered next, under 6 metres of soil and rock, was the unlooted Tomb II which caused such a commotion in November 1977. Located some 6 metres further north and towards the centre of the mound, Tomb II was a far larger and more ornate structure. Once again, it resided *below* original ground level and is referred to as 'Macedonian' in style due to its 'barrel-vaulted' design featuring an arched roof secured by a keystone, and its segregation into a main chamber and an antechamber separated by heavy marble doors. A walled trench known as a '*dromos*' had once descended to the entrance, framed by an 'illusionist' Doric stone facade: the columns either side of the doors were not structural, but simply decorative to provide the illusion of a grander building behind.[23] Above the entrance could be seen a vivid hunting scene that had miraculously defied the assault of moisture and soil; Chrysoula Paliadeli proposed that the artist was Nicomachus' son, the famed Aristides.[24]

The crowd watched on 8 November 1977 as Manolis Andronikos prepared himself for the descent into the tomb once the keystone was removed. He had been 'deeply stirred' as the structure emerged from the soil, and when he finally descended into the chamber, his disenchantment at the poorly plastered walls passed instantly when he was awe-struck by what gradually emerged below.

Above: Tomb II rising like a phoenix from the ashes in 1977 in the Great Tumulus, after it has been covered by protective corrugated iron roofing. The hunting fresco above the entrance can be seen. Below: the cutting away of the keystone.

His torch slowly illuminated a fine rusted-iron and gold breastplate, bronze greaves (which were the shin guards of an ancient infantryman), a solid-crested iron helmet, a gilded diadem and the remains of what would prove to be an elaborately decorated shield in ivory, glass and gold. Beside them rested various weapons with iron blades that were once attached to now-rotted wooden shafts of spears and the notoriously long deadly 'sarissa' of the Macedonian infantryman, the two-handed pike with which Philip and Alexander had humbled the armies of Greece and Persia.

Scattered around the chamber were cooking tripods of iron and bronze, alongside silver serving vessels, mixing bowls and unguent bottles of ceramic or alabaster for banqueting with the gods, among other less-easily identifiable grave goods.[25] Andronikos' attention was drawn to a long cylindrical object covered in layers of alternating cloth and gold: surely a royal sceptre.[26] Here lay all the objects for the after-life of a Macedonian king. But the most intriguing object of all was a closed marble sarcophagus, suggesting something precious inside.

The opening of the sarcophagus required the arrival of a technical conservator, so photographs could be taken of the tomb in its newly discovered state. Once gathered in the darkness of the resealed tomb, they managed to open the heavy marble lid and what emerged in the torchlight was breathtaking: a never-before-seen all-gold ossuary or funerary chest fashioned to hold the bones of the cremated dead, like those described in Homer's *Iliad*. More staggering still, it was embossed with the sixteen-pointed 'starburst' symbol of the Macedonian royal house. Placing the gold chest on the floor, Andronikos slowly lifted the lid in silence; inside lay carefully positioned charred bones, some coloured with a bluish-purple from what must have been a covering fabric. On top of the skeleton sat a heavy golden wreath delicately fashioned with acorns and oak leaves.

Both Andronikos and the General Inspector of Antiquities decided that the contents had to be removed immediately to the safety of the Archaeological Museum of Thessalonica, not least because bad weather still threatened the exposed tomb and some of the contents were clearly threatened by advanced oxidation; so a chemist was summoned and the position of everything noted.[27] But before the artefacts were lifted out, Andronikos had the chance to observe two of five small ivory carved heads initially found on the floor. A bearded face bore a remarkable likeness to images of King Philip II, visible, for example, on a Roman-era gold medallion from Tarsus, and the other face of a younger man appeared to be a lifelike rendering of his son, Alexander the Great.[28]

That evening, Andronikos drove in silence to the sanctuary of the Thessalonica Museum, under the escort of an Archaeological Service car, with the gold chest full of bones cradled firmly in the lap of the technical conservator on the back seat. When they were finally in a safe room, the chest was opened and the treasure displayed. Andronikos did not sleep that night, and many more that followed were filled with questions that might have answers too profound to voice.

On 21 November 1977, still punch-drunk from the contents discovered in the main chamber, and with the 'cold eye of the anatomist and the rigid logic of the mathematician', Andronikos planned how to access the tomb's second room, the antechamber which lay the other side of internal marble dividing doors wedged closed under another sagged lintel. Unlike the exposed roof above the first vault they entered, the antechamber exterior was plastered with a thick layer of stucco or lime plaster, so Andronikos decided to remove a block in the interior dividing wall.[29] Once it had been hammered through, he wriggled headfirst into the second room and shone his torch about him.

The antechamber was more carefully decorated, with deep red paint still gracing the upper walls and white on the lower. But the rendering had blistered and lifted, suggesting the plaster did not have time to dry before the room was buried under soil and deprived of air. Andronikos also appreciated the unusual scale of the room, which was almost as large as the first, whereas antechambers

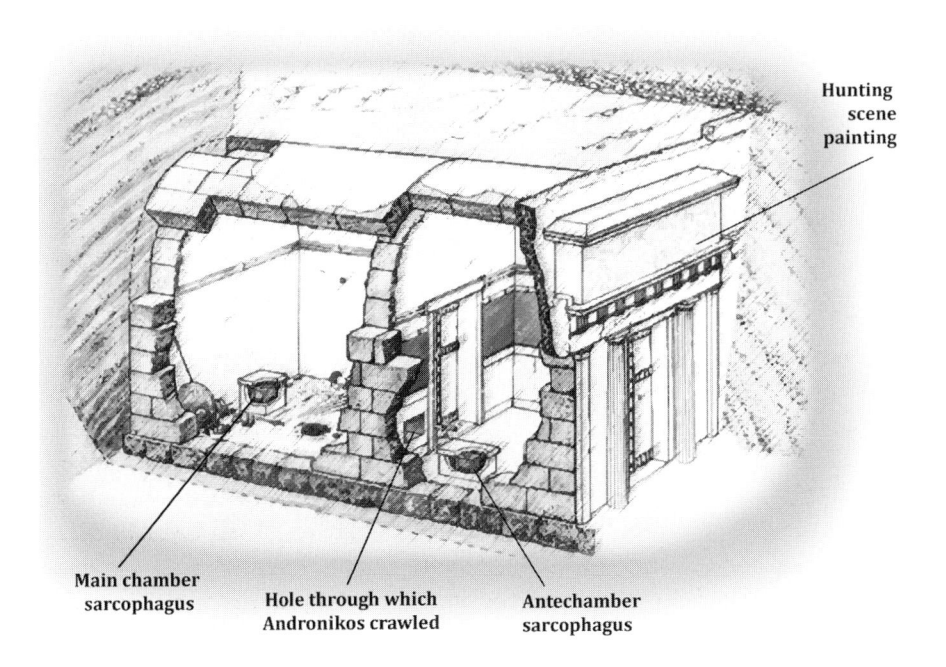

A cutaway view of Tomb II in its subterranean position. The rear roof keystone is shown removed, and visible to the right of the door adjoining the main chamber and antechamber is the hole through which Andronikos crawled.

were traditionally small repositories for artefacts.[30] The depth of this second room obviously facilitated the positioning of a funerary couch.

Stacked against the dividing doors was a pair of gilded bronze greaves, though they appeared uneven in length and in the shinbone shaping. Beside them rested remains of a stunning Scythian bow-and-arrow case known as a '*gorytos*', which was covered in silver and gold impressed with images from antiquity. In what appeared to be wood ash at its base were bronze arrowheads and delicate gold bands. Andronikos spied iron spearheads and a gilded throat protector known as a 'pectoral', as well as ceremonial drinking vessels, perfume vases in alabaster and an austere brooch of 'Illyrian' type. Then his torch beam landed on a further marble sarcophagus with a golden myrtle wreath on the floor beside it.

Questions came tumbling into his head: what was a Scythian bow-and-arrow quiver doing in a Macedonian tomb, and who did these weapons belong to? The following day, Andronikos and his team carefully lifted the sarcophagus lid and, sure enough, inside lay another gold funerary chest. It was slightly smaller and less ornate, but it was once again embossed with the starburst symbol of the ancient kings of Macedon, otherwise referred to as the 'Vergina Sun' or 'Star'.

The lifting of the antechamber marble sarcophagus lid. (*Image from Andronikos (1984) with kind permission of Ekdotike Athinon S.A. Publishers*)

The chest was tenderly laid on a plank so as not to disturb the layer of organic debris covering the floor. Andronikos raised the lid to reveal more burnt bones wrapped in the torn remains of a magnificent purple fabric interwoven with gold thread that had somehow evaded the ravages of time. A breathtakingly beautiful folded golden diadem rested at one end; he and his team had found the remains of a unique *double* burial.

Whoever the tomb occupants were had deserved armour and weapons of burnished gold, which still gleamed as bright as the day they were hammered into shape, banquet utensils of silver that had weathered to the duller tincture of argent, and bronze mixing bowls and jugs now coated in the bright lagoon-blue-green of oxidation. Organic matter that must have been wood, leather and cloth left stains, imprints and other telltale signs around the tomb, their story still to be pieced together with that of the still-controversial identification of the ancient city itself.

Andronikos' thoughts caressed the gilded artefacts that some craftsmen had fashioned for, he felt certain, the most famous of its kings, including two golden boxes containing the cremated remains of…[31] He dared not utter the name aloud in November 1977, not even to himself, but his twenty-five years of painstaking excavation at Vergina appeared to have finally paid off.

Dissecting the Double Burial

Apart from the difference in the internal plastering, a number of additional pointers convinced the excavator that the two chambers comprising Tomb II had been built, or completed, at different times. What Andronikos found within bore all the hallmarks of separate burials, which must have linked the occupants in some way, a clue back to a unique set of circumstances that might identify the bones.

Whereas plaster covered all of the exterior of the second room, the lower exterior walls of the main chamber remained exposed. However, a robust plaster layer covered the upper section and the roof, some 20cm thick in places, in which fingerprint indents of the workman could still be seen. This suggested that soil must have been piled up and around the base of the chamber before plaster was hastily applied to the top. Perhaps the most obvious clue to the two-stage construction was the vault of the antechamber, which rests a few centimetres lower than that of the main room and with no stones interlocking at the join. While it appeared that the side walls may have been erected for their full length in a single build, they never reached to the vaulted roof of the unfinished antechamber.[32]

Just as significant was a 'strikingly unexpected' feature on the west side of the roof: a crude brick structure had been erected above the main chamber before the roof plaster had dried, and traces of fire were visible. Andronikos initially believed this was some form of 'altar aimed to accept libations and sacrifices to honor the dead'. But he later revised his opinion after noting the disorganized piling of the bricks. He concluded a cremation of the inhabitant took place nearby, following which valuable objects found in the pyre debris were symbolically placed on the roof after the tomb had been sealed. Others believed the burnt bricks were actually part of the cremation structure itself.[33] Weapons had been sacrificed, ivory offerings thrown in the fire and even horse trappings were spotted, perhaps those of the captured assassins or Philip's famous chariot horses which were dedicated to the flames in Homeric style, Andronikos pondered.

A roof cremation seems unlikely when considering the scale of what took place. The pyre must have been a pyramid of wood many metres high which would have been burning for days, potentially reaching temperatures around 900°C. Such a pyre would have undoutedly affected the stones of the roof of the tomb and the soil around it, and would have left piles of ashes and charcoal and blackened everything with smoke and soot. Nothing of the sort was found on the tomb roof. Besides, the risk for the structure of the tomb from exposure to heat would have been very high.

But closer inspection of the remains turned up parts of the same gold oak wreath that lay in the gold chest full of bones and this supported the notion that the man in the main chamber was cremated in a ceremony conducted with special haste. The oak was the sacred tree of Zeus, and the kings of Macedon claimed descent from Heracles, his son. In older mythical dimensions preceding even the arrival of Caranus, another son of Zeus named Macedon fathered the eponymous race.[34]

There was one further peculiarity that betrayed very particular circumstances surrounding the construction of Tomb II: a quickly thrown-up wall of sun-dried bricks, which Andronikos predicted might be over 9-metres long before its full excavation, had once extended to the left and right of the entrance forming a protected 'yard' in front of the doors. This must have acted as a retaining wall to hold back soil until the antechamber and the trenched '*dromos*' were completed, which was most likely when the hunting scene would have been painted on the façade above the doors. Andronikos' final words on the issue left little room for doubt: 'It is clear that these two parts were built at different times and not as a unified whole.'[35]

The following season, 1978, saw the Great Tumulus yield another rare unlooted Macedonian-styled tomb, which was labelled 'Tomb III', and the same year saw the completion of the laboratory of Aristotle University of Thessaloniki at the site. But excavation work was briefly halted in the wake of the great Thessalonica earthquake late on the evening of 20 June, when fifteen seconds of violent shaking threatened the ancient structures. Discovered some 7 metres further north into the centre of the hill, Tomb III was but slightly smaller than Tomb II but similar in its 'Macedonian' design.

Nothing of the entrance frieze of Tomb III survived, as it appears to have been painted on either a wood or leather insert above the doors. The top walls of the antechamber were decorated on all sides with scenes of chariot races, which may denote the traditional 'Homeric' funeral games. A silver '*hydria*', or water pouring jug, housed the cremated remains of an adolescent thought to be age 13 to 16 years old. Precious items were scattered about the tomb, including a gold oak wreath, which once more suggested the presence of ancient royalty.[36]

The least contentious of all the structures because of the youth of the individual, Andronikos didn't hesitate to dub this the 'Tomb of the Prince'. Well-respected scholars assumed the deceased was Alexander IV, the murdered son of Alexander the Great and his wife Rhoxane, even though the sex determination of adolescent bones is difficult to establish.[37] But the identification was supported by the lack of a funeral pyre on the tomb roof, suggesting the youth had been cremated elsewhere and late reburied at Aegae.[38]

This grouping of Tombs I, II and III was soon referred to as the 'cluster of Philip II', the father of Alexander the Great, though Andronikos retained inverted commas around the labelling for safety's sake, admitting it was just a 'working hypothesis', but one he clearly favoured.[39]

The Chronology of Catastrophe

The discoveries at Vergina were first published in the 1978 September–October edition of the magazine *Archaeology*. When referring to the tombs, Andronikos concluded that they 'belong to a time span which does not exceed that of one generation'. He added that 'the date of all our finds was between 350 BC and, at the latest, 325 BC', though he conceded that the chronology could stretch down to 310 BC, a span broadly corroborated by the distinctive pottery sherds and artefact design. Moreover, 310 BC encompassed the murder of Alexander's sons.[40]

The dating realization was both 'fascinating and frightening' to Andronikos because, as he put it, 'from 359 BC to 336 BC ... there was only one king in Macedon, Philip II'. He added that Alexander the Great, who succeeded Philip in 336 BC and reigned until 323 BC, was buried in Egypt. 'Thus, we are almost forced to the startling conclusion: if the deceased had been a king, he was Philip!' he concluded, with an exclamation mark to emphasize the import.

Andronikos had finally let himself utter the king's name and visualize the Tomb II burial which took place in the autumn 336 BC: in the 'monumental death chamber ... laid on an elaborate gold and ivory deathbed wearing his precious golden oak wreath', 'King Philip II had been surrendered, like a new Heracles, to the funeral pyre'.[41] The bones were interred in a never-before-witnessed gold casket, like the mythical ossuary of Hector described in the *Iliad*.[42] Andronikos went on to suggest, with perhaps a little too much haste, that the female in the Tomb II antechamber was Philip's last wife, Cleopatra, the young niece of a powerful Macedonian baron named Attalus.

When proffering the tomb dating and identifications, Andronikos was not blind to his own use of a self-perpetuating logic in which both the argument and its conclusion were mutually justifying loops; it was the type of circular reasoning described in Aristotle's list of fallacies and is today better known as '*petitio principii*'.[43] Andronikos explained: 'The sequence of thought I have followed, from the chronological framework 350–310 BC for the objects which cannot be challenged ... leads us to the inevitable conclusion that Alexander buried his father in the great tomb after his murder in Aegae' in 336 BC. From this we 'formulate the very useful conclusion that all the objects in the tomb [Tomb II] date to before 336 BC'.[44]

Another example of his 'spiralling methodology', as he termed it, was his reference to the gold bow-and-arrow quiver from the antechamber: 'similar Scythian "*gorytoi*" which have been found in Russia have been dated to about the middle of the 4th century BC ... This date is confirmed by the Vergina *gorytos*.' Andronikos was unrepentant about his 'vicious circle of progression' which some felt was stretching the evidence, and he added: 'I believe that only by such a dialectical approach ... can academic thinking move to its ultimate conclusions.'[45] He did not foresee the backlash it was about to ferment.

Andronikos remained steadfastly confident of the 'cumulative value' of the evidence being gathered for the 'cluster of the kings', and in this respect he was vindicated. Two years later, in 1980, a fourth tomb was located to the west of the hero shrine close to the south-western edge of the Great Tumulus, though still sufficiently close to the three-tomb group to suggest a family link or association with the lineage. The walls of its single chamber were orientated on a broadly north-south axis, where Tombs II and III are eastwest, and it had been ransacked and mostly destroyed. But due to its unique design with subterranean pillars, Tomb IV is commonly referred to as the 'Tomb of the Free-standing Columns'.[46]

Given little attention in recent years, because it yielded almost nothing in its devastated state, Tomb IV has tentatively been dated to the third century BC, supported by the discovery of a coin from the reign of Antigonus II Gonatas in the pyre debris above the single-chambered roof. Some gold thread, perhaps from a cloth which once covered the bones, might indicate a cremation, while carved ivory heads found on the floor thirteen years later could have once adorned a couch. A horse's tooth looks like more evidence of another in-situ 'Homeric' funeral pyre, and large clay figures of humans and animals on the entrance path, shaped with exquisitely fine detail, could have fallen from a carved frieze.[47]

Despite later collateral finds in the natural soil below the Great Tumulus, which contained no grave offerings except two bronze coins of Philip II, it was Tomb II that remained the centre of intense debate; the unique double burial carried insights into the bigger picture of the 'speaking stones', as one archaeologist dubbed the chambers, which, nevertheless, remained conspicuously quiet thereafter.[48] The presence of distinct red earth had made it clear that an original smaller mound once covered the first two tombs, with Tomb II broadly at the centre, and this pointed to further historic cohesion and some chronological anchorages. Andronikos also pondered whether each structure might once have had its own small tumulus, in which case what he was excavating, like Heinrich Schliemann at Troy, was a 'many layered burial onion'.[49]

As early as 1978, Nicholas Hammond reminded the Vergina excavators that Homer described Achilles' wish that a second tumulus cover the remains of Patroclus and him, when his own death came. We have, once more, an allusion to the events portrayed in the *Iliad* and the *Odyssey*. The discovery of a rare 'double tumulus' in Argos raised the question of whether Caranus' migrating Argives brought this funerary practice with them to the north.[50] That would, of course, corroborate the Macedonian founding myth, one propagated by King Alexander I to remind the Greeks of their Dorian heritage at Argos, which ultimately extended to the sons of Heracles who, legend tells us, returned to claim the Peloponnese eighty years after the fall of Troy.[51]

The Advancing Case for Aegae

In 1981, the city's ancient theatre was discovered to the north-east of the palace at Vergina, some 60 metres away in a fold of the hillside facing the plains below. Only the front rows of stone seats remained intact, suggesting the tiers above may have been made of wood, but its unusual proportions, with an exceptionally large 'orchestra' or dancing floor, 'may speak for the needs of a royal dynasty', one commentator suggested.[52] Just to the south lay the remains of modest rectangular marble statue bases with an incised inscription still visible: 'Eurydice, daughter of Sirrhas, to Eucleia'. This was not difficult to decipher: the temple had been dedicated by Eurydice to Eucleia, the female spirit of good repute, otherwise known as the 'chaste bride'. She was a popular Greek deity who some believed was a daughter of Heracles, and she was also linked to the particular incarnation of Artemis worshiped in markets, where she was renowned for her fair dealing, presumably to inspire the traders to similar behaviour.[53]

'Eurydice' was common-enough name in Greece, but it was associated with queens in the late Argead line. The only Eurydice with the uncommon patronymic

'Sirrhas' was the wife of King Amyntas III; she was the mother of Philip II and grandmother of Alexander the Great.[54] Some sources claim she was of Illyrian stock, but if so, that had not put a stop to the hostility with these tribes to the north, who killed one of her sons in battle and perennially threatened the state.[55] Dedications from Amyntas' wife do appear historic. In an essay attributed to Plutarch titled *On the Education of Children*, perhaps the first ever commentary on 'the parental duty of tutoring at home', we find a further dedication by the then-mature Eurydice to the Muses who had aided her when she was learning to read and write for the benefit of raising her sons. So the mature female face carved on a larger-than-life-size statue unearthed in the Sanctuary of Eucleia may actually depict Alexander's grandmother.[56]

By now, it was clear that the palace at Vergina was not an isolated structure 'in the middle of nowhere', but part of a complex of buildings that suggested a royal city. The site had already given up a dedication to Heracles 'Patroos', 'the ancestral', hero of the Macedonian royals, found in a colonnaded circular room in the palace ruins.[57] Andronikos had already discovered the word 'Machatas' under the lip of a silver wine strainer found in the main chamber of Tomb II, a reference to either the manufacturing craftsman or the commissioning owner. The sole historic person we know of with this name is the brother-in-law of Philip II, a clue that has since been given curiously little air.

Although Aristotle – who resided at the Macedonian court – cautioned that 'one swallow does not a summer make', evidence was steadily building for the identifications originally proposed by Hammond and now endorsed by Andronikos: 'The long years spent studying tombs and burial customs, far from chilling his sensibilities, had sharpened them', he said of the 'moments granted to him to travel back through the millennia and come close to the living truth of the past'. Although Macedon's founding city was rarely mentioned in texts after King Archelaus I built a new political capital at Pella around 400 BC, probably to better administer the timber trade, the names 'Aegae' and 'Philip II' were finally being whispered with some conviction at Vergina by the excavation team.

Following the discoveries of 1977, the Greek government announced new funding for the ongoing excavations. What Andronikos had unearthed would put the hillside village of Vergina on the map, and the accumulated riches were soon referred to as the 'finds of the century'. The site was credited with UNESCO World Heritage Status, with an attached wording which may understate the extent of its true antiquity: 'an exceptional testimony to a significant development in European civilization, at the transition from classical city-state to the imperial structure of the Hellenistic and Roman periods'.

In recognition of his work, Andronikos, who started working alone at the site in 1952 as draughtsman, photographer, accountant and foreman, beside his archaeologist role, was awarded with the Grand Cross of the Order of the

Phoenix, Greece's highest civilian honour.[58] When later recalling that moment on 8 November 1977 on the roof of the ancient mausoleum, a tomb he knew was never designed to be opened again, Andronikos described with humble honesty his conflicted emotion as the keystone was lifted: the 'scientist's elation' laced with the 'desecrator's guilt'.[59]

Chapter 6

Of Scythians and Amazons

> Such were the funeral games of Hector.
> And now there came the Amazon,
> The great-hearted daughter of man-slaying Ares.[1]
> —Homer

> I have to speak of blood and war and death for friendship's sake;
> you will learn that all you have related is child's-play,
> when compared with the deeds of the Scythians.[2]
> —Lucian

Manolis Andronikos and his team quickly concluded that the gold chest found in the antechamber of Tomb II contained the bones of a woman, and logic suggested she was married to the man in the adjacent room: Cleopatra, the last wife of Philip II, Andronikos conjectured.[3] The gold and purple cloth, the elegantly flowered diadem and myrtle wreath each seemed styled for a female; myrtle was sacred to Aphrodite and could denote a person initiated into the Eleusinian Mysteries, though the ancient rites were open to both men and women.[4]

But the absence of jewellery from the antechamber was troublesome, and beside these beautiful artefacts lay the impressive accessories of war. Andronikos wryly commented: 'The problem created by the presence of a female burial and weapons … is certainly strange … This implies that the woman buried there could have had some kind of Amazonian leanings, or could have had some liking for, or familiarity with, the weapons.'[5]

There was an alternative explanation, and one Andronikos immediately proffered, though with a degree of reservation: the weapons, perhaps overlooked when the main chamber was sealed in a way which made it impossible to open, belonged to the man next door, as their upright position on the threshold against the dividing door might suggest. Any jewellery the woman owned was burned along with her body on the funeral pyre, Andronikos further ventured.[6] This was the explanation widely accepted by other well-known scholars who were starting to comment on the Vergina discoveries.

The centre of attention remained the weapon of intrigue: the spectacular gold-faced quiver, similar in design to others found in graves of the Scythian tribal lands in Ukraine and the Russian steppes. This two-compartment, hip-slung '*gorytos*' traditionally held both arrows and a compact Scythian recurve bow with its distinct 'cupid-bow' shape. It was a powerful weapon that could unleash arrows, often poison-tipped, at a prodigious rate on horseback, and Andronikos felt that 'it was not intended that a Greek should use it.'[7]

The Fabled Killers of Men

Assuming that the occupant of the Tomb II antechamber was a woman – nothing was anatomically certain at this stage and – if the golden quiver and weapons did belong to her, then, indeed, the excavators had a young warlike 'Amazon' on their hands. Here Andronikos was making a reference to the legendary tribe of female warriors who featured in ancient Greek legend, and whose latter-day descendants were said to be *gorytos*-wielding Scythian female mounted archers.

The words of the fifth-century BC tragedian Aeschylus suggest they were indeed considered together: 'The Amazons of the land of Colchis, the virgins fearless in battle, the Scythian hordes who live at the world's end.'[8] Around 380 BC, in an address attempting to drum up support for a unified invasion of Persia when Philip II was still a young child, the Athenian orator Isocrates had also rhetorically recalled a legendary Athenian victory over the invaders from the East, describing them as 'Scythians led by Amazons'.[9]

Tales of female fighters from the East had fascinated the Greeks ever since they featured in the *Iliad*. Women warriors symbolized a challenge to the patriarchal status quo; their freedom on the steppes and rugged nomadic existence perhaps evoking a lifestyle the Greeks viewed with a wistful nostalgia, enclosed as they were in city-state walls and suffocatingly strict social codes. Stories of Amazon-dominated 'gynocracies' ruled by sexually liberated female nomads who hunted with dogs, eagles and falcons on horses trained to kneel before them, must have been powerfully evocative of emancipation to Greek women. Quite literally, these colourful barbarian women wore the trousers in the ancient world; they were depicted in Scythian-Amazon art in which their britches are tucked into high leather boots. This gender-obscuring clothing was adorned with geometric patterns and animal motifs, as were their distinctive pointed felt or woollen hats. Dolls dressed as Amazons have been found in graves of young girls in Greece.[10]

The closed world of some 750–1,000 introspective and independent mainland Greek city-states was not receptive to the integration of barbarians or the concept of a national monarch, unlike Macedon to the north. But overpopulation and the need for foreign commodities meant the Greeks could never remain totally isolated; they founded over 300 overseas settlements where they lived closely with the indigenous peoples and developed a less xenophobic attitude. As a result, they absorbed into their own prehistory a 'gene pool' of foreign gods and the founding myths of the tribes they traded with, and perhaps the first tales of Troy; ever present were the tales of these fearsome women. 'Amazonomachy', art depicting Amazons in oriental outfits, is still visible today on the Parthenon, the Temple of Zeus at Olympia and at the Macedonian capital at Pella.[11]

In the mid-ninth century BC, if not earlier, Homer portrayed Amazons as 'women equal to men', and Aeschylus described them as living 'manless'. But it was Herodotus who provided detail on their Scythian integration and a trail to a legend in which some relevant truth may be embedded. Herodotus travelled around the western peripheries of the Persian Empire in the century before Alexander in search of vintage stories from pre-history and more recent accounts of the Graeco-Persian Wars.

In his wanderings, Herodotus captured detail of a mythic past, which was followed by the age of heroes who were born when gods conceived children with mortals. This 'Heroic Age', epitomized by Homer's epics, is commonly assigned to 1600–1100 BC. In the reckoning of modern scholarship, the name 'Homer' may not have been an individual poet at all; the name was 'shorthand' for the whole genre of Trojan poetry sung by the 'Homeridai', the guild of the 'sons of Homer', who managed to orally keep alive detail of a once-glorious past and great battles in the still-largely illiterate environment of his day.

Little but the now-standardized versions of the *Iliad* and the *Odyssey* and their Trojan War continuations, along with tablets dug up from the fallen Mycenaean-era cities, are available to inform archaeologists of the wars, bureaucracy and social codes of the world of the twelfth century BC when the battle for Troy supposedly raged. And without the steadying influence of literature, the content of the poems was then far from uniform in a language still evolving.[12]

After 1100 BC, the great palaces and extended state bureaucracies of the former Mycenaean world were replaced by rural settlements of fired clay instead of stone, in which isolated chieftains governed a more primitive society in Dark Age Greece. Out of these dimly lit centuries, a 'patchwork of light and darkness', walked the founding legends of Greece and Macedon, once again linked to Argos in Herodotus' version and three brothers from the house of Temenus.[13]

As a result, the Greeks made little of the segregation between 'history' and 'legend'; it was a blurred line where genres merged, courted and interbred under the genre of '*mythos*'. Clearly, this dispels the notion that the more ancient a source, the more authoritative it must be. Herodotus himself was never sure if he was encountering legend, folklore, the truly historical or a vexing laminate of each, and he justified his content with: 'My business is to record what people say, but I am by no means bound to believe it, and let this statement hold for my entire account.'[14]

It was within this fluid 'myth-historic' framework that Herodotus recounted the war between the Greeks and the Amazons, when Heracles was tasked with his famous Ninth Labour: winning the girdle of Hippolyta, the Amazon queen. Within the 'girdle' – perhaps a loin protector or chest-belt – she carried the sword and spear given to her by Ares, the same war god whose epithet, 'Enyalius', lay at the root of the Macedonian menacing war cry, 'Alalalai'. The Amazons indeed referred to themselves as the 'daughters of Ares'.

How, or from where, the name 'Amazon' originated is far from clear. Its etymology could stem from 'breastless women', an appearance that might more credibly originate from their binding up and flattening breasts with wide straps or leather jerkins as modern archers do. Alternatives include the Armenian for 'moon woman' or the Old Iranian 'Ha-mazon', meaning 'warrior'. Other etymologies stem from links to the early Black Sea settlement of Amastris, while compound words with various female attachments are enticing, but little can be proven.[15]

According to Herodotus, after a victory over the Amazons at the River Thermodon near their capital at Themiscyra on the southern shore of the Black Sea, the Greeks set sail for home through the Hellespont in three ships filled with the defeated warrior women.[16] Soon, the escaped captives turned huntresses, and after retrieving their weapons from the hold, they murdered the Greek crew, but found themselves adrift in craft they knew not how to handle and at the mercy of wind and tide. The Amazons were blown north to the shores of Lake Maeotis, today's Sea of Azov, bordering the country of the free and non-nomadic 'Royal' Scythians, where they beached the ships and ventured inland.

The Scythians watched on as these mysterious new arrivals seized a semi-wild herd of grazing horses and rode off in search of booty. They thought they were facing young beardless male marauders who spoke an unknown tongue and dressed in a strange costume, until a few of the pillagers were killed. Once the Scythians realized they were dealing with armed women, they promptly revised their plans. Now more intrigued than threatened, they decided to bait the intruders into dialogue rather than battle. Desiring to court these remarkable arrivals who seemed to share their horseback-orientated lifestyle, they drew ever closer to the Amazon camp.

First contact was made after they noticed that towards midday the women would wander off in twos or threes to wash or relieve themselves. A Scythian made advances to one who did not resist; she freely offered herself and, using sign language, signalled him to return the following day with a friend, and she, in turn, would bring a female companion. The rest of the Scythians followed suit, and soon the two camps were united with the men and women paired off. The Scythians were unable to master the Amazon language, and it was the women who adopted an imperfect form of the local tongue.

In time, the Scythians wished to return to their people and possessions, and they invited the Amazons to resettle with them in their traditional tribal homeland. 'We could never live among the women of your race, as our ways are too different,' came the Amazon reply. 'We are riders, our business is with the bow and the spear and we know nothing of women's work.' They suggested the Scythians go and fetch their belongings and migrate with them to new lands to the north of the River Tanais, the modern Don in the Ukraine. The men agreed, and the fused tribe became known as the Sauromatae; some speculate that they were ancestors of the Sarmatians, 'free people' in the Ossetian tongue, who appeared in the region around 400 BC.

The Sauromatae are said to have seared the right breast of their baby girls so that their right arms would be stronger, and they were still living in the region in Herodotus' day, enjoying a lifestyle in which women and men were hunting and fighting together on horseback.[17] One notable rule still epitomized the old Amazon code: a girl could not marry until she had killed an enemy in battle. Other sources claimed the Amazons partook in a once-a-year 'mating-fest' to increase their chance of begetting children, after which they killed or traded back the newborn males to the fathers in favour of raising girls; as a result, they were known as 'killers of men'.[18]

The Greek historian Hellanicus, who travelled to Macedon in Herodotus' day, colourfully described the Amazons as 'golden-shielded, silver-sworded, man-loving and male-child-slaughtering women' who *did* sear off one breast when young so that they could more easily draw back their bowstrings on horseback. There is little evidence to support this, and Amazons are depicted as fully breasted on vase paintings and reliefs. But the prominent role of the horse, 'hippos' in Greek mythology, is epitomized in the names of three prominent Amazon queens: Lisippa, Hippo and Hippolyta.[19]

In one of the many frayed strands of the emerging myths attached to the warrior women who inhabited the fringes of the Greek world, the Amazons did ally with the Scythians in the Attic War of legend, attempting to retrieve Antiope after she had been abducted by King Theseus, the hero who founded Athens.[20] This prompted a retaliatory war in which Heracles confronted her sister, Hippolyta, with Antiope a prize of war. A monument to her still stood in Athens when the travelographer Pausanias passed through in the second century AD.[21] Heracles all but exterminated the Amazons, none of whom returned to their homeland; only when the slaughter had finished did the hero allow the female commander, Melanippe, 'black horse', her freedom 'in exchange for her girdle', which some interpret as her rape.[22]

The Greek lyric poet Pindar claimed the Amazons founded a sanctuary to their chief goddess Artemis at Ephesus in Caria en route to invading Athens. The Greeks knew Artemis as the virgin huntress, and lingering tales of armed temple priestesses

68   *Unearthing the Family of Alexander the Great*

at Ephesus served to strengthen the link. But any goddess they worshipped was surely a more primordial eastern incarnation, perhaps closer to Phrygian Cybele, the Great Mother Goddess.[23]

The Great-Granddaughters of Zeus

The gold-clad bow-and-arrow quiver found in the antechamber of Tomb II at Vergina is clearly Scythian in design. Scythians enjoyed just as fierce a reputation as their Amazon counterparts who, according to Herodotus, were subsumed into their race. Scythians had already driven out the Cimmerians from Ukraine and the Russian steppes long before the historian's day, though traces of this former culture still existed.[24] Herodotus described the Scythian scalping techniques in which the skin of the enemy was violently shaken from the skull and kneaded to make a rag they would fasten to the bridle of their horse, while right arms of the enemy were skinned to make covers for arrow quivers.[25]

Scythian tribal regions stretched from the Danube around the northern reaches of the Black Sea to the borders of the Caspian. From there, the migratory lands swept east into modern Kazakhstan and the states to its south. 'Scythian' was therefore a loose appellation the Greeks provided to all Eurasian nomads sharing a common lifestyle and living in the swathe of land to the north of the Persian Empire, whether of Iranian, Turkic or Mongol stock; the Persians called them 'Saka' and the barren 'deserts' they inhabited were apparently ridiculed in Greek proverbs.[26]

The lifestyle and migrations of Scythian tribes appear frequently in Herodotus' *Histories*, as does their contact with the Persian Empire, though how they subsumed the Amazons rests on Herodotus' account alone. As they left no written records, we neither know their language nor whether they had a Scythian written script. Legend claimed they were descended from one of the three grandsons of Zeus; propitious golden gifts fell from heaven and signified which of them should rule the 'youngest of all the nations', forged just 1,000 years before Darius I crossed to Greece on the way to humiliation at Marathon in 490 BC.[27]

In this founding story, the beginnings of the Scythians also thread back to Heracles. He roamed Scythian lands searching for the 'proud horses of King Laomedon' until he met a viper-woman, half human and half snake, who possessed them. She demanded sons by the hero in return for the horses and his freedom, and Heracles complied. In due course, Heracles advised the serpent-woman to choose one of their sons as his successor to the lands: she should select the son who could draw his powerful bow and properly wear his chest belt. It was the youngest son, Scythes, who achieved the task and he became father of the eponymous race. In Herodotus' day, the Scythians still wore belts with little cups attached in memory of their hero-ancestor; they were possibly used to carry the

Of Scythians and Amazons 69

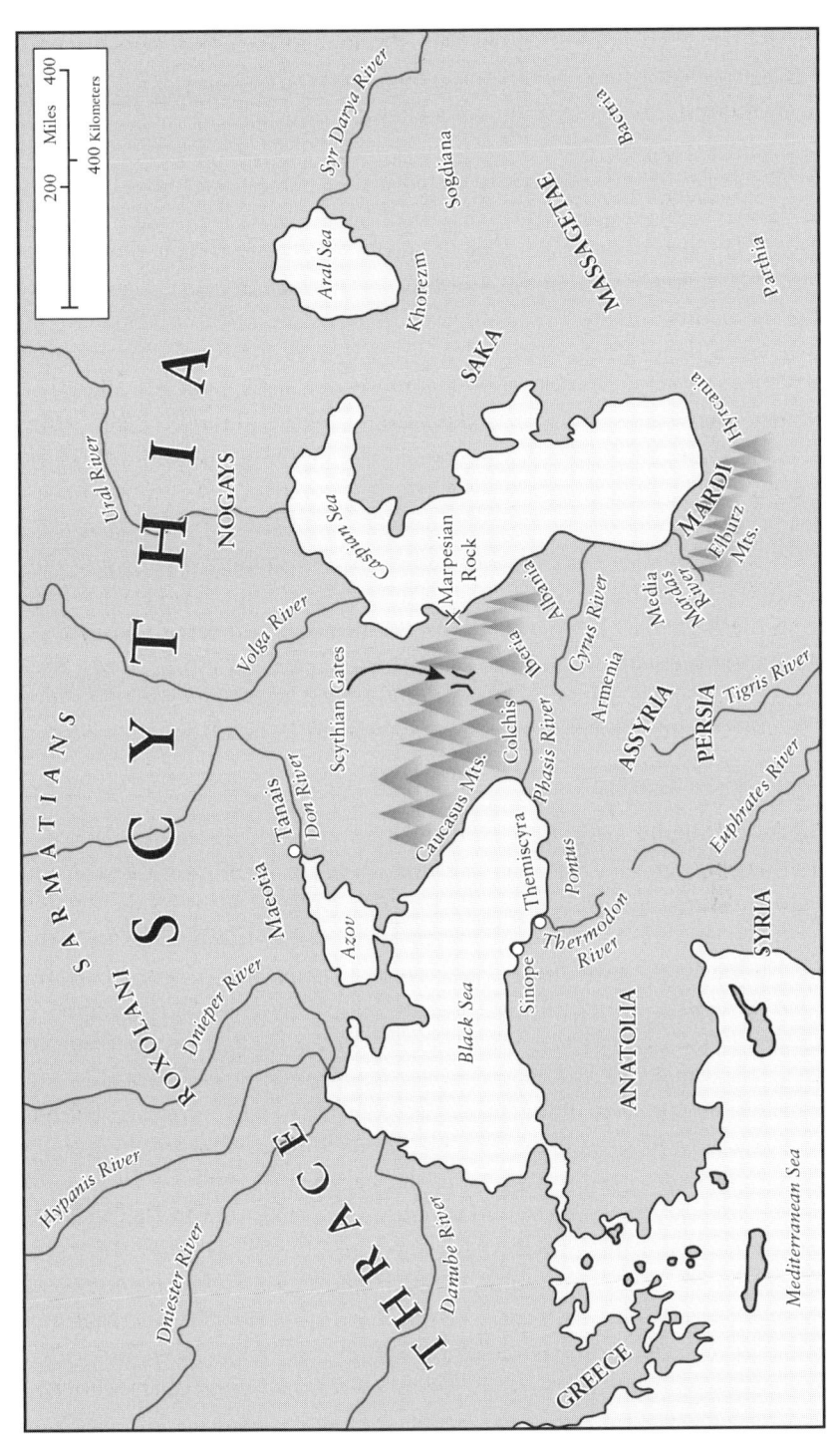

Traditional Scythian-occupied region stretching east from the Ukraine.

viper venom their arrows were dipped into, or for the swearing of blood-oaths in the saddle.[28]

Recent grave finds in burial mounds known as 'kurgans' do unite the women of the Scythian regions with a life on horseback and archery, either for hunting or war. In a series of excavations conducted before 1991, more than 112 graves of women buried with weapons were unearthed between the Don and the Danube, 70 per cent of them between the ages of 16 and 30 at death. Many of their bones were scarred with arrow wounds. The high proportion of females and the type of weapons accompanying them suggest 25 per cent of all Scythian fighters were women, a figure that appears to be rising with new DNA sexing of remains that were once thought to be men; some had unusually muscular right arms, suggesting frequent use of a bow.[29] The single earring commonly found in these graves might have differentiated these female fighters from the domestic workers of the tribe.[30]

Clearly, for a Scythian '*gorytos*' to have been buried in Tomb II at Aegae, there had to be some connection between the royal Argead line of Macedon and a Scythian tribe, or with a female warrior, at least. But unlike the warrior woman found in Tomb II, the Scythian burials were usually accompanied by jewellery: glass beads, earrings and necklaces of pearls, topaz, agate and amber, as well bronze mirrors and distinctive ornate bracelets.[31]

The New Penthesilea

The Roman historian Curtius Rufus, a rhetorician who fashioned his prose to please his Latin audience with his colourful and bittersweet history of Alexander the Great, proffered a condescending comment which might have, nevertheless, captured the prevailing attitude of the day: 'The Scythians differ from other barbarians, however, in not being intellectually backward and unrefined – some of them are even said to have a capacity for philosophy.'[32] A Graeco-Scythian philosopher named Anacharsis is said to have travelled to Athens in the early sixth century BC. Known for his straight-talking, he entered the company of the great law-giver Solon and gained the rare privilege of Athenian citizenship. Other traditions place Anacharsis as one of the Seven Sages of Greece who left a raft of wise epithets behind.[33]

The Greeks had settled in Pontus on the southern Black Sea coast as part of the so-called 'Great Migration' in the seventh and sixth centuries BC, with many settlements founded by the mixed-origin colony of Miletus on the coast of Caria.[34] Pontus was firmly associated with Amazon legend; its resident Greeks were perhaps Herodotus' principal source of information on their legends and to the alternative Scythian founding myth which linked them to Greek heroes. In 2011, linguists discovered a remote cluster of mountain villages in the region overlooking the Black Sea where 'Romeyka' could still be heard. This dialect proved to be the

Scythian archer on an Attic plate dated to 520–500 BC, showing the traditional hip-slung '*gorytos*' and compound bow. The mobile archer, shown without a beard and so possibly a female, is depicted as turning to reload and fire another arrow.

closest living language to Ancient Greek, spoken by a small community of a few thousand distinct for its fair-haired and blue-eyed women.[35]

Herodotus confirmed that Greeks and Scythians had coexisted around the Kingdom of Bosporus, a region we associate with the Crimea and the land to its immediate east. One tribe known as the Gelani was allegedly made up from Greeks driven out of their seaports and from the Scythian Budini among whom they then settled, so that their language and customs were a fusion of the two. The Callipidae were similarly attested to be a mixed group.[36]

Graeco-Scythian art, a hybrid of themes including Greeks battling with barbarians, had established itself in the region where these worlds overlapped, though it remains difficult to link the battle and banqueting scenes to any known mythology. Motifs on regional pottery represent this mixed tradition, and we should not forget the slave trade that saw captive Scythians shipped to Greece, Athens especially, where a Scythian not-to-be-messed-with 'police force' emerged in the mid-fifth century BC.

It was perhaps inevitable that tales of 'Amazons' from Scythia would enter the story of Macedon and the campaigns of Alexander. Fused to the past through his own heroic lineage and a classical Greek education steeped in myth, Alexander crossed the path of 300 alleged women warriors and their queen during his conquest of Persia. The name 'Alexander' – 'Alexandros' in Greek – loosely translates as 'repeller of men', but he was clearly not repulsive to women and reportedly enjoyed a thirteen-day tryst with the Amazon queen, Thalestris, in Hyrcania south of the Caspian Sea, satisfying her wish to beget a 'kingly' child.[37] The governor of Media named Atropates also sent 100 women from the region dressed as fabled Amazons to the Macedonian king.[38]

If Alexander was presenting himself as a 'reborn Achilles' on campaign, as the texts we have imply, then he, like Heracles, Theseus and even Cyrus the Great – each of whom struggled with pugnacious queens – needed an encounter with a warrioress like the legendary Penthesilea, the Amazon queen who journeyed to defend Troy to take on Achilles. Sitting astride her horse, Penthesilea had already dispatched eight Greeks and was baying for more blood when Achilles' javelin pierced her chest. Her beauty transfixed the hero when her helmet was removed, and Achilles fell in love with Penthesilea as she died in his remorseful arms. Her body, 'undimmed by dust and blood', was handed to the Trojan king, Priam, who placed it along with her horse and her dead companions, on a funeral pyre.[39]

Clearly, despite their valour, the Amazons of legend were more effective at loosing poisoned arrows from compact bows on horses, the great 'equalisers' in war, than fighting men in hand-to-hand combat, though depictions of them as foot soldiers do exist.[40] It does not lessen the romantic parallel when we read that Alexander enjoyed two amorous weeks in Hyrcania with Thalestris, when Achilles' encounter ended more abruptly at Troy. Pottery of the period is adorned by poignant images of the hero carrying her away, and the centrepiece of the spectacular ceremonial shield found in the main chamber of Tomb II at Vergina appears to represent just that: the scene of Achilles slaying Penthesilea.

The Romanized Greek historian Arrian recorded the presence of embassies from various Scythian tribes as Alexander journeyed through the Asian provinces of the Achaemenid Persian Empire forged by Cyrus the Great. When commenting on their forerunners, Arrian concluded of the Amazons: 'I cannot believe that this race of women never existed at all, when so many authorities have celebrated them.' His enthusiasm may be due to his birthplace, Bithynia, a region associated with their homeland.

In Arrian's career, under the rule of the Roman emperors Hadrian and Trajan, female gladiators featured in the Roman games. This continued interest possibly stemmed from female Scythians who had allegedly reappeared amongst the tribes from Pontus and the Caucasus to oppose Pompey the Great in the lengthy Mithridatic Wars which had ended in 63 BC. When captured, they were paraded as 'wild Amazons' before the crowds in his triumph in Rome. There is even evidence that female cavalry regiments, possibly Sarmatians, were incorporated into the Roman legions and fought as far afield as Hadrian's Wall.[41]

Surely, like the warriors of Roman times, the women Alexander encountered centuries before were the well-documented tall semi-nomadic Saka-Scythian-Sarmatians who inhabited the regions he was traversing, and not the true Amazons of old.[42]

The 'Father of History' and Pleasures on the Steppes

In Plutarch's biography of Demetrius the Besieger, the charismatic though somewhat tragic king of Macedon who fathered Antigonus II Gonatas, we find a curious statement: 'the Scythians … would twang their bowstrings as though summoning back their courage when it is dissolved in pleasure'.[43] The 'pleasure' may well have been marijuana, as excavations of Scythian tombs in 2015 discovered smoking paraphernalia lined with a residue containing the substance, as well as opium; it seems both intoxicants were used to supplement the alcoholic effects of fermented mare's milk.

Herodotus provided the earliest reports of this Scythian recreation which followed funeral rites: inside felt and leather tepee-like tents, they burned 'hemp' that gave off a smoke 'that no Grecian vapour-bath can surpass … transported by this vapour, they howl with pleasure'.[44] He also mentioned steam baths over red-hot stones, the 'saunas' of the ancient world; following their cleansing, the women would cover themselves with a blend of cypress, cedar and frankincense paste to reinvigorate their skin. In 1949, a sumptuous woollen carpet depicting Scythian horsemen was found frozen in a tomb beneath the Siberian steppe along with the corpses of embalmed nobles, suggesting some creature comforts made their way into the nomadic lifestyle. Reclined on these fine rugs and smoking psychedelic hemp was surely the 'high point' of an otherwise harsh existence.[45]

Born in Halicarnassus, modern Bodrum in Turkey, Herodotus was frequently criticized by fellow historians who branded him a 'teller of myths' who 'sometimes wrote for children and at other times for philosophers'.[46] Although often maligned for invention, Herodotus' book, the *Histories*, remains influential to our understanding of not just Amazons and Scythians and the fusion of their tribes, but a wider pre-history of the Graeco-Persian world, and it was just as influential to the ancient kings of Macedon from Alexander I onwards.

Time has since proven Herodotus a valuable door into an otherwise irretrievable past. Legends are, after all, often built around misplaced or forgotten historic events: Jason's journey in the *Argo* and the even the legend of King Solomon's Mines may all be echoes of real journeys distilled from explorers' travel logs along exotic trading routes. The quest for the Golden Fleece is likely based on the alluvial gold-panning technique used in the Kingdom of Colchis in modern Georgia, where sheepskins were laid in streams to catch flecks of gold. Even the legend of the Deucalion and Pyrrha, the 'parents of mankind' and sole survivors of the Great Flood – a tale closely paralleling Noah's Ark – originates in archaeologically sound foundations: evidence suggests that around 8,400 years ago, a land basin with a lake that is now the Black Sea suddenly flooded, driving refugees in all directions, some of them to northern Greece.

Similarly, the tale of the Wooden Horse of Troy likely had its provenance in more practical military strategy: Assyrian battering rams. They were ornately horse-headed in design and fully enclosed to protect the men who inched them forward to the walls. Pausanias, whose *Guide to Greece* was only taken seriously once it enabled Heinrich Schliemann to unearth the ruins of Mycenae in the 1870s, quipped of the legend: 'Anyone who does not suppose the Phrygians [Trojans] are utterly stupid will have realised that what Epeius [architect of the wooden horse] had built was an engineer's device for breaking down the wall.'[47]

A more recent myth concerns the name 'Amazon' itself. In 1500, the Spanish conquistadors were campaigning in South America searching for El Dorado. They navigated up the river system they variously named 'Rio Grande' for its size, 'Sweet Sea' for its freshwater or the 'Cinnamon River' in celebration of what were misidentified as cinnamon trees. Following explorations met with fierce club-wielding 'female' tribal warriors along its banks who were bold enough to threaten the musket-carrying Spaniards. These long-haired natives of the Icamiaba tribe may not have been women at all, but when hearing of their victory over his conquistadors, Emperor Charles V of Spain recalled the fabled women from Greek mythology and renamed the Brazilian river 'Amazon'.

A digression that takes us to the borders of the ancient Greek world must return us to Tomb II at Vergina. The discovery of both the Scythian bow-and-arrow quiver and the shield decorated in Amazonomachy in the adjacent main chamber clearly added colour to the early debate on the tomb occupants. But the antechamber female was real and anything but the stuff of legend. So the next step, as far as Manolis Andronikos, Nicholas Hammond and other commentators were concerned, was to highlight a Scythian connection along with any prominent women at the court of Philip II or Alexander who *were* renowned as warriors.

The Royal Dynasty of Macedon in the 4th Century BC

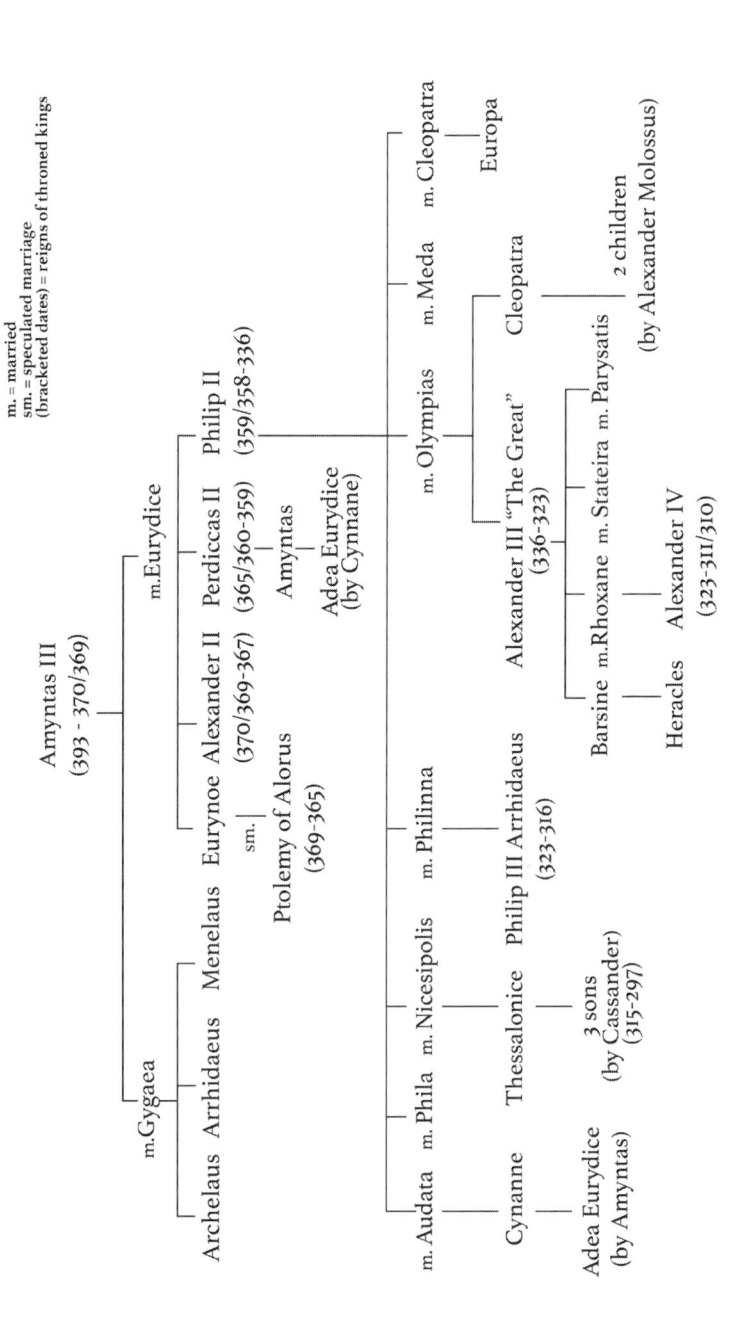

m. = married
sm. = speculated marriage
(bracketed dates) = reigns of throned kings

Amyntas III
(393 - 370/369)
m. Gygaea | m. Eurydice

Children by Gygaea: Archelaus, Arrhidaeus, Menelaus

Children by Eurydice:
- Eurynoe
- **Alexander II** (370/369-367) sm. Ptolemy of Alorus (369-365)
- **Perdiccas II** (365/360-359)
  - Amyntas — Adea Eurydice (by Cynnane)
- **Philip II** (359/358-336)

Philip II's marriages:
- m. Audata → Cynanne
- m. Phila
- m. Nicesipolis → Thessalonice — 3 sons (by Cassander) (315-297)
- m. Philinna → **Philip III Arrhidaeus** (323-316) — Adea Eurydice (by Amyntas)
- m. Olympias → **Alexander III "The Great"** (336-323), Cleopatra m. Alexander Molossus — 2 children
- m. Meda
- m. Cleopatra → Europa

Alexander III m. Barsine → Heracles
Alexander III m. Rhoxane → **Alexander IV** (323-311/310)
Alexander III m. Stateira
Alexander III m. Parysatis

The Argead dynasty of Macedon in the 4th century BC. The century ended with Cassander in power, anticipating 'Antigonid' rule, from 315–297 BC; he declared no formal title but was de-facto king after having Alexander IV executed in 311/310 BC.

Chapter 7

The First War of Women

> Once made equal to man,
> woman becomes his superior.
> —Socrates

The achievements of Philip II of Macedon and his son, Alexander III 'the Great', read as spectacular successes against overwhelming odds, in no small part due to the talented generals, philosophers and politicians who supported them and frequented the royal courts. Their successive reigns have always been a source of wonder and deep debate, whether they were considered 'nation-building kings' or 'empire-destroying tyrants'. And both men were wrapped in deep contradictions that historians could never fully decipher.

But it is Philip II who has undergone something of a renaissance at the hands of scholars in recent years, having emerged from the obscurity of being 'Alexander's assassinated father' and shaken off the ignominy of the various character assassinations he suffered; by Demosthenes, for example, the vocally anti-Macedonian Athenian. Although a self-conscious Roman Republic had little good to say about Philip when later cautioning on the power of kings and the tyrannical vices of 'empire', he is now spoken of as the real architect of Macedon's dominance and the king who put the 'Great' in his son's name.

Philip was what we might term in today's vernacular a 'lovable rogue'. Gifted with charm and wit, he was also sufficiently unscrupulous, calculating and ruthless to rescue the beleaguered nation from the meddling fingers of Persia, Greece, Thrace and hostile Balkan tribes. Yet Philip avoided battle with bribery when he could and wed his way out of war when women were available; as the Greek-Sicilian historian Diodorus neatly put it: 'The growth of his position was not due so much to his prowess in arms as to his adroitness and cordiality in diplomacy.'[1] Philip's irrepressible brand of statecraft was one that included 'bribery, intimidation, deceit, subversion, sabotage, assassination, marriage, betrayal, war – and on occasion, he even scrupulously kept his promise', as one modern biographer said of his diverse political arsenal.[2]

In his calculated dealings with Greece, Philip manipulated affairs so that he was operating under the guise of defender of Apollo's sanctuary at Delphi, undertaking 'Sacred Wars' as a representative of the justice of thirteen Greek city-states as both saviour and avenger. He once marched all his men into battle wearing sacred laurel wreaths to suggest the deities had backed them, and the outcome was beyond doubt. Philip was an opportunist who obviously knew the well-trodden adage: 'The gods help those who help themselves.'[3]

The Pellan Pike and PR Machine

As a teenager, Philip had been a hostage at Thebes in the reign of his oldest brother Alexander II, at a time when Theban military innovators had gained primacy in Greece after defeating Sparta at the Battle of Leuctra in 371 BC.[4] There he learned to compose and speak with the necessary rhetorical arts perfected in Athens, and he began developing his own thoughts on the almost ritualized battlefield tactics that had changed little over the previous centuries.

'Total war', hoplite style, was essentially a deadly shield-shoving match on the plains between close-packed infantry phalanxes whose tight formation offered the benefit of protection, but at the expense of manoeuvrability: their forward-facing ranks had no flanking guard nor rear protection, and cavalry troops rarely engaged in decisive pitched battles except as skirmishers or scouts. Auxiliaries were few, save smaller units of flying reserves to plug gaps in the line, along with shock troops to break a deadlock, and the bow was generally despised in Greece.[5] Set-piece confrontations before the Battle of Leuctra were static one-dimensional affairs in which the fate of a city-state hinged on bulldozing the enemy lines. 'Tactics', as the exiled Athenian mercenary Xenophon had observed, were 'only a very small part of warfare'.[6]

Learning from the recent new Theban infantry formation that toppled Spartan infantry domination, Philip innovated further. Working alongside Parmenio, the best tactician among his generals, he began to revolutionize warfare, creating a more-diverse army in which the whole was greater than the sum of its parts.[7] He hardened his mobile, waggonless infantry with 56km forced marches carrying weapons, armour and rations for thirty days in a training regime which enabled them to out-range any opposition.[8] His infantry flanks were protected by more highly mobile 'shield bearers', while the longer two-handed pike, the '*sarissa*', neutralized the shorter Greek spear.

Mobile skirmishes of every type harried enemy flanks with projectiles, while Philip's disciplined infantry moved with purpose, either advancing at an oblique angle or feigning a retreat. Both manoeuvres forced sections of the unsuspecting enemy front to advance at different speeds, and gaps inevitably appeared in their lines. It was at this point that his lance-wielding cavalry, now proportionally higher in number and operating as 'shock troops' rather than hit-and-run brigades, would

The leaf-shaped blades of each *sarissa* from five ranks of the pike bearers protruding; the scene captures the terror of the 'porcupine' of blades that an approaching line would be faced with, when points would be variously aimed at the vulnerable necks and groins of the enemy infantry.

punch through in wedge-shaped formations to cut the enemy to pieces in the flank and rear. The bristling Macedonian phalanx became the proverbial 'anvil' upon which the heavy cavalry dealt the decisive hammer-blow, and Philips' martial revolution would become the template for warfare for the next two centuries.[9]

In his first war against the Illyrians, Philip marched with 10,000 infantry and 600 cavalry; twenty years into his reign, he could field 30,000 foot soldiers and 3,000 horse, funded by the gold and silver from the annexed mines of Crenides and nearby Mount Pangaeum.[10] The high point of Philip's military career came with victory at Chaeronea, following which he manipulated Greece into a submissive League of Corinth, whose member states were required to sign up to an oath of common peace:

> I swear by Zeus, Gaia, Helios, Poseidon and all the gods and goddesses. I will abide by the common peace, and I will neither break the agreement with Philip, nor take up arms on land or sea, harming any of those abiding by the oaths. Nor shall I take any city, or fortress, nor harbour by craft or contrivance, with intent of war against the participants of the war. Nor shall I depose the kingship of Philip or his descendants.[11]

As its architect, Philip never signed the peace himself, which gave him an intriguing latitude for action, but it was this grudging 'peace' that finally enabled him to plan the invasion of Persia.

Gifted with an innate intelligence for what martial rule required, Philip also comprehended the value of bettering his court through education. The political capital of Pella was frequented by some of the greatest minds of the day, including Aristotle, who taught Alexander and his companions in a grove by the sacred Temple of the Nymphs at Mieza.[12] Aristotle espoused a philosophy that posed barbarians as inferiors destined to be ruled by Greeks. The Macedonians themselves had previously been referred to as '*barbaroi*', which is no doubt why Alexander I had previously promoted his Argive origins, and why Philip latterly filled his court with 'civilizing' scholars.[13]

At the state capital of Pella, Philip shared his palace halls in the Homeric intimacy of the warlords of old, as an ancient tenet demanded that kings be able to lead the most fearful phalanx and the most delightful symposium, since both are examples of good order. He would have taken comfort in the knowledge that the teenage royal pages who were serving his guests were the sons of his Macedonian nobles; in time, the most promising would become Philip's bodyguards and generals, but they meanwhile served as informal 'good-behaviour hostages'.

The kings of Macedon had traditionally exercised their power through a 'common assembly' convened to vote on crucial matters of state, such as trials for treason or the accession of a new king. Any democratic process suggested by its title was absent; this appears to have been a convocation of barons and men-at-arms, with not a noncombatant among them. Attending were officers who represented the peasant-stocked infantry, many of who started life as pastoral herders; 'milk-drinkers', Euripides would have labelled them. The cavalry commanders represented the more aristocratic elements of the state and the bodyguards at court.[14]

The barons of Macedon acted as a balance or conduit of authority between their warlord king – the 'first among equals' in this feudally managed state – and the growing power of the nobility on whom mineral extraction, harbour levies, timber felling and other commercial leases had been bestowed.[15] Although the king was deemed the 'guardian' of these state assets, his judicious distribution of the wealth assured him their support as they transformed into the court nobility. How far a king could extend his power independent of the assembly probably depended on his personal charisma, his diplomatic skills and the degree of leverage he had over his nobles. Success in battle was always a recipe for approbation and the traditional beating of spear on shield to signify approval; failure meant assassination from a rival branch of the royal house.

Philip was fully aware of the precarious nature of kingship, having witnessed the demise of his older brothers, so he made sure his public relations machine was rolling early in his reign, as was his judicious parcelling out of state lands. A historian once resident at Philip's court claimed that 800 of the king's 'friends' owned more land than the 10,000 richest Greeks.[16] New coinage was minted with likenesses of the gods and heroes linked to his family line, with Zeus and Heracles stamped besides images recalling Philip's chariot victories at the Olympic Games. Portraits and bronzes by the celebrated artists and sculptors Lysippus and Euphranor graced the court halls, and family statues were erected in the sacred grove at Olympia after victory at Chaeronea. No less intimidating was the poem of the day simply titled *Philip*, which, though comedic, captured the devastating ruthlessness of the royal army:

> Do you know with what men you must fight?
> We Macedonians dine upon well-sharpened swords
> And for starters we swallow lighted firebrands;
> Then for dessert our slaves bring in,
> After the first course, Cretan bows and arrows;
> And instead of chickpeas, broken heads of spears,
> We recline on weathered shields and breastplates;
> At our feet lie slings and bows and stones,
> And we wreath catapults about our heads.[17]

Philip's court at the political capital of Pella must have been a vibrant, intriguing, scheming and thoroughly perilous place to live during in his twenty-three-year reign, in terms of military threats from without and political intrigues within, bearing in mind, as Pausanias put it, that he was 'continually trampling on oaths to heaven … breaking treaties and dishonouring his words on every occasion', to achieve his political ends.[18]

The magnificent mosaics unearthed over the last decades at Pella in extravagant houses near the marketplace attest to a lifestyle of privilege if you resided in the inner sanctum of power. Apart from the generals, bodyguards, envoys and concubines Philip would have kept close by, his spouses must have lived in private accommodation near the palace, with resident ladies-in-waiting and family in attendance. His succession of wives would have visited the king's bedchamber after he had caroused with his generals in the great banquets, the 'workshops of war'. Philip's ability to juggle delicate matters of state obviously extended to his bed.[19]

A Harem for Political Purposes

Philip's marriages to foreign women established a 'harem for political purposes'; Olympias was one such conquest from the Molossian tribe of Epirus, broadly modern Albania, which bordered Macedon's western cantons.[20] And it was in her,

82 *Unearthing the Family of Alexander the Great*

A reconstruction of ancient Olympia from Pierers Universal-Lexicon, 1891. The circular building in the left corner is the Philippeion, constructed after Philip's victory at Chaeronea and housing the statues of his family.

possibly his fifth wife, that he truly found his match, and no less so in their son Alexander who was destined for greatness.[21] Royal women married young and many died young, often in childbirth, as had Philip's earlier Thessalian wife Nicesipolis; with them potentially died political alliances that would have to be repaired. It is unclear how many of Philip's spouses were still at the palace when Olympias ruled the roost; there may have been three previous wives still living, and Philip married twice again.

The last two marriages caused instability in his household and led to a rift in which Olympias and Alexander were temporarily estranged from court. Any wife, new or long-resident who might still bear the king children, posed a threat in an environment that did not specify 'chief wife' or official 'heir designate'. Although primogeniture – the accession of the first-born – was not a requirement of Macedonian monarchy, for purely practical reasons older sons usually ascended to the throne, though we should be careful to point out that actual 'thrones' were the abode of gods and priests, not specifically kings.[22]

Because of this, claimed Plutarch, who was ever on the hunt for the *scandaleuse*, and in her quest to protect Alexander, Olympias took the initiative against another of Philip's sons. The boy, Arrhidaeus, was born to an earlier 'obscure and common' wife named Philinna, who was reportedly a dancer: 'It is said that as a boy he [Arrhidaeus] displayed an exceedingly gifted and noble disposition, but then Olympias gave him drugs which injured his body and ruined his mind.'[23]

The continued threat from rival wives and their offspring reared its head again in an infamous episode at a rowdy banquet a year or so before Philip's murder. Attalus, the uncle of the king's newly wedded final wife, Cleopatra, is said to have prayed 'for a pure-blood heir from the union'.[24] If events truly played out as we read, this was a slap in the face to Alexander's half-Epirote bloodline, if not a barbed insinuation of Olympias' past infidelities. Alexander hurled a goblet at the smug baron for the insult and Attalus retaliated in kind. Philip was watching on in a drunken stupor and demanded an apology from his son. When Alexander refused, Philip drew his sword and lurched forward, only to fall in a heap between the reclining couches. Alexander quipped to the banqueteers in disgust: 'Here is the man who would lead you to Asia, but he can't cross from one couch to another.'[25]

The incident somewhat recalls the famous 'heroic' quarrel between Achilles and Agamemnon at Troy, and should perhaps be viewed with suspicion in its well-developed recounting. But Alexander was reportedly banished from the kingdom and journeyed to the newly safe haven of Illyria, after returning Olympias to the sanctuary of her native Molossian court ruled by her brother in Epirus.[26]

It could have been during this exile that Alexander attempted to undermine the marriage his father had arranged between his half-brother – the now-mentally impaired Arrhidaeus – and the daughter of Pixodarus, a powerful dynast in Anatolia; the union would have given Philip a base of support in Caria for his planned invasion of Persia. To scupper the plans, Alexander is said to have sent missives to Pixodarus in which he offered himself to the bride in Arrhidaeus' place.[27] Only the efforts of a respected intermediary united father and son before the wedding Philip had arranged for his daughter: the occasion at which Philip was stabbed to death at Aegae.

We have no proof that Olympias left Epirus to attend the wedding of her daughter, which might have coincided with the autumn equinox and the public festival or 'panegyris' that marked the beginning of the Macedonian New Year. If not, she certainly journeyed in haste to Aegae upon hearing the news of Philip's death. In what might have been later hostile propaganda, Justin claimed Olympias crowned the assassin, Pausanias, who is said to have been posthumously crucified by Alexander, and then she scattered his ashes on Philip's grave after consecrating his dagger to Apollo.[28]

With Philip lying in a pool of blood at the theatre entrance, Alexander ordered the immediate execution of the overconfident baron Attalus, who was now on duty on the Asian side of the Hellespont with the army bridgehead for the forthcoming Persian invasion. Attalus was summarily implicated in high treason and duly dispatched without being brought to Macedon for trial. Some months later, when Alexander and the army were securing the nation's borders, Olympias roasted Philip's new wife, the young Cleopatra, along with their newborn girl, over the coals of a brazier. This is just one version of the execution; Justin claimed Olympias killed the baby in her mother's lap and then forced Cleopatra to hang herself.[29]

It is difficult to know where to draw the line under sensationalism from Greek and Roman writers who were notoriously hostile to royalty, especially queens. Nevertheless, it appears that the unfortunate Cleopatra, who may have impudently assumed the royal family title 'Eurydice', suggesting her pre-eminence in the 'harem', was undoubtedly executed with any children, and probably with Alexander's consent, despite eulogistic writers claiming he was angry when he heard.[30]

Adding to the suspicion of their collusion in Philip's death, we have Plutarch's claim that Alexander had promised Pausanias, the assassin, revenge with the line from a Euripides play: 'The giver of the bride, the bridegroom and the bride, all at once.' It hinted at a triple murder in the making, and one that came to pass with the subsequent deaths of Philip, Attalus and his niece, the unfortunate Cleopatra.[31]

Cleopatra was the seventh of Philip's known wives, and in contrast to some of his earlier political marriages, Plutarch stated this was another 'love match', Olympias being the former. But there is no record that the young woman showed any martial inclinations or accompanied her husband to war, despite Andronikos' initial conclusion that her bones resided in Tomb II with the weapons and Scythian gold quiver.[32] Her credentials remained poor: Cleopatra was no celebrated Amazon-like warrior.

The Amazon and the Idiot

The career of another notable court resident could not have been more different. Philip's first or second wife, Audata, who may have been a relative of Philip's mother, was renamed 'Eurydice' after marriage in the Argead court tradition. Audata was of Illyrian extraction and believed to be from the family of the recently defeated Illyrian king, Bardylis, as the marriage is thought to have sealed the 'great new peace' that followed.[33] Illyrian women had a reputation for taking part in battles, and Philip's daughter by Audata reportedly killed an Illyrian queen in single-handed combat when she was still in her teens.[34] The pugnacious daughter's name was Cynnane.

When Cynnane reached childbearing age, Philip paired her in marriage with his own nephew Amyntas Perdicca, who was under his 'protection'; Amyntas had been under 10 years old at the death of his father, the former king, Perdiccas III, who was

Philip's older brother. Amyntas' youth gave Philip an immediate path to the throne, though some historians argue he initially acted as the boy's regent. Cynnane gave Amyntas a daughter named Adea, and this inter-family recognition made him a popular choice for the kingship at Philip's death. Plutarch tells us Amyntas was the successor favoured by many, so Alexander had been left with no choice but to execute him, along with any other contender for the throne:

> All Macedonia was festering with revolt and looking toward Amyntas and the children of Aeropus; the Illyrians were again rebelling, and trouble with the Scythians was impending for their Macedonian neighbours, who were in the throes of political change; Persian gold flowed freely through the hands of the popular leaders everywhere, and helped to rouse the Peloponnese; Philip's treasuries were bare of money, and in addition there was owing a loan of two hundred talents.[35]

By executing Amyntas, Alexander had deprived his half-sister Cynnane of a queenship, but as compensation, he paired her in marriage to a new ally, King Langarus of the Agrianians, a tribal confederation to Macedon's north. Langarus died the following year, 335 BC, before a wedding could take place, so the second-time-'widowed' Cynnane was left to school her daughter, Adea, in the arts of war.[36] Throughout Alexander's campaigning in Asia, Cynnane and the girl remained in Pella under the watchful eye of the nation's long-standing regent, Antipater, who had been left behind in Macedon to guard the state's interests with a modest defence force.

Twelve years on, at Alexander's death in Babylon in 323 BC, the nation faced a unique succession crisis: a new king had to be chosen by a national army stationed far from home. The familiar assembly was called, though what constitutional authority it carried overseas in Babylon is questionable. The infantry ranks and their officers squared off against the cavalry regiments led by the nobility of Macedon, with Alexander's former elite corps of bodyguards in overall command, as they had been on campaign. The peasant-stocked infantry demanded the elevation of Philip's mentally defective son, Arrhidaeus, who happened to be present in Babylon; Olympias' plan to destroy him early, if true, had backfired, for it was surely mental incapacity that had kept Arrhidaeus off Alexander's proscription list when Philip died.[37]

At the assembly gathering in Babylon, it was left to Alexander's former second-in-command, Perdiccas, to promote Alexander's son by his Bactrian wife Rhoxane, *should* a son be born, for she was seven months pregnant.[38] The boy was rejected by the crowd. Next to address the assembly was Ptolemy, who is credited with a speech which also rejected the 'half-barbarian prince' in favour of 'group rule' by himself and the seven notables who formed the king's personal bodyguard, 'those Alexander used to consult' on campaign. The crowd also rejected this aristocratic clique that was set to carve up the empire. Equally unacceptable was Alexander's older but absent son, Heracles, born of another Asiatic mistress, Barsine, who had Persian royal connections; Heracles was rejected by all except the lone voice of Nearchus, Alexander's admiral of the fleet, who had been married into Barsine's family at Susa the year before.

There next came a speech credited to the highest-ranking infantry officer in Babylon, who clearly despised the authority above him, and his barbed accusations epitomized the infantry-cavalry brigade divide. He openly defied Perdiccas and dragged the unwitting Arrhidaeus into the assembly in a bid to secure a position of power for himself.[39]

The growing tensions between the rival factions almost erupted into war on the plains outside Babylon, where the cavalry brigades affected a blockade to starve the infantry into submission. There had already been infighting over possession of Alexander's body, an emblem of authority, and spears had been hurled in the palace quarters. A fragile accord was eventually reached, whereupon Perdiccas had his war elephants suddenly trample the unsuspecting troublemakers, whose recalcitrant leader was hunted down and murdered in the sanctity of a temple.[40]

Under the terms agreed, if a son was born to Rhoxane, he would be titled 'King Alexander IV', and the mentally impaired Arrhidaeus would be co-king and assume the regal name 'Philip III Arrhidaeus'; in Plutarch's words 'a mute diadem, so to speak, passed across the inhabited world'.[41] The army that departed Babylon was resentful of the outcome. The Macedonians were in a hostile alien land, and tens of thousands of Greek mercenaries, many garrisoning the new settlements Alexander had dotted across the empire, were marching home to join a Greek army congregating south of Athens set to challenge Macedonian rule.[42]

Once news of Alexander's death reached Pella, Cynnane saw her chance. Defying the orders of the regent Antipater, she crossed to Asia, determined to propel her now-teenage daughter, Adea, into the scramble for power. Cynnane was killed when confronting the troops Perdiccas sent to intercept her. As commander-in-chief in Asia, he was just as motivated as Antipater to keep her out of the developing game of thrones.[43] But Perdiccas' troops were in uproar. Indignant at seeing one of Philip's daughters murdered before their eyes, they demanded that Adea be duly presented to the newly crowned co-king Arrhidaeus.

Perdiccas was left with no choice: Philip's pugnacious granddaughter would be wedded to Philip's half-witted son (her uncle), and 'an Amazon and an idiot' would rule Macedon. But as far as the infantry were concerned, having watched both Philip and Alexander take a succession of foreign brides, they had the first Macedonian-born queen in a generation.[44]

The Rise of the Regent's Son

The civil war that almost ignited at Babylon finally broke out when Perdiccas' secret marriage correspondence with Alexander's full sister – also named Cleopatra – was exposed. Perdiccas had already agreed to wed one of the many daughters Antipater was offering to the most powerful generals to secure his ongoing regency in Macedon.[45] After narrowly defeating the Greek uprising in Thessaly in what is known as the 'Lamian War', Antipater crossed to Asia with a home-grown Macedonian army, supported by the campaign veterans Craterus and Antigonus the-One-Eyed, to face the threat.

Perdiccas divided his forces; he himself journeyed to Egypt to confront Ptolemy for the hijacking of Alexander's funeral bier, and was murdered in his tent on the banks of the Nile by his own officers. The remaining generals in the region met the newly arrived Antipater, who was now almost 80 years old, in Syria, where a further assembly-at-arms decided on the redistribution of power in Asia and how to mop up Perdiccas' renegades who were still at large. Adea, who had assumed the queenly title 'Eurydice', was sufficiently plucky and audacious to challenge present authority. Defying the Doric form of her name, 'Hedeia', which simply meant 'sweet', her rabble-rousing caused the new guardians of the two kings to resign and almost swung the disgruntled troops her way until Antipater finally quelled them.[46]

Antipater died in old age a year or so after returning to Macedon with Adea and the two kings in tow, but neither the infant Alexander IV nor the mentally impaired Philip III Arrhidaeus were able to govern. On his deathbed, Antipater appointed not his own son Cassander, but a campaign veteran named Polyperchon to the post of regent, the highest in the land outside the kingship itself. Both Philip II and Alexander had trusted the long-governing Antipater throughout their careers, and his unselfish appointment of Polyperchon, rather than the overambitious Cassander, suggests their faith had been well placed.[47]

The no-nonsense conservative Antipater had also lately warned: 'Never permit a woman to hold first place in a kingdom.'[48] Antipater had put up with the political intrigues of Olympias for much of his regency, tensions that led to a corpus of correspondence from both of them pleading their cases to Alexander in Asia. Although Olympias' constant demands caused her son to quip that 'she was charging him a high rent for ten months' accommodation inside her', Alexander added that Antipater knew not that 'one of his mother's tears would wash out the complaints of a thousand letters'.[49]

The newly appointed regent, Polyperchon, proved ineffectual at controlling the capital, and Adea was able to manipulate her feeble-minded husband into war. She planned to take on Olympias and her supporters with the backing of the equally disgruntled Cassander, who had been promoted to 'second-in-command in Asia' the previous year but had no intention of operating under Polyperchon in Pella as *his* 'number two'. Cassander and Adea started rallying support in Greece and from Antigonus the One-Eyed, who now controlled all of Anatolia 'in the name of the kings'.[50]

Rather than be hemmed in by the old intractable regent, Olympias had years before departed Pella to govern her native Epirus, sending her own daughter Cleopatra back to Macedon in her stead; someone had to watch Antipater while Alexander was on campaign.[51] Olympias was still in Epirus when Alexander died in Babylon, and she had watched events unfold while planning her eventual return to Pella. Olympias had little option but to side with the 'royalist' Polyperchon, who was beckoning her back to court to take charge of her infant grandson, Alexander IV. Olympias put faith in her ability to raise an army in Epirus, where her nephew now ruled after her brother's death, and she strategically installed Cleopatra in the city of Sardis in Anatolia, from where she could broker her daughter's marriage to any 'loyalist' general in Asia who commanded a powerful army.[52]

Olympias next commenced a pogrom against the family of Cassander, murdering another of his brothers and, allegedly, 100 relatives. Her most significant retribution against his family was the overturning of the grave of Cassander's younger brother, Iollas, who had been Alexander's cupbearer on campaign, a role that demanded complete trust, as serving poisoned wine at banquets was an age-old means of regime change in the ancient world.[53]

Sure enough, Iollas and Cassander, along with their father Antipater, were soon implicated in rumours of a family plot which alleged Alexander had been poisoned at Babylon by Iollas' toxic cup. The accusations conveniently appeared in a propaganda pamphlet containing details of Alexander's final wishes which laid out how the king wanted power distributed across the empire. Often referred to in short as *The Book of Death and Alexander's Testament*, its timing and the content suggests that Olympias may well have had a hand in its drafting, as it clearly justified her mass murders.[54]

By now, however, Cassander was already bettering Polyperchon's army in southern Greece and had control of Athens. A domestic confrontation between the rival factions on Macedonian soil was imminent. When Olympias finally emerged from Epirus with her army through a pass in the Pindarus Mountains, she found the new young queen, Adea-Eurydice, with her ranks blocking the road to Pella. The contemporary historian Duris of Samos termed the confrontation the 'first war between women', and his description of the prelude to battle is preserved by the Roman-era antiquarian Athenaeus: Olympias marched out dressed as a follower of Dionysus to the haunting beat of a drum, while across the plain Adea-Eurydice 'came forward armed like a Macedonian soldier, having already been accustomed to war and military habits at the court of [her mother] Cynnane the Illyrian'.[55]

The amassed soldiers of the two armies faced a tough decision, but Adea's men, 'remembering the benefits that they had received from Alexander', defected to Olympias and the respected campaigner Polyperchon. The veterans clearly feared the wrath of Alexander's mother more than Philip's teenage granddaughter, and Adea was taken captive while attempting to flee to Amphipolis. Olympias assumed the guardianship of her grandson, Alexander IV, in Pella, and she gave Adea-Eurydice and her halfwit husband a rather interesting proposition: forced suicide by hemlock, sword or rope. One tradition tells us the defiant Adea strangled herself with her own girdle, while the hapless Arrhidaeus was put to the Thracian dagger.[56]

Olympias, who may well have orchestrated the assassination of her estranged husband Philip II, as some historians suspect, had now executed his son and granddaughter, as well as his last wife Cleopatra and her child. But in contrast to Cleopatra, who had no historical link to war, we are presented with the picture of a rather androgynous Joan of Arc-styled tomboy in Adea-Eurydice, the warrior queen born of an equally warlike mother, Cynnane.

The martial persuasion of women like Cynnane and Adea may not have been an uncommon phenomenon in light of established female warrior castes in Illyria and the nearby Scythian regions on the northern border of Thrace. In what is now north-east Bulgaria, archaeologists have found tombs with what appeared to be three classes of grave goods: those buried with men, artefacts belonging to women and a genderless third set.[57] Scholars now ponder the wider presence of what we might today term 'masculine' females whose orientations were deemed useful and celebrated in antiquity, rather than frowned upon: in the *Iliad*, Homer used the term '*antianerai*', 'man-like', when King Priam was describing the Amazons with awe.[58] Adea represents the pugnacious traits we might expect of this sect, and it would have been more fitting if she had been buried with the ceremonial weapons found in the antechamber of Tomb II, as commentators on the Vergina tombs were starting to appreciate.

Back in Pella in 317 BC, the primacy of Olympias and her infant grandson Alexander IV, supported by Polyperchon, didn't last long. Cassander, who had been fighting in the Peloponnese when the 'war of women' took place, proved remarkably effective at working with limited resources, perhaps using a political survival manual his father is thought to have penned, and he continued to exploit the oligarchies installed by his father, the former state regent, over the previous fifteen years, despite Polyperchon's hollow promises to finally 'free the Greeks' from Macedonian tyranny.[59] Within a year or so of Olympias' return to Macedon, Cassander had her under siege at Pydna and Polyperchon pinned down in Thessaly.[60]

The gruelling siege Olympias suffered at Pydna led to chronic starvation; even the war elephants had to be eaten, and after a bungled escape attempt, Alexander's mother was forced to submit. In a hastily convened assembly which was little more than a sham trial, Olympias was awarded a death sentence, though some 200 of Cassander's 'best soldiers' sent in to Pydna as henchmen were 'overawed by her exulted rank' and fled. Cassander was forced to call upon the relatives of Olympias' victims, which must have included his own extended family members, to stone her to death.[61] She 'uttered no ignoble or womanish plea' so that 'you might have perceived the soul of Alexander in his dying mother', it was claimed. Olympias' body was 'thrown out without burial', the ultimate humiliation of an enemy – like stripping a dying warrior of his armour – surely a retribution for her desecration of Iollas' grave.[62]

At this crucial point, Cassander needed all the legitimacy he could muster to govern a state in turmoil, so he extracted a useful captive from the Pydna siege: Olympias' ward Thessalonice, another of Philip II's daughters by the former wife Nicesipolis, who had died soon after giving birth. One source claimed Cassander forced Thessalonice into the marriage, yet nonetheless, Alexander's half-sister duly gave him sons with royal Argead blood.[63]

Cassander followed up by exhuming the bodies of the murdered Adea-Eurydice and Philip III Arrhidaeus from wherever Olympias had dumped them, perhaps a year or so before, and provided them lavish state burials at Aegae as a move to ingratiate himself with the court. It was at this point, or perhaps several years later when he executed Rhoxane and her son, that Cassander could have raised the original red-earthed modest tumulus that covered Tombs I and II. It would have signified the end of a branch of the royal line, as it marked the birth of his own.

The Political 'Amazons' of Macedon

The prominence of leaders like Philip and Alexander who changed the fate of nations has prompted a fundamental 'chicken and egg' question in historic debate: do great men make history, or does history make great men? The wording houses a rather obvious element of gender bias, but one which conformed to a historic reality: women were largely marginalized in the ancient narratives, which were exclusively written by men in the ancient world.

The histories of Greece and Rome have also been termed 'elitist' because they focus on kings, tyrants, statesman, generals and the wars they lost or won. Even Homer's *Iliad* had little room for the fate of the commoner. Aside from Thucydides' insights into the economic factors which fuelled the Peloponnesian War, the deeper social undercurrents that led to great upheaval were also ignored. But these ancient narratives could equally be termed 'misogynistic' in their lack of attention to historical women, the exceptions to the trend being accounts of the women of Macedon.

Macedon was still a patriarchic world, especially at the rowdy banquets and assemblies-at-arms where state decisions were made, but real power did occasionally manifest itself in the hands of women who proved ruthless counterparts to their kings and acted as 'state regents' when their husbands were absent. Some were later titled '*basilissa*' ('queen') in their own right, a title previously inferred only from their wife-of-a-monarch status.[64] They were politically active and even martially involved in statecraft, in which they 'could not be reproached either for cowardice or for scrupulousness'.[65]

If there had once been an 'oversupply' of Argead kings from the polygamy of the royal court of Macedon, there was now no shortage of dynastic daughters to be offered in 'military marriages' or under the terms of a treaty in the Successor Wars. Their status in these sovereignties must have seemed both threatening and archaic to the mainland women-suppressing Greeks, whose monarchs had disappeared with Homer's heroes and the Mycenaean world with its legendary kings and female protagonists at Troy.

The surviving accounts of the post-Alexander world are strewn with references to Macedonian-born Cleopatras, Eurydices, Stratonices, Arsinoes, Laodices, Berenices and Philas in a well-documented series of complex intermarriages in a deadly game of snakes and ladders.

Eurydice, the mother of Philip II, had been a devoted, if ruthless, widow who shepherded her boys through one succession crisis after another, courting generals and expelling usurpers, the rumours of filicide apart.[66] Antipater, the long-standing regent, is said to have been consulting with his daughter Phila about the most important matters of state since she was a child, a role she continued through her marriages to Alexander's foremost general Craterus and then Demetrius the Besieger.[67] Polyperchon's daughter-in-law Cratesipolis, which translates as 'city conqueror', was a renowned beauty who led the army when his son was killed in battle, and the wife of Antigonus the One-Eyed was involved in military negotiations in the Anatolian interior.[68]

Alexander's own full-sister Cleopatra most likely executed his policy when he was absent in Asia, in both a political and religious capacity in Macedon and Epirus, where women appear to have enjoyed a higher social status. We have notable examples: the years 330–326 BC saw Greece in the grip of a series of acute grain famines when Cyrene in North Africa, a vital grain centre for Athens, is recorded as sending 230,000 bushels of corn to Greece, including 72,600 to Olympias in Macedon and 50,000 to Cleopatra in Epirus as the recorded heads of state.[69]

Similarly, the warrioress of Tomb II at Vergina must have been a notable woman in Macedon. Following the release of Andronikos' first paper on the tombs in 1978, in which he pondered the presence of a woman with 'Amazonian leanings', a number of historians and classicists voiced their opinions on the identities of the skeletal remains, some with an incomplete knowledge of the chamber contents. But Philip II's final wife Cleopatra, and his pugnacious granddaughter Adea-Eurydice, along with their respective husbands Philip II and his son Philip

III Arrhidaeus, who died twenty years after him, remained the most popular contenders. It was now time to study the skeletons more closely to better establish the ages of the Tomb II occupants and determine if these frontrunners fitted the results. The 'first war of women' was about to be relived in the 'battle of the bones'.

Chapter 8

The Battle of the Bones

*We should not be surprised,
that each man selects the things fit for his pursuits
from the same material.*
—Seneca the Younger

To scientifically establish the age and gender of the two occupants of Tomb II, Manolis Andronikos invited Professor Nikolaos Xirotiris at the Democritus University of Thrace and fellow anthropologist Dr Franziska Langenscheidt to analyze the skeletal remains. Like him, they noted the care with which the male bones had been collected after cremation and looked to have been washed clean of pyre ash before being laid inside the gold chest. Not only had they been sorted according to size and length, but the skeletal arrangement was anatomically correct with the skull resting at the top. Even very small fragments had been retrieved from the funeral pyre remains on the roof of the tomb.[1]

Xirotiris and Langenscheidt published their report in 1981 and concluded that the main chamber bones 'most likely' belonged to a 'gracile' (of slender build) man between the age of 35 and 55 at death. He was between 160 and 170cm tall, but they warned that both the calculation of height and sex determination can be impaired by the effects of cremation, which causes bone shrinkage.[2] Nicholas Hammond's paper of 1978 had already stated that analysis of the teeth found in this gold chest belonged to a male over 32 years old.[3] Xirotiris and Langenscheidt further cautioned that certain infectious diseases in life, as well as malnutrition, can affect the robustness of bone structure. They added that 'gracility' of a face was often an identifying feature of upper-class society, though in this case it appeared the male had a well-developed muscular system.[4]

The remains of the women were scantier and still soiled with ash. The yellow-brownish colour of the bones suggested they had been burned at a different temperature than the whiter and better-preserved skeleton of the male, whose cremation looked to have been somehow 'temperature controlled'. The two were unlikely to have been cremated together, and this concurred with the separate funerals suggested by the two-stage construction of Tomb II proposed by Andronikos.[5]

Xirotiris and Langenscheidt concluded that the antechamber occupant had been a 'very delicate' female aged 20–30 at death, widening the previous estimate of 23–27 years given in Andronikos' first report.[6] Her height was calculated at around 155cm, though this was based on an unconventional method: measuring the diameter of the head of the radius bone between the elbow and wrist, with shrinkage factored in at 10 per cent. She was, they concluded, a 'skeletally mature young woman'.[7]

The report provided crucial age calculations in light of the tomb identities already suggested by Andronikos and Hammond: classical scholars, researchers and interested historians were now dealing with a middle-aged male and a much younger female who were almost certainly not cremated together. The age determination ruled out five wives from the early part of Philip II's twenty-three-year reign, each of them married between 359 and 356 BC, as they were too old when Philip died twenty years later in 336 BC. Excluded were his first Illyrian wife Audata, who was the mother of Cynnane, and the childless Phila of Elimea; also eliminated were Nicesipolis from Thessaly, who died shortly after giving birth to Thessalonice, and Philinna of Larissa, the mother of the mentally impaired Arrhidaeus.[8] Philip's fifth bride, Olympias, was a non-contender as she was around 60 when she was executed by Cassander in 316 BC.

The age of the Tomb II male at 35–55 years likewise culled candidates from the extended list of Argead kings of the period. Philip's father Amyntas III reportedly died at an 'advanced age' in 370/369 BC, despite the instability surrounding his reign, and Philip's brothers were too young.[9] The oldest, Alexander II, was assassinated after a reign of less than two years when probably in his early or mid-20s, and Perdiccas III died with 4,000 men fighting the Illyrians when of similar age. Moreover, Perdiccas' corpse was unlikely to have been retrieved from such a bloody battle for state burial: his surviving soldiers were 'panic-stricken' upon hearing that no prisoners would be taken alive.[10]

Alexander the Great died in Babylon, as all historians knew well. Although the existence of Alexander's lavish funeral hearse, and its unchallenged construction at Babylon over two full years, is suggestive that he requested burial somewhere else – Macedon, some believe – it never came to pass. Ptolemy diverted the corpse to the safe haven of Memphis up the Nile and it remained in Egypt well into the Roman era.[11]

The remaining contenders for the Tomb II male were Alexander's father, Philip II, who died in 336 BC, and his half-witted son, Philip III Arrhidaeus, who died twenty years later. Supporting the case for Arrhidaeus in this unique Tomb II double burial were the simultaneous funerals Cassander gave him and Adea at Aegae in late 316 or 315 BC, anywhere between six and seventeen months after their 'double-murder' by Olympias, for which we have no exact date. This became the mantra for this 'revisionist' Tomb II school of thought in the emerging Vergina debate.

A mid-nineteenth century artist's impression of Alexander's funeral hearse, an 'Ionic temple on wheels', on its way from Babylon towards Damascus, pulled by sixty-four mules following the description by Diodorus.

But the premise had its flaws. Although Adea-Eurydice had clearly demonstrated her military persuasion, Arrhidaeus, who might have been epileptic or more convincingly autistic, if not truly rendered a halfwit by Olympias' 'mind-destroying' drugs, had no military experience we know of, and it is doubtful he could have been trusted with weapons. If the contents of the tomb were emblematic of the life and status of the occupants, as commentators were inclined to believe, then the sumptuous armour, shield and tools of war were unlikely to be his.[12] But the biggest problem remained the foreign intruder in Tomb II: the gold-faced Scythian bow-and-arrow quiver in the antechamber with the female.

The Symmetrical Uncertainty

Although the identifications had been narrowed down by the Xirotiris-Langenscheidt report, the outcome was still complicated by a rather unfortunate symmetry: both Philip II and his son, Philip III Arrhidaeus, were of similar age when they died, in their mid- and early 40s. Furthermore, both were married to far younger women who were in their late teens or early 20s when executed. The dubiety this caused led scholars to become 'obsessive on the vexed identity' of the male, as one historian put it, and there commenced a bitter 'battle of the bones'. The emerging commentaries became as divisive as the tenets of Darwinists and Creationists when opposing ranks faced off in an endless 'tug of war' waged through a series of academic papers in the years that followed.[13]

The partisans supporting Alexander the Great's father, Philip II, as the occupant of Tomb II were initially the better equipped, because two more of his surviving brides potentially fitted the age range of the female. Nicholas Hammond had first suggested that her bones could belong to Meda, a daughter of the Thracian king Cothelas of the semi-nomadic tribe known as the 'Getae' living south of the Danube. She was married to Philip II in the latter years of his reign and her fate is unknown.[14] Another attractive option was a presumed daughter of King Atheas of the Danubian Scythians, who at one stage planned an alliance with the Macedonian king. As Hammond voiced it, it 'seems almost certain, her hand was given in marriage to Philip when Atheas, despite having a son, promised to adopt Philip as heir to his throne'.[15] The once-friendly relationship with Atheas broke down, but scholars conjectured that a daughter, given freely or taken with the 20,000 captive women, could then have become Philip's concubine or possibly his seventh wife of what would then be eight in total.[16]

Both the Getae and Scythian women, Hammond further argued, had a custom of ritual suicide to honour the death of their king. Herodotus reported that in the case of the Thracians, a favourite wife would have her throat slit after being praised by funeral onlookers, while those not chosen to die lived in great shame thereafter.[17] Thracian and Scythian lands bordered one another close to the Danube, where their customs, language and even a mutual love of tattooing themselves appears to have merged and spread.[18] The ritual death of a spouse from either tribal region would explain the double burial in Tomb II, though not its two-phase construction.

The theories surrounding these women were not devoid of additional problems: while the preparations for Philip II's funeral are recorded in surviving texts, along with the names of the assassins and their accomplices, there is no mention at all of *any* wife being buried at Aegae with him. If his entombing had been accompanied by ritual suicide, or even voluntary death in a funeral pyre, 'suttee' as it is termed, it would have been a memorable event that ought to have featured prominently in surviving accounts.[19]

As a parallel example, we have another episode of 'suttee' which took place in the early Successor Wars, some seven years after Alexander's death: a wife of the fallen Indian general Ceteus entered the pyre alive, and the morbid fascination of the Macedonian onlookers was vividly embedded in the post-battle accounts. Diodorus was also clear on the origins of the rite: the requisite suicide in India evolved from the very-real need to deter wives from poisoning their husbands.[20]

Still short on evidence that might provide a robust identification for the Tomb II female, both teams proffered new arguments that focused on the male. In their attempts to either endorse or disqualify Philip II, they targeted the wounds he suffered in battle. One contemporary list of the injuries comes from an oration titled *On the Crown* by Demosthenes, who survived the reigns of both Philip and Alexander, despite his open hostility to the Macedonian state.

When famously orating from the natural-rock outcrop known as the 'Pnyx' which served as an auditorium above Athens, Demosthenes once said of Philip II: '[He] united the functions of a general, a ruler and a treasurer … as the absolute autocrat: commander and master of everyone and everything.' It was not meant as a compliment to the tyrant who, Demosthenes claimed, enjoyed punishing his body for the sake of power. He further exclaimed that the Macedonians did not even make decent slaves. But in Demosthenes' own frustration at being hamstrung by a spider's web of laws and by city-state politicians always a step behind Philip's more agile *machtpolitik*, he warned the infighting Athenians that they were 'boxing like barbarians'.[21]

Demosthenes' exquisite court defence, *On the Crown*, was delivered in 330 BC, six years after Philip's murder at Aegae, but when the world had irrevocably changed: it was the year in which Alexander burned down the Achaemenid capital of Persepolis, having defeated Darius III in a final battle at Gaugamela in northern Mesopotamia, and Macedon now governed the Graeco-Persian world. Demosthenes had practised his public speaking with a mouth full of pebbles by candlelight, so his words smelled of 'the lamp wick', claimed his newly pro-Macedonian opponent Aeschines, whose legal counterpunch failed. Demosthenes managed to overturn the allegations that six years earlier he illegally received state honours, in this case a crown, for improving Athens' defences after defeat to Philip at Chaeronea in 338 BC.

Philip's bones, it was argued, should be witness to the wounds referenced in *On the Crown* and other corroborating texts: the blinding of his right eye by a projectile, a shattered right collarbone, a blow sustained to the arm or hand and a wound to the upper leg or thigh which left him lame.[22] Plutarch was among those who confirmed the last, and he said in his usual rhetorical fashion: 'Alexander urged his wounded father, who limped and was troubled by his lameness, to go forth and remember his valour with every painful step.'[23]

Justin additionally explained how this particular injury came about: when Philip was returning from the Scythian campaign against King Atheas – father of the hypothesized daughter – the Thracian Triballi tribe refused to allow him passage unless they received a share of the spoils. The dispute escalated into a battle, in which Philip's leg was run through so violently that his assailant's spear or javelin killed his horse. Once Philip had fallen and was initially thought to be dead, the Macedonians lost their campaign booty, which included 20,000 young Scythian men and women, a similar number of horses and a vast number of cattle.[24]

The analysis by Xirotiris and Langenscheidt, however, found no evidence of these traumas on bones of the Tomb II male. The advocates of Philip II, who now included the well-known Alexander biographers, Professors Robin Lane Fox and Peter Green, along with the prolific writer and historian Stanley Burstein of California State University, were understandably devastated.[25]

But a more fundamental challenge emerged to threaten *both* sides of the Tomb II debate: the very identification of the ruins at Vergina with the ancient city Aegae was being called into question. Greek archaeologist Photius Petsas had a well-known and long-standing antagonism with Manolis Andronikos dating back to their student days and competing excavations. Petsas had been vocal on the 'incorrect identification of Vergina' issue since 1977, when a transcript of his interview on the topic was published in the *New York Times*.[26] He was not alone; another professor at the Aristotle University voiced similar reservations in a paper published in November of that year.[27]

Potentially more damaging to Andronikos' reputation was a letter to an Athens newspaper on 13 February 1978 by Dr Zachos of the University of Paris, who was one of the first to propose the alternative identification of Philip III Arrhidaeus and his young assassinated wife, Adea, for Tomb II. Dr Zachos' correspondence alleged that when Andronikos announced he might have found the remains of Philip II, he was following a political agenda: the 'nationalism' evoked by the discovery aimed at securing victory for Konstantin Karamanlis' New Democracy party in the 20 November general election of 1977. What Zachos failed to remind his readers was that Andronikos' public statement, which 'armed the quiver of Hellenism', took place on 24 November, four days *after* the vote.[28]

Further challenges to the Philip II identification soon emerged. In 1980, another Alexander the Great biographer, Winthrop Lindsay Adams of the University of Utah, followed by the archaeologist and art historian Dr Phyllis Williams Lehmann and a list of other commentators, threw their support behind the case for Philip III Arrhidaeus and his young wife, the warlike Adea-Eurydice, as the Tomb II occupants. Adams drew attention to Cassander's 'legendary knowledge of Homer', which explained the Homeric reverence evidenced by the style of funeral he provided them. Adams pointed out that a source had claimed Cassander, just like Alexander, 'was so fond of Homer that he had the greater part of the epics at his tongue's end. Cassander even made copies of the *Iliad* and the *Odyssey* with his own hand.'[29] This was a further vexing symmetry that poured fuel on the debating flames.

The newly emerging papers still centred on the notorious double burial in Tomb II, but arguments were becoming broader in scope. The architectural claim of Thomas Boyd, which first appeared in 1978 in the *American Journal of Archaeology*, percolated into the debate: the barrel-vault design of Tombs II and III followed architectural concepts and techniques Alexander's engineers absorbed in Asia, so the tombs and their Doric façades must post-date the death of his father Philip II. They were certainly built after Tomb I, the simpler 'cist tomb' design, Boyd believed.[30]

The new pro-Adea-Arrhidaeus arguments appeared to dismiss important elements of Andronikos' discoveries: for example, his conclusion that Tomb II was built in two distinct phases, which failed to correlate with their simultaneous 'double burials'. Also sidelined was the importance of the small ivory carved likenesses of a bearded Philip II with his sightless right eye, and a clean-shaven Alexander with a melting glance and the familiar neck tilt we read of.[31] Andronikos had already proposed that the carvings might be based on the statues of the royal family in the Philippeion at Olympia, which Philip II had commissioned from the master sculptor Leochares and dedicated to the sanctuary following his victory at Chaeronea.[32]

Andronikos remained undeterred, and in a rather beautiful pictorial book published in 1984, he expanded upon his original conclusions. He cited further evidence from Justin's chapters which pointed to the funeral ceremony of Alexander's father: the friends of the assassinated King Philip II 'grieved that the same torch that had been kindled at his daughter's wedding should have started the funeral pyre of the father'.[33]

This statement by Justin was intriguing because on the floor of the main chamber of Tomb II sat a never-before-seen open bronze cylinder which narrowed to a conical pipe, into which a wooden shaft could be inserted. Inside the cylinder

Two small heads carved in ivory and recovered from Tomb II, thought by Manolis Andronikos to depict Philip II and Alexander the Great.

there were still traces of smoke, with wood fragments and fine gold leaf beside it.[34] It was clearly a torch designed to be borne aloft by a ceremonial torchbearer, perhaps, as Justin claimed, the very same torch used at Cleopatra's wedding just before Philip's murder. In reply to Andronikos' theory, the opposing scholars pointed out that Justin's wording was a well-used poetic simile, and not proof of Philip's cremation at all.

Andronikos' 1984 publication was a visual treat presented with the due care of an excavator under siege. But an air of frustration had crept into his prose when referring back to the past seven years of speculation by onlookers less familiar with the archaeology: 'Sometimes they have not paid enough attention to this information, sometimes they misinterpret it; on most occasions, the arguments employed have been selective and certain factors have been isolated in order that more general conclusions may be reached.' Reiterating the frustrations that had already appeared in an article he published in 1980, Andronikos was unhappy that words and opinions he never uttered had been inserted into new academic papers.[35]

But with the exception of those still holding the 'anti-Aegae' view, and in light of new finds in the palace ruins at Vergina, which occupied three times the floor space of the Parthenon in Athens, few commentators now doubted Andronikos'

The Battle of the Bones 101

basic contention: the Great Tumulus tombs were the burial sites of the Macedonian 'royalty'. Clusters of graves suggested a family line and the mound was conspicuous in its size. Besides the remains of the funeral pyres found above these vaulted tombs, a prominent unifying factor was the original modest tumulus that appeared to have once covered Tombs I and II, with Tomb III possibly inserted later.

The strongest evidence for royalty remained the quality of the artefacts, augmented by the calibre of art and frescos: as kings had been distinguishable in life with their more spectacular weapons and armour, so we can distinguish the regal nature of the dead, Andronikos believed. The diadems and heavy gold wreaths, the purple fabric on the bones and starburst embossing the gold chests, as well as the lion reliefs and Heracles' club visible on the shields, all pointed to the Argead clan.[36] The presence of thrones, however, remained vexatious: some commentators argued they were for gods and priests, yet it may be contended that the king represented the high priest of the state.[37]

Then there was the presence of the cenotaph or hero shrine, which meant someone of national importance was being revered. The Philip III-Arrhidaeus camp argued that would be the occupant of Tomb I, the closest structure which sat just a few feet away, which they suggested housed Philip II. Arguing to the contrary – that Philip II's bones, armour and weapons resided in the grander Tomb II – Andronikos speculated that the thirteenth god-like statue Philip II had paraded in the theatre before his death, fashioned in a likeness of himself, could have been posthumously deposited in the shrine to reinforce his deification.[38]

In September 1985, after several years of architectural consultations between Manolis

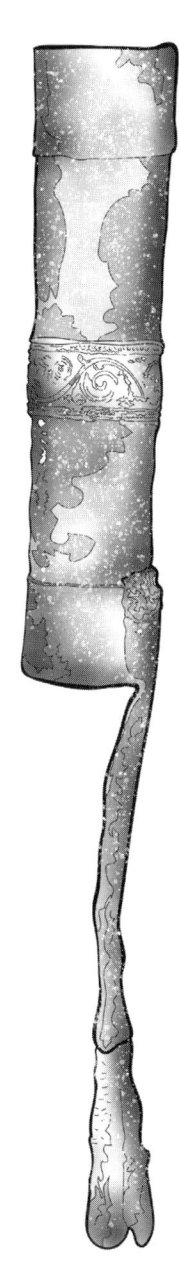

Illustration of the bronze conical torch identified by Andronikos from the main chamber of Tomb II; traces of fire were still visible.

Andronikos, the Directorate for the Restoration of Ancient Monuments and the Central Archaeological Council, designs for a 'shelter in the style of a tumulus' were adopted and approved: Vergina would have a museum-cum-mausoleum. The Greek Archaeological Receipts Fund would provide 30 per cent of the development money and a European Community programme would fund the remainder, 1,614.2 million drachmas, approximately US$7 million at the time.

Andronikos did not finish excavating at Vergina with the levelling of the Great Tumulus from 1977–80, and in 1987 he unearthed another barrel-vaulted tomb some 400 metres to the south and halfway to the more elevated site of the palace ruins. This was situated in what is termed the 'cluster of the queens', so named because all the tombs appear to house women. Although it had been looted and greatly damaged in antiquity, this tomb seemed to be the earliest of the 'Macedonian-styled' vaulted structures found so far. Sherds of ceramics and a vase inscription in the funeral pyre remains above it were clearly dated to the year of the Athenian chief magistrate in 344/343 BC, some eight years *before* Philip II died, that is assuming the artefacts were contemporary with the sealing of the tomb.[39]

In one corner of the chamber sat an ornate marble-and-gold-embellished throne painted with scenes of the Underworld framing Pluto and Persephone. A remarkably realistic architectural formation of a façade on the rear wall featured false windows and a door framed by Ionic columns, an image so authentic-looking that the ancient tomb robbers believed it led to another chamber and chipped away at the plaster until their folly became apparent.

Inside the tomb lay a marble chest or larnax which may have once held the cremated remains of a woman, while in the soil infill close to the antechamber door were human skeletal remains: deceased tomb robbers, Andronikos curiously proposed. The dating of 344/343 BC led him to label the structure the 'Tomb of Eurydice', after the energetic, if controversial, mother of Philip II. She is thought to have died shortly before 346 BC, when the orator Aeschines visited Philip's court as part of an Athenian embassy sent to conclude a peace. Demosthenes later accused Aeschines of taking bribes there to support the Macedonian cause.[40]

Like nearly all ancient burial chambers, the Great Tumulus tombs were devoid of written dedications to their occupants, but there was one further inscription that both intrigued and carried a warning on dating their construction from the artefacts found within: 'I am from the games of the Argive Hera', exclaimed an engraving on a bronze tripod in the main chamber of Tomb II. The Heraean Games at Argos, dedicated to the goddess Hera, may predate the Olympics; and unlike the more famous athletic festival at Olympia, men *and* women could participate, though females could not compete naked. Bronze tripods were among the prizes, and the Tomb II example was stylistically dated to 450–25 BC.[41] Andronikos concluded that it was 'separated in time from all other finds' and must have been a family heirloom. Its presence in the chamber suggested a Macedonian royal had triumphed at the games long before the tomb was built.

In the same year, 1987, a Greek archaeologist termed the preoccupation with the tombs a 'Vergina Syndrome', noting how unfolding drama had eclipsed more modest finds throughout Greece and dragged the magnet of historical attention its way.[42] The year also saw Andronikos publish more 'reflections' on the third-party commentary that he felt 'rejected new evidence by trying to make it fit the old theory'.[43] The Great Tumulus cluster of tombs at Vergina, he argued, showed clear elements of continuity in design and clear signs of innovation in the chain of development.[44]

In reply to the architectural arguments of Boyd, which proposed vaulted roofs post-dated Philip II, Andronikos argued that the Greeks had known about vaulted buildings since the philosopher Democritus invented the arch decades before Philip II even came to the throne. After all, everyone knew that flat roofs could not withstand a weight of earth piled on top![45] Andronikos went on to question how the Greeks could *not* have known how to build arched structures which appeared in the Near East well over 1,000 years before. Ionian masons worked on Persian palaces centuries before Philip II, and in the words of Plato: 'Whenever the Greeks borrow anything from non-Greeks, they finally carry it to a higher perfection.' Greek assimilation and adaption of Phoenician alphabetic writing around 800 BC is another salient example.[46]

Vaults, Diadems, Sceptres and a Beaten Helmet of War

Eugene Borza, a well-respected Macedonian specialist and the professor of ancient history at Pennsylvania State University, had been publishing his own views on Vergina since Andronikos' pictorial emerged in 1984. In a new article released in 1987, he tantalizingly voiced 'the possibility' that Tomb II might contain the very weapons, armour and insignia of Alexander the Great. The items under scrutiny included the iron-and-gold cuirass or breastplate, an iron collar or pectoral, ivory and glass shield with its decorative Amazonomachy which now sits on display in the Vergina museum.[47]

We know from ancient texts that Alexander did reportedly take a 'sacred shield' from the Trojan Temple of Athena after some priest or acolyte convinced him it was 'original' and used at the battle for Troy. When Alexander arrived at the site in the summer of 334 BC, there was an established and flourishing tourist industry around the remains of what the Greeks termed 'Ilium', where a number of tumuli had sprung up in the shadow of the citadel ruins, allegedly those of the heroes who fought in Homer's *Iliad*. Athens had strategically founded its first overseas colony, Sigeium, there to 'co-opt the legendary framework' of these burial mounds containing the cremated bones, it was claimed, of Hector, his victim

Patroclus and his avenger Achilles, around whose mound Alexander and his companion Hephaestion raced in celebration.[48]

Like Xerxes, who had visited the mound of Troy in 480 BC when dedicating 1,000 cattle to the gods, Alexander probably needed little convincing of the veracity of the Trojan 'tourist' artefacts, set as he was on leaving his own footprints in legendary soil.[49] He would also have been aware of the vivid description of Achilles' 'fivefold' shield from the *Iliad*, which was richly decorated with the stars of the firmament and rustic scenes of the land, though there was no suggestion the relic proffered to Alexander was this particular item.[50] Alexander's bodyguard and shield-bearer, Peucestas, carried the display shield into each battle, surely as a talisman, because it must have been too old and ornate for use in extended combat.[51]

Borza's detailed paper outlined a number of other premises relevant to the chronology of Tomb II, though some of them were expansions of arguments already proffered by other scholars. Underpinning the notion that barrel-vaulted tombs appeared after the reign of Philip II, Borza believed the vivid hunting scene fresco painted above the entrance of Tomb II was inspired by the well-stocked Persian game parks – '*paradeisoi*', from which the word 'paradise' derived – that Alexander and his entourage had witnessed in Asia. Logically, therefore, it was painted for the funeral of his half-brother Philip III Arrhidaeus who was entombed by Cassander some seven years after the Asian campaigns had ended.[52] Thankfully, when Andronikos stumbled upon the fresco in November 1977, a team of wall painting restorers were working at the nearby village of Palatitsia in a post-Byzantine church, as this hunting scene and the wall murals in Tomb I remain prominent among the few works of art that have survived from the period.[53]

But according to Eugene Borza, now following the logic of two Italian historians who published in 1980, there was a further link in Tomb II to Alexander's Persian campaign: the diadem found on the floor, as this was a symbol of kingship adopted in Asia and not seen in Europe before.[54]

The most personal element of Borza's paper was a direct challenge to Andronikos concerning the illusive sceptre he first mentioned in his 1978 report. A sceptre, Borza claimed, would have been passed down through the generations of kings, as it was in the *Iliad* from the gods through Pelops, Atreaus, Aegisthos and on to Agamemnon, the king of Mycenae.[55] Similarly, an Argead sceptre would not have been buried with Philip II, but passed on to his son Alexander the Great, and, in turn, on to his successor, Philip III Arrhidaeus, at Babylon.[56]

Imagery of such regalia appear in Diodorus' account of Alexander's funeral carriage as it departed Babylon:

> On the first of these tablets was a chariot ornamented with work in relief, and sitting in it was Alexander holding a very splendid sceptre

in his hands ... Upon this chest there had been placed a cover of gold, matching it to a nicety, and fitting about its upper rim. Over this was laid a magnificent purple robe embroidered with gold, beside which they placed the arms of the deceased.[57]

Borza went on to argue that a sceptre could, however, have been interred with Philip III Arrhidaeus because he was the last male of Philip's direct line. In personal correspondence, he asked Andronikos to explain why references to the sceptre had disappeared from his later reports. Andronikos replied and explained that he had been mistaken in the original identification. Borza remained suspicious and inferred that once Andronikos had realized the relic weakened his argument for Philip II, he spirited it away. The gloves were coming off in the 'battle of the bones'.[58]

Eugene Borza presented a further challenge to Andronikos by bringing attention to the rather special Thracian or Phrygian-styled iron helmet found in the main chamber of Tomb II. Its uniqueness lies in the material, for helmets were usually beaten in bronze and no other iron example has been found.[59] The craftsmanship of the iron helmet, which features the head of the protective deity Athena below the tall solid-iron crest, was, as Andronikos had already pointed out, exceptional, because gamma rays revealed it had been fashioned from many pieces soldered together and hammered into its final seamless shape.[60] Original in-situ photos of Tomb II from 1977 revealed the helmet had been damaged on the left side, which resulted in a missing section, though it had since been repaired before being put on display at Vergina.[61]

As with the shield from Troy, Borza's line of questioning led back to historic events: in his biography of Alexander, Plutarch described an iron helmet worn at the Battle of Gaugamela where it 'gleamed like polished silver'; it was the workmanship of Theophilus, who is otherwise unknown.[62] When Alexander started wearing it is unknown, although no helmet is visible in the famous 'Alexander mosaic' found at Pompeii (see the image at the top of the book cover) which is thought to be a copy of a lost fresco painted by Philoxenus of Eretria for Cassander portraying events at the Battle of Issus, the second of the three great set-piece conflicts that toppled Darius III.[63]

The great victory at Issus near the narrow pass known as the 'Cilician Gates', where southern Turkey meets northern Syria today, prised open the heart of the Persian Empire and, more importantly, gave Alexander his first significant Persian treasury haul. With Darius' entourage at Issus and at close-by Damascus were all the trappings of Persian royalty: his golden chariot, funds to pay the vast army, as well as 7,000 pack animals and Darius' 329 concubines. Also captured were the Great King's family, who Alexander all but adopted. He is wisely said to have kept all the women isolated from his men and himself.[64]

Alexander was almost bankrupt when he first crossed to Asia, with sufficient funds in the state treasury for only a few months of campaigning. So taxes formerly directed to the Persian regime from the cities he 'liberated' in Anatolia, whether founded by Greeks or otherwise, were redirected to the Macedonian regime.[65] The Battle of Issus changed everything, and additionally gave Alexander the trophy of Darius' breastplate, which must have been far too large for him, as Darius was said to be a giant among men. Sometime before the next confrontation at Gaugamela, the 'gleaming' iron helmet appeared.[66]

Borza proposed that this particular helmet design, as well as the illusive sceptre, can also still be seen on a series of coins known as 'Porus Medallions' which were struck soon after Alexander defeated Porus, the raja of today's Punjab region of India. But the clue back to the artefacts in Tomb II lies in the first major battle with the Persians, three years earlier, at the Granicus River in 334 BC, not far from the Trojan ruins; one tradition claimed it was fought on the 1,000th anniversary of the fall of Troy. But according to Plutarch, Alexander was almost killed by a blow to the head from the battle-axe of a Persian commander.[67]

The axe-damaged helmet must have saved Alexander's life, as did his senior officer named Black Cleitus, who severed the outstretched arm of another Persian noble attacking Alexander from behind.[68] After hard fighting to ford the river, the Persian line collapsed, and it quickly turned into a rout. Spoils of battle, including 300 suits of Persian armour, were sent as votives to hang in the Acropolis at Athens. Thousands of Greek mercenaries in the Great King's employ, and who stood their ground to the end despite the Persian flight, were massacred or sent in chains to the mines of Macedon.[69]

Borza contacted Andronikos again and asked if there was any evidence that the helmet from Tomb II had been repaired in antiquity, presumably on the assumption that Alexander wore that particular helmet in future engagements after the Granicus battle. Andronikos duly replied, stating he understood the import of the question and further promising that technicians would investigate, but no further information was forthcoming.

The Cult of Alexander

If Eugene Borza was right, and if Tomb II *did* contain the very helmet, weapons and armour of Alexander the Great, an explanation was required as to how the regalia ended up in the burial chamber at Aegae. Once again, the chain of historical evidence does permit the notion: at the assembly gathering in Babylon after Alexander's death, the dead king's crown, robe and arms were exhibited as a sign of continuous royal authority. It was here that the unwitting and cowed Arrhidaeus was first dragged into the fray by dissatisfied infantry officers and proffered to the crowd as an alternative 'figurehead' king.

Following initial skirmishing over possession of Alexander's body, and once a truce had finally been reached between the divided infantry and cavalry factions, a second assembly was called at which 'King Philip III Arrhidaeus' was officially presented to the army outfitted in Alexander's robe – and presumably other weapons and regalia – besides the set that departed Babylon with Alexander's funeral bier.[70]

Perdiccas took Arrhidaeus with him when he invaded Egypt after Ptolemy hijacked Alexander's body, so we may speculate a set of his royal insignia were passed to the regent Antipater at the conference of generals in Syria following Perdiccas' death. The regal possessions would have been returned to Macedon when Antipater escorted Arrhidaeus, along with his new wife, Queen Adea-Eurydice, back to Pella. When Cassander gave them state burials in 316/315 BC after wresting control of Macedon from Olympias and Polyperchon, the armour, weapons and insignia could thus have been interred with them in Tomb II.[71]

Borza's well-constructed paper of 1987 caused quite a stir, but it contained nothing definitive on dating, and many of the arguments had been offered before and could be folded back on themselves. The various ceremonial insignia described are not *identical* with those now on display at Vergina: as far as the helmet is concerned, for example, Plutarch stated that the blow to Alexander's head sheared away one of the helmet's plumes, but the Tomb II example has no sockets for colourful plumed attachments.[72]

It seems that several ceremonial sets of insignia may well have been made for the king's court and they were portered around the empire for future king-making. Similar items reappeared in the Successor Wars in the possession of Alexander's former secretary, Eumenes of Cardia, who inherited significant regions to govern in the post-Alexander world. This remarkably tenacious and resourceful Greek had been elevated from court scribe to cavalry commander by Alexander, and he was given plenipotentiary powers across Anatolia under Perdiccas. Eumenes had already suffered a gruelling siege by Antigonus the One-Eyed from which he had extracted himself by artfully rewording a loyalty oath, and he needed all the leverage he could muster with the Macedonian officers now under his command, including an unpredictable brigade of veterans known as the 'Silver Shields'. Eumenes resorted to placing a diadem, sceptre and arms beside a throne when invoking Alexander's spirit in councils of war, and his 'cult of Alexander' made its way into history's pages.[73]

This brings us back to the Tomb II sceptre. Andronikos' description of a rod with a bamboo core with 'alternating layers of cloth and gold' hardly sounded like a construction fit for purpose: Achilles once 'dashed his gold-studded sceptre on the ground' to command attention, so they were not of the delicate structure Andronikos described. It was an innocent misidentification, as he had already explained.[74]

108   Unearthing the Family of Alexander the Great

The contention that the hunting scene painted above the entrance was based on the Persian game parks witnessed on Alexander's campaign is curiously undermined by one of Borza's own observations: Macedon in the late sixth century BC was a dependency of the Persian Empire, annexed as it was before Darius I's invasion of Greece. This was a period when Eastern traits in art and architecture would have indelibly left their mark. Examples of Persian-styled furniture with lion's-paw feet have been found at both Pydna and Pella, and to quote one expert on the issue: 'Even in Greece, following victories at Salamis and Plataea, Persian spoils influenced aspects of Greek material culture.' In fact, ever since the Euboeans dared cross the Aegean to Syria in the eleventh century BC to colonize in the face of the domestic catastrophe which heralded the Dark Age, Greek art had been infused with Eastern traits.[75]

The sister of the double-dealing King Alexander I had married the Persian ambassador Bubares, and sanctuary had been given to the exiled Persian noble Artabazus by Philip II when Alexander was a youth. Artabazus is also said to have had a hunting reserve on his estates in Phrygia.[76] We know that hunting reserves existed in Macedon itself, at least before the Roman invasion, with Polybius commenting that 'there was an abundance of big game of every kind in them'.[77] Yet there is nothing overtly Persian about the scenery in the Tomb II hunting frieze.[78]

The behaviour of Persian women in Macedon is documented as well: they demanded the luxury of the Achaemenid world and imported subservient ladies-in-waiting, 'ladder-lasses' they were called when crouching down to act as steps to help their mistresses into carts.[79] Additionally, we have examples of the 'Medizing' of the Macedonian court. It is thought that the tradition of enrolling royal pages, as well as the polygamy of the kings and the title 'chiliarch' for a second-in-command – a grand vizier of sorts – were all titles or roles adapted or adopted from the Achaemenid rulers, as was the emergence of the king's personal bodyguard corps.[80]

Persian weights and measures were still being used in Macedon, though not exclusively, until Alexander adopted the Attic system more widely in 335 BC.[81] Arrian provided a further example of eastern influence. When referring to the duties of the royal pages he stated: 'They would also take the horses from the grooms and lead them up to wherever the king [Alexander] was to go riding, then, Persian-style, assist him to mount and join him in the competitive business of the hunt.'[82]

Dining on Xerxes' Camels

A significant intrigue within the Tomb II hunting frieze is the depiction of lions in the quarry: there were no lions in ancient Macedon, Eugene Borza argued, so the scene must be set in Asia. But as Nicholas Hammond, Robin Lane Fox and other scholars have since pointed out, there is clear evidence for the presence of lions, in the fifth century BC at least, along with the danger they presented:

Pausanias and Xenophon placed lions, leopards, lynxes, panthers and bears in the region, and Herodotus tells us that lions preyed on Xerxes' camels when his army transited Macedon in 480 BC.[83]

If Herodotus' claim was allegorical to represent the 'symbol of the fierce resistance' of Alexander I, whom the historian clearly admired, lions were, nevertheless, attested to have roamed 'near' the country's eastern borders and on Mount Olympus. Pausanias tell us that in a victory over a neighbouring tribe, Caranus, the founding king of Macedon, 'set up a trophy after the Argive fashion, but it is said to have been upturned by a lion from Olympus, which then vanished'. This may be another symbolic accommodation to a kingly legend, but lion motifs adorned the coins of Alexander's grandfather, King Amyntas III.[84] Just as Homeric themes lived on, the Tomb II mural might have captured the essence of the once-iconic test of bravery, even if by the fourth century it was the wild boar that was actually hunted in that rite of passage. The lion and boar were considered comparable in ferocity, and hunting them was considered good training for war, though lions were exclusively hunted by kings.[85]

So, regarding the hunting frieze, like all the other arguments surrounding the Tomb II identifications, the 'slippery paths' of art were now clouding the Vergina debate.[86]

Two further pieces of evidence undermined the notion that barrel-vaulted tomb design post-dated Philip II. The first was Andronikos' discovery of the similarly shaped structure in 1987, labelled the 'Tomb of Eurydice', Philip's mother, with the artefacts within it dating to *ca.* 344/343 BC, eight years *before* Philip's death. The second was a description of the ideal mausoleum found in Plato's *Laws*, written sometime around 350 BC, which described this type of construction. But these datings remain open to question: Plato's term for 'vaulted' is somewhat ambiguous and the artefacts found in the 'Tomb of Eurydice' may also have been handed down, like the tripod found in the main chamber of Tomb II.[87]

The vaulted archway found in the ruins of the city of Priene and a similar archway at Nemea next entered the debate in defence of existing Greek knowledge of the construction technique. But these corbelled arches did not constitute true 'barrel vaults', came the reply from the Philip III Arrhidaeus-supporting camp.[88] Moreover, if they *did*, scholars argued with dexterity, 'Cassander presided over the Nemean Games in summer 315 BC, so he must have copied the design from here', long after Philip II died. But the structures are also uncertainly dated, so the 'proofs' from both teams floundered once again.

Still unresolved was the term 'diadem' in the context of 'royalty' when resonant of the priestly duties a king performed as an intermediary with the gods: did a diadem mean a metal circlet, a conical mitre as worn by Cyrus, a ribbon or a crown?[89] Descriptions of Alexander's diadem suggest it was a cloth fillet attached to a typical Macedonian hat known as a 'kausia', and not the circlet

A horseman and lion on a silver stater of Amyntas III.

of metal found in Tomb II; but solid bronze diadems have been found in older Macedonian graves.[90]

As Professor Hallie Franks of New York University pointed out when commenting on the paraphernalia connected to Alexander and the items Borza believed found their way to Tomb II when Cassander buried Adea and Philip III Arrhidaeus there, it is unclear what exactly Cassander 'would have stood to gain from taking out of circulation the very symbols of Alexander's royal authority'.[91]

When all the opposing views had been aired, nothing seemed certain except the Socrates 'paradox': 'all I know is I know nothing for sure.' Like the brilliant sophists of ancient Athenian debates, scholars were still able to argue everything both ways. Borza's paper, like Lehmann's of 1980 – both of them aggregates of earlier ideas from various scholars – was soon refuted by the well-known period scholar and Alexander author Ernst Fredricksmeyer of the University of Colorado and by the French historian Pierre Briant.[92]

Reconstructing the Face of a King

At the end of the archaeological field season of 1984, Dr Jonathan Musgrave from the Centre for Comparative and Clinical Anatomy at the University of Bristol took a look 'in haste' at the bones from the simpler cist grave labelled Tomb I.[93] At that time, they were stored at the Archaeological Museum of Thessalonica, which had originally been built to house the contents of the six unlooted tombs discovered by chance at Derveni to the north of Vergina in January 1962 during a construction project. A site was linked to the ancient city of Lete, and the contents was built to house them.

The following year, 1985, Musgrave published a short paper titled 'The Skull of Philip II of Macedon' in which he outlined in a postscript his 'tentative' findings on the Tomb I bones, concluding that the chamber housed a well-built male in the prime of his life, a young woman and a newborn baby or foetus. The bones were then passed to Nikolaos Xirotiris and it appears they remained in his laboratory at Democritus University in Thrace for almost two decades.

What Musgrave unwittingly did in his haste was to give ammunition to the faction backing Philip III Arrhidaeus and Adea-Eurydice as the residents of Tomb II. By concluding that the Tomb I bones were those of a middle-aged man, a young woman and a baby, Musgrave had all but described the events surrounding the death of Philip II, whose young wife Cleopatra and her newborn were executed by Olympias. If they were buried in Tomb I, Arrhidaeus and Adea *must have* resided in Tomb II. But that was not what Jonathan Musgrave believed at all.

Something significant was needed to reverse the growing momentum of the Arrhidaeus-Adea camp with their strengthening contention that some of the Tomb II artefacts belonged to Alexander the Great. Musgrave himself provided the momentum shift the same year when he was invited by two professors at the University of Manchester, which had already made its name in autopsies on Egyptian mummies, to take a further look at the Tomb II male skull. Their conclusions on the visible wounds were rather different to those provided by Xirotiris-Langenscheidt in 1981. Discounting the effects of heat from the funeral pyre which would have caused bone cracking, Musgrave believed there was clear evidence of trauma consistent with the eye wound Philip received at the siege of the city of Methone around 354 BC, eighteen years before he died. Philip's royal surgeon was famously praised for removing the eye and leaving no infection.[94]

Following a series of searching questions, and to their 'disbelief and delight', Manolis Andronikos gave the Tomb II cranium, which he termed his 'most important skull', to Professor Richard Neave, an expert in forensic facial reconstruction at the University of Manchester. His colleague was the historian and archaeologist Professor John Prag. They, in turn, consulted with Musgrave, 'an erstwhile classicist turned anthropologist at the University of Bristol … who had made his specialty in the study of human remains from Greece'.[95]

Musgrave assisted Neave and Prag in the construction of wax facsimiles of the skull set into clay blocks, with missing portions recreated through a similar modelling process.[96] Several casts of the cranium were made, after which an expert make-up artist added skin colour and hair. The reconstruction was 'deliberately carried out without reference to the ancient portraits' of Philip II, according to a sound bite designed to stress the unbiased nature of the work.[97]

The full facial reconstruction was a stunning achievement considering that the back of the skull had actually exploded in cremation. Musgrave explained that the brain, blood and cerebrospinal fluid must have boiled in the fire for that to have occurred. Prominent on the remodelled skull was the high forehead and steep nose first noted by Xirotiris and Langenscheidt, with some notable asymmetries of the jaw and chin, a probable physical imbalance from birth that would have been noticeable all his life. A surgeon working with them had also spotted a small nick at the inner top corner of the right eye socket and that a piece of bone was missing at the suture, suggestive of an angled blow.[98]

Based on this, Musgrave and his team added a gaping, shiny red and still-wet-looking slashing scar from the middle of the forehead down, emphasizing the damage Philip suffered to the right eye. Apparently the make-up artist from Granada Television styled it on the look of a wound on a Canadian lumberjack who happened to be visiting a friend at her workplace.[99] In the minds of these experts in Manchester there was no longer any doubt: it *was* Philip II who was cremated and interred in Tomb II, and 'Andronikos would have the answer he hoped for'.[100]

The team was heavily criticized for exaggerating the facial wound: this was far too subjective an addition for a forensic reconstruction and was now leading in its inference. The head had, after all, been fashioned from damaged bones with much guesswork involved. Neave only had five cranial fragments to work with, all significantly warped or shrunk, and, despite the earlier statement, he admitted the team had been working on a subjective basis: they believed they *were* reconstructing the face of Philip II, and they had used likenesses of the king when finishing the modelling, especially the nose. To counter the growing criticism, Prag released a non-scarred face in 1990 which, unfortunately, did not 'convey the excitement and fire of the first version'.[101]

That year, Musgrave endorsed the Xirotiris-Langenscheidt gender and age prognosis for the Tomb II bones in a paper colourfully titled 'Dust and Damn'd Oblivion: a Study of Cremation in Ancient Greece'. But that still left the door open for both Philips and their wives. As with the Tomb I remains, Musgrave had never been able to take more than a cursory look at the bones himself, the male cranium aside, and he was largely working off photographs. Yet he remained steadfast in his conclusions. In 1991, in the publication *Ancient World* he opened his paper with: 'My aim is to persuade you that the bones from Tomb II belonged to Philip II and, probably, Cleopatra, and not, as others have suggested, to Philip III Arrhidaeus and Adea-Eurydice.' Musgrave's goal was clear, though his introduction was interpreted by critics as 'fitting the evidence to the occasion'. But he was not the only one presenting a new case for an old identity.

Under the Metaxas dictatorship in Greece in the late 1930s, the Slavic-speaking people of northern Greece, many descended from the Slavic tribes who settled in Macedonia in the sixth century AD, were subject to harsh treatment. The Second

World War and the Greek Civil War of 1946–49 saw Macedonia occupied by Bulgarian and Yugoslav communist forces. In 1944, Tito established the People's Federal Republic of Macedonia with its capital at Skopje, with the aim of bringing it under Yugoslavian control.

Yugoslavia dissolved in 1991, and out of the fallout emerged a new socialist republic to Greece's north. Its borders fell between Albania and Bulgaria in what would have been largely ancient Paeonia and western Thrace in the time of Philip's predecessors. Arguably a slither of ancient 'Upper Macedonia', the northern cantons annexed by Philip II in his expanded realm, fell into the new state. This was a geographical anomaly voiced in *The Falsification of Macedonian History* published by the former Secretary General of Northern Greece in 1984.[102] Despite the questionable geopolitics, the new Republic of Macedonia immediately adopted a twelve-point Vergina starburst of the Argead kings to adorn its national flag.

Greece saw the republic's name and its flag as national identity theft and demanded both be changed. Street protests followed on both sides of the border and airport names were changed in line with the nationalist cause. The new regime was duly recognized by the United Nations in 1993, but only under the title 'Former Yugoslav Republic of Macedonia' ('FYROM'). Claiming ancient roots in the region under a tide of nationalism, FYROM accused its neighbour of stealing the biggest part of 'Aegean Macedonia' and incorporating it into northern Greece.[103] The response from Athens was a blockade of the new Balkan player staking identity claims to the kings buried below Vergina.[104]

On 5 July 1993, in what, in hindsight, appears a suitable riposte to the political turmoil, an inaugural celebration was held with the completion of the exterior of the 'tumulus-styled' Museum of Royal Tombs of Aegae. It was reasoned that 'preventative conservation' under an earthen covering, with 24-hour air filters inside and crystal screens separating the façades of the exposed tombs from the public areas, would stabilize the temperature and humidity, providing the structures with something of the environment they had survived in for the previous 2,300 years. It was a world of shadows painted in shades of grey with subtle illumination to preserve the atmosphere of a Netherworld into which the tomb inhabitants had passed.

During the museum's construction, some twenty-five more simple tombs had been found in the vicinity of the new building, apparently housing the graves of commoners, not royalty, and all immediately back-filled 'in order to gain a more accurate picture of the area that remained a cemetery for centuries'. As work was about to commence, the chief architect overseeing the project, Dr Dimacopoulos, eloquently articulated the philosophical challenge he and the museum faced:[105]

> In the case of these monuments of Vergina, it is obvious that there is an innate contradiction arising out of the desire of many to see and enjoy

the aesthetic experience of a heritage for which its creators had planned the exact opposite – that is, the deliberate concealing of it from the world of the living.

The ancient tomb builders were outvoted, and museum construction continued.

In 1993, Professor Chrysoula Paliadeli entered the debate. One of Andronikos' original assistants and in many ways his successor, she would become director of Vergina excavations at Aristotle University, which had been sponsoring archaeological digs at Vergina since 1982. Professor Paliadeli was more qualified than any of the external voices to commentate on the finds, and she convincingly countered another of Eugene Borza's contentions: the Macedonian beret-style 'mushroom' cap or 'kausia' visible in the hunting fresco was a design borrowed from the ancient Afghans and known there as a '*chitrali*'.[106]

The Greeks were the '*Yauna*', 'Ionians', to the Persians, but the Macedonians were distinguished as '*Yauna Takabara*', those 'wearing shields on their heads', due to the distinctive round shape of either the hat known as a 'kausia' or the broad-rimmed 'petasos'; they were variously described as being made of felt, wool or leather.[107] Paliadeli's paper showed that the ancient texts describing their provenance, materials and function were confused and contradictory, while accounts clearly suggested that the 'kausia' personified a 'Macedonian': the hats were linked to royal pages and high-ranking generals of the kings' courts, and at times they were bound with diadems.

Turning Borza's argument on its head, it is not impossible that a derivative of these Macedonian hats was adopted in the East after Alexander had passed through, or when his successors established kingdoms in the regions surrounding Afghanistan. After all, inhabitants of the remote mountainous areas of what we term the Hindu Kush and northern Pakistan later revelled in the story that Alexander was their ancestor.[108] The tribes known as the Hunza and Kalasha, with fair hair and blue eyes, claim Greek and Macedonian descent. Perhaps unsurprisingly, a delegation from FYROM invited the Hunza royal family to Skopje, where they were feted and 'treated like long lost cousins', much to the ridicule of the Greek press.[109]

The Ballad of Valla

In 1994, a new geographical cat was thrown amongst the anthropological pigeons when a further challenge to the 'royalty' of Vergina and its tombs emerged. In *The American Journal of Archaeology*, Panayiotis Faklaris, one of Manolis Andronikos' former assistants at the Aristotle University of Thessaloniki, published a paper that again undermined the premise that ancient Aegae had been discovered.[110] Calling into question the sources that made Nicholas Hammond link Vergina to the ancient capital,[111] Faklaris proposed the real Aegae was situated on Mount Bermion, above what were once referred to as the Gardens of Midas, following clues in the statements given in the texts of Herodotus and Diodorus.[112]

Faklaris' contention placed the actual founding settlement of Aegae close to the modern villages of Kopanos and Lefkadia, east of Naousa, where classical graves and a fourth-century BC theatre had already been excavated, close to the ancient settlement of Mieza where Aristotle schooled Alexander. He argued that Léon Heuzey's conclusion from almost a century-and-a-half earlier had been correct all along: Vergina was the site of the ancient city of Valla. But in a 1996 paper, Elizabeth Carney of Clemson University, a renowned scholar and author of a number of influential books on royal women of Macedon, demonstrated quite clearly that the non-contemporary sources were confused over the border between the ancient Macedonian cantons of Pieria and Bottiaea: differing texts placed Aegae in either, depending upon whether the dividing line was considered to be the Haliacmon River or the Pierian hills.[113]

Terracotta figurine circa 300 BC of a boy wearing the Macedonian hat known as a 'kausia'. (*British Museum*)

Despite all this, by the time the Archaeological Museum of Vergina opened its doors to the public in 1997 under the reconstructed tumulus, the curators led by Dr Angeliki Kottaridi had no doubt about the labelling of the tombs: Tomb II *was* the resting place of King Philip II of Macedon, in the antechamber *was probably* his obscure Thracian wife Meda, while Tomb III *did probably* hold the bones of King Alexander IV, the murdered teenage son of Alexander the Great. The 'official' literature that followed was even more unequivocal on names, causing Eugene Borza to comment on one title: 'The text is marred not only by the worst sort of nationalistic archaeology, but also by serious lapses in reasoning.'[114] Yet these identifications ensured the museum was a commercial success, and this is how they remain today. But the truth has always been rather more obscure.

In the inaugural year of the museum, two more Greek historians questioned the 'royal' nature of the Great Tumulus burials. They considered the tombs within a wider context of other notable 'rich graves' occupied by veterans of Alexander's Asian campaign, like those uncovered at Derveni. Derveni Tomb 'B' yielded the spectacular krater or mixing jug which remains the museum's centrepiece. Similar pottery to examples from Vergina were found in tombs there, along with wreaths, purple cloth on cremated remains, fine weapons and armour, and coins clearly dating to sometime in the reigns of Philip and Alexander.

But as Professor Stella Drougou pointed out, none of them can accurately triangulate when the burials took place, whether during or after either the reigns of Philip or Alexander. The richness of the Derveni finds simply reinforced the notion that the 'warlord kings' of Macedon were simply 'first among equals' among the tribal nobles that managed the state.[115] And unlike Aegae, none of the ancient cities associated with the ruins at Derveni, Aenea and Agios Athanasios, where a sixteen-pointed 'Argead starburst' had been found, were recorded as the burial ground of royals.[116]

Despite Andronikos' early contention that the architectural 'binary system' of subterranean tombs positioned by an adjacent above-ground shrine – like those in the Great Tumulus – was unique in Macedon, later excavations showed that the practice was not so rare. A close-by cluster tumulus in the Vergina necropolis is one example, as are Tombs 'A' and 'D' at Aiane and two more at Pella.[117] Hero shrines had also been erected by the numerous tumuli found outside the ruins of Troy, from where the burial practices of Macedon were supposedly archetyped.[118]

Five years on from Faklaris' paper, in 1999, Chrysoula Paliadeli replied to the Vergina identity challenge with an article published in *The Annual of the British School at Athens*. She detailed the many geographical and archaeological markers that now made it clear that the ruined city was indeed ancient Aegae. The fortress walls had by then been unearthed, along with more cemeteries and the Sanctuary of the Mother of the Gods, with over 1,000 graves in total, besides the burial clusters of royal women and earlier Temenid kings. In all, some 500 tumuli had been exposed covering over 900 hectares between Vergina and Palatitsia, revealing the extent of the ancient capital, which, with its suburbs, covered some 6,500 hectares. Taking all this into account and responding to earlier tomb arguments from Borza's fulsome papers, Professor Paliadeli labelled his 'evidences' as 'misunderstandings' from his 'inadequate or preconceived archaeological knowledge'. His pages, she concluded, definitely needed some 'refining'.[119]

Ever since Andronikos had first tentatively referred to Tomb II as the 'Tomb of Philip II' in 1978, both his supporters and his critics had aired their views in the *American Journal of Archaeology*. But in the absence of definitive evidence, the editors of the publication in 1983 – noting, in particular, the incessant back-and-forth rebuttals between Fredericksmeyer and Lehmann over the previous three years – then in 1987 and now in 1999, called for a moratorium on further 'Vergina papers' until new discoveries could significantly advance the debate. As Dr Miltiades Hatzopoulos explained, 'a precarious equilibrium had been reached' when the fighters had run out of new ammunition. The *American Journal of Archaeology* recognized the stalemate for what it was.[120]

'Cherish those who seek the truth, but beware of those who find it'

In 1999, Dr Costas Zambas, a civil engineer who designed and supervised the restoration of the left earthen retaining wall of the yard at the tomb entrance, argued that the joint on the extrados (the outer curve of the arch) which divides the vaults of the chamber and the antechamber was not a proof that the two parts were constructed in different phases, as Andronikos supposed. Zambas, in fact, observed even more differences between the two rooms such as their heights inside and outside, the differing profile of the vaults, the number of stone blocks used and the distinct form and level of their decorative zones. Nevertheless, his conclusion was that the tomb could have been constructed as a whole and the variances of the two rooms part of the initial design. He pointed to a more-sound example in the Tomb of Judgment at Lefkadia. Zambas also noted during the restoration work that the brick retaining wall did not continue behind the side wall of the antechamber, as Andronikos estimated, but stopped 20cm from the surface of the façade.[121]

But it was only in the following year that a truly new debating catalyst arrived. In April 2000, Dr Antonis Bartsiokas, a paleoanthropologist at Democritus University, published a paper in the journal *Science*. He claimed the eye-wound trauma seen by Musgrave and team on the skull of the Tomb II male was nothing more than bone cracking in cremation. Xirotiris and Langenscheidt had apparently been correct in their contention: no injury could be seen. Further, he agreed that *none* of the other wounds mentioned by Demosthenes were visible on the skeleton.

The few hours Bartsiokas spent looking at the Tomb II bones in 1998 at the Vergina laboratory, using what is termed 'macrophotography' to capture extremely high-resolution images of minutiae, additionally led him to conclude that they had been 'dry cremated', that is burned when the flesh had already rotted away and the bones had become 'degreased'. This is distinct from a 'green' or 'flesh-boned' cremation of the newly dead, and the difference can be detected from the bone colour and warping. This was, of course, more manna from heaven to the Philip III Arrhidaeus partisans: dry-boned cremation ruled out Philip II, who was consigned to the flames by Alexander just days after being stabbed at his daughter's wedding.

Bartsiokas went on to argue that a dry-boned cremation fitted the circumstances of Philip III Arrhidaeus and Adea-Eurydice, who were cremated by Cassander some six to seventeen months after Olympias had them executed in 316 BC. On the back of Bartsiokas' report, new influential members of the academic community joined the 'Philip III Arrhidaeus league'. Nevertheless, serious questions were soon raised about Bartsiokas' conclusions: why his photographs excluded the 'long' bones, the left femur for example, which *did* show sign of in-flesh cremation.[122]

The following year, sometime between 13 August and 9 September 2001, modern-day tomb raiders descended on Vergina and headed for the Tomb of Eurydice. It was as if the looters from antiquity, those who had once been fooled by its realistic false door, had returned to finish the job. Due to summer staffing shortages, the evening guard shift had been dispensed with. Only the monthly checking of environmental monitoring equipment in the tomb detected the theft. The looters had hacked off seven statuettes from the back and armrests of the marble throne in the rear of the tomb, some of them figurines of female dancers, along with three coloured statues of sphinxes. The Tomb of Eurydice was never opened to the public, and as there was no sign of forced entry, security guards were interviewed on suspicion of an inside job. No one was ever convicted.

In 2007, in a comprehensive paper titled 'The Chronology of the Macedonian Royal Tombs at Vergina', Eugene Borza teamed up with Olga Palagia, the Professor of Classical Archaeology at the National and Kapodistrian University of Athens, to present a renewed case. Between them, Borza and Palagia had by now authored, reviewed or lectured on almost every aspect of the ancient Macedonian world, and here they combined many of the isolated arguments from the past thirty years, including Borza's previous papers.

Professor Palagia had already elaborated her intriguing theory on the hunting scene frieze above the entrance: it is not Alexander's bearded father sitting on the horse, as Andronikos had imaged, but the halfwit Arrhidaeus, who could not be trusted with a razor. Moreover, the naked youths were not royal pages or bodyguards, but Cassander's younger brothers, thus it was a memorial to a royal hunt that took place in Babylon just before Alexander died, when Cassander was said to be present. Tomb II was therefore the resting place of Philip III Arrhidaeus and his wife Adea-Eurydice.[123]

The erudite nature of their new and expanded paper, overly pressed arguments aside, was articulated in great detail. It concluded: 'In the nearly three decades that have elapsed since the commencement of the excavations of the royal tombs at Vergina no credible new argument has been offered to support the identification of Philip II as the occupant of Tomb II.'[124] But this was equally true of the opposing view. The Borza-Palagia paper regurgitated the earlier insinuations on Manolis Andronikos' impartiality, but Andronikos was now unable to reply, having died in 1992. Borza had already voiced his disappointment with that state of affairs: 'It would be unfortunate if the interpretations of the finds from Vergina were frozen in time from the moment of Andronikos' death.'[125]

The Cottage Industry of Verginana

Dr Miltiades Hatzopoulos is something of an expert on ancient Macedon and the author of many books and academic papers on the classical world. I had drawn frequently from his *Macedonian Institutions Under the Kings* when researching the royal line. Back in 1996, he had provided a somewhat optimistic commentary on the excavations at Vergina:

> Half a century after the start of systematic, large-scale excavations, the huge labour by archaeologists, who have dragged from the earth ruins hidden in the past, and the patient work of all the scholars, who have concentrated the expertise on their finds, have revealed an inhabited land that had been terra incognita and given a face to the people, enigmatic until that point, whom Alexander led to the ends of the earth.[126]

But watching on as various teams of archaeologists and historians drew polarized conclusions, and occasionally commenting on the bias that had crept in, Hatzopoulos issued the less laudatory summation in 2008 of the 'cottage industry of Verginana', as he termed it: 'It is true that the issue has been obscured by precipitate announcements, the quest for publicity, political agendas and petty rivalries, which have led to an inconclusive series of down-datings and up-datings, finally disqualifying all the 'scientific' criteria – including forensic medicine – invoked.'[127]

In particular, Hatzopoulos cautioned that the twenty years between the deaths of Philip II and his son Arrhidaeus is 'too short a period for the kind of precision attainable' from looking at ceramic pottery and metal ware, from which many commentators had based their dating conclusions. Moreover, he reiterated that the Athenian specimens used as dating parallels 'were not strictly identical to the Vergina ones'.[128] This included the tentative dating of four 'spool-shaped' salt-cellars found in the Tomb II main chamber, as they resembled condiment pots found in Athens which had been dated to 325–295 BC.[129] But similar-designed objects, which are rather bland and unadorned, have been found in northern Greece and dated by experienced excavators to a century or more earlier, long before the alleged 'late dating' artefacts from Attica.[130]

Hatzopoulos also considered Bartsiokas' conclusions prejudiced by his support of Borza's 1987 paper, including the contention that Tomb II may hold the paraphernalia of Alexander the Great.[131] His apt comment recalls a familiar and now pertinent refrain: 'bias sticks to a historian's thinking like soil to a gardener's spade.'[132] Although a wealth of new 'objective' forensic disciplines are at the disposal of scientists and anthropologists, those employing them are far from impartial, and commentators have highlighted how we prejudice our rewriting of the past, unconsciously at times. As the saying goes, 'cherish those who seek the truth, but beware of those who find it.'[133]

In 2010, Robin Lane Fox joined the Musgrave-Prag-Neave team for a final fulsome rebuttal to the Philip III Arrhidaeus camp. Along with Hugh White from the department of pathology of Southmead Hospital in Bristol, they produced a tour de force refuting Bartsiokas' finds which questioned the competence in the 'poor reconstruction of the skull'.[134] Lane Fox had published a biography of Alexander the Great back in 1973 with a remarkable degree of insight, and more recently he had advised Oliver Stone in his making of the 2004 film, *Alexander*, which, unfortunately, flopped. Lane Fox penned the historical backbone to the new paper, while Musgrave and the expanded team provided an extensive medical autopsy.

Their report comprehensively overturned Bartsiokas' arguments, which had 'made it all sound so simple', and also those he published in 2007–08 with Elizabeth Carney, who had correctly pointed out that 'identification of the occupants of Tomb I has tended to depend on whom one preferred for the occupants of Tomb II'.[135] At this point, Bartsiokas had not personally examined the Tomb I bone collection, even though he felt qualified to state: 'Skeletal and taphonomic evidence ... shows ... it belongs to Philip II, his wife Cleopatra and their newborn daughter Europa.' He was regurgitating Musgrave's ageing and gender conclusions from 1984.

Musgrave and team pointed out that Bartsiokas' conclusion that the Tomb II male had been 'dry burned' – cremated without flesh – was self-defeating for his arguments. Philip III Arrhidaeus' corpse *would have still been in the process of putrefying* when it was dug up and reburied by Cassander some months after he was killed: apparently it takes several years for a cadaver to completely lose its flesh, though local conditions such as temperature and soil humidity affect the process of decay.[136] This led to a fundamental question: would ancient Greek or Macedonian religious custom and taboo have allowed for Cassander to exhume the still-putrefying corpse of Arrhidaeus, onto whose putrescent head a gold crown must have been placed for the funeral, judging by the gold pieces found in the pyre? In the ancient mindset, a dead body was a pollution or defilement that had to be immediately buried or burned for good.[137] So this scenario seemed highly unlikely.

Philip's contentious eye wound remained at the centre of the Lane Fox-Musgrave-Prag-Neave paper. Musgrave believed the condition of the skull may have deteriorated in the fifteen years since he had seen it back in 1984, explaining why Bartsiokas was no longer able to identify the trauma. This was a rather surprising proposition for a cranium that had already weathered 2,346 years, and one Bartsiokas summarily rejected.[138]

Clearly, none of the new arguments by either camp had produced a smoking gun. But they were all worthy of a chair in the Vergina debating hall, having been put forward by well-respected scholars, who, together, have attempted to deepen the world's knowledge of ancient Macedon, even if, as Hatzopoulos pointed out, evidence had been 'over-solicited' and 'abusively interrogated'.[139] Opposing views should be embraced as part of this fascinating emerging story, but instead a caustic schism had developed which, in some cases, harked back to decades-old personal rivalries and political divides. 'Archaeology is not a science, it's a vendetta,' was the rather-apt summation of Sir Mortimer Wheeler, the British archaeologist who died a year before Andronikos found Tomb II.

New academic papers emerged after 2010, but they were based on old and faulty information or simply regurgitated the past. Any meaningful commentary would need to incorporate results of the new study of the Tomb II skeletal remains by Professor Theodore Antikas and Laura Wynn-Antikas, which had commenced in late 2009 and would be by far the most comprehensive analysis to date. By now they had based themselves at the Vergina laboratory, an hour's drive from their home in Makrygialos, and each day they were 'living' in the bones.

Chapter 9

Bones Don't Lie!

>The most useful piece of learning for the uses of life is to unlearn what is untrue.
>—Antisthenes

Like Manolis Andronikos and millions of other Greeks, Theo Antikas' parents had been refugees forced to resettle from Turkish territory, in their case from Constantinople during the population exchange of the 1920s, and the fierce tides of Hellenic politics never calmed in the decades after.

Theo's widowed mother had insufficient funds to send him to medical school, so he joined the army medical corps. In 1969, after serving for many years, Theo found himself on an army scholarship at the University of Illinois, undertaking a PhD in human physiology and teaching post-graduate veterinarians.

Much to his disappointment, the army recalled him to Greece and there followed a brief period of incarceration. In 1975, Theo decided he would run as a member of parliament for a district of Thessalonica, a political post that legally required him to resign his military position, now as captain and Director of the 1st Horse Division in Thessaly. However, the Minister of Defence refused his resignation and demanded his return to active duty, despite a ruling by the Supreme Court to the contrary.

Theo sent a letter to a Thessalonica newspaper to expose his predicament. The Defence Minister visited Theo to demand an answer to his insubordination, and in a heated debate Theo reminded him that unlike vets, politicians have short shelf lives, and he advised the minister to 'return to his home in Epirus and make cheese'. The result was sixty days in a military prison, where Theo posted a sign in his door which read: 'Finally, I have a roof over my head.' He spent the time writing a book titled *30 Years with Animals (Or the misfortune of being a veterinarian)*.

Theo's resignation was finally accepted, and in the early 1980s he promptly left for France, where he ran a veterinary clinic, taught laser surgery and therapeutics and became the chief vet for the French Pony Clubs. He based himself in an apartment in Paris, where he and Laura first lived together.

From 1995, they lived in Litochoro on the foothills of Mount Olympus, a stone's throw from the ancient shrine at Dium where the lush summer evergreens are crowned by winter snow. The year 2005 saw them return to the US: they worked in the Skagit Valley, which is back-dropped by the Cascade Mountains, in the north-west corner of Washington State with its mellow maritime climate. Laura was curating at a local museum, while Theo held both the posts of Visiting Onassis Professor in the History Department at the University of Washington and Adjunct Professor in the Biosciences Department at Skagit Valley College.

On 1 May 2005, Theo posted a formal request to the Ministry of Culture, via Professor Chrysoula Paliadeli, for a re-examination of the Tomb II bones, along with the creation of a database in which bones would be numbered and catalogued, as there had been many discrepancies in the skeletal references since their discovery in 1977. This was not the first request: Dr Yannis Maniatis, a physicist and experienced materials scientist who founded the Archaeometry Laboratory at the National Centre for Scientific Research Demokritos in Athens, had been petitioning for a multidisciplinary forensic study on all the Great Tumulus bones since 2004. He and Theo now recommended that the study be undertaken by a 'neutral' institution such as the Smithsonian Institute in Washington D.C., ideally by a renowned anthropologist with no preconceived ideas or knowledge of their historical background or the ongoing 'battle of the bones'. Dr Douglas Ubelaker, who assisted the FBI in forensic cases, was the suggested candidate.

They also wanted the bones to undergo radiocarbon dating and DNA tests. Professor Paliadeli, who had published her own book on ancient Macedonian tombs and monuments in 2003, and in 2005 co-authored a sumptuous and worthy continuation to Andronikos' earlier pictorial history of Vergina, accepted the recommendation and appreciated the import of the work.[1] The Smithsonian anthropologist was contacted, but there were insufficient funds to contract him. Various applications for studies on the bones were made in the following years, but all were rejected by higher authorities with responsibility for the tomb finds, and no funding was forthcoming.[2]

In late 2008, Theo and Laura returned to Greece, though it would take ten years for her to be granted naturalized Greek citizenship, a decade during which she felt like 'Penelope weaving and waiting 10 years for the return of Odysseus'. They finally moved into their newly built house in November, a month which encompasses 'St Martin's Summer', when sheep are led from higher pastures to warmer winter grazing, and gossamer threads of fragile autumn sun are bordered by chill mornings as olive pickers take to the fields. Their own grove sat above the ancient battlefield of Pydna on the outskirts of modern Makrygialos. 'You can still hear the screams,' claims Theo, recalling that some 20,000 Macedonians died on the day that King Perseus' army fell to the short sword of the legions of Rome.

The Roman historian Livy, who surely drew from Polybius' now-lost eyewitness account of the build-up to the battle, provided some intriguing insights into the mindset of the vanquished Macedonians: perplexingly, having crushed every opponent from the Balkan kingdoms to southern Greece, and every tyrant, king or satrap from Asia Minor to the Indus Valley, they were said to be 'shocked' at the brutality of the Roman war machine, and yet awed by the precise arrangement of its military camp.[3] At Pydna, wounds caused by the slashing weapons of Aemilius Paullus' legionnaires, in particular, were gruesome compared to the more familiar puncture marks from spears and lances. Such organized brutality was not a trait that had coexisted in the 'barbarians' the Macedonians had previously encountered.

Despite the groans Theo fancies still echo from the battlefield at Pydna, the Macedonians were among the 'silent people of the ancient Mediterranean basin', as Eugene Borza termed them, referring to their lack of literary output, and to that of the Carthaginians and Spartans beside them. It's a useful generality, though not wholly accurate, and neither is it a pointer to Macedonian illiteracy, as Borza believed. It is simply because none of these accounts survived that the picture of 'literary silence' prevails.[4]

In late 2008, the bones at Vergina had still not spoken with any clarity, so Yannis and Chrysoula submitted a new proposal for an integrated analysis of all the tomb finds – the bones and associated materials. As Theo was back in northern Greece, he could undertake the bone anthropological study with Laura. Once again, their request fell on the ever-receptive ears of Professor Paliadeli, who had become a Member of the European Parliament with roles representing the Committee of Culture and Education as well as European History. She had been instrumental in helping the application for European research funds for ongoing research, but this also proved unsuccessful. However, in September 2009, she advised Theo that through her ongoing efforts, the Research Committee at the Aristotle University had provided a small grant for the project, even though Greece was heading into the worst financial crisis since the Romans marched on Pella.

The funds provided, a modest 6,000 euros, were to cover several months of work. As Professor Paliadeli frequented Brussels in her new parliamentary role, Athanasia Kyriakou, an archaeologist at the Aristotle University of Thessaloniki, acted as her 'right hand woman' and the point person for communications with the Antikas team.[5] Dr Kyriakou frequently lectured on the Vergina tomb finds, and more recently she had introduced a study of the gold wreaths with an observation that sounded particularly pertinent to the ongoing Vergina debate: 'Remarkable finds very often pose puzzling questions and demand synthetic answers that merely constitute suggestions for conceptualizing the past.'[6]

There followed discussions on protocols for the new Antikas study, with the sketching out of a working methodology for dealing with these irreplaceable human remains, after which Theo and Laura personally met the bones at their storage place at the Vergina laboratory in January 2010. They had all the necessary experience, both in terms of fieldwork and in the laboratory going back to 1995, since when they had analyzed hundreds of skeletons from the Iron Age to the Byzantine period in Greece. Their work and publications, in particular the paper concerning the animal remains from the funeral pyre on the roof of Tomb II, provided the Antikas team with valuable experience at the site.

Theo and Laura had also worked at Pella, where an eight-chambered rock-cut tomb was found, the largest in Greece. Among the human skeletal remains, animal bones had to be identified. Many were found to be astragali, the lower leg tarsal bones of sheep and goats, which also had other uses in the ancient world: as gaming dice known as 'knucklebones', or as ritual objects to ward off evil spirits. Some even had inscriptions carved on them. Laura had become familiar with the signs of human intervention such as stringing holes and polishing that might suggest their purpose.

There are not too many couples who relish the prospect of working as a team, but the project at Vergina presented a once-in-a-lifetime opportunity. Besides, Theo felt he was following his grandfather's adage, 'don't be lazy; put your wife to work'. Laura had her own philosophy on the challenges of the task ahead: 'shrouds don't have pockets'. She was referring to the limited funding that saw them digging into their own shallow bank accounts to complete research only ever intended to cover cataloguing the skeletal remains of the male, but which soon extended to the Tomb II female, the 'Amazon' Andronikos discovered. Laura was pointing out that you cannot take money with you into the Underworld, or, as the followers of Pythagoras would have termed it, with each new transmigration of the soul into the next body. Shrouds once covered the dead in the ancient Greek world before they entered the purifying funerary fire, the difference being that the valuables of life *were* buried then with the deceased for the afterlife.

Methodology on Morphology

A major challenge to the Antikas study was the past treatment of the bones, which, whilst well-meaning, had been damaging. Many were covered in heavy preserving solutions of silicon-based polymers, while resins and adhesives had been used in bone moulds for the age and gender studies. Alginate residue with plaster appeared in facial reconstructions, and plasticine was used in the late 1980s and early 90s to support the bones on display at the Archaeological Museum of Thessalonica. Each of these left some form of contamination, as did the wooden support sticks inserted in the reconstruction process. Twenty years earlier, Theo had written to the Minister of Culture pointing out that the skeleton of 'Philip II' then on display at the museum in Thessalonica, sat 'like the head of a saint' in a glass cabinet close by the entrance to the toilets.

The male skeleton from Tomb II on display at the Thessalonica Archaeological Museum, September 1990. (*Image courtesy of J.H. Musgrave*)

As part of the new forensics, Theo was overseeing computed tomography (CT) scans at the medical diagnostic centre in Veria run by Dr Kostas Kotridis, who was generously lending his resources and time at no cost. CT scanning had been used since the 1970s to 'unwrap Egyptian mummies' and probe the internal organs of the 'bog corpses' found in remarkable states of preservation in Northern Europe: the haunting face of Tolland Man, hung with a leather noose and thrown into a Danish bog 2,300 years ago, is one such example.

Modern CT scans, a quantum leap in diagnostic imaging, provide greater clarity through 3D visualizations than earlier conventional 2D X-rays which had been used on Egyptian mummies since 1898, by Howard Carter, for example, from 1904 onwards and upon discovering the tomb of Tutankhamun in the Valley of the Kings in 1922. More recently, CT scans had thrown light on the ash-entombed victims of Pompeii. This non-invasive scanning can also be applied to funerary objects that are too delicate to open or dissect in any other way.[7]

CT scans can highlight more obvious trauma such as injuries from hard labour, battle and execution blows, and help to determine the age of the deceased by identifying the bone fusions or separations that occur as the human skeleton matures. The technique can also reveal evidence of dental disease and attrition, bone density and cancer, bacterial infection, tuberculosis and rickets, all of which leave evidence on, or inside, bones.

Yet, with all the modern technology at hand, on occasion there is no replacement for intense scrutiny with a simple magnifying glass. Using no more than a hand-held lens, the Antikas team determined the Tomb II male suffered from a respiratory problem, a chronic condition that could have been pleurisy or tuberculosis, evidenced by the pathology they found on the inside surface of his ribs. Further visible 'wear and tear' markers on his spine indicated he had experienced a life on horseback.

At this point, the Tomb II skeletons were provided with new nametags for cataloguing purposes: the male was labelled 'RTIIA' – for royal tomb 'II', 'A' for male – and the female became 'RTIIB'. Theo and Laura next interviewed as many of the anthropologists, archaeologists, historians and conservators as they could track down to build an oral history from those who had previously dealt with the bones. What soon became clear was the poor state of documentation after the earlier handling, along with an almost complete lack of photographs. Moreover, the few images of the skull that had been captured in the early 1980s showed marked differences to the same bone joints and reconstructions photographed a decade or more later.

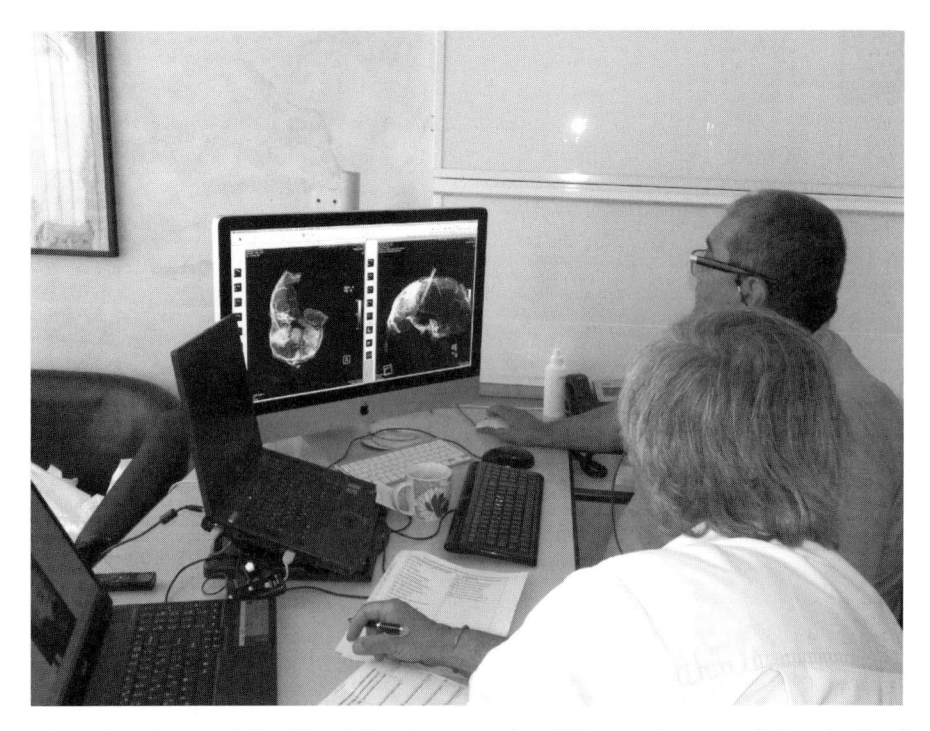

Theo Antikas and Dr Kotridis viewing the CT scan image of the skull of the male from Tomb II at his laboratory in Veria.

In March 2011, at the annual convention of Archaeological Works in Macedonia and Thrace, the Antikas team presented the planned methodology for their study and database. They had decided to analyze cremations from other tombs dating to broadly the same era, including those from Derveni and Pydna, to compare the morphological changes and fragment sizes to better interpret the Vergina bones. Their overall methodology was a 'good model' for future archaeological finds, commented Dr Michaelis Lefantzis, who would later oversee the architectural work at the Casta Hill tomb site at Amphipolis.

Each bone was catalogued with a unique number, with entries on weight, condition and morphological changes such as colour, warping or cracking. Any signs of foreign materials such as rare minerals were noted, along with comments on the conservation condition from previous handling. Laura next photographed each bone fragment from every anatomical plane, capturing over 4,000 images.

A major part of the meagre budget was spent on storage and transportation materials, and Chrysoula Paliadeli added modest funds from her own resources to cover their travel costs. Laura's curating experience and the protocols developed when she was a technician at the Smithsonian Museum of Natural History were now put to good use. There, in a small office crammed with text books, she once had a formative meeting with one of the 'fathers' of modern forensic anthropology, Professor John Lawrence Angel, whose work on the skeletal remains in Greece birthed 'paleodemology', which encompassed the study of population changes and other cumulative data from which longevity and health in the ancient world could be determined.

Under Laura's direction in the laboratory at Vergina, Tyvek tags were used to assign each bone and fragment a unique number. These were attached to the bones using dental floss, a new technique employed for this project, because it could easily slide over its surface without causing any damage. Ethafoam supports lined with polyester Pongee silk were constructed to hold many of the delicate and larger bones. The storage cabinet's glass was overlaid with a UV-adjusted plastic film to protect the fragments from sunlight, and though standard practice was to write the catalogue number on the bones themselves, Laura decided this was unwise as it added more foreign material.

Some 350 male bones had been found in the gold chest in the main chamber of Tomb II. His skeleton weighed in at 2,225.8 grams, remarkably close to the mean weight, 2,283 grams, of adult male cremation remains today, a testament to the care with which the bones had been collected from the funeral pyre.[8]

Human teeth and bones were also found in the pyre debris, both burned and unburned. All the teeth were loose and found lying with animal remains and ivory from a couch. But no tooth crowns were found with the bones in the gold chest in the main chamber from which age might have been determined; and though some roots were intact, they are not helpful in ageing. Hammond's 1978 paper

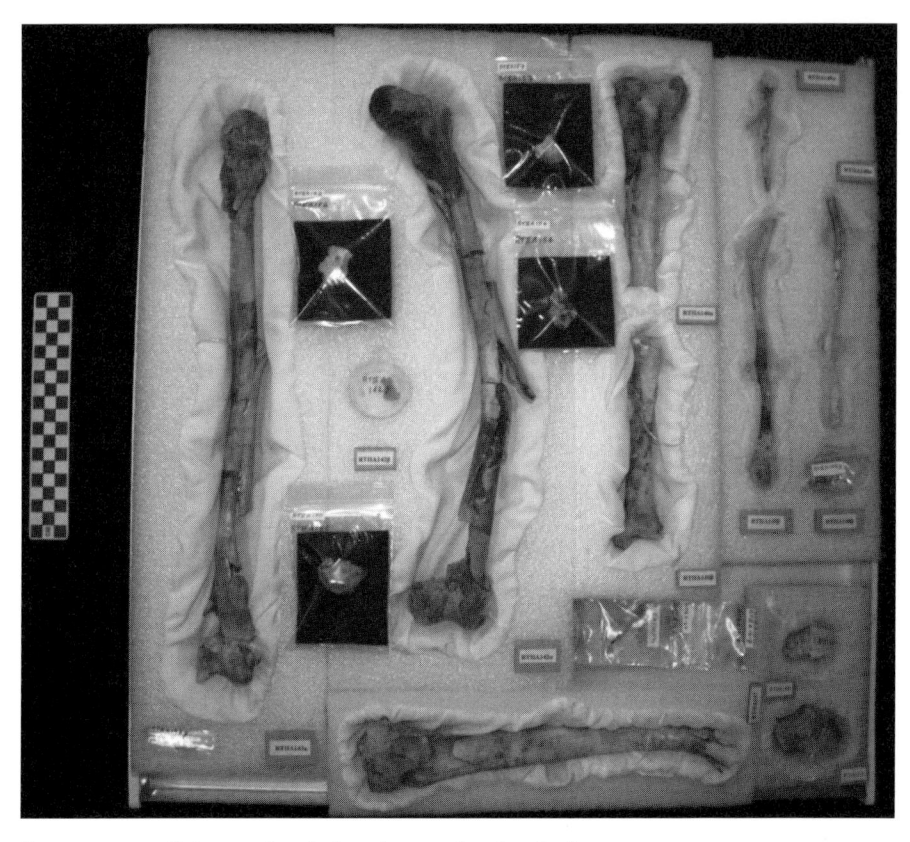

Fragments of the male skeletal remains in their new storage mounts.

had been wrong in the prognosis that these teeth suggested a man over 32 years of age. More problematic was the question of whether the additional human remains found in the pyre debris on the roof of Tomb II belonged to the buried male or to other 'sacrificial victims', possibly Philip's assassins, who were allegedly executed near the tumulus of the tomb. Because of these uncertainties, these teeth and bones were excluded from the RTIIA catalogue of remains.

The incorrectly reconstructed facial bones of the male were an additional dilemma. The Antikas team decided to leave them as found because any further handling might have caused more damage. Additionally, at some point when the skull and the rest of the skeleton were on exhibit, the upper and lower jaws were glued together, and they now had to be separated in order to be catalogued and photographed. A year on, the careful process of disarticulation took place, Laura videoing the two-hour operation in which she used a tiny brush and ethanol. Finally, she sought permission to remove some of the wooden sticks that held the Macedonian royal together.

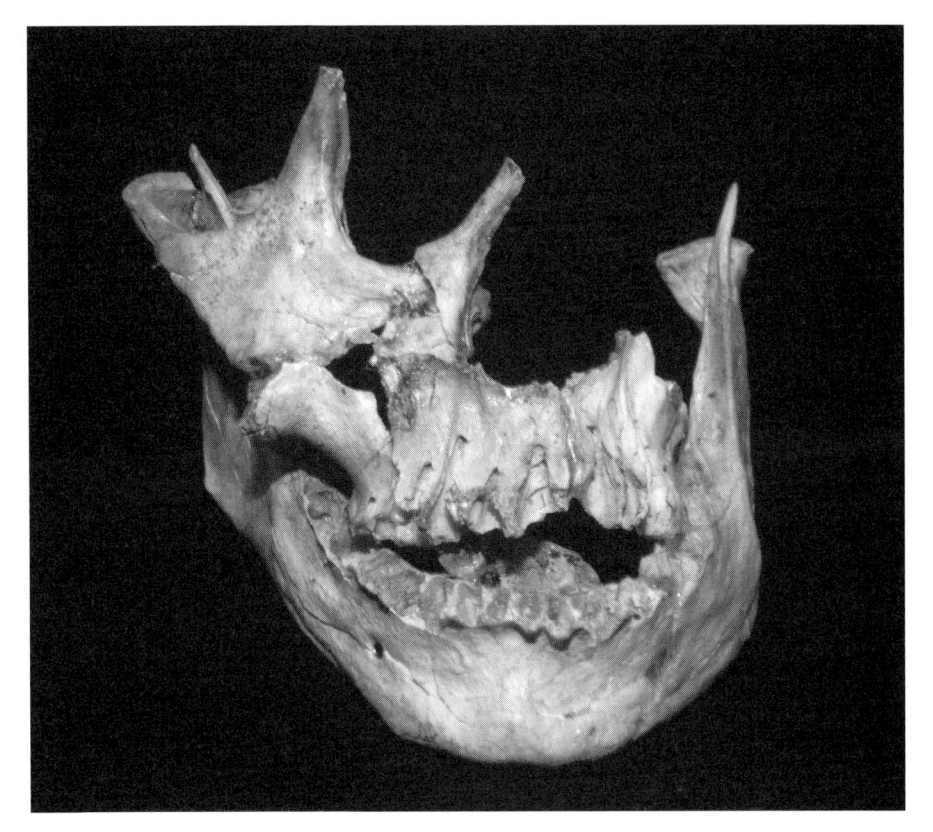

The jaw and facial bones of the Tomb II male.

Despite the poor condition of teeth, there was a positive for the skeleton: the Tomb II bones had been cremated. In many cases, burned remains preserve better than those buried in soil, because they are less affected by microbial bacteria. Additionally, cremated bones are usually preserved in some form of ossuary, in this case gold caskets, where they are protected from the intrusions of flooding, scavenging animals, plant roots, from the soil itself or later intrusive human activity above.

The warping and colour of the male bones made it clear that the deceased had been given a flesh-boned cremation, backing up Musgrave's earlier conclusion and undermining Bartsiokas' report, which seemed to be fighting the evidence: the gold oak wreath found in the chest had some pieces missing, and gold acorns and a leaf had been found in the ash of the funeral pyre on the roof. Gold droplets were also seen on the shoulder blade and upper vertebrae, so it appears the man was wearing the wreath in the early stage of the cremation, unless the gold came from some other adornment.[9]

Demosthenes' Shattered Remnant

'Absence of evidence is not evidence of absence' is an old aphorism that has been somewhat more cynically described as 'impatience with ambiguity'.[10] But in the search for the identity of the Tomb II male it had particular relevance, because scholars were presented, once again, with a confounding symmetry: both Philip II and Philip III Arrhidaeus had died from blade wounds. Philip II was stabbed by Pausanias at Aegae, and his son was executed with a Thracian sword by Olympias' executioners.

The identity arguments had so far rested on finding signs of trauma that matched the injuries Philip II is known to have sustained, thanks to Demosthenes' speech and corroborating texts. But as Theo and Laura pointed out, just as Xirotiris and Langenscheidt had thirty years before, these wounds would only be visible if an assailant's blade had sliced against bone.[11] It is quite possible for mortal flesh wounds to leave no skeletal scars.

The injuries Demosthenes listed were less than clinically described. He was a rhetorician who squeezed ever drop of drama from every flammable word he uttered in a political environment in which death or exile could be dished out to Athenian orators under the charge of 'impiety' or 'pollution of the city'. Moreover, Demosthenes was defending a career of mischief-making that had only resulted in failure for the state. The 'shattered remnant', as he termed Philip II in his speech *On the Crown*, was obviously not quite as debilitated as Demosthenes made out, for Philip led his army to victory at Chaeronea in Boeotia in 338 BC after sustaining all his wounds and just two years before he died. Clearly, the good-luck motto Demosthenes reportedly painted on his shield before the battle was of little use against the tight ranks of Macedonian pike-bearers.[12]

One of Philip's injuries would be troublesome to pinpoint because the ancient Greeks did not differentiate between the hand, arm or elbow, an apparent idiosyncrasy in a world in which Aristotle categorized everything in his bold attempts at zoological taxonomy and classification. Nevertheless, the Antikas team found evidence of a hand wound not identified by Xirotiris' study. It appeared to have been delivered by a sharp blade and was still healing when the Tomb II male died. Philip II had wounded his hand (arm or elbow) during battle with Scythians, so this correlated well. Finally, one of the traumas mentioned by Demosthenes may have been found.

Theo was critical of the previous arguments over one wound in particular: the loss of Philip's eye, which was reported by no less than twenty Greek and Roman sources, though traceable back to rather fewer contemporary reports.[13] Endorsing the Xirotiris-Langenscheidt conclusion from 1981, and Bartsiokas' later report, no evidence of this was visible on the skull. But the Antikas team did find signs of a condition that could have been sinusitis on the bones above and below the eye socket, possibly the byproduct of the trauma. They tactfully pointed out that if an arrow, spear or javelin had entered Philip's eye with sufficient force to cause a still-visible notch on the bone, he would have most likely died on the spot.

There was a good precedent at hand for their contention. Earlier, in 2004, the skeleton of a soldier was found in a grave close to Vergina. Theo, Laura and two colleagues were called in to analyze the remains and they published a paper on their autopsy. The shape of the wound made it clear that a catapult bolt had severed the soldier's spinal cord and killed him instantly, leaving no one in doubt of the potential penetrating effect of these lethal weapons.[14]

Siege-engine technology had come a long way since the tyranny of Dionysius of Syracuse and then Philip's own engineers who threw up towers over 100ft tall, but the term used for these mechanical catapults was generic and could refer to any of the projectile-throwing devices which were torsion-powered by skeins of twisted rope.[15] The rather impartial compiler of history, Diodorus of Sicily, who had little motive to manipulate historic events that took place three centuries before him, reported that an arrow was responsible for the loss of sight in one of Philip's eyes,

Theo Antikas and Laura wrapped-up for winter conditions in the Vergina Laboratory cataloguing the Tomb II bones. In the foreground sits the skull of the male from the main chamber, arguably Philip II.

which, nevertheless, had to be removed. This is not necessarily suggestive of injury to the socket bone.[16]

We know a projectile of some kind caused the damage at the siege of the city of Methone, a drawn-out campaign that occupied Philip II from winter 355 BC to summer 354 BC.[17] The historians Duris of Samos and Theopompus of Chios were somewhat more inclined to embellish and add colour to broadly contemporary events: they tell us that Philip was inspecting his siege engines and the so-called 'tortoise' sheds which provided shelter to the besiegers, enabling them to fill in the city's protective ditch, when his eye was penetrated.[18] Duris even named the culprit, Aster, which suspiciously means 'shooting star', claiming he hurled a javelin at Philip. Duris claimed that flutes had been playing the choral hymn 'Cyclops' before the projectile struck home.[19]

Philip's bodyguards would not have allowed their king within easy range of the city walls without protection, so it is more likely that a spent arrow at the very end of an ambitious arcing trajectory, and with little penetrative force left, pierced Philip's soft eye tissue, which was successfully scooped out of its socket by his surgeon.[20]

Aster worked himself into a legend which claimed the javelin was inscribed with Philip's name. In yet another version of events, Philip retrieved the projectile, carved on it a threat to the assailant, and hurled it back to the city walls, proverbially having the last word in the encounter. Thereafter, Philip apparently flew into a rage if anyone mentioned his lost eye. This garnishing was no doubt inspired by the fact that the king's bronze arrowheads indeed had 'of Philip' imprinted on them.[21] These serve as salutary warnings on the reliability of the ancient sources and their rhetorical flourishes that put a straightforward story through 'curling tongs', as Cicero put it.[22]

The facial reconstruction work of Prag, Neave and Musgrave back in 1984 remained a reconstructive visual treat and one that graced the cover of books and articles on Philip II. But it was now clear that their prominently long eye scar needed to be removed from whoever was buried in Tomb II. Demosthenes' 'shattered remnant' may have been rather less unsightly, from the shoulders up at least. Further age-related changes to the male skeleton, which had not been brought to light before, allowed the Antikas team to narrow down the estimate of the Tomb II male to 45 +/- 4 years at death, squarely in the middle of the previous Xirotiris-Langenscheidt age range estimate of 35–55.[23]

Age Profiling the Amazon

Early analysis of the Tomb II female by Xirotiris and Langenscheidt, and then by Musgrave, concluded she was aged 20–30 when entombed. One reliable method of aging a skeleton is to analyze the 'symphysis', a pubic joint whose morphology, including the extent of billowing, changes as the body matures. Yet none of the former studies had seen this crucial joint. But on 12 February 2012, the Antikas team found the 'inferior' portion of the symphysis with the female bones in the laboratory at Vergina.

Laura journeyed to Bristol in September to take an oral history from Jonathan Musgrave, she showed him a photo of the joint, and with a quick look he confirmed it appeared to be from a 'mature' female. This ruled out the 20-year-old end of the Xirotiris-Langenscheidt and Musgrave estimate, as did the fact that the breastbone-end of her collarbone was already fused, a process that usually happens between the ages of 24 and 29.[24]

On 16 October 2012, the 'superior' portion of the symphysis was found among the many fragments in the two large drawers containing the remains of Tomb II female: the complete joint was now available to provide a more accurate examination. There commenced the long process of employing the ageing-formula guidelines. Twelve generic casts of pubic symphyses from six different phases of life were analyzed under what is known as the 'Suchey-Brooks (1990) Scoring System' with its benchmark of statistics. The casts were made by Diane France, a doctor of forensic anthropology at Colorado State University, whose well-known expertise had already made her the subject of a biography titled *Bone Detective* in 2004.

After eighteen months of analysis, which also took into consideration activity and degenerative changes to her skeleton as well as the fusion of her collarbone, the Antikas team could unequivocally state that the Tomb II 'Amazon' was aged 32 +/− 2 years at death, though they believed she was closer to 30.[25] This was one of the most significant discoveries in decades; a single bone joint having rendered redundant many of the theories from both opposing teams in the 'battle of the bones', as the world would soon find out.

Artefacts, Artifice and the Limping Warrior

'Gender bias' is a term the Theo and Laura team associate with the unconscious process of linking artefacts to gender determination without pondering alternatives. To make their point, they cited an article that appeared in 2013 with the strapline 'Oops! Etruscan Warrior Prince Really a Princess'.

The Etruscans were responsible for much of early Roman culture and military innovation, and new linguistic investigations suggest they may well have been refugees from fallen Troy.[26] Some of the paintings on the walls of Etruscan tombs dating to the sixth century BC look somewhat Greek in style, with Phrygian and Lycian points of comparison from Anatolia, while Etruscan offerings from the seventh century BC have been found at Olympia, suggesting continuous contact with Greece.[27]

In September 2013, archaeologists in Italy announced a stunning find: a completely sealed and unlooted tomb from the sixth century BC had been found cut into rock at Tarquinia in Tuscany. It held what initially appeared to be the skeleton of an Etruscan prince holding a spear, along with the remains of a woman, each lying on separate funerary beds cut out of the rock walls. Several pieces of jewellery, a perfume flask and bronze-plated box were also recovered from the tomb. Archaeologists quickly identified the spear-wielding corpse as a male warrior, and they logically assumed the jewellery belonged to the female across the chamber, presumed to be his wife.

Analysis of the bones revealed the prince was, in fact, a princess aged 35–40. Opposite her lay a weaponless male of 20–30 years. One theory presented the spear as a symbol of their unity, while another suggested it represented her high social status. Hamstrung by the model of modern society and straitjacketed by perceptions of the lives of traditional Greek and Roman women, archaeologists failed to factor in the unique social code of Etruria, where women enjoyed greater social, recreational and even sexual freedoms. Depictions of Amazons are, unsurprisingly, ubiquitous in Etruscan art.[28]

Back at the Vergina laboratory, the Antikas team had been poring over the same Tomb II bones for days with magnifying glasses, while carefully making data entries for the most minute of detail on their wear and tear in life, or at the point of death. Laura felt she knew the bones intimately: 'scatter them in a field with a thousand others and I would recognize them', she claimed. And on 13 April 2013, the laborious task of cataloguing paid off.

Laura had been systematically studying every long bone fragment when she turned over the woman's left tibia or shinbone; as she stared at it she trembled and reached for her phone. What Laura had found was a major fracture that appears to have been sustained some years before the woman died. Theo was equally thunderstruck when the call arrived and immediately jumped in his car. He arrived at Vergina with his head still spinning and headed for the laboratory.

The discovery of the terrible shinbone fracture, which had caused a shortening of the left leg, was more than a 'eureka' moment. What Theo subsequently verified united the female to the armour lying around the antechamber of Tomb II, because the left greave of the gilded pair, which had always looked rather delicate and 'feminine' in proportion, was 3.5cm shorter and also narrower than the right. That, in turn, linked the female to the weapons in the room. They wondered how this trauma had been previously overlooked.

The discovery dispelled the still-widely held belief that these ceremonial weapons of war belonged to the man on the other side of the marble doors, a theory first offered by Manolis Andronikos, who saw the uneven greaves as a potential link to Philip II's limp, his 'personal signature', as he described it.[29] Andronikos had also offered an explanation for the difference in size of the gilded grieves: they were designed for the posture of an archer, where the shorter left shin guard facilitated a kneeling position to draw a bow.

The notion that the weapons and armour belonged to the adjacent male had prevailed, despite the fact that an Alexandrian scholar of the first century BC claimed Philip's leg wound was to the right upper leg or thigh, not to the shin of the left. Justin also placed the wound in Philip's thigh, as Adams had pointed out back in 1980.[30] The long-accepted theory also ignored the fact that three further pairs of greaves found in the main chamber with the man were far larger than the antechamber shin guards; moreover, they were of equal size.

'Weapons were for men what jewels were for women', read the display case for Philip II in the museum at Vergina. This was, arguably, another case of 'gender bias' that had thrown the best-intended archaeology off track.

With the newly exposed pathology, the Antikas team painted a picture of a limping woman constantly plagued by pain. Her uneven bronze greaves covered with gold plate – a gilding almost unique in the ancient world – may have served a function more practical than ceremonial: the shin guards would have hidden her rather unsightly fracture, or even served to help support her and reduce the evidence of a limp. This particular injury had been described by Hippocrates of Kos, the 'father of western medicine' and the supposed architect of the eponymous oath sworn to the medical gods on ethical standards:

> Of the bones, the inner of the so-called shinbone is the more troublesome to treat, requiring greater extension, and if the fragments are not properly set, it cannot be hidden, for it is visible and entirely without flesh.[31]

Hippocrates' extract, which likely originated in the later notes compiled by his students, went on to describe the pain patients would suffer when applying tight bandages, and it reiterated the risk of not setting the bones properly. This is suggestive that shinbone wounds were a common outcome of battle, explaining the need for protective greaves.

Laura was frustrated that there were no references in the ancient texts to a woman at the court of Macedon with a pronounced limp. But this was unsurprising: there are scant references, for example, to the fate of the wounded on Alexander's campaign in Asia, those I had described in my treatise as:

> the snow-blinded, frostbitten, the leprosy-afflicted, or the malaria-ridden who languished forever in a mud-brick 'Alexandria' rather than returning to families across the Hellespont. None of those unfit for battle, the bone-shattered, limb-lost and dysentery-emaciated infantrymen, were feted by fanfare or captured in bronze or paint. For there was no rhetorical value in the men bypassed by the goddess Fortuna.

I went on to quip that Alexander was indeed fortunate to have died 'so thoroughly' in Babylon, for a partial recovery, or even maiming, might have taken the 'Great' out of his name.[32]

Equally to blame for the loss of such detail is the brevity of the surviving accounts. They are essentially epitomes of earlier far weightier histories which themselves were abridgements of once-voluminous originals, and often excerpted with little forensic curiosity. The pages of Diodorus' only-partially intact books dealing with Alexander and his successors are reckoned to be just a tenth of the length of his sources, so it follows that he dispensed with 90 per cent of what he read. Justin's précising was even more severe, and he admitted he left out 'what did not make pleasant reading or serve to provide a moral'. Plutarch was clear that he only extracted detail that helped paint the biographical picture he wanted on his developing canvasses.[33] And unsightly wounds generally lacked necessary rhetorical gravitas.

The physical deformities we *do* read about in ancient Greek accounts were not dealt with sensitively, as they might have prevented eligibility to the priesthood, where ugliness and physical abnormality were deemed divine disfavour. Deformities and lameness would have also prevented participation in military service and thus reduced a man's value to the city-state.[34] The comic poet Aristophanes claimed that the not-so-humorous exposure of children was 'commonplace' in Athens, where unwanted, sickly or impaired infants were left to die in rude cradles or shallow pots in the streets.[35] But disfigurement as the result of a wound from battle might be seen as a mark of honour. Either may have been the plight of the Tomb II 'Amazon', but Laura was correct: there is no reference to a lame wife or daughter of the late Argead kings. A new avenue or investigation had certainly appeared, but her anonymity remained.

On 20 May 2013, the Antikas team was allowed the rare privilege of opening the display case in the Vergina Archaeological Museum to measure and weigh the uneven greaves, which felt 'light as a feather' to Laura. The larger right greave weighed 475.6 grams and the shorter left 423.3 grams. They were indeed ceremonial and not meant for war, though traces of fabric on the inside suggested they had been lined, possibly with leather, for comfort. Scholars and the growing tribe of Vergina commentators now had a limping '30-ish-year-old-Amazon' on their hands.

Like the Tomb II male, it was clear from the 'riding markers', most clearly seen on her spine, that the female warrior had been astride a horse most of her life. The Antikas team highlighted the fact that '25 per cent of Scythian horseback archers consisted of women aged 20 to 30 years who fought alongside their husbands', a statement backed up by the weapon-filled graves found between the Danube and Don rivers. In their opinion, this narrowed the identity of the Tomb II 'Amazon' field down to a total of one: a Scythian princess.

The Philip II camp was understandably elated with their report. But there remained the mystery of the Tomb I bones, which had unfortunately been buried in soil since the tomb was looted in antiquity. The study of these fragments fell outside Theo and Laura's remit, and certainly outside their meagre budget, so any analysis would have to wait; or so they at first imagined.

Of Wise Curators and Museum Basements: The Tomb I Bombshell

Back in 1932, an old curator of Egyptian art informed an incredulous young student: 'Some of the best excavations have been made in museum basements.' He went on to explain his mantra: small objects are easy to file away during digs, and they are just as easily forgotten.[36]

On 8 July 2014, a young archaeologist working alongside the Antikas team at the Vergina Laboratory discovered three wooden crates in a storage room, inside which were three plastic bags filled with well over 100 bone fragments, labelled as originating from Tomb I. These bones had never been studied and no one knew they were there. A week or so later, on 17 July, yet more containers were found in the underground storage room containing plaster fragments, human bones and animal remains with butchery marks. Laura was incredulous and started photographing them for a separate database.

Despite being focused on Tomb II, Laura had been searching both locally and in Thessalonica for the Tomb I bones ever since they drafted their cataloguing methodology back in 2010. On 30 March that year, she had even asked Dr Angeliki Kottaridi, who was now the director of the Vergina Museum amongst other roles that oversaw archaeological sites in the region, if she knew the whereabouts of the Tomb I bones. She did not, despite her interest in the chamber, which, she believed, once held the remains of Philip's early wife, Nicesipolis.[37]

In defence of the original curators who handled the excavation finds, the Great Thessalonica Earthquake of June 1978 had put an abrupt stop to work on Tomb I, after which all energies were redirected to the greater finds in Tomb II. It was probably in this commotion that the bones were sidelined to thirty-six-years of obscurity in the storage room.

Back in 2013, Theo had taken an oral history from Professor Xirotiris, who had retired from his post at the Democritus University of Thrace. He stated that the Tomb I bones – still thought to be of an adult male, a female and a baby, as per Musgrave's 1984 conclusion – might be still sitting in his laboratory, which was now occupied by Professor Bartsiokas and inaccessible to him. Theo and Laura had then given up hope of ever finding the skeletal remains.

In July 2014, after the Antikas team had analyzed some seventy of the fragments found in the laboratory at Vergina, it became clear these were not the collection

Xirotiris had referred to, the same bones Musgrave looked at 'in haste' back in 1984, because the skeletal remains of at least seven individuals could be identified: four babies aged 8–10 lunar months, along with a foetus, had to be added to the adult male, female and baby.[38] The notion that Tomb I housed solely Philip II, Cleopatra and their newborn child now needed to be scrapped. An ugly fact had yet again slayed a once-attractive idea.

But the most important skeletal bones from Tomb I were not among the Vergina collection, which suggested more bones were elsewhere. So Theo, Laura and Yannis Maniatis began a new quest to locate them. They obtained some documents from the Archaeological Museum of Thessalonica which referred to 'return bones to Vergina' decades before, but from just which tomb was unclear. But after tracing the documentary history back, everything did suggest that the most important Tomb I bones must be in the Anthropology Laboratory of the Democritus University of Thrace. Yannis telephoned Bartsiokas and asked him directly if he had the bones; Bartsiokas refused to confirm either way, 'because it was a matter for the Ministry of Culture'.

For the time being, the team was left with only the newly found fragments from Tomb I. It was clear they had been inhumed – buried in the flesh in soil or laid in a chamber – and not cremated, which could suggest they were later intruders and not those of the original occupants. Although it was clear that Tomb I had been opened and looted in antiquity, most likely by the Gallic mercenaries operating under Pyrrhus of Epirus, archaeologists now faced the sober prospect that it became a 'dumping ground' for the dead, babies especially. Human bones had been found at different levels in the soil, suggesting different entry dates, and there was no guarantee those found near the floor belonged to the original occupants; they may have been tomb raiders who fought and died over the spoils.

This curious theory was voiced in 1980 by Robin Lane Fox, who erroneously attributed the idea back to Manolis Andronikos, but nevertheless, Professors Stella Drougou and Chrysoula Paliadeli had voiced it more recently.[39] The 'grave robber' scenario seemed to be corroborated by what had been found in another looted tomb in a cluster linked to the structure reported on by Léon Heuzey in 1861. Outside the tomb but immediately in front of the entrance lay a skeleton in a fine state of preservation which belonged to someone who had been forcefully pushed backwards. He appeared to have been killed by a blow to the head, 'perhaps by his accomplices who desecrated the tomb', which appeared to belong to a woman. Who she might have been is rendered even more interesting by the gold coin from Caria in Anatolia found in the hand of the 'grave robber': certainly, this currency did not circulate locally in Greece or Macedon. The coin, perhaps part of an embassy gift, had been minted by Pixodarus, the dynast Philip II had attempted to ally with through a marriage to Arrhidaeus.[40]

Professor Elizabeth Carney was rather more dismissive of attaching the 'phantom' raider idea to Tomb I: 'we would have to believe that a robber either happened to die of natural causes in the tomb or had a fatal quarrel with his companions ...' who 'left him there unburied but stripped of everything not biodegradable...' and 'that animals entering through two small openings so gnawed, fragmented, and removed his bones that they finally exactly resembled the state of ... legitimate occupants'. Moreover, we would need to accept 'that enough time passed for all this to occur before the tomb was resealed'. She was right; it required a 'series of remote possibilities'.[41]

Reuniting the Bones with the Prince

Tomb I bones were not the only remains to emerge from the obscurity of storage. In 2010, shortly after the commencement of the Antikas team study, a glass container with plastic lid was found to contain yet more forgotten remains, simply labelled '38–30'. Theo and Laura debated whether it was a code: perhaps a longitude-latitude fix, or a grid reference from the digs. The bones were dirty

A further looted tomb at Vergina with what appears to be the skeleton of a tomb robber killed in the process of looting, as its position suggests.

grey-to-brown in colour and some were poorly burned, and they appeared to be similar in appearance to those found in 1978 in Tomb III, the 'Tomb of the Prince'. Their morphological changes also pointed to an adolescent.[42]

Back in 1990, Jonathan Musgrave verified the original conclusions that the skeletal remains in Tomb III were those of a youth, probably male, with the dental age of 12–14, consistent with the age of the adolescent King Alexander IV, born in late 323 BC and murdered on Cassander's orders sometime between 311 and 309 BC. It was an identification favoured by the scholars Nicholas Hammond and Peter Green.[43] Like all the remains studied in the early years following the 1977/78 finds, the bones found in the glass container in the Vergina Laboratory in 2010 were covered in preserving chemicals and consolidants, but they now needed to be reunited with the remains from *one* of the three tombs. Theo and Laura interviewed everyone they could, but their provenance remained a mystery.

Eventually, the Antikas team thought of a rather obvious solution. Back in 1978, the adolescent's bones in Tomb III had been found in a silver water pourer known as a 'hydria', in this case manufactured in two parts that separated halfway down and clipped together. One means of determining where the '30-38' fragments originated would be to submit them to X-ray florescence (XRF), which could identify any trace metals on a sample.

A permit for the analysis was applied for in December 2012, and in March 2013 some thirty-five of the fifty-or-so small bones were analyzed by Christos Katsifas, a chemist in the Laboratory of Physico-chemical studies and Archaeometry at the Archaeological Museum of Thessalonica. Every fragment had traces of silver, and these could only have come from contact with the Tomb III silver hydria. The 'prince' was being pieced together at last, but absolute proof of ownership would only result from comparative DNA testing, if DNA could be isolated from ancient cremated bones.

The agonies and ecstasies and the twists and turns of the ongoing osteological investigation were far from over. With the tomb candidates further narrowed down by the work of the Antikas team, new avenues of forensic investigation, human, heroic and seemingly divine, were about to add their colour to the tapestry of mysteries that still shrouded the Vergina tombs.

Chapter 10

Orphic Masks and Burial Rituals

> That is the gods' work, spinning threads of death
> through the lives of mortal men,
> and all to make a song for those to come.
> —Homer[1]

The ancient Greek world was steeped in superstition and '*deisidaimonia*', a 'sanctimonious piety'. Not only did the gods above need pacifying, but also the '*daimons*' below. Thunder was Zeus' anger, sea storms Poseidon's wrath, and the dark mood of Demeter was responsible for crop failure and famine, if not due to a pestilence spread by Apollo. When looking to the sky, comets were considered celestial portents, while eclipses were harbingers of death. Man could do no more in the face of such threats than beseech divine favour, so animals were sacrificed before battle and libations poured into the earth to ensure good fortune at any and every significant event.

But the dialogue with lofty Olympian deities and chthonic gods often went deeper and darker than that, with the more ancient of the mysticisms rooted in atonement, exorcism and purification rituals, in which tombs and mausoleums played an integral part.[2]

Over 1,700 curse tablets have been found across Greece and Macedon taking the form of inscriptions on lead sheets invoking spells to the spirits of the Underworld, commonly Hermes, Charon, Hecate, Pluto the lord of the dead and Persephone, who was otherwise known as Kore. Tablets were thrown down wells, many folded and pierced with nails, or buried in graves and temples, occasionally accompanied by carved likenesses. Invocations were made in indecipherable languages, supposedly the demonic tongues, and those targeted by such curses wore charmed amulets to ward off disaster.[3]

Thessaly was known as the commercial centre of witches whose dark services were for hire, and Ephesus in Anatolia had a reputation for magic and magicians. The Sacred Disease was thought to possess epileptics, magnetic lodestones housed trapped souls, and in Athens there was a court for trials of inanimate objects, which could be held responsible for murder, including figurines. Shepherd's tales even accommodated the existence of werewolves.[4] Across Greece, a number of well-known locations were renowned as prophecy places of the dead in caves staffed by

Sibyls, the invocators of spirits where necromancy was practised, and requests were tendered to the gods below.

Unsurprisingly, funerals incorporated dedications to the deities associated with death.[5] Ghosts frequented the subterranean burial chambers where the deceased commenced their journey to the realm of Hades, and they were not to be intruded upon without consequences.[6] Xerxes' sacrilegious entering the tomb in the temple of the Bel Marduk in Babylon was said to be the true cause of the Persian defeat at Plataea.[7] Subterranean riches, the precious metals and ores, also belonged to Hades, so the looting of the tombs at Aegae by the Celtic Gauls was seen as defiling the voyage to the afterlife, explaining why Andronikos had carried with him a keen sense of the 'desecrators' guilt' when opening Tomb II in November 1977.[8]

In contrast, the ongoing above-ground Antikas-team forensics at Vergina were firmly grounded in the more rational challenges of the day, though the handling of the bones still lent a sacral quality to the research. But the limited funding, the time delays in obtaining permissions and the laborious task of cataloguing undocumented and missing fragments had now dragged Theo and Laura's meagre funding into several years of largely unpaid work.

They had initially been allotted a specific room at the Vergina Laboratory for their study, but were relocated three times with the whole bone collection. Work had to stop completely between August 2013 and January 2014 when the exhibits for a new museum at Vergina occupied all available space. Theo and Laura finally ended up working in a cold storage room in less than ideal conditions and poor lighting, outfitting themselves in balaclavas and winter coats and arming themselves with magnifying glasses that steamed up with winter breath.

There were times, Laura admitted, when they simply hit the wall. To maintain motivation, they reminded themselves this was not simply a matter of cataloguing bone fragments, but part of the process of reconstructing one of the most momentous burials in the classical world. The parable of the mediaeval stonecutters comes to mind: when questioned by a traveller on their toil, the first of three medieval masons, clearly unhappy with his lot in life, grudgingly answered: 'Why, can't you see? I am cutting stones.' The second replied somewhat stoically: 'I am building the east wall.' The third workman, who could be heard whistling while he chiselled, looked up at the traveller and smiled: 'Why, I am building the greatest cathedral the land has ever seen.' Like the task at hand at Vergina, it was simply a matter of perspective. And just when they faced another dead end, the gods handed the Antikas team a further breakthrough. This time it came in the form of a rare, white earth mineral.

Hunting the Huntite Origin

The Antikas team noticed an unusual material both on, and with, the male Tomb II bones. In April 2013, their colleague, Dr Yannis Maniatis, was given permission to conduct a study. He had never seen anything like it before. The forensics involved the scrutiny of a Scanning Electron Microscope (SEM) and Infrared spectroscopy (FTIR), while the bones underwent SEM and X-Ray Fluorescence (XRF) to determine the composition of anything attached.[9] Sure enough, the material was present on many of the fragments, though fragile and puzzling in appearance, as it was formed from many layers of white, beige and purple – potentially explaining the purple stains on the bones – and it was clearly of human construction.

After months of chemical analysis of the brilliant white layer, which had an infrared spectrum not readily identified to *any* of the common white materials used in antiquity, Yannis was able to confirm it was the mineral huntite, containing egg-white as a binder. FTIR revealed that the purple layers were textiles, now dissolved, dyed with the pigment known in the ancient world as 'Tyrian Purple', alongside raised deposits of what were contaminants of lead, possibly from melted objects thrown into the funeral pyre. Clay plus huntite was present in the beige layer, and the Department of Industrial Chemistry at Pisa University also identified beeswax and pine resin there.

Huntite is one of the whitest naturally occurring minerals, and was used in Egypt as a pigment in tomb paintings, masks and the clothes of funeral participants, and most notably in the plaster found in decorative mummy cases known as 'cartonnage'. It is the major white pigment found in the tomb of Pharaoh Tutankhamun. But it had never before been found in Macedon. No further record exists of its use in the ancient Hellenic world, despite the fact that huntite is today extracted from the Kozani Basin just 70km from Vergina, which extends either side of the Haliacmon River. Yannis, who had worked in the Research Laboratory of the British Museum and at the University of Heidelberg in Germany, had reached out to one of the Austrian geologists at the company now mining at Kozani with questions on its chemical composition and was awaiting a reply.

Stable isotope analysis, employing mass spectrometry, can identify specific isotopic ratios of elements and metal ores within chemical compounds, creating a fingerprint or signature of carbon and oxygen isotopes that can pinpoint the exact geographical origin of the compound by comparison with other samples from various regions. Preliminary isotope tests suggested the huntite may well have been sourced locally. Research told me that the mineral had also been mined in antiquity in one of the shafts named 'Mine 19' at Lavrion in Attica, south of Athens, as well at Hierapolis in Phrygia, now central Turkey. But as far as we know, Egypt had no deposits, so the pharaohs must have imported huntite, though there is no mention in the ancient sources of such a trade with Macedon.

However, back in 1989, Professor Panayiotis Faklaris, who had been excavating the walls of Aegae for decades, found a 'scarab' at Vergina. These were amulets and administrative seals shaped like scarab beetles, and originated in Egypt.

Scarabs were usually made from stone and then fired and glazed for colour, and often engraved with names of pharaohs or officials, often copying phrases from the ancient *Book of the Dead*, whereafter some were placed in tombs. Faklaris' find was remarkably dated by an Egyptologist to the Twelfth Dynasty in Egypt, so 1991 BC to around 1800 BC. If it was a contemporary import, and not later Mycenean trade in 'already-ancient' artefacts, the Vergina scarab could suggest that undocumented trade links existed between Egypt and Macedon in the pre-Mycenaean Bronze Age, and the commerce may have included huntite.[10]

We know that by the reign of Pharaoh Psammetichus, from 664–61 BC, Greeks had already settled in the Nile Delta at Naucratis and at the trading city of Heraclion, which was later inundated and only recently located under a few metres of ocean off the Egyptian coast. But the scarab is a relic of an enterprise we understand little of, stretching back into prehistory, possibly fostered at sea by the Minoans of Crete or Phoenician traders, and then inland across the Peloponnese into Thessaly and further north. Mycenaean-styled pottery has certainly been found in many parts of Macedon.

Yannis was baffled as to why huntite was so rarely used in Macedon, that is, if the ancient residents knew huge deposits existed. Its brilliant white colour would not have gone unnoticed, nor its fire-retarding properties which led Yannis to speculate it had been used to either douse the fire at the end of the cremation or to help preserve the bones from the flames. Often found sitting in front of a scanning electron microscope until the early hours of the morning, Yannis was able to determine that the huntite on the male bones *was* made with a technique resembling Egyptian cartonnage. But the mineral thermally decomposes over a temperature range of about 450–800°C, releasing carbon dioxide and leaving a residue of magnesium and calcium oxides; and as no trace of either were found, it was clear that the huntite had *not* been burned in the pyre, a conclusion backed up by the intact Tyrian Purple which decomposes at an even lower temperature.

When Philip II walked into the theatre at Aegae on the day he was stabbed to death in 336 BC, a thirteenth statue was being paraded after those depicting the twelve Olympian Gods: a clear likeness of the king who had 'enthroned himself' among them, in Diodorus' words. And on that day, Philip was said to be wearing a white cloak, perhaps signifying his own role as the nation's chief priest, or possibly something more divine.[11] On the island of Lesbos is an inscription dating to 340/339 BC, just a few years before Philip's death, which mentioned the destruction of temples to 'Zeus Philippios', suggesting a similar deification. This was a far cry from the aftermath of his victory at Chaeronea, when a slave was ordered to declare thrice each morning, 'Philip, you are only human', to thwart any self-idolatry thoughts.[12]

Underpinning Philip's elevation to Mount Olympus, or perhaps prompting it, is a speech by Isocrates, the great orator who called for Philip to lead the Greek

Orphic Masks and Burial Rituals 147

invasion of Persia: in an open letter to the Macedonian king, he promised that if Philip rallied Greece to war, 'nothing will be left for you but to become a god'.[13] Philip seems to have adopted Isocrates' notion ahead of his departure to Asia, and on the fateful day he was stabbed he may have also been wearing a symbolic white mask of huntite. Facemasks were certainly worn at religious festivals, often made with stiffened linen and clay.

If not worn in life, we have the tradition of 'death masks', including those in silver and gold sheet like the so-called 'Mask of Agamemnon' found by Heinrich Schliemann at Mycenae. Other examples were found in the early 1980s in graves

The so-called 'Mask of Agamemnon' found at Mycenae by Heinrich Schliemann in 1876. Hammered out of a single sheet of gold, it dates to 1150–1500 BC, too early to belong to the traditional dating for Agamemnon. (*National Archaeological Museum of Athens*)

at ancient Chalastra, near modern Sindos outside Thessalonica, where horse skeletons suggest the settlement may have been a recruiting ground for Macedonian cavalrymen.[14] Masks of gold foil have also been recovered from numerous graves at Archontiko just 5km from Pella, and their more practical application may have been to hide an already-putrefying face until burial or cremation.[15]

Yannis concluded that some kind of white layered artefact, a votive tablet or funerary mask of huntite, had been placed on top of the already-cremated bones in the golden chest in the main chamber. The gold oak wreath found in the gold chest looked to have been squeezed to one side to accommodate it, and gold of a very high purity, 98.5 per cent, had adhered to the composite material, suggesting they were in contact. The Argead kings may have been connecting themselves with their Argive roots stretching back to the Mycenaean world and Homer's Bronze Age heroes, traditions either preserved in clan memory that spanned the Dark Age or inspired by the more-recent spread of the Homeric epics.[16]

Yannis and team might have finally found clues to an even older mysticism embodying Orphic funeral rites in which a whitened mask was placed on the bones of the dead. The Tomb II double burial was becoming even more unique, but huntite was not the only material witnessed on the cremated remains.[17]

Fireproofing a King

In 1870, Heinrich Schliemann began digging into the hill at Hissarlik in Turkey that he believed was the mound covering Troy. On 14 June 1873, after 249,000 cubic metres of soil had been removed, he unearthed the treasure which 'crowned his labours with golden splendour'. The zealous German archaeologist outfitted his beautiful Greek wife in what was surely jewellery from the legendary court of King Priam, and for a moment Sophie Schliemann became Helen of Troy.[18]

According to Homer's *Iliad*, at the close of an epic battle, Achilles had his fearsome warriors, the Myrmidons, prepare a funeral for his closest companion Patroclus. They drove their chariots and horses thrice around his body and past the corpse of Hector, the Trojan prince who slayed him, and whose body would be fed to the dogs as part of Achilles' revenge. That was until King Priam charioted across the plain to offer ransom for his dead son: heroic respect and disrespect were mixed in one funeral cup in the *Iliad*.

Thousands of Greeks, the 'Achaeans' to Homer – although he also collectively termed them 'Argives' and 'Danaans' in the convention of his day – gathered for a feast, with oxen, sheep, goats and cows slaughtered in preparation for Patroclus' farewell. Achilles asked Agamemnon, the king of the invading army, to have his men fell the nearby forest to construct a great funeral pyre, and Achilles cut short his own hair, as mourners did, before laying his 'manslaughtering' hands upon his dead friend in his grief.[19] When he had taken sufficient wine to drown his sorrow, Achilles fell into a sleep in which Patroclus' ghost appeared to him and spoke:

> You sleep Achilles, you have forgotten me; but you were not
> Careless of me when I lived, but only in death. Bury me
> As quickly as may be, let me pass through gates of Hades.
> The souls, the images of dead men, hold me at a distance
> And will not let me cross the river and mingle among them,
> But I wander as I am by Hades' house of the wide gates.
> And I call upon you in sorrow, give me your hand: no longer
> Shall I come back from death, once you give me my rite of burning.

Achilles reached out to embrace his friend, but the phantom disappeared into the ground like a ghostly vapour exhaling a final thin cry.

As epitomized by Patroclus' plea, the ancient Greeks believed a spirit was unable to enter the Underworld unless it had been buried or cremated with due funerary rites, else the soul was destined to wander forever in a kind of 'no man's land' without passing to the other side through the proverbial Veil of Lethe, where all memory is erased. So the Greeks built the great pyre for Patroclus that day: axes fashioned a wooden platform, bronze-bladed saws felled towering oaks and mules hauled the split trees to the shoreline, where the ceremony would take place.

The timbers were piled up to make, as Homer described it:

> a pyre a hundred feet long this way and that way, and on the peak of the pyre they laid the body, sorrowful at heart; and in front of it they skinned and set in order numbers of fat sheep and shambling horn-curved cattle; and from all great-hearted Achilles took the fat and wrapped the corpse in it from head to foot, and piled up the skinned bodies about it. Then he set beside him two-handled jars of oils and honey.

Homer was very specific with what he believed took place at Troy.[20]

Four strong-necked and whinnying horses were driven onto the conflagration at the four corners of the wooden structure, as if the deceased was being sent into the Elysian Fields at full gallop.[21] Patroclus owned nine hunting dogs, and Achilles cut the throats of two and set them on the pyre along with twelve captive Trojans who were sacrificed to the 'iron fury of the fire'. The winds were summoned and finally the wood was alight. Achilles drank wine all the night, while the flames raged higher, and poured libations from his two-handed mixing bowl. At dawn, the embers were doused with wine and Patroclus' white bones were gathered up from the ash and placed in a golden jar, then coated with fat and covered with a thin fabric veil. Achilles called for traditional funeral games and fetched from his ships prizes for the victors: tripods, 'horses, mules, pretty women and worked iron'.[22]

When Manolis Andronikos opened the first gold chest in Tomb II back in November 1977, he immediately noted the remarkable condition of the male bones compared to cremated remains found in other similarly dated graves, and even the female bones next door. How this overall state of preservation was achieved, with an almost intact skeleton, has long been a mystery, like the task of retrieving Patroclus' bones from the centre of a pyre as large as Homer imagined.[23]

Finding human remains would have been extremely challenging, especially with the adjacent jars of oil and wrappings of animal fat which would have raised the temperature around them beyond any controllable level. Patroclus' remains would have been indistinguishable from the wood-pyre debris, while the adjacent bones of Trojan captives, along with the sacrificial animals, further complicated the separation. Could Patroclus' corpse have been wrapped in some way that separated, or protected, it from the rest of the conflagration?

The answer, at Vergina in any case, could be 'asbestos'. The Antikas team found traces of another material on one of the ribs of the Tomb II male that defied immediate identification, but it appeared to be mineral-based and a clue to its origin may lay in ancient texts. The Roman Pliny the Elder claimed that the ancient Greeks wove shrouds of asbestos in which they wrapped the bodies of kings so that their remains could, indeed, be isolated from the pyre debris. The Latin name of the material translated as 'unquenchable' due to its invincibility in heat. Pliny's claim has always been one of those quaint and yet not readily believable nuggets we might expect to find in the accounts of less-reliable ancient antiquarians. But Pliny said he witnessed Romans throwing tablecloths and napkins of 'incorruptible' asbestos into fires at the end of feasts, after which they were retrieved cleaner and whiter than when first used.[24]

Apparently, the Romans were not blind to the downside of the side-effects of asbestos – 'asbestosis', the chronic inflammation and scarring of the lungs – just as they were aware of the dangers of poisoning by lead, '*morbi metallici*' or 'death metal', as it was known in Latin. That did not put an end to the mining of the fireproofing material and using the malleable metal for water pipes and lining aqueducts.[25] Well before Pliny's day, Aristotle's student Theophrastus described the uses of what might also be asbestos, and there is a history of ancient extraction at Karystos on Euboea in Greece, as well as at Mount Troodos in Cyprus.[26]

An asbestos shroud would explain why even the smallest of male bone fragments ended up in the gold chest found in Tomb II at Aegae, but whether the practice could have stretched back to Bronze Age Troy remains conjecture. However, in the conclusion to the *Iliad*, Achilles is otherwise referred to as being burned 'in the clothing of the gods'. Asbestos would have seemed divine if it withstood the appetite of fire, and perhaps Homer imagined the warrior's still-smouldering asbestos shroud being unwrapped to douse and wash the bones in wine before being placed in an ossuary for eternity.[27]

Once more, Theo, Laura and Yannis might have finally identified evidence of this illusive, and yet wholly practical, cremation accessory. Yannis received permission from the Ministry of Culture in Athens to study the materials on the Tomb II bones, which might now include the set of six naturally occurring silicate minerals known in the modern world for their fire-proofing properties.

The Ritual of Gypsum

While 'whitening' huntite had been identified on the male bones, the mineral gypsum was detected on the female remains found in Tomb II. This supported the idea that the cremation of the 'Amazon' was distinct and conducted under very different conditions. But what did gypsum signify?

I turned up a paper delivered in 1915 at Princeton University by Professor W. Sherwood Fox. It opened with the following: 'The whiteness of gypsum, clay and dust is so commonly referred to in connection with certain Greek rites and myths that it seems natural to explain their symbolism on the same grounds as the symbolism of other white objects of religious import … the sun and its purifying light as opposed to darkness and miasmas.' Professor Fox went on to explain that gypsum and lime were about 'bringing about new birth or instilling new life into a plant, animal or man'.[28]

The ceremonies he referred to were the rites of Dionysus Zagreus, the Orphic rites, and a festival in which gypsum was sprinkled on the soil as a fertilizing agent, and all were linked in some way to the goddess Aphrodite. Pluto of the Underworld, who was not one of the Twelve Olympian Gods, was sometimes depicted as white-haired. A Roman source tells us that Pluto fell in love with Leuca, 'White', the most beautiful of the nymphs, and he commemorated their love by creating a white cypress tree in the Elysian Fields.[29]

The analysis of the gypsum conducted by Yannis and his student Theodora Arvaniti as part of her PhD thesis concluded, once again, that the substance was not the product of natural mineralization but the result of human activity using gypsum in the form of powder or plaster for an object which came into contact with the bones after cremation. Because like the traces of huntite, the gypsum had not been burned.[30]

A study of the remains from the nearby sites of Aenea, Agios Athanasios, Derveni and Pella also turned up traces of gypsum. From the few samples analyzed, it seemed to be more prevalent on female remains, whereas huntite has only been found on males who were nobles or royalty judging from the artefacts present.[31]

The common denominator remained their 'whiteness', whatever their actual function was. Laura recalled that when Heinrich Schliemann discovered the

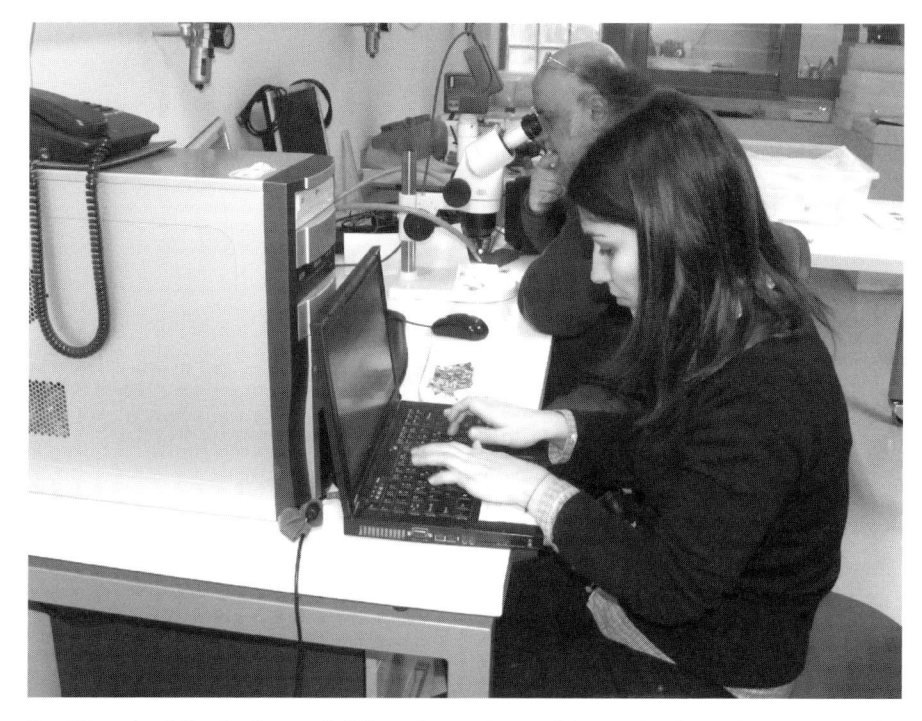

Dr Yannis Maniatis and Theodora Arvaniti analyzing the composite materials from Tomb II in the laboratory of the Archaeological Museum of Thessalonica.

shaft graves at Mycenae, a layer of white clay was found to cover the bones.[32] Curiously, in Argos, the proper colour for a cloak to be worn at funerals was white, and not the black of Athens.[33]

Housing the Homeric Pyre

Homer's epics recalled the highly ritualized cremations of the heroes of the Late Bronze Age. Macedon itself has been described as a 'sub-Homeric enclave' that followed archaic codes.[34] Yet the oldest graves at Aegae dating back to the Early Iron Age, and the more recent burials stretching into the Dark Age that followed, are evidence that inhumation was a more common practice than cremation, in contrast to the custom in other parts of Greece. The grandeur of funerary flames had all but disappeared from these dim-lit eras in Macedon. The later cemetery clues suggest that a revival of the ancient custom of burning bodies took place in the sixth and fifth centuries BC at Aegae when new wealth was arriving, as suggested by the greater finery of grave goods.[35]

Recalling Patroclus' huge pyre on the beach of Troy, these grand and highly orchestrated cremations prevailed through the reigns of Philip II and Alexander,

Aerial view of the ruins of ancient Aegae showing the palace and theatre. (*Alamy.com*)

Fresco depicting the mythical theme of the Abduction of Persephone on the north wall of Tomb I. (*CC BY-SA.2.0*)

(*Above*) Entrance to the subterranean Archaeological Museum of Vergina. (*Author photo*)

(*Below left*) Façade of Tomb II showing the entrance doors and the remains of the hunting scene frieze above. (*Alamy.com*)

(*Below right*) Artist's reconstruction of the entrance of Tomb II with details of the hunting frieze. (*Aristotle University of Thessaloniki - Vergina Excavation Archive*)

(*Above left*) Gold chest or '*larnax*' found in the main chamber of Tomb II, holding the bones of the male. (*Aristotle University of Thessaloniki - Vergina Excavation Archive*)

(*Above right*) Iron-and-gold cuirass found in the main chamber of Tomb II. (*Aristotle University of Thessaloniki - Vergina Excavation Archive*)

(*Below left*) Ornately decorated gold, ivory and glass shield found in the main chamber of Tomb II. (*Aristotle University of Thessaloniki - Vergina Excavation Archive*)

(*Below right*) Solid-crested iron helmet found in the main chamber of Tomb II. (*From Andronikos (1984) with kind permission of Ekdotike Athinon S.A. Publishers*)

(*Above left*) Gold wreath found in the main chamber of Tomb II fashioned with acorns and oak leaves. (*Aristotle University of Thessaloniki - Vergina Excavation Archive*)

(*Above right*) Facial reconstruction of the Tomb II male. (*Image courtesy of the University of Manchester and Richard Neave*)

Gilded silver adjustable diadem from the main chamber of Tomb II. (*Aristotle University of Thessaloniki - Vergina Excavation Archive*)

Gold diadem found in the Tomb II antechamber chest; 'the most beautiful piece of jewellery to have come down to us from the ancient world'. (*Aristotle University of Thessaloniki - Vergina Excavation Archive*)

(*Above left*) Gold-and-purple fabric found in the Tomb II antechamber chest with the female bones. (*Aristotle University of Thessaloniki - Vergina Excavation Archive*)

(*Above right*) Gold myrtle wreath found in the Tomb II antechamber. (*Aristotle University of Thessaloniki - Vergina Excavation Archive*)

(*Below left*) Gilded greaves and quiver or '*gorytos*' leaning against the dividing door separating the antechamber from the main chamber. (*From Andronikos (1984) with kind permission of Ekdotike Athinon S.A. Publishers*)

(*Below right*) Gilded pectoral found in the Tomb II antechamber. (*From Andronikos (1984) with kind permission of Ekdotike Athinon S.A. Publishers*)

(*Above left*) Theo beside Laura holding the shorter left greave of the pair found in the antechamber of Tomb II, in front of the display cabinet in the Archaeological Museum of Vergina.

(*Above right*) Façade of Tomb III, The 'Prince's Tomb'. (*Alamy.com*)

(*Left*) Silver water pourer or '*hydria*' and gold wreath found in Tomb III. (*Aristotle University of Thessaloniki - Vergina Excavation Archive*)

(*Below*) Tomb IV or the 'Tomb of the Free-Standing Columns'. (*Aristotle University of Thessaloniki - Vergina Excavation Archive*)

(*Above left*) So-called 'Tomb of Eurydice' and the gold-ornamented marble throne. (*Aristotle University of Thessaloniki - Vergina Excavation Archive*)

(*Above right*) Gold oak wreath from the burial finds close to the ancient market place or Agora of Aegae. (*Aristotle University of Thessaloniki - Vergina Excavation Archive*)

(*Below left*) Mosaic from the floor of the Casta Hill Tomb at Amphipolis. (*Alamy.com*)

(*Below right*) The Derveni Krater. (*CC BY-SA 2.5*)

Lion hunt mosaic from Pella. (*Alamy.com*)

Banquet scene on the frieze above the entrance of the Agios Athanasios tomb. (*CC BY-SA 2.5*)

for both male and female royals. Diodorus stated that Philip's ceremony 'surpassed all expectations in its magnificence'.[36] Dr Jonathan Musgrave admitted that, following his intuition, he had 'stuck his neck out' in 1984 with the proposal that the male 'skeleton from Tomb II shows every sign of having been burnt in some sort of enclosed chamber', the Prag-Neave report even likening it to 'an oven'. The evidence that emerged suggests that they were correct in conceptualizing an enclosed environment, perhaps built from the bricks found on the tomb roof, and that may well account for the successful collection of the bones.[37]

The prospect of a grand cremation close to Tomb II was fascinating and I had tried on a number of occasions to visualize it. That became easier when I saw an artist's reconstruction of a similar structure suggested by the pyre remains above a tomb at Derveni. Ancient Macedonian convention, it seems, was to conduct a cremation near the tomb of the deceased and heap the notable possessions which had survived the fire on the roof.[38]

The Derveni funeral looked impressive, but the Vergina pyre could have been an even more elaborate affair. Andronikos unearthed the brick structure on the roof of Tomb II. It covered the length of the main chamber and some 3.5 metres of its width to hold the cremation remains. As he described the scene of the nearby cremation itself, 'several hundred unfired mud bricks were used … on which an

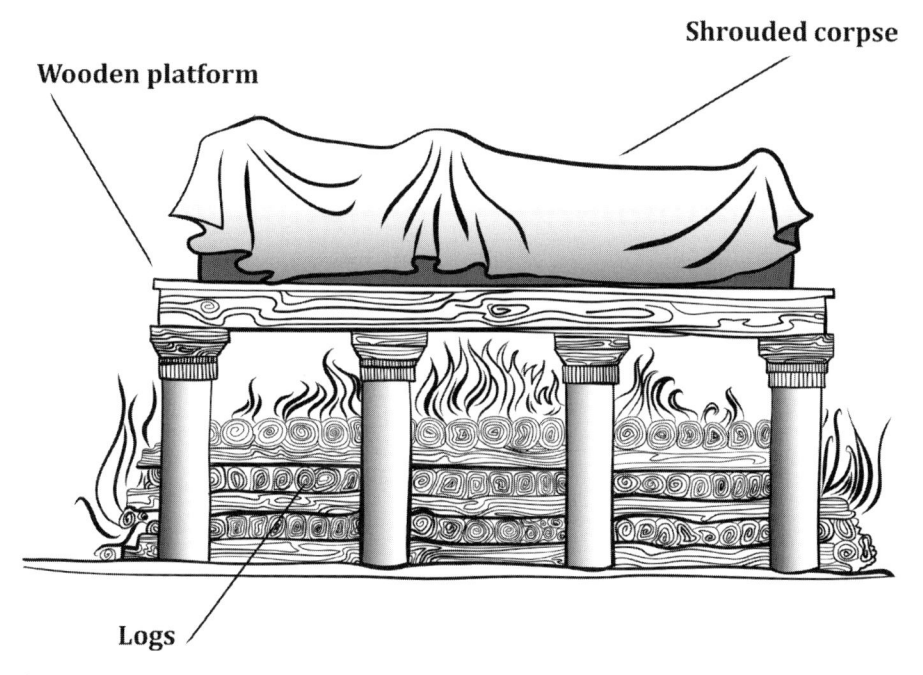

A depiction of the funerary cremation structure at Derveni Tomb A. The body is shown resting on top in a covering shroud.[39]

ornate chryselephantine couch and the body were placed ... for the construction of a small building in which they were burned, complete with door with a lion head knocker.'[40] Chryselephantine is an artistic fusion of ivory covered in places by gold leaf, the height of finery in commemoratives.

Besides the remains of a fine couch, there were weapons, funerary wreaths, smashed plates and libation jugs, along with grapes, almonds and charred lambs, goat kid, and the four horses and two dogs, the latter once more evoking the funeral of Patroclus at Troy.

As further evidence of the protocols surrounding the funeral of Philip II, we have a fragment of a papyrus found in Egypt, translated in 1923, which mentions cedar wood being gathered for the occasion, either for his pyre or the funerary bed, perhaps due to its fragrant smell.[41]

If we are truly witness to the imprint of Philip II's funeral near his tomb, it must have been quite a sight to behold in October 336 BC, with not just the burning of the king, but the execution of the assassin's accomplices. The prisoners would have been marched out and shot with javelins, stoned to death or run through with a blade in front of the gathered crowd, and perhaps left to rot where Andronikos found two skeletons in the reddish earth. The two twisted swords found in the ash might even be their weapons, as those on trial in Macedon retained the right to be uniformed and armed.[42] Even Philip's diviner was put to the blade for wrongly having pronounced favourable omens for the day he was killed. It was an unwritten rule that the families of the guilty would have been executed as well, to prevent inevitable revenge killing.

Carpenters may have been putting finishing touches to the quickly-thrown-up platform on which the wrapped corpse was to be placed. When it finally burned through and the wooden enclosure fell, the bones would have dropped into the crude brick structure below, which we might liken to the 'oven'. Justin's statement that Philip's assassins were executed at 'the tumulus of the tomb' corroborates its proximity to the tomb.

It would have been an occasion of great excitement, fear and grisly curiosity. Finally, with great ceremony, the priests would have consigned Philip II to the flames and the procession then wound its way along the oblique descending pathway that brought the corpse to the door on his journey to meet Hades.[43] The quick plastering and lack of decoration inside the Tomb II main chamber suggests the whole affair, as Andronikos speculated, was undertaken with great haste.

I wondered how the priests, the seers and those involved in a post-cremation ceremony on the roof had mounted the vault to deposit the remains there. A simple answer lay in Andronikos' first report: the tomb sat *below* ancient ground level, as indicated by the surrounding soil colour. Tomb II must have been constructed in the middle of an excavation pit, in which case wooden planking would have sufficed to bridge the gap between the adjacent terrain where onlookers stood

Orphic Masks and Burial Rituals 155

broadly level with the roof. If the pit around the sunken tomb was too wide for planks, earth would have been shovelled back into the pit and piled up around its walls to roof level to provide an access rampart.

I asked Yannis how the six gold acorns from the gold oak wreath could have ended up inside the bricks on the roof. Like Andronikos, he believed the bones were collected first for the ceremony when the the tomb was closed. Then days later when the pyre ash had cooled down, other noteworthy objects, including two burned swords, an iron spearhead and a bronze horse bridal, were recovered from the cremation debris and piled on the roof to symbolically reunite them with the hero interred below. The paucity of charcoal and ash inside the brick pile corroborates this scenario. A few of the bricks did show traces of fire, indicating that they were close to, or part of, the pyre which took place nearby.

CT scans by the Antikas team identified droplets of gold on the man's shoulder blade and upper vertebrae, those closest to the skull. Andronikos suggested they came from the partly melted oak wreath found inside the gold chest, which then must have been placed on the head of the deceased in the early stages of the cremation. As flames licked the corpse, the wreath must have been swiftly removed and then placed in the gold ossuary. This is consistent with finds from grave 'A' at Derveni, where remains of a wreath had also been collected from the pyre and interred with bones.[44]

Intriguingly, the Armenian version of the colourful *Alexander Romance* states that Philip was indeed 'buried with his crown', which we could reinterpret as 'cremated wearing a wreath'.[45] But as Yannis pointed out, a pyre would need to reach 1,064°C before it could melt gold. Although jars of oil or flammable material might raise the temperature this high in a localized area, a pyre is unlikely to burn this hot, certainly in the early stages, and no priest or attendant could have approached the corpse in that heat. Did the oak wreath remain in the flames throughout, until it was collected from the cooled ash?

There were also traces of fire on the spectacular chryselephantine ceremonial shield with the Amazonomachy at the centre. Homeric custom, it seems, was to present the king to funeral onlookers and the army in a potentially shrouded state but fully panoplied with weapons, armour and insignia, before whipping away the more spectacular items for interment in the tomb. Evidence in the ash tells us a less-spectacular shield was left to the flames.[46]

Back in 2003, when Laura was working on the remains of a nearby Iron Age site, she had been asked by one of the conservators to take a look at some of the ivory fragments associated with this ceremonial shield that was found inside Tomb II, as they were not reunited with the pieces now on display. One of the fragments appeared odd and stood out: what the conservator showed Laura was, in fact, a human phalange, a bone from the extremity of either a hand or foot. The human skeleton comprises 206 bones, and 106 of them are found in the hands and feet. Only 18 phalanges were identifiable in the remains of the Tomb II male, because fingers and toes are notoriously difficult to pinpoint in the pyre debris.

Laura pondered whether the bone from the Tomb II male had been accidentally mixed in with ivory in the Vergina laboratory, or whether an already semi-cremated finger was ripped off an already crisping hand when the shield was lifted from the funeral flames. In the heat of the fire, the body often assumes a 'pugilistic-boxer-like' pose, when arm muscles tighten and fists look raised and clenched.[47] What a sight it would have been for the crowd if an unshrouded corpse appeared to move in a defiant last gesture!

Preservation and Putrefaction: the 'Clothing of the Gods'

When mentally reconstructing the ancient funeral on the roof of Tomb II, I felt that an important question had been overlooked in the heat of the identity debate: was the main chamber already built, or semi-completed, when the occupant died? Yannis had been in touch with Dr Costas Zambas, an expert on ancient architecture, and in his opinion, it would have taken well over a month to dig the trench, cut and dress the stones and construct the vaulted main chamber from scratch, even with a wealth of skilled labour at hand.[48] Greeks did not let bodies putrefy, and in the October heat a corpse would not have lasted more than three to five days before starting to decompose. Although Greek funerary custom was to bandage a corpse in linen wrappers, this was not associated with an attempt at preservation.[49]

In Trojan legend, Hector's body remained unburned for some twenty-two days after his death, and Achilles' seventeen, so some putrefaction-delaying process must have been known to the Bronze Age Greeks, or to Homer at least. There is a curious archaic Greek word used three times in the *Iliad* – '*tapxuein*' – which suggests the preserving of bodies, and here with a substance likened to 'ambrosia', or the 'nectar' of the gods, but possibly based on some forgotten technique.[50] The shaft graves at Mycenae also provided signs that the inhumed, but not cremated, dead were embalmed in some way.[51]

Whatever the process entailed, it appears to have been distinct from Egyptian-like mummification in which fluids were extracted from the body. It also appears different from Herodotus' rather vibrant description of the Scythian pre-burial practice involving slitting the belly of the deceased open, cleaning it out and filling it with aromatic substances, after which the corpse was covered in wax, ahead of it being carted around for display for a considerable time.[52]

Kings knew that death was only ever an arrow, spear, poisoned cup or hunting accident away, and they may well have planned their own burial chambers in advance, like the pyramids of the Egyptian pharaohs and Mausolus' 'mausoleum' at Halicarnassus. Although we have no evidence of such forethought in Macedon, the Hecatombid dynasty of Mausolus was well known to Philip and his son, both of whom formed strategic alliances with the fabulously wealthy clan heads in Caria. If Tomb II at Vergina was almost ready at the time of Philip's death, it would have been completed rapidly on Alexander's orders, explaining the unfinished state of the internal plaster in the main chamber and lack of decoration therein.

Finally, if conforming to contemporary tradition, Alexander ought to have placed a coin on his father's body to complete his ceremonial obligations.

Pases' Half-Obol

It was customary for the Greeks to place a coin, usually an obol, in the mouth of the deceased to pay the fare to the boatman Charon who ferried the dead across the River Styx, the last river to navigate before arriving in the Elysian Fields where the heroes hoped to gather for eternal banqueting. Obols have been found in mouths, hands or on top of skeletons dug up in Macedon, including the soldier killed by the catapult bolt who happened to be clenching a hoard, whom Theo and Laura called 'fistful of dollars'. In the case of cremations, obols have been discovered with the ashes and bones in ossuary urns and chests. But there was no evidence of coins with the bones unearthed from the Great Tumulus tombs. Were royalty given a free ride by Charon, or did their valuable artefacts negate the need for a payment coin? I could turn up no references to this special dispensation in either ancient or modern texts.

Greek mythology held that Hermes escorted the souls of the dead to the Acheron, the river of woes, which flowed through the kingdom of Epirus in dark narrow gorges, where it disappeared into the ground at several places, hence its chthonic association. Being the entrance to the Underworld, the Acheron was considered a location of prophecy, places to the dead and their associated cults. Olympias' homeland Epirus remained a land steeped in 'pagan' rites and bewitchment. But without an obol for crossing the Styx, which was guarded by the hungry many-headed dog Cerberus, 'the bloodless, bodiless and boneless' were condemned to endlessly wander along the banks of the river of lamentation, certainly not a suitable ending for the Macedonian royals.[53]

The small silver obol was valued at one-sixth of a drachma, an insubstantial sum: slaves cost around 180 drachmas in the early fourth century BC, paupers on state benefit in Athens received 2 obols per day, unskilled labourers 3 obols, and the stipend for a day's jury service was the same.[54] The single obol was later associated with low-value bronze coinage.[55]

The Roman-era satirist Lucian later ridiculed the funerary custom, even though it had perpetuated itself across the Roman Empire:

> So thoroughly are people taken in by all of this that when one of the family dies, immediately they bring an obol and put it into his mouth

to pay the ferryman for setting him over, without considering what sort of coinage is customary and current in the lower world and whether it is the Athenian or the Macedonian or the obol from Aegina that is legal tender there, nor indeed that it would be far better not to pay the fare, since in that case the ferryman would not take them and they would be escorted to life again.[56]

Lucian's impeccable logic aside, the absence of coins in the Great Tumulus tombs was still odd. Perhaps we have a case of 'Pases' half-obol', I ventured. In a book titled *On Magic*, an ancient grammarian named Apion explained that Pases had once excelled everyone as a magician. He could make lavish dinners and servants appear and vanish again. He owned a half-obol coin with which he paid merchants for his goods, but the coin always returned to his pocket when he wished for it.[57]

Instead of tradable currency, 'ghost coins' have also been found in graves. These were gold-foil sheets with a coin impression, and were sometimes accompanied by scrolls containing instructions to navigate the afterlife, a sort of 'passport' to the Underworld.[58] With this in mind, I wondered if a rather more precious gold coin, a fee fit for royalty and 'business class' across the Styx, had been placed in the mouth of the Tomb II male before the fire was lit; in which case, the coin rather than the crown might account for the melted droplets on his shoulder blade and upper vertebrae. Yannis, reiterating that this would have required extremely high sustained temperatures, proffered a simpler alternative: the deceased was wearing either gold-embroidered clothes or jewels, or golden ceremonial weapons part-melted before being whipped away. XRF spectrums of the precious metal had been taken and Laura agreed that isotope analysis was now needed, if permits could be obtained.

Then I recalled the depth to which these burials at Aegae emulated the old Homeric code, and a simpler explanation was at hand: when the battle for Troy raged in the twelfth century BC, metal currency was unknown, and neither had it appeared by Homer's day, in the ninth or eighth centuries BC. Herodotus believed coinage originated a century later in Lydia with King Gyges or his son, probably from the need to hire Greek mercenaries with a form of remuneration that could be hoarded. The poets mentioned the litany of possessions of these often-impoverished hired fighters, including haversacked cheese and onions, a wallet, blanket and wine cup, with armour and weapons inherited or taken from the dead.[59] On campaign they received a modest basic pay and a ration allowance, and needed a form of payment they could return home with, or which could be exchanged for non-perishable goods.

Until coins first appeared, an 'obol' denoted the singular of '*oboloi*', meaning roasting spits in ancient Greek, and they would have been traded as quasi-currency, either for raw metal ingots or consumable commodities. This suggests that when coins finally appeared there was equivalence in value between them.

The notion of payment to the ferryman was a late arrival on the mythological scene, sometime in the fifth-century BC as far as we can tell, far more recent even than the appearance of the 'puppet theatre' of the Olympian Gods and their particularly 'human' set of emotions: greed, jealousy, lust and impatience were ever on display. This 'immortal aristocracy' had dispelled and eventually replaced the darker more monstrous beliefs and chthonic orgies and rituals of pre-Hellenic Greece. Olympian Gods were behind the forces of nature and they were hands that dealt victory and failure in Homer's battles of heroes and mortal men.[60] But if on the day of the funeral in question the Macedonians were conforming to the older Homeric codes, no obol would have featured in the rites at Aegae.

The Comparative Weight of Evidence

The currency struck by Philip II and then Alexander had not been absent from the 'Battle of the Bones', and Yannis drew my attention to what some considered compelling proof that Tomb II post-dated Philip.

A pair of silver stemless two-handled banquet cups were found in the main chamber with the male, and they appeared to be of distinctive Macedonian design. Like certain other metal artefacts, they had been engraved with their weight in drachma and obol equivalents, so that accurate weighing of the vessels by Andronikos and team was able to determine the gram-per-drachma standard of the currency of the day. The inscriptions had baffled Andronikos, but later interpretations suggest a drachma weight consistent with the heavier silver currency Alexander introduced after his father's death.[61]

While Philip's gold 'staters', worth something like 144 bronze obols, conformed to the Attic standard of Greece, and thus became popular currency internationally in the Eastern Mediterranean and Near East where Greek trade penetrated, his parochial silver coins did not, in this bimetallic currency system. They were worth a twelfth of gold equivalents on a weight-for-weight basis and were lighter than the Athenian equivalent, which traded at a ratio of a tenth. The parsimony means that circulation of his silver appears to have been restricted to Macedon and the Balkans.[62] At some point, Alexander increased the weight of the silver currency by 20 per cent, so conforming to the Attic standard, but numismatists are unsure of just when, although evidence suggests this commenced some three years into his reign and from mints in Asia.[63]

Like all the other Tomb II 'proofs', the currency-standard argument is clouded by the possibility that the silver cups in question did not originate in Macedon: they could have been campaign loot or gifts from outside the state.[64] I pointed out to Yannis that Philip's pending plans to invade Persia also had a bearing on the debate. Philip knew he would have to pay both Greek mercenaries and regulars in the invasion force with coin that they would accept, as well as bribe Greek city governors in Anatolia to avoid lengthy sieges. And he could hardly remunerate his own Macedonian state levies, who may have previously enrolled for nothing more than food and lodging, with anything less than Attic-standard coins if fighting alongside them. One scholar suggested Philip prepaid his men the difference, or he planned to make up their pay from loot, but that is an awkward argument when a simpler solution was at hand.[65]

Philip may well have planned or even commenced minting silver on the Attic standard in preparation for the crossing to Asia by the time he was assassinated at Aegae. The Amphipolis mint, closer to the gold and silver mines of Mt Pangaeum, was a relatively recent endeavour to supplement currency being churned out at Pella. As with much else he did, army reforms included, Alexander may have simply been following his father's initiative. Certainly, Alexander continued minting coins with 'Philip-styled' markings, both gold staters and silver tetradrachms, for some years into his reign.[66] Numismatists have long pondered over the complete absence of coins conforming to the old lighter Macedonian silver standard from hordes found in Asa, and they concluded none of Philip's silver was used in the campaigns. However, the unearthed coins that have been credited to Alexander may well be from Philip's lifetime mints at Pella and Amphipolis. Similarly, the stemless silver cups found in Tomb II may well have been made and weight-stamped at the end of Philips' reign to the new Attic standard.

Very little reporting on the economic factors either side of the death of a king was ever clinically clear, even the death itself. Succession issues are clouded by the world-shaking nature of the event and the political and military fallout. Any financial reforms that came with them were even more ephemerally reported by ancient pens. The silver artefacts from Tomb II remained as vexing as the gold.

From early 2010 to late 2013, the ongoing forensics at Vergina had been witness to Orphic masks and burial rituals, heat-proof shrouds on great wooden pyres and the stuff of the Homeric age. Burials were steeped in superstitions and an honour code of the Late Bronze Age world or their Argive forerunners that fuelled the imaginations of the Argead kings. And the very nature of the precious metals used in funerary goods and coins had entered the debate. On a 6,000-euro budget, long before depleted in what by now amounted to four years of studying the Tomb II bones, Theo, Laura, Yannis and their team had turned up intriguing insights into the mindset of the royalty of Macedon, in both life and death. Now they felt it was high time the world was informed.

Chapter 11

Entering the Chthonic Debate

> Man's most valuable trait is a judicial sense of what not to believe.
> —Euripides

On Thursday 13 March 2014, Theo and Laura arrived in Thessalonica to present their findings at the annual conference of Archaeological Works in Macedonia and Thrace. They checked into the Museum of Byzantine Culture, which lies across the street from the Archaeological Museum and by pleasant parklands close to the city's seafront promenade, where a statue of Manolis Andronikos had been posthumously erected. Here a few select rooms are kept available for visiting scholars.

The paper they presented was titled 'New Finds on the Skeletons in Tomb II at the Great Tumulus of Aegae: Morphological and Pathological Changes'. Yannis Maniatis, who had already published or co-authored more than 200 scientific papers and books from his expertise at analyzing ceramics and other archaeological materials with a scanning electron microscope, next discussed the composite material found on the bones.[1] And in a third presentation, Professor Chrysoula Paliadeli provided an overview of the entire project on behalf of Aristotle University.

In May 2014, immediately after the 40th International Symposium on Archaeometry at the Getty Museum and UCLA in America, Carol Thomas, a professor of ancient Greek history at the University of Washington and a long-time friend of Theo and Laura, invited Yannis over to present his findings. Laura accompanied him to Seattle, where they announced that one of the materials adhering to many of the bones was the rare mineral huntite, which may have been used in the painting of a multi-layered structure that might have been a mask.[2]

Back in 2001–02, Laura had been contracted by Dr Kottaridi to excavate and study twenty-six skeletons from the Iron Age site of Tzamala in the hills outside of Veria where the new Egnatia Highway was being constructed broadly along the ancient Roman Road. To improve her knowledge of the Iron Age, Laura came across a useful book on the era that was co-authored by Carol Thomas.[3] Laura had been planning a visit to her parents, who were also based in Washington State, so she contacted Carol to inform her of the ongoing work and excavations, and she suggested they meet.

The statue of Manolis Andronikos in Thessalonica.

In the autumn of 2002, Laura arrived at Carol's office at the University of Washington, which was lined with books on classical Greece, and she immediately felt at home. From that first encounter, their friendship continued to grow. Carol and her husband visited northern Greece on numerous trips and trekked through the hills of ancient Macedon, during which Theo and Laura imbibed them with a sense of the importance of the work at Vergina and the settlements nearby.

In May 2014, after the presentations in Seattle, Carol, who had by now written her own book on the era of Alexander the Great, offered to help cover some of their personal expenses and provided a much-appreciated contribution to continue their work.[4] The success of these initial lectures, both in Greece and America, resulted in a further specially organized conference on 10 October 2014, hosted by the Archaeological Museum of Thessalonica. Here Theo expanded on the identity of the Tomb II 'Scythian Amazon', and Yannis followed with his preliminary results on the mystery composite material, while a textile archaeologist presented his initial findings on the fabric stains found on the male Tomb II bones.

The event, delivered in Greek, generated a huge amount of interest. 'It was overwhelming and unexpected,' Laura recalled. TV channels and reporters crowded into the auditorium, resulting in a flurry of newspaper clippings in the Greek press, though none were translated for international consumption at this stage.

The poster announcing the results of the Tomb II bone study and the preliminary results from the analysis of the composite material and textile stains on the cremated bones of the male.

The interest in Macedon's archaic past was heightened by archaeologists making their first entry into the massive tomb structure at Amphipolis in the summer of 2014. The Casta Hill tomb lay inside a 155-metre high mound surrounded by a 500-metre perimeter wall which lay outside Amphipolis' fortified city walls. Originally founded as Ennea-Hodoi, 'Nine Ways', the Athenians gained control in the 450s BC as the settlement bridged the Strymon River and controlled access to the timber and pitch trade in the interior.[5] They soon renamed it Amphipolis, and though it changed hands in the Peloponnesian War, its residents always thought it was impregnable until Philip II besieged it in 357 BC when he proclaimed it formally 'independent', whereafter it became a Macedonian stronghold.

Yannis had recently radiocarbon-dated the wooden bridge, with the conclusion that its foundation timbers remained in use for a remarkable 2,500 years.[6] The ancient ruins of Amphipolis had been described as far back as Léon Heuzey's expeditions in the nineteenth century, but excavations of the Casta Hill tumulus did not commence until the 1960s, when a section of the perimeter wall was revealed. A building atop was unearthed a decade later and thought to be a grave marker, and in 2012 the entrance, guarded by two imposing griffins, was finally found.

On 12 August 2014, as excavators prepared to go in, the Greek Minister for Culture and Sports enthusiastically exclaimed: 'We have been waiting for this tomb for 2,300 years.' The Prime Minister, Antonis Samaras, hurried to the site with TV cameras in tow and promised that the dig in the 'land of *our* Macedonia would be completed within a couple of days'. The Bishop of Thessaloniki promptly added: 'Whoever may be buried inside the tomb, he is bound to be Greek.' These were deliberate slights to the parliament of the 'other Slavic Macedonia' at Skopje in FYROM. 'Amphipolitics' was hitting the news and conveniently diverting the country's attention from rising unemployment and Greece's European Union bailout programme which was supposed to end that year.[7]

There followed a new frenzy of nationalism, during which some commentators proposed that the massive tumulus at Amphipolis, which covered 2 hectares, could only be the burial site of Alexander the Great, despite the well-documented journey of his corpse to Egypt. It soon became apparent that the Casta Hill tumulus was a natural hill and not a man-made mound. Moreover, it had probably been turned into a tomb in the generation *after* Alexander. So the family of the great king may have been the occupants, proposed Dr Katerina Peristeri, the chief archaeologist, recalling that his wife Rhoxane and their son were murdered at Amphipolis on the orders of Cassander.

On 3 December 2014, in the wake of the archaeological fervour at Amphipolis, during which Yannis appeared on almost every TV channel in Greece explaining the forensics that ought to be brought to bear on bones and materials, the full

The barrel-vaulted entrance of the Casta Hill tomb at Amphipolis guarded by marble sphinxes. (*Alamy.com*)

Antikas team project paper, a result of six years of painstaking microscopic analysis and the cataloguing of bones with 4,500 digital photos, was submitted in English for the first time to the *International Journal of Osteoarchaeology*. It was titled 'New Finds from the Cremains in Tomb II at Aegae Point to Philip II and a Scythian Princess' and was finally published on 15 April 2015.

The introduction explained:

> This paper contains new finds regarding age, gender, palaeopathology and morphological changes to bones. Recent evidence indicates the man in the main chamber is Philip II of Macedon, father of Alexander the Great, and the woman in the antechamber his seventh wife/concubine, daughter of Scythian King Atheas killed in battle against Philip in 339 BC.

The report also stated why their work was needed: 'These cremains had been studied insufficiently and/or misinterpreted, causing debates among archaeologists, historians and anthropologists for over three decades.'

The publishing of the revised age of the Tomb II woman at 32 +/− 2 years caused consternation when the audience began to appreciate that this conclusively ruled out the most prominent Tomb II female candidates on both sides of the thirty-six-year 'battle of the bones'. Gone was the young Cleopatra, Philip II's final wife, who was never a convincing candidate when considering the 'Olympias factor': Alexander's mother brutally executed Cleopatra with her child and was hardly likely to have provided her with a royal burial which would have only highlighted the crime.

Commentators soon realized the revised ageing also discounted the equally young warrior-like Adea-Eurydice and, by association, Philip III Arrhidaeus, Adea's half-witted husband, who had no other female companion we know of and certainly no other wife. Moreover, the leg fracture suffered by the female provided indisputable evidence that the antechamber weapons belonged to her.

Following its release, key extracts from the paper were posted on the internet and in a report in *Forbes Magazine* thanks to Dr Kristine Killgrove, a professor of bioarchaeology. Theo communicated with *Discovery News* in October and underpinned the report's conclusions with: 'No Macedonian king other than Philip II is known to have had relations with a Scythian.' A write-up was also posted in the Ancient Origins website with the banner: 'Remains of Philip II, father of Alexander the Great, Confirmed Found'.

New Bones, Old Information and Fortuitous Reacquaintances

Almost simultaneously, in June 2015, and completely out of the blue, a new paper by Dr Antonis Bartsiokas and his new associates appeared. A couple of years before, he had inherited the office of Nikolaos Xirotiris at the Democritus University of Thrace located at Komotoni. It was now clear that with the laboratory came the 'stray' Tomb I bones; what the Antikas team and Yannis suspected about their whereabouts had finally been confirmed.

Since inheriting Xirotiris' office, Bartsiokas, a paleoanthropologist, had been studying the skeletal remains in Thrace without anyone's knowledge or consultation, though he implied Professor Panayiotis Faklaris had provided him with the bones. Bartsiokas must have been aware that the Antikas team were due to publish their finding on Tomb II, because their programme of analysis and methodology had been published back in 2011.

Theo, Laura and Yannis had themselves requested permits to study the reunited Tomb I bones with a combination of scientific techniques, and they had sent a detailed application to the Ministry of Culture in August 2014.

The recommendation of the Ephorate of Emathia, under Angeliki Kottaridi, was negative. The Ministry asked the Ephorate for an explanation without receiving a reply, which delayed the whole process and enabled Bartsiokas to complete his analysis on the most important Tomb I bones.

Bartsiokas' latest report was compiled with four Spanish researchers, though none of them were specialists in human skeletons from this particular era.[8] He was completely unaware that the Antikas team had recovered additional Tomb I bones from storage at Vergina, and so he was working on the assumption that the grave contained the skeletal fragments of the three individuals Musgrave had first identified. The bones, Bartsiokas still believed, were from Philip II, Cleopatra and their newborn. Adhering to Eugene Borza's hypothesis, once more, he proposed that Tomb II with Philip III Arrhidaeus and Adea-Eurydice might therefore contain the armour and weapons of Alexander the Great. This was, by now, all very familiar territory.

Bartsiokas also felt able to state, from the dental attrition of the upper and lower jaw, that a male in Tomb I was 'around age 45', and this was more consistent with the age of Philip II than his son Arrhidaeus, who was closer to 40 when he died. Bartsiokas added that the male bones he had been analyzing from Tomb I were found 'touching the floor or very close to it', a seeming contradiction to his 2007–08 paper which made it clear that the tomb excavator, Panayiotis Faklaris, who originally cleaned and lifted the bones, found them above 12cm of soil. Plaster and imprints of vases were also found *under* the remains, with traces of a fire in the cracks in the floor stones, possibly from funeral pyre ash which fell through the opening above when the tomb was looted.[9]

Bartsiokas explained this away: the soil falling through the broken roof when the tomb was robbed caused this layer of sediment.[10] That was surely the case, but the incoming earth would have accumulated on *top* of the bones. Moreover, there seemed to be no certainty where the remains of the newborn baby, supposedly the daughter of Philip II and Cleopatra, were found and at what depth in the soil. The excavator's report of 1978 simply identified three distinct piles of bones in the 'lower extremities', alongside bones which were 'disarticulated', and so not attached to the others. This meant that any attempt to link the owner of the jawbones to any other bones was highly speculative.

But Bartsiokas had a secret weapon up his sleeve: he was in possession of a thighbone and shinbone, which showed evidence of a 'terrible' knee wound. The bones had fused together at the knee at an angle approaching 80°, hardly the work of a royal surgeon, and they had never come to light in previous references to Tomb I.[11] Like all the others in his possession, they had not been cremated, so Bartsiokas reiterated that Justin's reference to Philip II's funeral pyre was a Roman lie. Bartsiokas summed-up with an explanation of the prominent hole through this joint: '[It] ties in perfectly with the penetrating wound and lameness

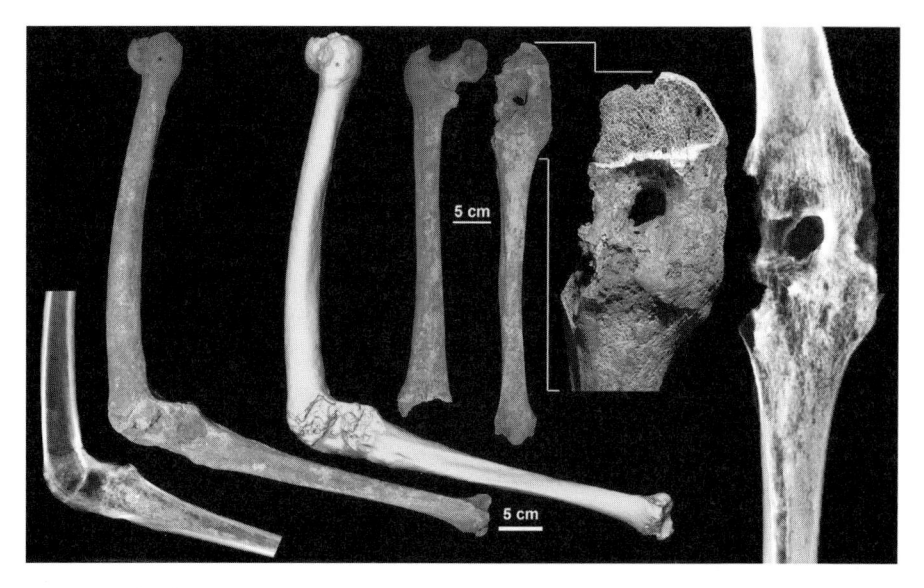

168   Unearthing the Family of Alexander the Great

The 'terrible' knee wound Bartsiokas introduced into his report, showing the fused position of the shinbone and thighbone and the puncture hole. (*From Bartsiokas-Arsuaga-Santos-Algaba-Gómez-Olivencia (2015), with permission of PNAS*)

suffered by Philip II ... thus the 40-year-old mystery concerning the royal Tombs of Vergina has finally been solved.'[12]

What remained puzzling was that neither Musgrave nor Xirotiris, in whose office the bones had sat for over twenty years, had ever seen this prominently large left knee joint with its quite obvious hole and horrendous angle of bone fusion. Nor are they shown on the excavators' diagrams of the three groups of bones in situ. From the remarkable size of the leg bones, Bartsiokas further calculated the person had been 180cm tall, a colossus for the era.

No ancient text suggests that Philip II was strikingly tall. His son, Alexander the Great, was sufficiently modest in height, at perhaps 160–165cm, for Curtius to refer to his 'slight stature' and for Darius' newly captured mother to mistake his taller companion, Hephaestion, for the king.[13] The Persian nobility appreciated stature as well as beauty, explaining her mistake, and Darius III himself was said to be 'the tallest of men'. The captive queen mother's faux pas prompted Alexander's famous reply concerning his second-in-command in an attempt to alleviate her embarrassment: 'he too is Alexander'.[14]

In a more credible estimation, Musgrave had calculated the height of the Tomb I male at 165.18cm, based on the length of the left femur. However, Bartsiokas now claimed that the femur came from the leg of a *woman*, despite the fact that the size of the head of the bone fell squarely in the male range. She was a 'robust' female, Bartsiokas explained. Professor Xirotiris was sufficiently dubious when he read Bartsiokas' report to publicly state that he doubted these large leg bones originated in Tomb I at all, with all the inferences that carried.[15]

Attributing Bartsiokas' thigh- and shin-bones to Philip II carried further challenges. The fusion of the bones, at close to an 80° angle, makes it clear that whoever sustained this trauma would have been unable to walk upright, and he must have moved with his left leg dragging behind the right with an impossible gait. Yet Philip led the right flank of his army into battle at Chaeronea just a year after sustaining his leg wound in battle against the Triballi in Thrace in 339 BC. Then I recalled Pausanias' description of the tomb-looting Celts: 'the tallest men in the world'.[16] Could the bones have come from the upper soil infill and belong to a tomb robber? Still, no noteworthy bone like this appeared in the excavators' reports.

When Bartsiokas' paper emerged, Theo and Laura were shocked. It instantly became clear what had happened to the bulk of the bones from Tomb I: Andronikos had given them to Xirotiris in the 1980s for analysis after Musgrave had taken a 'hasty' look at them in 1984 at the Archaeological Museum of Thessalonica. Since then, they had never been studied, nor had they left Xirotiris' office in Thrace to be returned to Vergina with the other bones from Tomb I. The bagged remains found in the basement of the Vergina laboratory in July 2014 were smaller and less-easily identifiable remains from Tomb I that had never been sent away.

Like Musgrave and other commentators, Bartsiokas was unaware that the remains of at least seven individuals emerged from the soil of Tomb I, with four additional babies and one foetus now identified. Nor was he aware that the pubic joint of the Tomb II female had enabled accurate re-ageing, which ruled out the young Adea-Eurydice, and so Philip III Arrhidaeus, the Tomb II occupants he was so energetically still arguing for. Bartsiokas' new paper was redundant before it was ever published.

The Antikas team and Yannis began the task of reuniting the Tomb I bones still sitting in Thrace with those found at Vergina; but this would prove a painfully drawn-out process.

Theorizing with Theo

It was mid-2014, coincidentally, when my own manuscript delving into the succession mystery surrounding Alexander the Great was nearing completion. I came across the Ancient Origins article announcing the Vergina finds when researching the royal burials, and there in the accreditations I saw Theo's name. I had not been in contact with him since 2008, when he was based in the US and he had kindly agreed to edit my original Masters thesis on Alexander's 'lost testament'. I had no idea that he had since returned to Greece and was working on the Vergina bones.

On Sunday 3 May 2014, I contacted Ancient Origins to obtain Theo's new contact details. The founder explained that the source of her article was *Discovery News*, with which she had no direct link. So I set about trying to find an updated bio or CV that might have Theo's latest home address or email. I finally tracked him down through an academic website and fired off a somewhat hesitant approach.

Theo replied as enthusiastically as ever, congratulating me on the forthcoming book, and he was thrilled that I followed his advice to publish my 'controversial' ideas on Alexander. From our previous discussions, I knew he was authoring a book on the Macedonian poet Poseidippus of Pella and that he had read his own manuscript through some twenty-three times, so I asked if he had published since. Theo replied:

> I am now on its 33rd re-read ... had to stop for six years due to the very demanding, copious study of the cremated bones from the royal Tomb II at Aegae, and those at Pydna. Presently, we are off to Pella where an eight-chamber rock-cut tomb has been unearthed – the largest in Greece – and only Zeus knows how many skeletal elements will come out of it ... There is no further budget for bones, so we have asked if the Pella remains can be transferred to Dium to minimise our travel expenses. We desperately need to find a financial donor. Never a dull moment.

Through the following weeks, Theo and I exchanged long emails and he was patient with my barrage of questions concerning the Vergina finds. I finally met him in Kent when he was visiting his son for Christmas in 2015, and our correspondence extended to January 2016, when I *thought* my own manuscript was finally ready.

Theo always ended his emails with an uplifting salutation. Fluent in ancient Greek, as well as English, Spanish, French and Latin, fillets of each entered his prose: '*Kalimera Hermano, Tolle Lege, Tyche Agathe* to you', was not an unfamiliar greeting. Tyche, the god of good fortune, would certainly be needed in the coming months.

Throughout the remainder of 2016, I worked on the editing, typesetting, image collection and permissions, plus all the attendant tasks and protocols required in publishing a book. I was also incorporating the helpful critique and suggestions offered by Professor Carol Thomas, who had seen my working manuscript. Inevitably, all this took longer than I had expected, and at times, reflecting on the never-before-voiced controversies that underlined my conclusions of Alexander's death and the Successor Wars that followed, I felt like a turkey voting for Christmas when signing off the final text and sending it to print.

Remaining true to a promise I had made to Theo some years before, I booked a flight to Thessalonica on 30 January 2017: he would have the first signed copy. It was that extended meeting in Makrygialos following my visit to Vergina that truly immersed me in the tomb debate. There followed a new offensive of emails in which our theories and opinions, unifying or amicably divisive, filled up pages of correspondence with red and blue text inserts, as Theo and Laura added their comments to mine.

I had asked Theo what made him and Laura take on the anthropological study when much had already been written, and on such a limited budget. He explained that they could not simply let the bones lie there because there was so much still to be told and so many unanswered questions; *too* many for their liking. The archaeologists who haul out gold and silver receive the international attention, and that's understandable, Theo philosophized, as it focuses interest in the right place:

> Look at how the world was transfixed when Howard Carter unearthed the riches of Tutankhamun in November 1922. But it's the behind-the-scenes 'bone work' that tells the greater story: how they lived, how they died, how they were buried, what illnesses and injuries they suffered, and now there is the possibility from DNA testing to determine if they were related. And all this might tell us who they are.

Laura was no less animated on the issue, and she added that osteological studies provide archaeologists, historians and classicists with solid evidence to base their theories on, but unfortunately their contribution to the story is not always recognized or understood. Archaeologists, 'historians with a spade', study the artefacts and buildings, but anthropologists study the people who made them. Only by combining the constructions of the human hand and the biological information can we have a greater understanding of an ancient culture.

I had already heard from other sources that finding bones in a tomb is an archaeologist's worst nightmare, because excavators wanting quick and unhindered results had side-lined the bones in the past in favour of the more newsworthy grave goods. 'Accidental' finds during construction projects had led to police and even builders tossing remains aside.

After meeting Theo and Laura, I was thoroughly intrigued. On 3 March 2017, a month or so after our memorable encounter, I came up with the idea of documenting the full story of the excavations at Vergina, and I soon found myself drafting *Unearthing the Family of Alexander the Great*.

Chapter 12

Finding Material Witnesses

> I know you won't believe me,
> but the highest form of human excellence
> is to question oneself and others.
> —Socrates

Three weeks after returning from Greece in late January 2017, I received a curious question from Laura: had my research on Alexander turned up any references to a companion with an 'overbite' or buckteeth? She explained: there is a man depicted like this on the far right of the Tomb II hunting frieze, with an open cape, holding a spear and wearing a traditional felt hat, the Macedonian 'kausia'. Laura had already discussed her theory with Professor Chrysoula Paliadeli, who had written a monograph on the mural, and she agreed this was a fascinating portrait that might depict a real person.[1]

Ptolemy's Nose and a Hunter's Buckteeth

I could not recall any references in the ancient sources to a bucktoothed friend, general or bodyguard of Philip or Alexander, but then we are extremely light on any personal descriptions of their entourages. I wanted to check Laura's observation for myself. Manolis Andronikos' visually stunning book from 1984 remains one of the best pictorial records of the Great Tumulus excavations, and when I homed in on a close-up of the controversial hunting fresco that had featured so prominently in the chronology debate, sure enough, I found the hunter with prominent teeth. But something else struck me: the naked youth to the right-centre of the fresco was the spitting image of Ptolemy, Alexander's boyhood friend.

Ptolemy's campaign career proved to be illustrious: a royal page at the palace, he was considered a 'syntrophos' at court, literally a 'foster-brother' to the prince, and ended up as one of Alexander's personal bodyguards, traditionally seven in number, though possibly extended to eight by their return to Babylon in 323 BC. This elite group commanded the most prestigious cavalry and infantry brigades, dined with Alexander and acted as his advisers as if being groomed as future governors of the huge expanses now under Macedonian control.[2]

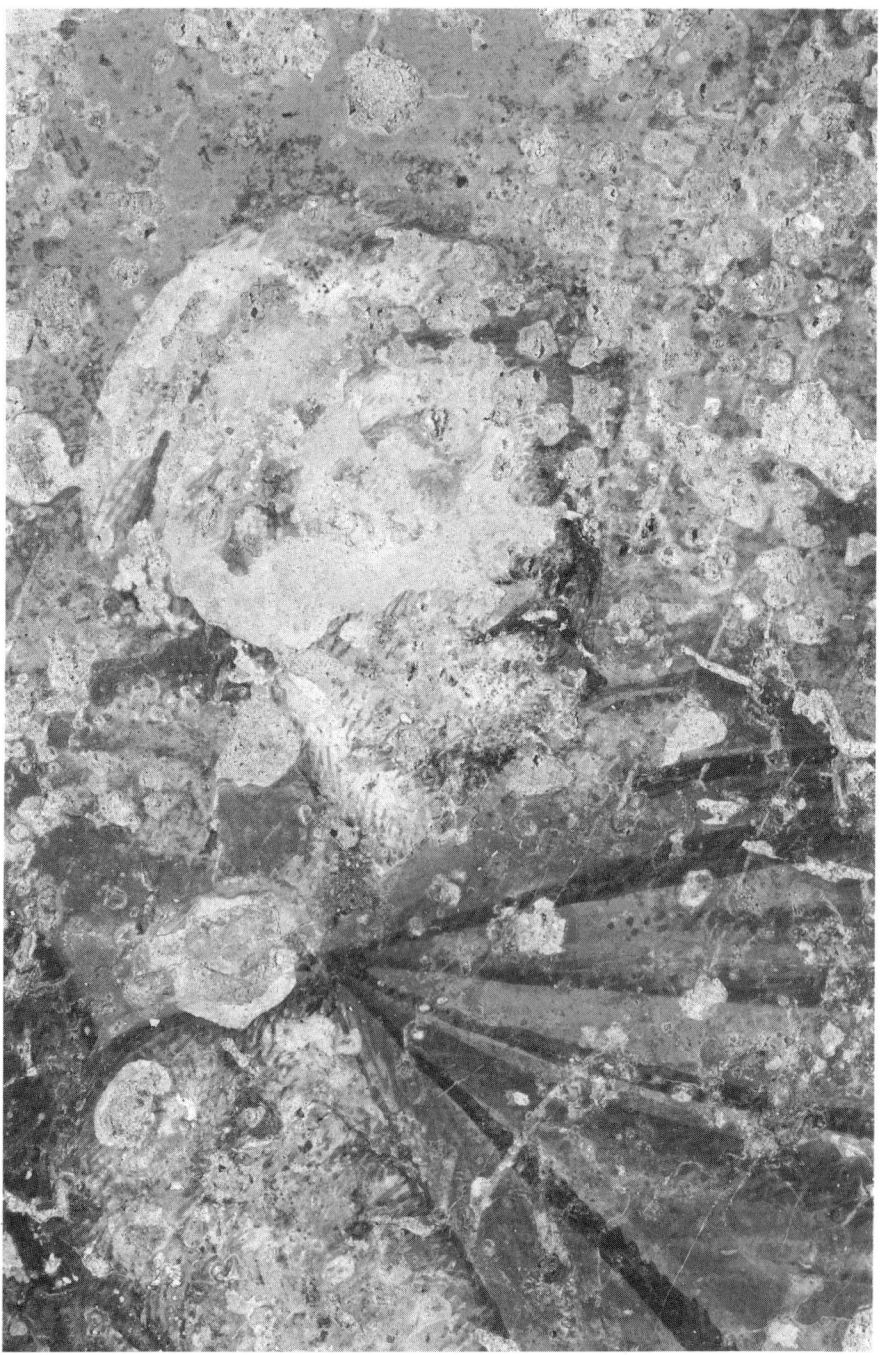

The 'bucktoothed' hunter in the frieze above the entrance of Tomb II.

When Alexander died, Ptolemy assumed control of Egypt. Like all other provinces in the conquered East, this initially represented a governorship in the name of the two kings in Pella: Alexander IV, the son of Rhoxane, and the mentally impaired king Philip II Arrhidaeus. But eighteen years later, and thanks to Cassander terminating both of Alexander's sons, he became the self-declared 'King Ptolemy I' and de facto pharaoh of the ancient land. It was in this period that Ptolemy assisted the island of Rhodes when under siege by Demetrius the Besieger, earning himself the epithet 'Soter' ('Saviour') in the process. The famed Colossus of Rhodes, the massive 100ft-tall brass statue of the Titan-god close to the harbour entrance, was erected in celebration using funds raised from the sale of Demetrius' abandoned siege equipment.

Ptolemy's mother was one of Philip II's former concubines who was rumoured to have been passed on pregnant to Ptolemy's father, Lagus: if the whisper is to be believed, Ptolemy was Alexander's half-brother.[3] Of course, this might have been a valuable hearsay that the Egyptian dynast spread himself. But Ptolemy had a distinctive hooked nose, more prominent than Philip's, and a similarly shaped chin, a profile effectively captured by engravers on his coins. The well-known bust of Ptolemy in the Paris Louvre is a fine example.[4] I emailed Laura my observation and she confirmed that the resemblance to Ptolemy was striking, and later informed me that Chrysoula Paliadeli had made the same connection in her 2004 monograph and in the rich pictorial history she published with a fellow excavator in 2005.[5]

Andronikos had already noticed another significant familiarity: at the centre of the hunting scene painted above the Tomb II entrance sits a youth on horseback sporting a pink-purple tunic, who, he felt, bore a likeness to the teenaged Alexander. The youth's pivotal position in the painting reinforces the idea, as does the green laurel wreath upon his head. Three additional youths are depicted attacking a lion, a clear suggestion that 'royalty' was present: the Ptolemy-resembling figure, another wielding an axe and an older bearded man on horseback to his left, Philip II, Andronikos believed.

I pondered the possible family attachment of this grouping in which 'four human figures form the framework for the rest of the composition', in Andronikos' words.[6] If Philip II and Alexander are accounted for, with Ptolemy in between, we needed an identity for the man with the axe to Ptolemy's immediate right. I suggested that he could be the bodyguard Leonnatus, and explained to Laura that his father, Anteas, was a relative of Eurydice, Philip II's mother, so Leonnatus was a member of the Lyncestian royal house. Moreover, his love of hunting was apparently legendary, according to a passage in the Roman-era text of Athenaeus which describes the length of his quarry nets.[7]

Our discussion extended to the third horseman. For similar historical reasons, I proffered either Alexander's second-in-command Hephaestion or Perdiccas,

Above. Ptolemy I Soter tetradrachm minted in Alexandria ca. 300–285 BC showing his distinctive hooked nose and chin. (*Classical Numismatic Group Inc.*) There is a resemblance to the profile of the youth in the hunting scene, below. (*Aristotle University of Thessaloniki – Vergina Excavation Archive*)

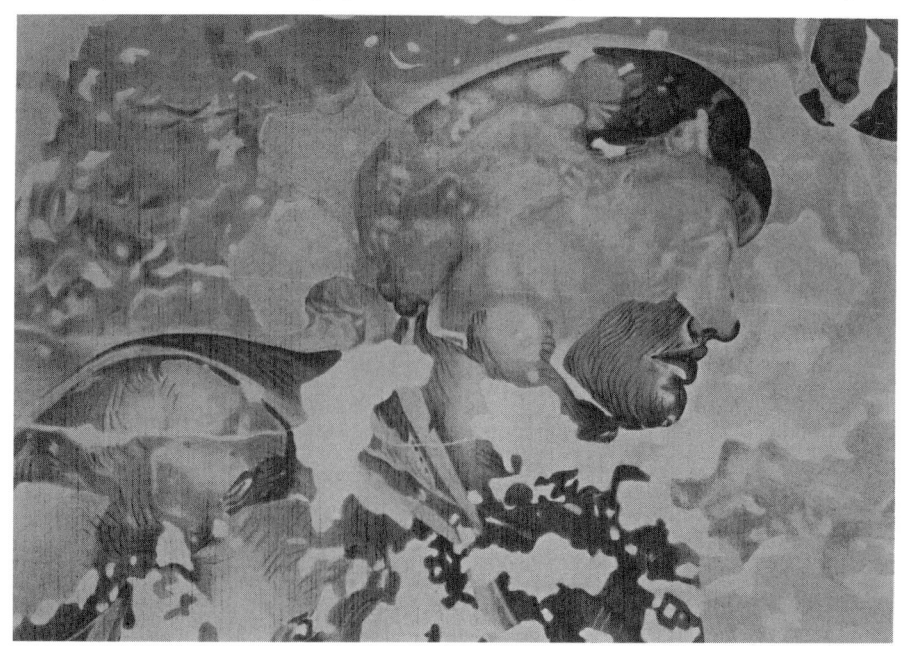

who assumed the role following Hephaestion's death. Both were commanders of the elite brigade of Companion Cavalry, an equestrian status potentially suggested by their mounts in the hunt.

I wondered whether the painting above the Tomb II entrance might reveal more, and recalled Aristotle's ideas on physiognomy in which he boldly proposed it was possible to deduce a person's character from their physical appearance.[8] Aristotle, who was no Adonis himself with his small eyes and thin legs, cared little for political correctness. He believed that people with large foreheads were 'sluggish', those with small craniums were 'fickle', the broad-headed 'excitable' and the bulging-headed 'spirited'. Blinkers were 'unreliable', people who didn't were 'impudent', and protruding ears were a sign of those disposed to 'foolish talk'.[9]

The faded condition of the hunting fresco does not give us too much to go on, but the youths are well muscled and most are portrayed in 'heroic nakedness', except for two of the mounted men: those supposedly Philip and Alexander. The hunt takes place in a rocky, mountainous landscape where a sash and a votive tablet are attached to one of the trees, which, with a single-statue pillar, suggests the sacred or even mythological nature of the grove, as does the antiquity of the dead and leafless forest, if not simply redolent of a bleak midwinter.[10] The whole composition epitomizes bravery in the attacking of a lion and a boar without the assistance of a hunting net, the very Platonic essence of the courage expected of descendants of Heracles the 'huntsman'.[11]

In a monograph on the frieze, Professor Hallie Franks of New York University pointed out that Alexander chastised his companions for 'going soft' and using nets. Although a hunting net is visible, it remains unemployed in the wings and is perhaps being depicted as 'refused'. Professor Franks was referring to a statement by Plutarch, whose biographies were steeped in rhetorical devices, but nevertheless, his entry is interesting in its additional symbolism linking kingship with the 'king of animals', the lion:

> He [Alexander] saw that his favourites had grown altogether luxurious and were vulgar in the extravagance of their ways of living. For instance ... Philotas had hunting-nets a hundred furlongs long ... Accordingly, he exerted himself yet more strenuously in military and hunting expeditions, suffering distress and risking his life, so that a Spartan ambassador who came up with him as he was bringing down a great lion, said: 'Nobly, indeed, Alexander, hast thou struggled with the lion to see which should be king.' This hunting-scene Craterus dedicated at Delphi, with bronze figures of the lion, the dogs, the king engaged with the lion, and himself coming to his assistance; some of the figures were moulded by Lysippus, and some by Leochares.[12]

According to Athenaeus, it was not customary in Macedon to recline at a dinner symposium until you had speared a wild boar without using a net. In what might have been later derogatory propaganda, not impossibly spread by Olympias and her backers, it was claimed that Cassander was still banqueting upright with his father at the age of 35. This is a state of affairs that can only have been truly witnessed if his father, the regent Antipater, was prepared to humiliate his oldest surviving son, whom he was clearly grooming for high office.[13]

Two Italian historians commenting on the Tomb II entrance painting suggested that the shaven appearance of the hunters may represent the clean grooming style Alexander introduced.[14] Back in 2005, in correspondence with Professor Paliadeli, Theo had pointed out that nine hunting dogs and three horses feature in the hunting scene and that the remains of a similar number of dogs and horses had been found in the funeral pyre on the roof, a theme reinforced in his 2002 paper titled 'Horse and Heroes in the Tomb of Philip II'.[15] He and I had more recently discussed this further.

'David, it's truly amazing. In the Tomb II pyre debris, we found the bones of four horses and two dogs. Even the horses' trappings and bits were still there. *Four* horses. What does that remind you of?' asked Theo, who reminded me that almost every god, goddess, or lesser deity in history was immortalized by his or her closeness to horses.[16] I nodded in sage agreement that is was redolent of the funeral of Patroclus at Troy.

'Yes, *Iliad* verse 23.171.' Theo continued to quote Homer verbatim: 'Achilles sacrificed "four horses with high arched necks ... swiftly upon the pyre, groaning aloud the while. And there were nine dogs of the table that had belonged to the lord Patroclus. Of these he cut the throats of two and set them on the pyre."'

Theo had told me some time ago that he had memorized the complete *Iliad*, a feat that requires the recounting of some 15,693 now-standardized lines of dactylic hexameter, as the meter of archaic poetry is known. But it was an accomplishment I never expected to hear in such fluent motion. What Theo had found in the pyre remains from the roof of Tomb II was not just a burial in Homeric style, it was an *exact* re-enactment of Achilles' burial of Patroclus.

'Who knew the *Iliad* off by heart?' Theo asked.

'Alexander,' I replied, thanks to a statement in Plutarch's biography, though as it had already been pointed out, Cassander was also renowned for memorizing Homer's verses.

'*Exactly.* So here we have the tomb of Philip II, whose funeral was overseen by Alexander.' '*Possibly,*' Theo added, with due scientific caution in the wake of miscalculations and precipitous announcements that have since proved unfounded.

Hounds and hunting were the invention of the gods Apollo and Artemis, who passed their knowledge on to Apollo's son Charon, and he, in turn, had as his students the warriors who fought at Troy.[17] At the Argead court in Pella, the 'royal huntsmen' were the teenage pages in the process of transition to soldiers of the king's personal cavalry brigades.[18]

With the dogs and horses in mind, I wondered if the number of hunters depicted in the fresco might be just as symbolic: there are ten in total. Excluding the possible identifications of Philip and Alexander, we have the likely number of Alexander's personal bodyguards by the end of his campaign.[19] So I pondered whether the hunting scene might depict this remarkable group of future dynasts who later carved up the empire and almost fought to the last man. If this was the case, the Tomb II frieze must have been painted towards the end of Alexander's reign and over a decade after Philip II died. But that didn't rule out Philip as the main chamber occupant if Andronikos was correct and the two chambers of Tomb II were built at different times, or the tomb remained empty and incomplete until it was finally sealed years later, in which case the hunting scene above the entrance was the final part of the tomb to be adorned after the interment of the female warrior.[20]

Signs in a Symposium

In 1994, another huge tumulus, some 90 metres wide and 18 metres high, was partially excavated near the town of Agios Athanasios, 60km from Vergina as the crow flies and just 15km east of the ruins at Pella. The tumulus is thought to be related to the site of the ancient Macedonian city of Chalastra on the west bank of the Axius River. Two 'Macedonian-styled' tombs had already been found in the area of the tumulus in the 1960s, and were dated to the years following Alexander's death.

Two unlooted tombs were revealed in the eastern slope of the tumulus. One was a chamber tomb and contained a silver-on-cypress wood larnax decorated with two silver discs embossed with sixteen-point stars on the hinges of the lid. The chest contained cremated female bones wrapped in familiar gold and purple cloth, and a 7-to-7½-month-old foetus, suggesting the woman could have died from childbirth complications.[21] Outside the entrance were signs of a funeral pyre in which debris from an ornate wooden couch could be seen. This was all suggestive of Macedonian nobility with 'royal' connections.

Towards the centre of the tumulus, which appears to have been constructed over an original natural hill, lay another grander Macedonian-styled barrel-vaulted tomb which had unfortunately been plundered via a hole in the west wall. Despite the loss of the contents, traces of iron armour and ivory inlay from a reclining couch could be identified, along with a gold coin of Philip II, probably from an issue struck after his death. A still-vivid scene portraying a typical Macedonian symposium was painted on the frieze above the entrance, the only wall-painting ever discovered in mainland Greece depicting the lively court banquets we read about in ancient texts.

As described by the excavator, Dr Maria Tsimbidou-Avlonitou, it had been painted in crimson, purple and light blue against a darker background by a 'rapid yet skillful hand' that clearly understood colour, harmony and contrast.[22]

Six men wearing wreaths can be seen in the banquet art, some reclining and others sitting upright. More riders and guests are arriving, clearly outfitted as armed Macedonian soldiers. Women are portrayed between the dining men, one of them seated and curiously playing an ancient lyre or 'cithara', as this was a role usually reserved for males. As a teenager, Alexander was said to be an accomplished lyre player who once entertained an Athenian delegation with his music, but Philip thought his skill effeminate and asked his son if he was not ashamed to pluck the strings so well, and Alexander never performed again.[23] But here, a second woman plays a flute, so the imagery suggests the host was sufficiently wealthy to hire professional musicians.[24]

Various foods, roasted and sweet, adorn the tables, and an assortment of furniture decorates the room, which can be dated by the contents to the mid- or late fourth century BC, though these could have been long-standing family possessions. As the excavator noted, the presence of a naked male in the role of a wine pourer or 'cup bearer' makes the scene redolent of the so-called 'death feast' reliefs, as well as the banquet descriptions found in Plato's *Symposium* and Athenaeus' *The Dinner Sophists*, a diverse collection of anecdotes, pithy maxims and moralizing epithets set in a banquet setting.

The size of the Agios Athanasios tumulus and the cluster arrangement of its tombs in many ways paralleled those of Vergina, so I was keen to apply the same logic to the banquet painting and see if it might portray actual characters.

Antipater, the long-serving state regent of Macedon, had six sons that we know of, one of whom, Iollas, became Alexander's chief cupbearer. Antipater also had at least four invaluable daughters, who were brokered in marriage to powerful generals after Alexander's death. The oldest, Phila, was noted for her wisdom and her ability to deal with the troublemakers among men: she was a key adviser to her father and a steadying influence on her husbands, who included Craterus and Demetrius the Besieger, with whom she bore Antigonus II Gonatas.[25] On the right of the painting, the armed Macedonian soldiers are watching on, some younger in appearance and others wearing the 'kausia' leather cap worn by generals, which again suggests high status: the banquet host had his own security corps or personal bodyguards.

I wondered if the necropolis at Agios Athanasios was the burial site of the 'Antipatrids', as the family line is known. In his long-standing service to the kings, Antipater had accumulated sufficient power and wealth to commission a burial mound of such proportions. We additionally know that two of his sons were buried soon after his death, one at the hand of Olympias.[26] Immediately after, Cassander established himself as king in Macedon, once he had wiped out the remainder of

Alexander's line, so any regal artefacts attached to the tombs are readily explained: Cassander surely felt his father deserved all the trappings of state. These include the iron greaves which are unique, like the Vergina Tomb II iron helmet, as all other examples are fashioned in bronze, even those gilded over.[27] The conservators working at Agios Athanasios were also able to reassemble an iron-and-leather-coated cuirass, almost identical to the Tomb II example.

Along a similar path of logic, Professor Olga Palagia suggested that the banquet scene not only represented real individuals, but an actual event concerning the very same family: in 294 BC, Demetrius the Besieger murdered Cassander's son, King Alexander V, at a banquet at Larissa in Thessaly. It was the culmination of mutual suspicions and infamous double-dealings colourfully portrayed by Plutarch. Demetrius got wind that Alexander V had already set in motion *his* execution at a symposium. So the presence of soldiers in the scene, Palagia argued, recalls the armed escort Alexander fatally left outside so as not to arouse the suspicion of his guest.[28]

Coming from quite different perspectives, we both linked the Agios Athanasios painting to the Antipatrid line, although the excavator, Dr Tsimbidou-Avlonitou, cautioned me that the tombs appear to predate the symposium event described above. But if the association is correct – and as he had already done at Aegae – Antigonus II Gonatas might have symbolically raised this second 'great tumulus' over his relatives' tombs, for Phila was his mother. In which case both mounds were part of Antigonus' dynastic aspirations: his attempt to protect that 'glorious past' to 'shore up a less certain present', for the age of the Argeads and Antipatrids was over, and it was time for his own Antigonid dynasty.[29]

Excavations at Agios Athanasios, whose modern town was populated in 1922 by refugees from thirty-two formerly Greek-inhabited villages now in Turkish territory, halted due to limited funds and impending town planning which authorized the building of new residences on the perimeter of the site, despite objections from the Greek Archaeological Service.[30] I contacted Dr Tsimbidou-Avlonitou with a number of further questions concerning the excavations of 1994. Could more structures still reside under whatever remained of the tumulus? Have new digs been undertaken? What state is the banquet frieze in, and has any restoration taken place?

Maria was kind enough to reply and sent me stunning visuals of the façade and its current protective shelter, but I could sense her frustration with what occurred since, a 'long story' as she put it. A proposal for a protective shell was first submitted in 1998 but construction did not commence until 2008, fourteen years after the tomb was first unearthed. There were many technical problems and bureaucratic setbacks, and it was eventually completed in 2012. Dr Tsimbidou-Avlonitou was finally able to present a paper in March 2013, titled 'Aghios Athanasios 2008–2012: Towards the End of an Odyssey'.

A small part of the tumulus remains and overlooks the town today, though the original exploratory trenches dug in 1994 had revealed nothing more. The site is nowadays temporarily open to the public for only two days a week and only accessed occasionally for visits by archaeologists. Somehow, I felt the tombs of Agios Athanasios were yet another unfinished page in Macedon's still-incomplete story. And what might conceivably be the burial ground of Macedon's most famous regent, with its unique banquet images, sits again in a sidelined, solitary silence, as it did for 2,300 years.

Purple Stains on Blue-Blood Bones

Manolis Andronikos found the remains of a partially intact purple-and-gold fabric on the Tomb II female bones at Vergina, which matched, down to its very pattern, the material found in the silver larnax from the unlooted Agios Athanasios cist tomb.[31] Once again, this pointed to a central workshop that was outfitting the royals and nobility, both in life and after death.[32] But only stains from a fabric could be found on the male bones in Tomb II. The fact that one type of cloth survived when the other did not is suggestive of different materials or some distinct funerary treatment, because conditions in the main chamber and antechamber of Tomb II were virtually identical throughout the subterranean centuries.

The deep purple colour may have once held sinister connotations: the similarly coloured cloak laid at Agamemnon's feet in the *Iliad* was suggestive of a path to slaughter, as was the same-coloured robed procession of the Furies which represented gory sacrifices made. In time, purple came to represent royalty, the principal power behind the 'spilling of blood'. Dyeing fabrics in purple pigment, most famously made from murex sea molluscs by the Phoenicians, and then adorning fabrics with gold thread, required expertise and wealth above the average household. Rather, this signified precious commodities and the purse of royalty. The expression 'royal purple' has been found on an inscription from Knossos on Crete dating to the thirteenth century BC.[33]

The Phoenicians, who would have been locally known as 'Canaanites' in the Levant, had settled 2,000 years earlier at Sidon, Arados, Berytos and Byblos in today's Lebanon, where they also occupied the strategically important island-city of Tyre. Since the sixteenth century BC, trade in the production of murex dye had flourished there; the 'land of purple' is, in fact, the etymology of 'Phoenicia'. Alexander captured Tyre after a seven-month siege in which every available innovation of mechanical warfare and artillery was exploited. The gradual silting over of his 600-metre-long attack causeway is what joins Tyre to the mainland today.

The Greeks viewed these aquiline-featured Phoenician traders with a fair degree of suspicion. In the *Odyssey* they were termed 'greedy rascals with thousands of trinkets in the hulls of their black ships', while Herodotus all but blamed them for starting the Trojan War.[34] Routes to their westernmost trading posts, some beyond the Mediterranean and their Atlantic base at Cadiz founded at the close of the twelfth century BC, extended as far as the tin mines of Cornwall and were closely guarded. The Tyrian Phoenicians who founded Carthage in modern Tunisia blocked the sea passage through the Pillars of Hercules, today's Strait of Gibraltar.

'Tyrian Purple' was worth its weight in silver, claimed the historian Theopompus, who was acquainted with Philip's court.[35] According to Plutarch, when Alexander captured the Achaemenid city of Susa, he found '5,000 talents' weight of purple from Hermione in the Peloponnese, which, although it had been stored there for 190 years, still kept its fresh and lively colour. The reason for this, they say, is that honey was used in the purple dyes. Darius, it appears, maintained a deposit of high-value purple assets among his coined money.[36]

In Homer's *Odyssey* we find further detail on the cremations of the heroes, which might be pertinent to the perished fabric on the remains of the Tomb II male: Achilles' cremated bones were gathered and washed in unmixed wine and unguents before being placed in a golden jar with Patroclus' remains.[37] I wondered if similar cleansing agents were responsible for the demise of the fabric on the male bones. The woman's skeletal remains were still covered in ash, so they had clearly not been washed, and perhaps that accounts for the survival of her textile. However, inspection suggested the woman's cloth was made from wool, whereas his had been made from more perishable linen.[38]

In June 2017, Laura approached Dr Margarita Gleba, a European Research Council Principal Associate at the University of Cambridge, who lectures on archaeological textiles and the social aspect of textile production in antiquity, especially in the Mediterranean. With excavation experience in Turkey, Italy and Ukraine, Margarita enthusiastically accepted the challenge of analyzing the stains on the male bones.

Theo, Laura and the team about them still had no funding of their own, and certainly none to offer Margarita, who agreed to travel to Vergina using her own resources. Her first opportunity to study the textile stains would be in November 2017, when she planned to attend the 8th International Symposium of Ancient Macedon, if permission for the analysis was forthcoming. Meanwhile, a new 'material' debate was raising its head at Vergina.

The Cotton Conundrum

In 1979, two years after Tomb II was unearthed, fragments of a burned textile were found in the pyre remains on the roof. In 1997, after the removal of the excessive consolidants of silicon-based polymers used in its preservation, the textile was analyzed by Georgianna Moraitou, an archaeological conservator at the National Archaeological Museum of Athens, before being mounted for exhibition in the Vergina museum. The tabby-woven fabric was provisionally identified as cotton.[39] But as I pointed out to Laura, the presence of cotton would be significant, or perhaps problematic, to the chronology of Tomb II, depending on whether you conformed to the Philip II or Philip III Arrhidaeus camp.

The Roman geographer Strabo tells us that it was Alexander's campaign philosopher, Onesicritus, who detailed the very first sighting of cotton plants when the Macedonians entered India. Historians and geographers of the time referred to anything east of the Persian Empire as 'India', although most of Alexander's campaigning by the Indus actually took place in what is now Pakistan. India was then considered the 'third part of the world' in their rudimentary geography of Eurasia and the East, along with the belief that a great 'stream of ocean' encircled the joined landmasses.[40]

The Macedonians were both impressed and terrified with much they saw in the exotic monsoon-ridden region, and 'India' soon became a byword for exaggeration. Descriptions of plants and animals were inflated and entered the campaign accounts as hardly credible 'wonders', with 200ft-long serpents and 300-year-old elephants among them. Strabo was unimpressed and thought 'all who write about Alexander preferred the marvellous to the true', and the campaigning in India only magnified their art.[41]

The significance of finding cotton in India was rooted in a rather more practical application: Alexander was so impressed with the coolness of the new fabric that he had cotton tunics made for all his men, dispensing with their less practical woollen vests. But the arrival of the Macedonians in India post-dated the death of Philip II by a decade or more, so the presence of cotton in the remains of the Tomb II funeral pyre would demand some explanation, *if* he was the occupant.

It is possible that the newly wealthy Macedonian royals were importing rolls or garments of cotton from the East earlier than has been documented. Finds from the Indus Valley confirm the Harrapan civilization, which thrived from 3300 BC until it vanished around 1600 BC, had already mastered cotton production. A century before Philip's death, Herodotus also described a material on 'wild growing trees' whose 'wool exceeded in beauty and goodness that of sheep, from which the Indian make their clothes'.[42]

But cotton did not feature in the domestic histories of Greece or Macedon, a contention seemingly corroborated by an extract from Curtius' account of Alexander's campaign: after three years battling in Asia, Alexander received from home a 'present of Macedonian clothes and a large quantity of purple material' when he arrived at Susa in the heart of the Persian Empire. He gifted the delivery to Darius' captive mother, Sisygambis, and added that 'if she liked the clothes, she should train her granddaughters to make them'. Sisygambis was mortified:

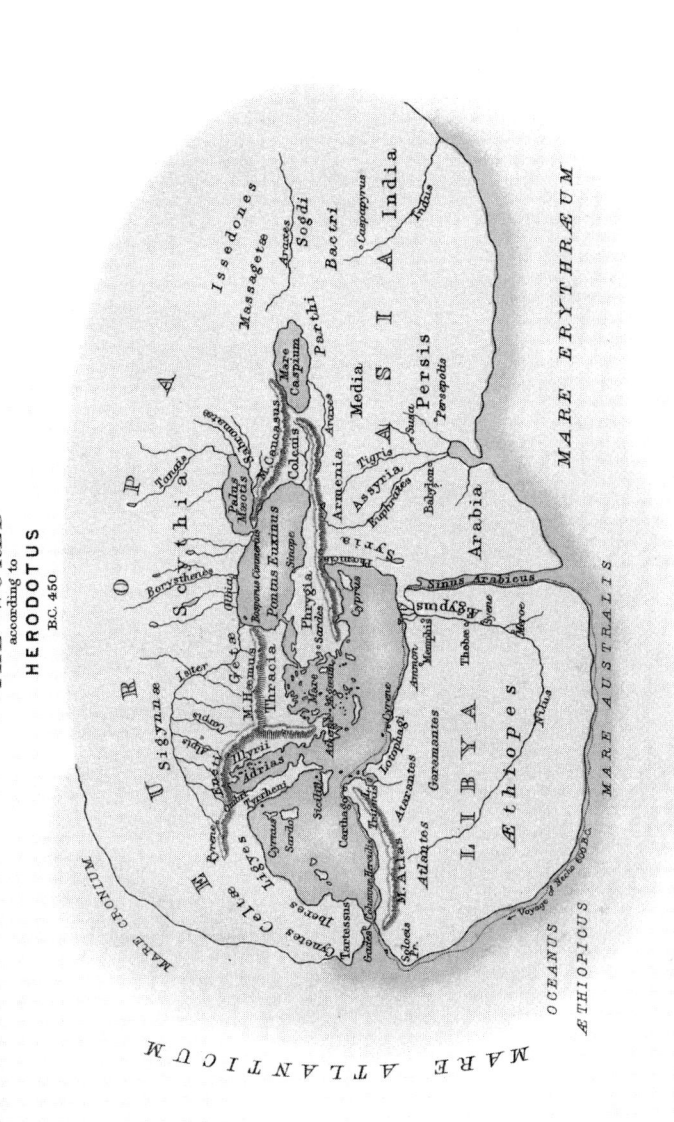

A map of the known world drafted according to Herodotus' geographical descriptions ca. 450 BC. When the Macedonians arrived in India, they started to appreciate the boundless East, with the Ganges clearly referenced in extant texts. Whether the land of the Seres, China, was mentioned to them we can only speculate.

'tears came to the queen's eyes, signifying her angry rejection of the gift – for to the Persian women, nothing is more degrading than working with wool,' added Curtius.[43] If cotton was already available in Macedon, surely the garments sent to Alexander in the heat of the East would have been of that cooler, finer fabric.

In Greece, body wraps known as 'chitons', as well as the outer cloak or 'himation' and the cape known as a 'chlamys', were each made of wool. Since Mycenaean times, the other principal textile in circulation was linen made from the cellulose fibres of flax, which was once grown in the Greek mainland, though it required all-too-rare tracts of fertile soil.[44] The wearing of Ionian linen tunics, rather than the Doric shirts of wool, had been introduced from Caria in Anatolia, and linen is thought to have been the mainstay of the sail-making industry for ships and fishing nets.[45] Linen corselets and cuirasses are ubiquitous in references to the chest armour of Greece, Etruria, Egypt and Persia from Homer's *Iliad* onwards, with evidence that the material was stiffened with vinegar to make it more resilient to blades.[46]

If cotton was found to be present in the royal tombs at Aegae, it would be the 'only Hellenic fabric of its kind identified at present', commented Georgianna Moraitou in a 2007 paper.[47] Moreover, Strabo's account of its sighting in India is certainly suggestive of the 'wonder' material seen for the very first time. In the opinion of Dr Stella Spantidaki, an expert on Greek textiles, cotton and hemp were listed as 'unknown to the Greeks and used by foreigners'.[48] Laura and I delved into her publication, '*Textile Production in Classical Athens*'. It cited a 2009 paper by a well-respected Athens-based textile conservator who had identified 'the rare phenomenon' of cotton fibres in a fifth-century BC grave in the Kerameikos, the ancient cemetery of Athens, and at Trachones in Attica.[49] This would also make these the first competing discoveries of cotton in ancient Greece, but these fibres had already been confused with silk in earlier studies, an even more unlikely resident at fifth-century Athens.

It wasn't until the Hellenistic era following Alexander's death that silk first appeared in Europe, carted down the Silk Road with the help of the settlements Alexander had founded or simply renamed along its route. According to Strabo, the city of Alexandria 'Eschate' ('the furthest') in the Fergana Valley brought the Greek settlers and the Graeco-Bactrian Kingdoms into first contact with the silk traders in the Han dynasty of the 'Seres', as the Chinese were known. The Romans would later develop a voracious appetite for silk, obtained from the Parthians who most likely encouraged the belief that silk grew on trees, a myth dispelled by the naturalist Pliny when he outlined the role of the silkworm. But like cotton, silk was not a feature of the domestic world of Philip II or Alexander.

Laura and I made contact with Dr Spantidaki at the ARTEX Hellenic Centre for Research and Conservation of Archaeological Textiles. She informed us that the cotton prognosis for the Kerameikos grave find was, in fact, far from certain, with a wool-flax composite the only fibre firmly identified. Dr Spantidaki seemed to share my dubiety on the presence of the cotton in fifth-century Greece, and she stressed that the fabrics needed new examinations.[50]

This opinion was endorsed by Margarita Gleba at Cambridge, with whom I discussed the cotton trade with Macedon in the mid-fourth century BC, when the tombs at Aegae were built. She informed me that cotton does not come into widespread use until the Roman period, and she was puzzled by the obsession archaeologists have with finding silk and cotton, because the textiles that the ancient cultures could make using wool and linen were absolutely exquisite, in her opinion.

Dr Gleba also commented on the purple murex dye: The earliest production of purple was actually not in Phoenicia but on Crete and Italy, dating to 1900–1800 BC. The abundance of purple in Macedonian graves suggested to her that it was produced locally; many production sites have been identified across the Aegean and the molluscs were ubiquitous. The dye cannot be readily transported long distances due to specificities of the chemical reactions: it has to be used as soon as the purple-bearing gland is extracted from the mollusc, followed by an incubation period in tin or lead containers, which were not easy to transport.[51] Further, the gold threads found in the purple funerary fabrics are quite peculiar in construction, from what she had seen in images. Once again, this pointed to the domestic production in precious materials and purple dye in Macedon itself.

It was difficult to imagine that in the world of DNA sequencing, radio carbon dating and stable isotope testing, something as basic as identifying the type of fabric used in the Tomb II funerals could provide key evidence in dating the burials; but that might just be the case. Georgianna Moraitou's report also concluded that scanning electron microscopy (SEM) was now needed for a more secure identification of the burned fabric from the pyre, though more would be revealed about the fabric stains from Tomb II once Dr Gleba visited Vergina in the coming months.

The Whispering Papyrus

Laura and I soon found that our enquiry into cotton was not the end, but rather the beginning of the story of man-made materials recovered from the Vergina tombs. On 10 May 2017, Theo and Laura attended a speech at the Archaeological Museum of Thessaloniki by Professor Richard Janko, a classicist at the University of Michigan, one of the world's leading papyrologists and a renowned linguist of the Homeric epics. When engaging him after the conference, they heard him mention something rather intriguing: he was studying papyrus from the Great Tumulus at Vergina, including fragments from Tomb II.

Despite their familiarity with the bones, Theo and Laura were completely unaware that any papyri had been found in the Great Tumulus tombs, except for 'imprints' recovered from the main chamber of Tomb III, the 'tomb of the prince'. These were formed when imprints of ink from a now-decomposed papyrus transferred onto wet plaster, but with the writing reversed. Found in 1978, these fragments had finally been removed from Tomb II in 1990.[52]

We discussed the possible source of the Tomb II papyrus, because nothing of this nature was mentioned in Andronikos' reports. I could recall only one relic which might explain the presence of the writing paper of the ancient world: the mysterious sceptre Andronikos first mentioned in 1978. He described it as 'a long cylindrical object, poorly preserved, whose core, according to the chemical analysis, was some kind of bamboo. The outside of this object was covered in cloth and gold in alternating layers; it seemed unavoidable to interpret it as a sceptre.'[53] I had always thought the description sounded unsuited to the sturdy staff that was representative of a king's office, and pondered if what Andronikos described was, in fact, a papyrus scroll wrapped around a bamboo core known as an 'umbilicus'.

I relayed my thoughts to Laura, who passed them on to Professor Janko, who happened to be in London following his trip to the Vergina Laboratory on 28 June. He invited me to meet him at the Institute of Classical Studies in Senate House, close to London's Russell Square, and on the balmy afternoon of 8 August we met in the downstairs café which looks across to the British Museum.

Richard Janko had been based at the University of Michigan as professor of Classical Studies since departing the University of London, which shares the premises at Senate House, where resides arguably the world's finest library on ancient Greece and Rome. Having graduated from Cambridge with honours and a dissertation on the language of the Homeric hymns, Professor Janko now reads in eight tongues, including ancient Greek. He and Theo, I mused, would have a field day travelling through both ancient and modern Europe together.

Professor Janko had already published a study on the famous Derveni Papyrus found in Tomb 'A' at Derveni in 1962, which remains the 'oldest European book' in existence. The now-famous text commented on the Eleusinian and Orphic Mysteries, whose founder, Orpheus, was said to have been buried in Macedon after being dismembered and decapitated by raving Thracian women. The text reveals that the author of the papyrus was critical of excessively literal religious interpretations: a clear monotheist, he claimed that 'God' is the 'mind', and he labelled those who initiated themselves into the mysteries without further thought as 'gullible' and 'money wasting'.[54] However, his blasphemy apparently accommodated benign '*daimons*', which, he thought, were the souls of the dead.

Orphic texts have been found on gold tablets in tombs at Vergina, Pella and Amphipolis, among other locations,[55] and one scholar has since proposed that

Fragments of the Derveni Papyrus, the 'oldest book' in Europe, found in 1962, explaining the author's views on the Orphic Mysteries. (*Alamy.com*)

these carefully prepared papyri, with religious or sacred texts, were used to light funerary fires.

The story of papyrus starts in Egypt and the earliest surviving examples we have date to around 3500 BC. Its preparation was described in detail by Pliny, who took much of his information from Theophrastus, a student of Aristotle and his successor at the Lyceum in Athens. The inner rind of the papyrus or 'biblos', which gave us the word 'bible', was cross-braided and bound with glue, then pressed and dried to make it ready for ink. Like modern textured paper, papyrus had a front and reverse, with one side more receptive to being written on and the other having a coarser surface. This observation is helping modern researchers unravel the original texts from reused scrolls known as 'palimpsests'.

A standard papyrus scroll was made from twenty sheets glued together and was some 56 metres long when fully unravelled. Major works often ran to unwieldy lengths, 10 metres or more: the last two books of the *Iliad* alone ran to somewhere near 8 metres. The scrolls were best preserved rolled up and housed in jars, a state described by the Latin word '*volumen*', from which 'volume' derives. The inks of this period, applied with reed pens, were generally still charcoal-based with soot, gum and water, and were easily erased by accident or deliberately amended.

It is not unusual to find archaic Greek papyrus manuscripts written 'boustrophedonically', where the direction and orientation of letters was reversed on every line: imagine the continuous pattern left in the soil by a cart yoked to an ox ('*bous*' in Greek) ploughing a field and turning back at each end. We also have verses or even signatures written as acrostic poems, in which the first letter on each line formed a new word when vertically arranged, and which only made sense as such. Lines of ancient text lacked punctuation marks, and later script known as 'uncial' was continuous with no gaps at all between individual words. These alphabetical challenges, along with fragmented and faded text, have hindered the deciphering of ancient manuscripts, which, in the era under scrutiny, were written in the still-developing Greek. It was becoming infused with Macedonian to form the '*koine*' or 'common tongue' which was widely used in the Hellenistic era.

Professor Janko was kind enough to provide me with a draft of his paper on the Great Tumulus papyri in which he cited my theory. As far as the possible misidentification of the sceptre, he postulated that the scroll may have fallen out of a gold cloth container and its core partly unravelled, perhaps when the wooden couch it once lay on disintegrated, so that it was tapered and elongated when Andronikos found it, explaining its 'sceptre-like' length.[56]

Having photographed the papyrus fragments, Professor Janko computer-enhanced the images and then attempted to reassemble the pieces in a search for coherent wording which might help date the tombs. Tomb II had yielded up 168 papyrus fragments in various shades of silvery black, which could, if arranged together, be fitted into a 22 × 22cm sheet. But the pieces were from different parts of a far lengthier scroll, with no cohesive words or sentences, though single letters could be identified.

Richard Janko concluded that what little writing could be seen on the Tomb II fragments in optical light revealed that the letter 'Sigma' had been written in an old style as Σ, which was more in keeping with a text penned in the reign of Philip II than later. Another potential chronological clue to the Great Tumulus burial dates was the recovery of a further Sigma from a papyrus fragment from Tomb III amongst 112 pieces retrieved there. Here, in the tomb of the 'prince', the same letter had metamorphosed into what is referred to as a 'lunate C'.[57]

From comparisons with other more-firmly dated Greek papyri, we know this newer form of Sigma first appeared a generation after the reign of Philip II. As many scholars on both sides of the Vergina identity debate had accepted that the Tomb III bones are those of the son of Alexander the Great, who was murdered and buried in secret on Cassander's orders between 311 and 309 BC, then it becomes axiomatic that the Tomb II script, with the older Sigma, was written a generation before. Once again, that points back to Philip II and not his son Philip III Arrhidaeus, who died in 316 BC, far too close to the 'prince's' death for the Sigma to have evolved.

But the day the royals were killed, and the year they were finally entombed, were not necessarily correlated. I pointed out to Laura, and later to Richard Janko after he had published, that Tomb III is unlikely to have been sealed before 294 BC, some forty-two years after the death of Philip II, because neither Cassander, who died in 297 BC, nor his sons, who ruled to 294 BC, could have provided burial honours to Alexander IV, who had been murdered on Cassander's orders. That would have simply brought attention to the family crime.

Unfortunately, my observation was no friend to Manolis Andronikos' original statement that the three tombs forming the 'cluster of Philip II' date to a single generation, and not later than 310 BC, though Andronikos maintained reservations that Alexander's son resided in Tomb III. Yet the late closure of the tomb, sometime after 294 BC, provides more than an adequate generation gap for the Sigma to have evolved from the older style Σ to a lunate C.

The coherent wording on the papyrus from the prince's tomb was intriguing. The reflective coating of the consolidant used to preserve the fragments made photography difficult, as did their colour and curvature. But Professor Janko managed to reconstruct what looks like a list of chattels buried with the adolescent: soft tunics, drums and another unnamed boy's item. Written beside them were references to planks and pegs, while the iron head of a hammer had been found on the Tomb III floor. This appeared to be a list of construction materials a workman might have used, in which case the papyrus was written when the tomb was sealed.[58] We know remains of wooden tables and couches were found on the floor, and they may too have been assembled on site. Hooks were most likely hammered into the walls where possessions were hung, like those illustrated on a Hellenistic tombstone from Veria.[59]

Questions still remained about where the fragments from Tomb II had been found, whether in the main chamber or antechamber. The answer could help establish when the female was cremated. If the 'early' Sigma had been found with her, it would suggest her burial was broadly contemporary with the man's, but if the papyrus was recovered from the main chamber, it left the door open for a much later funeral for the antechamber 'Amazon'. That was significant in light of what I had first proposed in 2015 for her identity, which conformed to none of the conventional arguments proffered so far, and it assisted what I was about to suggest again in expanded form. But Professor Janko was wise to caution that Tomb II could contain heirlooms from an earlier date, including a generation-old papyrus.

What became clear from Richard Janko's work was that *all* the tomb contents, famous and obscure, needed to be analyzed together if the Vergina mystery was to be solved. Yet the thick mass of decomposed organic material gathered up from the tomb floors, comprising the remains of wooden furniture, leather, clothes, tapestries, foodstuffs and possibly even more papyri, are still sitting in storage at the Vergina Archaeological Museum.

The ongoing studies were now revealing clues of chthonic import. Inanimate materials were providing further pointers to the tomb datings, and artists' portraits along with possessions were yielding insights into the mindset of those who buried the dead. Although these ancient funerals were clearly orchestrated to ensure safe passage to the afterlife, emerging evidence was beginning to suggest that the kings and queens of Macedon believed in the possibility of a return ticket as well: reincarnation.

Chapter 13

Afterlife in Amphipolis

> Dying, I should willingly come back to life again for a little while,
> Onesicritus, that I might learn how men read these things then.
> If they praise them and admire them now,
> you need not be surprised;
> each imagines he will gain our good will by great deceit.
> —Alexander the Great[1]

We have a remarkable story of tomb reincarnation attached to Philip II's court. A young woman named Philinnion, the daughter of a couple from Amphipolis, died soon after marrying a suitor named Craterus, perhaps the prominent general who later accompanied Alexander the Great to Asia, though it was a popular name. Philinnion was buried in the family tomb, but six months after her death, she returned to life and for many nights she slept with a lover, Machates, who originated from the state capital at Pella but was staying with her grieving father in the Amphipolis family home.[2]

A household nurse soon detected Philinnion's presence, and after being reproached for her behaviour by her incredulous parents, Philinnion died a second time, after professing that her actions were the will of the Underworld gods. Everyone saw Philinnion's corpse as it lay in state in her father's house, but in their disbelief that it could truly be the daughter, they went to the family burial site and dug into the sealed communal tomb. There was no trace of Philinnion's body, except for one gold ring and a wine cup given to her by Machates just days before.

There was considerable fear in Amphipolis, where an assembly recommended that her corpse be burned and ritually purified with fire outside the city limits, followed by sacrifices to the appropriate gods. Poor Machates committed suicide in his grief. The governor of Amphipolis and another prominent citizen sent a number of letters to Pella in which they described the event to the king.

Could the 'Machates' of the tale be the 'Machatas' of the royal house of Elimeotis in Upper Macedonia? He was the brother of Philip II's second wife Phila and the name which appeared on the vessel Andronikos found in Tomb II.[3] It is perhaps a fanciful link to make, but what the story clearly evidences is that ghosts or apparitions, 'phasma' to the ancient Greeks, were thought to inhabit the portals to the Underworld. They were said to occupy the sites of the battles at Plataea and Marathon, where a white marble column and 15-metre-high mound over the mass grave were erected to commemorate the slaughter. And some of these inhabitants allegedly returned to life.

The theme of reincarnation is associated with griffins or winged lions, like those painted below the stunning wall frescos of Tomb I. As at the massive Casta Hill mausoleum at Amphipolis and the unique banquet tomb at Agios Athanasios, griffins have been found guarding the entrances to burial chambers. Commenting on the theme of afterlife, the excavator at the site of Finikas close to Thessalonica added: 'In Greek funerary art the gesture of the handshake in a scene is usually interpreted as the "farewell of the warrior", or his return.' A reunion in the Underworld stresses the non-absolute nature of death, which instead represented a transition to a new form of life.[4] But reincarnation was symbolized most vibrantly in the myth of Persephone, in which the 'Macedonian preoccupation with death' infused the art in their tombs.[5]

The Abduction of Persephone

In fifth-century Athens, while wives remained on 'house duty', the men famously consorted for sexual and intellectual stimulation with courtesans known as '*hetairas*'. With the exception of the unique social code of Sparta, Greek women were not considered 'true citizens' of the state save in their ability to bear children, preferably boys. Even then, the predominant ideology was that women were simply carriers of male seed and played little part in the child's final form and character.

Plato stereotyped a wife's domestic role with 'weaving and watching over rising cakes and boiling pots'. Women of the time were 'trained to see and hear as little as possible', added the Athenian-born Xenophon in his dialogue on household management, and they passed their days in the 'gynaeconitis', the female-only chambers towards the back of the house or upstairs.[6] The spindle and the loom were carried in wedding processions as a token of a wife's domesticity, and a popular tenet of Greek city-state society stated: 'A man outside the home, and a woman inside it.'[7] The women of Athens were barred from politics and comedy at the theatre, restricted to watching tragedies instead, while even the market place was a male-dominated area of business.[8]

Daughters were frequently married soon after puberty into a household of a man they had never met nor courted, often with a significant age gap between them and with a bride price paid to sweeten the transaction as he symbolically grasped her by the wrist to signify her bondage.[9] Their plight became the subject matter of the tragic poets Sophocles and Euripides, who pitied the maidens 'driven away from home and sold as merchandise':

> Of all creatures that have breath and sensation,
> We women are the most unfortunate.
> First at an exorbitant price we must buy a husband
> And master of our bodies …
> And the outcome of our life's striving hangs on this,
> Whether we take a bad or a good husband.
> For divorce is discreditable for women
> And it is not possible to refuse wedlock.[10]

The neglected domestic women, with the status of 'slave-wives' in some circumstances, turned to the ancient cults of the earth-goddess Demeter and her maiden daughter Persephone.[11] They attended associated festivals in their honour such as the Thesmophoria and the Eleusinian Mysteries, where powerful female elements were promoted and worshipped as part of a woman's 'secret emancipation'. A circular 'Thesmophorion' has been excavated at Pella, where the cult of Persephone was established.

Ancient texts tell of women consuming pine bark and needles, pomegranate seeds and the herb pennyroyal, which were associated with the *Homeric Hymn to Demeter* as well as other cults, and modern research confirms each contains sex hormones with contraceptive effects. They sit in contrast to the quince, for example, which was eaten at the threshold of her husband's home upon marriage day to symbolize fertility.[12] It seems these otherwise 'muted' women may have sought to control the balance in domestic affairs through this covert means of controlling pregnancy.

The worship of female forms was introduced, or advanced, in Macedon by King Archelaus I at the close of the fifth century BC, when dedications to the Muses were commonplace.[13] These primordial goddesses, daughters of Zeus and one of the Titans, represented the arts and sciences that Archelaus introduced to his court through visiting scholars and performers from across the Greek world. Here Euripides wrote his tragic play, *The Bacchae*, perhaps inspired by the orgiastic rituals he saw in honour of Dionysus. It was Eurydice, the wife of Amyntas III and mother of Philip II, who brought with her the cult of Eucleia, with a shrine to the goddess built at Aegae.

Eurydice's daughter-in-law Olympias, who was variously known as Myrtale, Polyxena and Stratonice before adopting the better-known name resonant with Philip's successes at the Olympic Games, was no less drawn to the divine mysteries. She had allegedly met Philip as a youth on the rugged isle of Samothrace, where she was initiated into Orphic rites.[14] For centuries, the Samothracian Mysteries lured visitors to the island's almost harbourless rocky shores and to its lush interior forests, mountain and waterfalls, which were powerfully evocative of a sanctuary of the Great Gods and cults stretching back to the dawn of time.

Olympias became a maenad, a follower of the god Dionysus, whose entranced disciples known as the 'raving ones' tore apart wild animals with their bare hands. Natural intoxicants and hallucinogens might have been responsible for the euphoric condition: possibly eating 'magic' mushrooms and the chewing of laurel leaves, whose narcotic effects were otherwise restricted for the use of the priestess Pythia at Delphi and her divine trances.[15] Olympias' rituals and the attached oaths of secrecy could have been imported from her native Epirus along with the snakes which made their way into her bedchamber and reportedly disgusted Philip. Serpent gods and priestesses had featured in earlier Minoan and Mycenaean cults and were considered incarnations of the dead. It was probably through these strange primeval rites that Olympias retained a spirit of independence at the court of competing wives at Pella.[16]

Stone and marble effigies of snakes were found in the Sanctuary of the Mother of the Gods at Vergina in 1990. This very ancient deity was the goddess of nature and life and death who preserved the key to the Underworld, as worshipped in the East with the associated mysteries and nocturnal ceremonies. In the sanctuary unearthed at Aegae, a 1.8 metre larger-than-life-size coiled snake, representing the god Zeus Meilichius and his chthonic cult, was a noteworthy resident.[17]

The ever-pious Plutarch claimed that Philip lost his eye at the siege of Methone as a punishment from the gods for spying upon Olympias' secret ceremonies.[18] But Plutarch was demonstrably hostile to Philip's Molossian bride, possibly because her paganism offended him in his role as the senior Priest of Apollo at Delphi. Plutarch was not a 'historian' per se; he was in search of vices and virtues of men 'from a chance remark or a jest that might reveal more of a man's character than the mere feat of winning battles', and he believed in reincarnation, like the Pythagoreans before him.

When Philip was a hostage at Thebes in his teens, he was schooled, it is claimed, in the teachings of Pythagoras, who believed in the transmigration of the soul.[19] In tales dating to the period, souls were drawn out of the body by wands, emerging in the form of snakes or seen flying out of people's mouths as ravens.[20] Pythagoras himself believed he had once been Ephorbus, the warrior killed at Troy by the Spartan king Menelaus; as proof, he tracked down the beaten shield that Menelaus had dedicated to the temple of Apollo. Similarly, Empedocles, the Greek cosmogenic philosopher from Sicily who lived in Herodotus' day, claimed to have once been a boy, a girl, a bush, a bird and a scaly fish leaping out of the sea. One may wonder whether Scythian recreational drugs made their way to the philosophers of Hellas.[21]

The Abduction or Seduction of Tomb I

The theme of the Abduction of Persephone by Hades, the Underworld god otherwise known as Pluto, was painted on the northern wall of Tomb I, and this too could denote resurrection from the dead. Orphic symbolism in the myth of Persephone implied hope of a rebirth, as she and her mother Demeter were associated with immortality. So it appears that the royalty of Macedon might have believed in an afterlife in more literal terms than the Greeks.

Like the legendary abduction of the sea nymph Thetis by Achilles' father Peleus, which was a popular motif adorning the pottery of the day, an alternative explanation for the Tomb I art might be the symbolic removal of a woman from her parents' home to the bridegroom's house as part of the wedding contract.[22] The theme surrounding Persephone may be a metaphor for a forced or political marriage, followed by resistance to, and repudiation of, male authority, outcomes not unknown in the dynasties either side of Philip and Alexander. As told by the *Homeric Hymn to Demeter*, Persephone's mother, Demeter, was able to shape her daughter's destiny and reunite with her, despite her father Zeus offering Persephone to his own brother Hades, who was both her paternal and maternal uncle.

Marriage to an uncle was acceptable at the time, and we recall that Philip II offered his own daughter Cleopatra to the brother of his wife Olympias, who became the king of the Molossians in Epirus. As significantly, Philip offered a further daughter, Cynnane, to her own cousin Amyntas and the army felt justified in demanding the marriage of Adea to her uncle Arrhidaeus in the aftermath of infighting at Babylon. But rather than a bride given in well-intended wedlock, we see distress and fear in the faces of the women in the Tomb I abduction scene, underlining their helplessness in the face of a crime.[23]

If the Tomb I art is somehow emblematic of the life and deeds of the person buried, we need to question who chose it as appropriate. Manolis Andronikos suggested the artist was the celebrated Nicomachus of Thebes, as he is known to have painted this very theme. Another well-respected professor of classical art, who has authored books on its significance in the period of Philip and Alexander, observed that 'the spontaneity of the painting and its rapid execution indicates it must have been undertaken *al fresco*, when the plaster was wet'.[24] Lime-plaster dries slowly, allowing the paint to penetrate and impregnate it, which stabilizes the colour.[25]

The figures on the opposite walls, a sorrowful Demeter and the Three Fates looking on in sadness at Persephone's plight, appear just as hastily sketched: the Tomb I internal decoration, at least, was possibly a last-minute affair. So did the Abduction of Persephone represent the plight of the female occupant, as the presence of the marble shell and ivory comb in Tomb I might suggest? Or did it represent the deed of the male tomb occupant who fettered her, violently or otherwise, resulting in Zeus hurling a thunderbolt in approval, or in anger?

If Philip II was interred in the adjacent Tomb II, and assuming Tomb I is indeed the older structure as is generally believed from its simpler cist-grave design, then his father King Amyntas III, who died in 370/369 BC, is a strong candidate for the original occupant; the adjacent above-ground shrine might have been another 'Amyntaeum'. The evidence is, however, thrown into disorder by the bones the Antikas team found in the Vergina Laboratory, which meant we now have the remains of at least seven individuals, with no certainty of which bones are original, except for dating hierarchy suggested by their proximity to the stone floor, and whether they were cremated or not.

In the so-called 'Tomb of Eurydice' at Vergina, unearthed by Manolis Andronikos in 1987 and never fully excavated, we once more see Persephone and Hades painted on the marble throne, but here they are in a 'relationship of equality'; no fear or sign of unwillingness is present.[26] A further subterranean chamber, which has been linked to one of the wives of King Alexander I in the cluster of the queens at Aegae, contained at least twenty-six figurines of Demeter and Persephone. If a family relationship between these tombs was being implied, we might ponder what would have adorned the walls of the main chamber of Tomb II if its doors had not been shut for good in such obvious haste.

Funerary theology linked to the Abduction of Persephone also appears on a 4.5 × 3-metre floor mosaic in the multi-chamber tomb at Amphipolis, the city significant to the story of Macedon's emergence as a superpower, as well as Philinnion's reincarnation. Philip II was already worshipped 'as a god' at Amphipolis, just as Amyntas III had been revered at Pydna,[27] but it remains uncertain whether the depictions can in any way connect these burial sites more specifically.

The Casta Hill mausoleum at Amphipolis housed the bones of a woman aged around 60 and a little under 5ft 2in tall, along with a newborn baby, fragments of a cremated adult and the skeletal remains of two men aged approximately 35–45; each of them was 5ft–5ft 7in tall, and the younger appears to have suffered mortal wounds to the chest. Olympias was around 60 years old when she was executed on Cassander's urging, leading to speculation that Alexander's mother was reburied at Amphipolis, potentially explaining the presence of the additional 'Abduction of Persephone' mosaic. Fragmentary inscriptions and a now-lost tomb epigram last seen a century ago, suggest that her kin, the Molossian Aeacids from Epirus, had previously provided her with a modest tomb at Pydna sometime in the decade after Cassander's last son ruled Macedon and possibly when Pyrrhus controlled the region.[28]

The absence of any precious artefacts in the looted multi-chamber tomb at Amphipolis, the broken marble doors which had their protecting entry stones removed, as well as the scattered and fragmented nature of the bones lying strewn across the floor, suggest Pyrrhus' Celtic Gauls may have also ransacked the chambers before the tomb was resealed, that is, if the Romans under Aemilius Paullus, who entered Amphipolis in 167 BC, were not responsible for its looting.

In 2016, the site archaeologist, Dr Katerina Peristeri, claimed to have unearthed markings inside denoting the name 'Hephaestion', Alexander's closest companion and former second-in-command, who, many historians assume from their intimacy, was the king's lover. Further evidence of Hephaestion's presence is a 7-metre-tall statue found decades before which some assumed once adorned the mound, though probably marked a spot closer to the Strymon River. Known as the 'Lion of Amphipolis', it resembles the still-standing lion monument at ancient Ecbatana, modern Hamadan in Iran, reputed by some to be a further commemorative to Hephaestion, who died there the year before Alexander passed away in Babylon.[29] Alexander was so grief-stricken at his companion's death that he executed the doctor treating him. 'To lighten his sorrow', he reportedly destroyed the Temple of Asclepius at Ecbatana and sheared the manes of his horses and mules in typical Homeric mourning. Plutarch added that Alexander embarked on a 'blood-soaked hunt' of the nearby hill tribe as a 'sacrifice to the shades of his dead friend'.[30]

Hephaestion's corpse, after being embalmed we may presume, was taken to Babylon, where a lavish funeral pyre was to be built in seven tiers from the prows of 240 ships, with an almost 2km section of the city demolished to house the structure. It cost the lordly sum of 12,000 talents of silver or gold, almost a dozen years' total income of the city-state of Athens. We don't know how much of the monument was completed, but Perdiccas had the project cancelled at the assembly after Alexander's death when the succession issue was being debated.[31]

Alexander had requested permission from the oracle of Zeus-Ammon at Siwa in Egypt to have Hephaestion worshipped as a hero or god, but how his body might have ended up in the Amphipolis tomb is unexplained, although one scholar has speculated that his cremated remains returned with the fleet Alexander sent to Macedon.[32] A stone relief found near Pella confirms his heroization around 320 BC, but when considering the significance of inscriptions mentioning Hephaestion, we must recall that other returning wealthy veterans had served in the elite cavalry regiment which carried Hephaestion's name.[33]

I had often been asked to comment on Alexander's sexuality and his intimacy with his second-in-command, and always pointed out that the Greek world had a rather different view of gender relations than we have today. It was not unusual for a mature Greek male to take a younger male lover, an '*eromenos*', and the famous 300-strong crack-infantry regiment of Thebans known as the Sacred Band, which was wiped out by Philip and Alexander at the Battle of Chaeronea, was said to be comprised of 150 paired lovers who fought fiercely alongside their partners. It was their final, valiant stand at Chaeronea, when the other allied forces fled, that sealed their fate and their immortal fame.

A reconstruction of the multi-chambered tomb in the Casta Hill tumulus at Amphipolis. The blue mosaic floor can be seen with the Abduction of Persephone inlaid in stone. (*CC BY-SA.4.0*)

Pausanias of Orestis, the bodyguard who stabbed Philip II to death at Aegae, was apparently one of the king's paramours. He was said to be seeking revenge for being jilted in favour of another male youth of the same name, as well as for his more recent sexual assault by the baron Attalus and his muleteers in the course of a drunken banquet.[34] Little was made of the sexual peccadillos between men in the world of Philip and Alexander, who is said to have taken a eunuch from Darius III's court as a lover on campaign. And yet many of the scandal-ridden episodes stem from the 'Vulgate', or 'popular', biographical tradition that exploited any episode related to the steady moral decline of the 'storm-tossed' Alexander in the latter years of the campaign.[35] Like much else associated with the ever-campaigning kings, the truth behind their exploits was proverbially buried under successive layers of propaganda.

Perhaps the multi-chambered tomb at Amphipolis was designed to be the resting place of notables associated with Alexander, with its imagery providing them a form of immortality. Alexander's admiral Nearchus, the court notable Laomedon, another prominent ship commander named in India, as well as Aristonus, who was one of Alexander's bodyguards and who supported Olympias to the end when defending Amphipolis against Cassander, were each associated with the city. Only 'bone-work' might unravel who was buried in the Casta Hill tomb.[36]

The Reincarnation of Alexander

One further latter-day colourful tale of reincarnation comes from the Roman historian Cassius Dio and concerns Alexander himself. In AD 221, more than half a millennium after his death in Babylon, a mysterious figure appeared at the Danube with an entourage and claimed to be Alexander the Great. Entranced by the apparition, none dared oppose his progress; on the contrary, they provided him with food and lodging. After performing nocturnal rituals and burying a wooden horse, the figure departed once more.[37]

The disappearance of Alexander's tomb in Alexandria probably gave impetus to such stories, which came on the coat-tails of his own well-documented search for immortality. One popular tradition upholds that Alexander requested burial in the Siwa oasis in Egypt to be reunited with his immortal father, the composite god Zeus-Ammon. On his earlier visit to the temple, the priest had apparently addressed Alexander with '*O, Pai Dios*' ('Oh, son of God') rather than the standard '*O Paidion*' ('O my son'), a fortunate slip of the tongue of legendary proportion.[38]

Although his earthly father gave Alexander the legitimacy he needed to take control of Greece and the Persian invasion force, Philip, despite his own best efforts at becoming a 'thirteenth god' himself, had apparently not provided the immortal identity Alexander ultimately sought.[39] The Roman-era satirist Lucian ridiculed the association to Zeus-Ammon in his *Dialogues of the Dead*:

> Philip: 'You cannot deny that you are my son this time, Alexander; you would not have died if you had been Ammon's.'
>
> Alexander: 'I knew all the time that you, Philip, son of Amyntas, were my father. I only accepted the statement of the oracle because I thought it was good policy.'
>
> Philip: 'What, to suffer yourself to be fooled by lying priests?'
>
> Alexander: 'No, but it had an awe-inspiring effect upon the barbarians. When they thought they had a God to deal with, they gave up the struggle; which made their conquest a simple matter.'[40]

After hijacking the funeral bier, Ptolemy interred Alexander's mummified corpse at Memphis up the Nile. Statues of the Greek poets and philosophers most influential to the conqueror were found arranged in a semi-circle by excavations in the Avenue of Sphinxes in 1850/51 and may mark the very site.[41] Later in Ptolemy's reign, or in the kingship of his son Ptolemy II Philadelphus, Alexander's corpse was moved to the Sema in Alexandria, the communal mausoleum of the new dynastic line. Thereafter, various tales emerged about the whereabouts of the talisman that was Alexander's body in Egypt. The corpse was said to have been moved by Ptolemy IV, the great-grandson of Alexander's general, to the royal compound and may well now be under water, as the Ptolemaic royal burials were on the waterfront of Alexandria.[42]

Various new reports circulated: some claimed that Alexander's sarcophagus was eventually stripped of its gold, after which the corpse was interred in an alabaster tomb; another propagated a myth claiming that the empty green granite sarcophagus of the last Egyptian pharaoh, Nectanebo II, once held the body. That sarcophagus now sits in the British Museum. I had already written to the curators explaining that the museum's plaque was incorrect in stating that Alexander 'boosted his title to Egypt's throne by claiming Nectanebo was his father'. Alexander linked his divinity to the composite god of Siwa, not the demonstrably mortal and unsuccessful last Egyptian pharaoh of Egypt; this was a later association most likely perpetuated by the Ptolemies. Despite a grateful reply, the British Museum plaque has not been changed.

Over the last century, a number of archaeologists have insisted that they found Alexander's final resting place, either in Alexandria or at Siwa, where antique references to tomb sightings lent hope to excavations. One archaeologist, Liana Souvaltzi, reported that when she commenced her digs at the desert shrine in 1989, 'a miracle happened': 'two of the most dangerous snakes in the area slithered through my feet. This was considered to be a sign from Ammon.'[43] Possibly with an overdeveloped sense of the portentous, she was recalling Ptolemy's story that the god Ammon sent two hissing snakes to guide Alexander and his lost party to the temple in the remote desert oasis.[44]

The complete disappearance of Alexander's corpse from the Sema in Alexandria at the end of the Roman era lends an appropriate air of the supernatural to his legacy. Yet the words of Pericles, rendered timeless by Thucydides, suggest that Alexander should not be distraught: 'illustrious men have the whole earth for their tomb'. 'The mind boggles' at the arrangements Alexander 'might have made for his own obsequies', suggested one leading Alexander scholar, and yet a laconic, humble and somewhat piercing inscription found on Cyrus' single-storey tomb was said to have deeply moved the king:[45]

> Passer-by! I am Cyrus son of Cambyses,
> who founded the Persian Empire,
> and was King of Asia.
> Grudge me therefore not my monument.[46]

After reading it, Alexander was 'reminded of the uncertainty and mutability of life'.

A nineteenth-century photo of the Tomb of Cyrus the Great on the Murgab Plain near Pasargadae.

Tombs of the Achaemenids at Naqsh-e Rustam near Persepolis. (*CC BY-SA 4.0*)

In what have been termed Alexander's 'last plans' – the list of pending construction and campaign projects supposedly found at his death in the royal archive – he is said to have ordered the construction of a 'tomb for his father to match the greatest pyramids of Egypt'; we might interpret this as a 'great tumulus'.[47] Until Alexander had seen Cyrus' understated tomb, his father's vaulted chamber must have seemed a very modest memorial, embarrassing even, considering that he had campaigned by Mausolus' great resting place at Halicarnassus, the Great Pyramid at Giza and the spectacular rock-cut tombs of the Achaemenids at Naqsh-e Rustam near Persepolis. Luckily for Manolis Andronikos, the Argead kings of Macedon *were* supposed to confine themselves to the smaller realm of Aegae.

Clearly, much of what has been written about Philip and his son over the centuries is highly dubious, especially the reporting of Alexander's death, his tombs, afterlife and the succession instructions he left, which amounted to none as far as the historians old and new are concerned. My enthusiasm to overturn the 'standard model' of Alexander, as I termed it, had been the impetus behind my treatise on the great king. But what I learned next in my research of the Vergina excavations reinforced my own hunch about the gold-accessorized 'Amazon' of Tomb II, whose identity, I felt, now needed a 'reincarnation' of its own.

Chapter 14

The Queen's Gold and the King's Craftsmen

> The second hardest thing in nature is the greed for gold, which is the most stubborn of all things.
> —Pliny the Elder

Since man first stumbled upon its gleam, gold has caused passions to rise and wars to be fought over the wealth and power it came to signify. The appeal of gold lies in its visual beauty, its rarity and its virtual indestructability through the ages. If iron was synonymous with bladed weapons of war, gold was the international tender of royalty in ancient Macedon.[1]

Once rare ore-bearing sites had been identified, extracting gold in a ready-to-use state was relatively simple in antiquity, either as nuggets from veins in rocks or as alluvial deposits from riverbeds. References to 'pure gold', however, are an anachronism, as it naturally contains impurities of silver, copper and often traces of iron, along with tin, mercury and platinum group elements. Early unrefined gold objects from the sixth and fifth centuries BC are often pale or lemony in colour at around 75 per cent purity, and would better be referred to as 'electrum' alloy.[2]

The Fortunate Folly of the Five Gold Rings

Beside the Scythian gold-faced bow-and-arrow quiver, or '*gorytos*', found with the woman in the antechamber of Tomb II, five gold bands or small hoops were recovered from the ash of rotted arrow shafts, with one band slightly larger than the others.[3] A couple appeared to be prised open and out of circular shape, but they were carefully closed again into perfect rings before being put on display in the Vergina Archaeological Museum.

Manolis Andronikos believed that the bands were once wrapped around sheaves of arrows; seventy-four arrowheads lay in the ash, which suggests fourteen or fifteen arrows must have been clasped by each. But I couldn't help thinking that the feather flights would have been ruined when pulled through these modestly sized gold bands, which I doubted could have clasped anywhere near this many arrows.[4] Furthermore, three sizes of Scythian-shaped arrowheads were identified, suggesting there ought to have been three arrow clusters, not five. The Vergina museum curators have since revised Andronikos' explanation, and the display plaque now states that the rings were the decorative part of a now-decomposed ceremonial bow.

Theo agreed with the new prognosis, but I pointed out that Scythian compound bows were flat in cross-section, not round, and made from laminated wood with horn, and traces of the latter ought to have survived. Construction of these extremely powerful recurve bows could take several years of seasoning the wood and then gluing layers together, so they were more often passed down the generations rather than being buried with the dead. When the strings were drawn back, Scythian-styled bows were held away from the chest in a technique known as the 'floating anchor', and they vibrated violently each time an arrow was loosed. I could not envisage the delicate gold bands staying attached to such a weapon, ceremonial or not.[5]

Laura concurred and suggested the hoops might be decorative elements from a Scythian whip, which made more sense.[6] One ring was slightly larger, and two more appear to taper slightly. After we had stared at the collection for some time, it became apparent that the five rings could be rearranged to confirm to a gradually tapering handle.[7] Like the small Scythian axe known as a 'sagaris', horsewhips were a common accessory and were reputedly effective against former slaves, claimed Herodotus, whose tale of Amazon-Scythian integration was not always one of marital bliss.[8]

According to his *Histories*, the settled rather than pastoral tribes were known as 'Royal Scythians', being descended from Zeus' chosen grandson. During a twenty-eight-year absence when tribesmen were fighting Medes and Cimmerians in an audacious encroachment into the Persian Empire, the left-behind Scythian women consorted with their captive slaves, who had been blinded in their cruel but practical tradition. The children from this union had now grown to manhood, and learning of the circumstances of their birth, they resolved to take control of the tribe and oppose the returning men who had enslaved their fathers.[9] Earthworks were thrown up around the settlement, with a defensive ditch in front, and positions were manned in readiness for an attack by the homeward-bound campaigners, who failed to breach the perimeter despite repeated attempts.

One pragmatic Scythian realized that their strategy was self-defeating: if they won the battle they would lose their very own slaves. 'I propose, therefore, that we stop using spears and arrows, and go for them each one of us with a horsewhip,' he said. The plan was artful: when slaves were confronted by traditionally armed Scythians, they were compelled to fight as equals, but if approached with nothing more than a horsewhip, they would recall their lowly status and submit. Sure enough, the defenders lost their courage and fled.

Despite the attraction of Laura's suggestion, and before I had seen the gold bands from Tomb II close up, I threw in an additional idea: five in number

A Scythian wielding a 'sagaris', the distinctive axe, as depicted on an Attic amphora dated to 510–500BC. (*Louvre*)

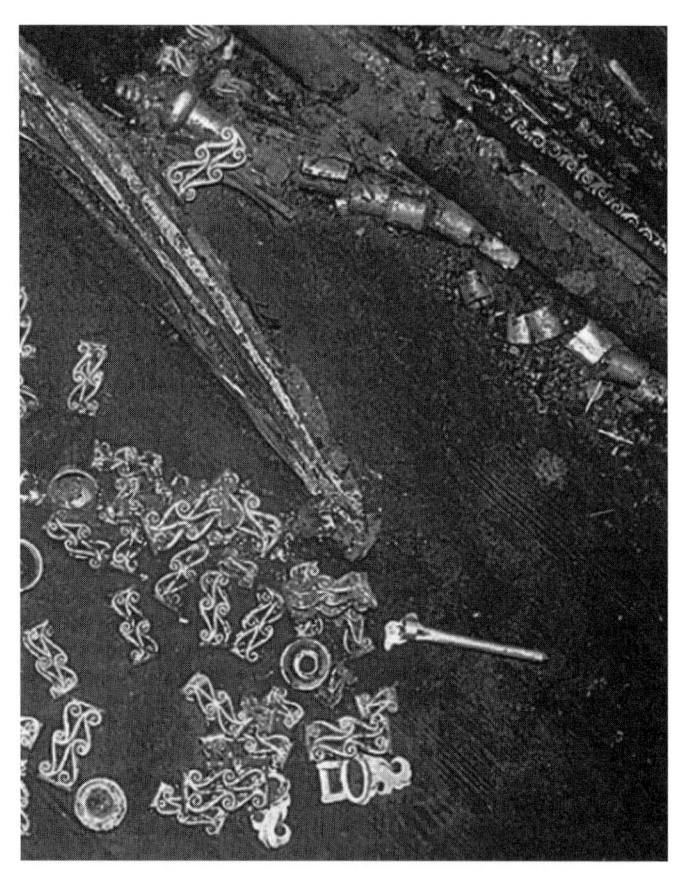

208 *Unearthing the Family of Alexander the Great*

Above: the remains of a whip with gold bands found in a Scythian burial site. Below: an illustration of an intact Scythian whip.[10]

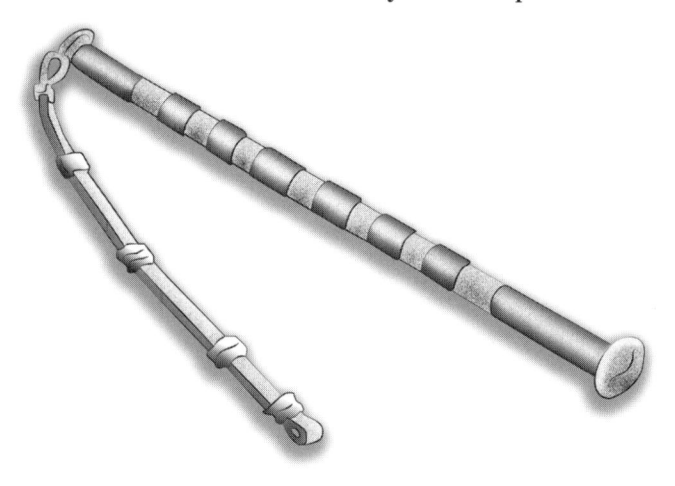

with one slightly larger, they might be archers' rings for the fingers and thumb, ceremonial in function but based on a well-documented ancient tradition. Archers' rings were ubiquitous in the ancient world, being worn on the thumb to lock the bowstring when it was drawn back with an arrow already attached. But they were of a distinct shape that protruded out on one side to provide an element of protection to the thumb.

Then I found references to a particular firing technique in which the bow string was gripped with the three lower fingers of the right hand, with the index finger pointing towards the target. One translation of the technique suggested that in this 'peculiar draw', the little finger, the ring finger and the middle finger were locked on the string, with the index finger again positioned along the arrow. But it was what came next that caught my attention: 'finger-tips of gold, copper and iron are used by archers employing this technique.'

The explanation appeared in a 1972 technical paper on Sassanid cavalry equipment and tactics in which the author, an emeritus professor of Iranian studies, concluded: 'It is evident that if the Sassanian archer wore rings upon his fingers, it was with these that he was accustomed to draw the bow.'[11] The Sassanid Empire appeared post-AD 224, well after the era of our entombed 'Scythian Amazon', but Sassanid bowmen, early Parthian horse archers and the formidable Massagetae before them, whose promiscuous queen Tomyris is said to have beheaded Cyrus the Great, shared common geography with Scythians and a heritage of lethal cavalry bowmen.

My curiosity was further sharpened when I read that five bronze rings had been found in a grave in ancient Colchis in what is now Georgia, dating to the end of the second millennium BC. Lyn Webster Wilde, who journeyed to Ukraine to search for evidence of the legendary Amazons, described the grave in some detail: the woman, clearly a warrior, had been buried in a sitting position with a short sword resting on her knees, with an iron dagger placed on two small stones in front of her. A lance-point was lying next to her, under which the jawbone of a horse was found; the rest of the animal may have been eaten at the funeral. Two bracelets, pearls and earthenware vessels were found besides the rings. Her skull showed signs of a serious wound in the process of healing.[12]

Managing a highly tensioned Scythian bow obviously required finger protection, and modern archers use leather finger guards. Wear and tear can be seen on the bones of two right-hand fingers of a woman warrior found at Chertomylk near the Dnieper River in south-central Ukraine, indicating unprotected heavy bow usage. Women with weapons were found in fifty-three of the graves, including a girl aged 10–12 buried with chain-mail armour. After reading this, I thought that the five gold rings might have come to ceremonially symbolize an archer's draw hand.[13]

On 8 April 2017, I contacted Lyn in rural Wales. She described the chill that ran down her spine when she first heard about the grave, as the woman was of sufficient status for a male, perhaps a servant, to have been killed for burial beside her. Lyn suggested that I contact Professor Renate Rolle, the German archaeologist who, in her opinion, knew more about these warrior women than anyone alive, having published her finds in 1989 after many years excavating in the steppes of Russia and Ukraine. Lyn had herself sought Renate out in 1997 and found her there on a dig. I found Renate's contact details at Hamburg University and was told she had retired, so I was directed to a colleague who was then working on an archaeological site in Jordan.

I decided to contact Adrienne Mayor at Stanford University, a historian of ancient science and classical folklorist who had also published her own research on tribal warrior women who epitomized the legendary Amazons. During our discussions, and by pure coincidence, Adrienne informed me that she had been corresponding with the Antikas team since 2008, and more recently in her quest to include detail on the Tomb II female in her book. Adrienne was extremely helpful and she, in turn, put me in touch with an archeologist and a curator of the Hermitage in St Petersburg, where artefacts are stored from an ever-increasing number of graves found in the Scythian regions.[14] Corpses from some of the female graves had either been mummified or preserved in permafrost, an environment that preserves the skin, enabling the intricate animal tattoos to be seen for the first time under infrared light.[15]

I ended up corresponding with Dr Andrey Alexeev, head of the Department of Archaeology of Eastern Europe and Siberia, and he graciously provided his opinion: the types of ring from Vergina are very rare. He had only witnessed anything similar at one 'barrow' tumulus, known locally as a 'kurgan', and they were, indeed, found on the fingers. But these particular rings were stylized like solid bracelets, not rings that could be closed or prised apart. Curiously, the burial site at Chertomylk dates to 340–320 BC, coinciding with the Vergina tombs. I felt it was just as significant that no decorative bands from Scythian bows had been found in any graves.

My investigation into archers' rings was off to a promising start until Laura warned me that the five bands found from the Tomb II antechamber looked too large to have been worn by the 'Amazon', or anyone else for that matter. Moreover, close-up images of the rings revealed they had sharp edges, as if they were digging into whatever they once clasped. Yet the vexing sense of scale in reconstructions of ritual weapons and armour needs to be put in perspective. I had already noted an Etruscan ceremonial shield on display in the British Museum, which appeared far too large to have been practically wielded in battle. Similarly, at Vergina, the reconstruction of the Tomb II gold, glass and ivory shield with its Amazonomachy at the centre appears oversized when compared to the corselet of its owner. Theo informed me that the original conservator tasked with piecing it together in Thessalonica agreed.

I wondered how the scale of the rings compared in the overall sense of things, and though my foray into ancient archery may have been a self-indulgent folly, there was one further idiosyncrasy that had yet to be explained.

On one recent visit to the Vergina museum, Laura was able to photograph some of the exhibits relevant to her study. Her close-up photographs of the five bands revealed the joint on each was, in fact, a 'tear' line; the joins were ragged and uneven, and the fracture looked to have been caused by stress. They *were* originally solid bands, and not adjustable rings. The only explanation I could proffer was that whatever the rings clasped, originally circular in shape, had expanded in the tomb's humidity before finally decomposing, causing the soft gold to tear at the weakest point and prizing some of them apart. Their provenance remained unclear, in my mind at least.

Alongside the weapons found with the female warrior, Laura questioned why there was no trace of a shield. I replied that if she was a Scythian or a 'horseback warrior', the answer would be straightforward: mounted archers were often depicted without shields, and those who did carry them held the small Thracian crescent-shaped 'pelta', the root of the name given to lightly armed skirmishers known as 'peltasts' in Greece. Images we have suggest they were lightweight and made either of wicker or hide stretched across a wooden frame. These would have decomposed in the tomb over 2,300 years.

Artefacts and Artifice: Fingerprinting Gold

My off-target theorizing had fortunately drawn me deeper into the world of Scythian artefacts. I soon learned that one of the fifty burial sites at Chertomylk in Ukraine had yielded another gold-encased Scythian bow-and-arrow quiver. Close inspection made it clear that though it was stamped with a different pattern than the '*gorytos*' found in Tomb II, the overall placement and segmentation of images was almost identical. The scarcity of these gold and silver quivers, along

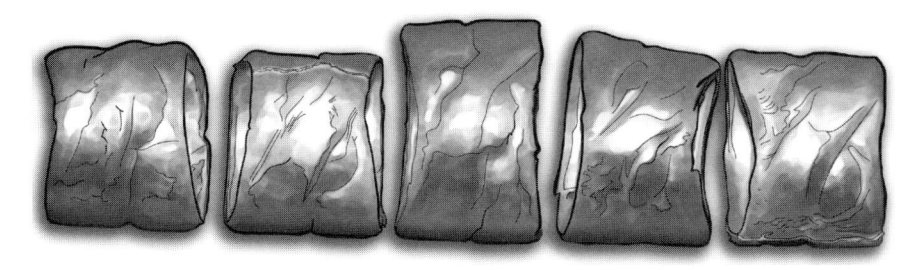

A close-up artist's rendering of the five gold bands. The tears are visible at the top of the second band and at the bottom of the fifth band and appear stress-induced.

with their resemblance in appearance and the similar dating of the graves to the era of Philip and Alexander, struck me as relevant to the identity of the 'Amazon'.

The relative proportions of the impurities found in gold – the silver, copper, iron, tin, mercury and platinum group elements, for example – could, in theory, provide a 'diagnostic fingerprint' to the source of a noble metal.[16] One example of this type of forensic approach concerns the Bronze Derveni 'Krater', or water jug: the head curator of sculptures at the National Archaeological Museum of Athens pointed out that the high-tin bronze alloy from which the spectacular jug was fashioned was commonplace in Macedon, but not Athens, where it was originally thought to have been manufactured, judging from its design. So the provenance of the metal challenged scholarly opinion on where the jug was made.[17] Herodotus, Thucydides and Strabo each confirmed that an industry of fashioning precious metals into final form existed in ancient Macedon.[18]

I wondered whether the golden artefacts found at Vergina had undergone similar analyses. I was informed that Dr Michael Vavelidis at the Department of Mineralogy, Petrology and Economic Geology at Aristotle University had presented a paper on the Vergina tomb finds in 2009/2010.[19] I was stunned by the results: archaeometric studies of the metal confirmed the silver in the Tomb II quiver was mined in north-east Chalcidice in ancient Macedon.[20] Dr Vavelidis' opinion had also been published on 13 March 2008 in the national newspaper *Ethnos*. Regarding the 'provenance of precious metals used in the royal burials' at Vergina, the gold was from the nearby Haliacmon River, and the silver used in other tomb artefacts came from the mines at Lavrion south of Athens.

Assuming Dr Vavelidis' conclusions were correct, either a locally based craftsman in Macedon was fabricating Scythian-styled goods for export to wealthy Scythian chieftains, or raw ingots of gold and silver were being shipped from Macedon to Greek artisans in the Bosporus, where they were fashioned into the ornate artefacts found in the Scythian graves. By 480 BC, Greek settlers had established the political federation of the Kingdom of Bosporus in what is now the eastern Crimea, driven by exactly this type of commerce. Stonework in Scythian tombs suggests the Bosporan Greeks had built them, along with the conclusion that 'the Scythian elite was highly Hellenised'.[21] A thriving destination was the well-known metalworking centre of Panticapaeum, identified with modern Kerch on the Crimean Peninsula.[22]

Greece had relied on grain from the Bosporus region ever since Persia annexed Egypt and the Nile Delta ports. The Mediterranean coastline and its interior had also been off limits to the Greeks once Carthage and the Etruscans blocked both sea and land routes to the west and north of Italy by 535 BC.[23] The Persian navy had for a time closed the Black Sea as well, so grain imports from Sicily and the northern Adriatic had to be sourced, until the armies of Darius and Xerxes were defeated at Marathon and Plataea.[24] Favourable trading contracts had since been re-established with the Kingdom of Bosporus, so that in Philip's reign more than one-third of all grain imports to Greece originated there. It was in this benign environment that Greek traders flourished on the northern shore of the Black Sea, which they renamed the 'Euxine' or 'Hospitable Sea', with Ionian Greeks having taken refuge in the region from their troubled outposts in Anatolia.[25] The remains of their settlements can be seen at Sinope, Olbia and at Chersonesus by modern Kherson, where sixth-century BC ruins have been termed a 'Ukrainian Pompeii'.

I replied to the Hermitage curators and asked if any 'archaeometallurgy' testing of the Chertomylk gold had been undertaken, to establish if we are indeed looking at quivers made from the same metal deposits. I knew that any fresh analysis of these artefacts, under lock and key in the Hermitage and at Vergina, would not prove easy, but before the Hermitage replied, I discovered a paper which provided me with an even stronger conviction that the golden quiver from Tomb II had local origins, not Scythian.

In a jointly authored article by a senior research assistant at the Leningrad Division of the Institute of Archaeology and a senior lecturer at Saratov University, I found a revealing statement: 'there can be little doubt that all three gold scabbards and the four gold arrow quivers found in Ukraine, all of them ceremonial rather than for daily use, belong to the same series of manufacture ... produced if not at

Above, the gold Scythian arrow quiver, or '*gorytos*', found at Chertomylk. Its overall layout and positioning of images is remarkably similar to the quiver found in Tomb II at Vergina. (*Hermitage Museum. Alamy.com*)

the same time, then with only a short interval between them.' It went on to state that they belonged to the very same burial set as the gold quiver from Vergina. Each of them dated to the same decades, broadly 350–325 BC, and each had been commissioned from a 'Greek' centre of manufacture.[26]

One of the gold scabbards now resides in Gallery No. 158 at the Metropolitan Museum of Art in New York, with a description which reinforced the common origins: 'Although the scabbard is of Scythian type, the decoration is Greek in style and undoubtedly of Greek workmanship. Similar sheet-metal goldwork from the royal cemetery at Vergina in northern Greece and from kurgans ... of Scythian rulers in the North Pontic region have been linked to the same workshop.'

Mikhail Treister at the German Archaeological Institute in Berlin is an expert on Scythian grave goods. In a 2008 paper he discussed one of these four gold quivers, which had been found in a grave or a 'barrow' at Karagodeuaskhsh in Russia, probably belonging to a king of the Phateli tribe. In our subsequent correspondence, he was careful to point out to me that the '*gorytos*' has survived in fragments only, yet the pattern appeared very similar, if not identical, to the example found at Vergina, and was potentially hammered on the very same matrix or mould. Andronikos had come to the same conclusion in his 1984 publication and I had overlooked it.[27] Mikhail Treister's paper concluded that there is no 'other plausible explanation' except that these are 'evidence of diplomatic contacts on the highest level'.[28]

However, in the correspondence that followed, Dr Treister warned me that it is 'naive' to think that the analysis of gold can point to the originating mine or river. This seemed to contradict Dr Vavelidis' conclusions, and I was now confused. To try to throw light on the matter, Laura put me in touch with Christos Katsifas, the chemist who found silver on the stray Vergina bones which were reunited with 'the prince' in Tomb III. As Christos explained it: 'serious scientific groups with funding have tried to approach the subject with no final conclusions.' He explained that provenance studies of ancient gold artefacts are difficult: the high hopes of the scientific community for platinum group elements quickly evaporated as did the search for trace element patterns, and isotope analyses remain inconclusive. Dr Vavelidis had apparently never published the results of his isotopic study so the basis for his statements remained unknown. I needed to know more.

Professor Paul Keyser is a physicist and classicist who has published on ancient science and technology, and his interests include isotope determination of ancient coinage and even the history of alchemy. The detailed explanation he provided for me corroborated Christos' comments: determining the origins of silver is 'possible, but chancy; but the provenancing of gold is not yet possible, although there are prospects of at least determining a few facts about the kind of source of the gold and the type of processing that was performed' on it.[29] 'Plan on spending

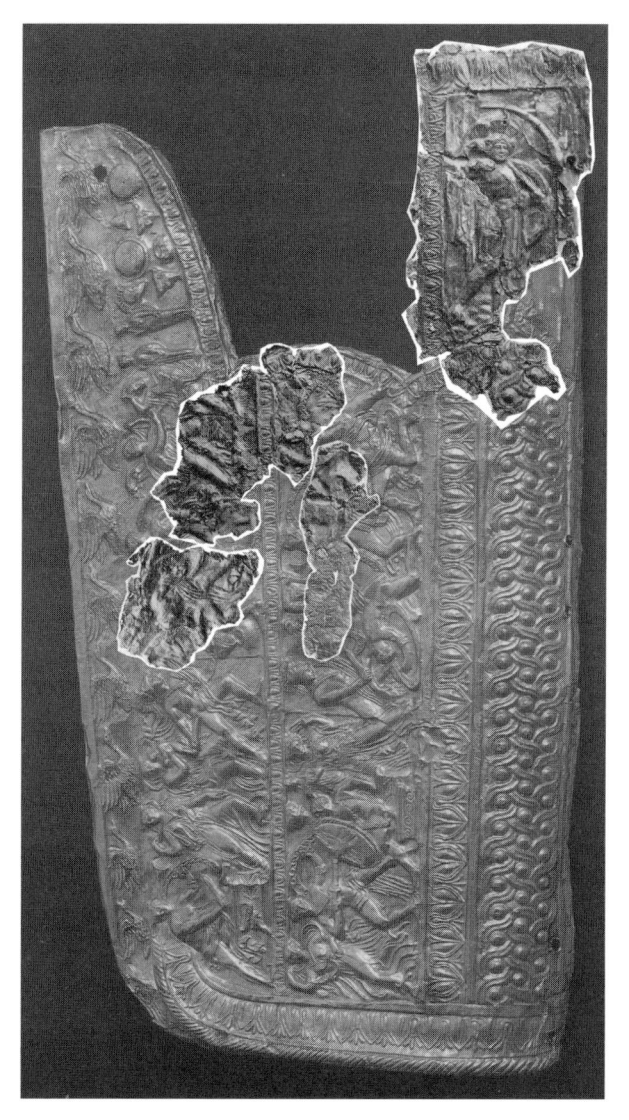

The Tomb II quiver in gold with the superimposed fragments from the *gorytos* found at Karagodeuaskhsh in Russia. The fragments appear to be an exact fit. (*Permission of M. Treister; image from Treister, 2005*)

several thousand dollars, and many weeks; be willing to accept an ambiguous or inconclusive result,' he finally cautioned.

Silver was known by the ancient metalworkers to be present in lead ores, often as sulphides, and it had to be separated out using a process known as 'cupellation'. This involved smelting the ore and draining the base metal 'slag', which had a lower melting point than silver and which oxidized in the process; any gold present settled with the silver. Extraction by this means would retain a small but detectable amount of lead, which can be analyzed in a mass spectrometer, and paired ratios of impurities are then compared with known mining sources.

But the problems of identifying the 'signature impurities' are complicated when native mixes of gold and silver existed naturally in the form of electrum alloy, as is common. Electrum was often 'enhanced' by craftsmen to adjust its properties and colour, either by 'whitening' and 'diluting' with more 'cupelled' silver, or 'reddening' and 'hardening' it with copper, for example.[30] Many noble metals and alloys found in tombs and graves had been manipulated, one way or another, before being fashioned into artefacts or currency. Some ancient artefacts were even 'recycled' and melted down to be used in new pieces of jewellery or ornaments. A notorious example of a more devious manipulation was the silver-plating of baser-metal coins, and it is still possible to see 'test cuts' on the edges of ancient currency to reveal the inner material, the most effective method of assaying metal and detecting fraud until Archimedes developed the theory of specific gravity. So, in the case of many grave goods, any useful 'diagnostic fingerprint' was lost in either the smelting process or the craftsman's art.

I also understood the problems of using 'invasive' forensics which could destroy the irreplaceable artefacts being analyzed: any 'bulk' study of metal wares would demand cutting cross-sections before exposing them to a beam of subatomic particles or to a similarly destructive 'wet' chemical analysis.[31] A surface study of an object using non-intrusive X-ray fluorescence provides results on only a microscopically thin layer of the material's skin. If a metal had been buried for centuries in acidic soil, the most reactive 'baser' elements that needed analyzing would have already leached out of the surface layer and the results would be distorted by a process known as 'surface enrichment'.[32] Professor Keyser's final words on the matter were that unless researchers have made a major advance that they have published, they have no basis for saying anything about the provenance of the gold.

Dr Alexeev at the Hermitage was cited in the Russian study on the Chertomylk gold finds and quivers, and he had his own hypothesis on the Vergina gold and silver artefacts: these ceremonial weapons were diplomatic gifts exchanged during the reign of Alexander the Great, when Macedon was trying to penetrate the Black Sea, and they were manufactured on his orders. Alexander's coinage has been found in Bosporus-region graves.[33]

The historians Arrian and Curtius detailed the diplomacy between the Scythian and the Macedonian campaign expedition travelling through Asia. We have scant record of the treasures Alexander sent back as trophies from his campaign across Persia, apart from 500-talents' weight of frankincense and 100 of myrrh to his austere tutor, Leonidas, who had once chided him as a child for wasting the precious incense.[34] We also know he sent 1,000 talents for his regent Antipater to wage war against Agis of Sparta, along with a research grant for Aristotle, and we hear of Persian armour from the great set-piece battles shipped to Greece as votives for its temples. But undocumented precious goods may well have been sent to his mother sister, and half-sisters, including Scythian booty.

However, what scholars did agree on undermined this notion: the Vergina golden quiver was from the same artistic tradition as those found across Scythian lands in Ukraine and the Russian steppes, all dating to the same tightly triangulated period, and all probably from the very same *Greek* workshop. The correlation includes the gold thread and purple fabric found on the bones of the Tomb II 'Amazon', which is dated to a similar example stored in the Hermitage.[35]

Dr Alexeev reminded me that grave artefacts were not necessarily manufactured where the gold originated: they could have been fashioned by Greeks in the Crimea using Macedonian gold.[36] I discussed this with Adrienne Mayor and we both questioned the likelihood of this, bearing in mind that the Scythians had their own rich ore deposits, as did northern Thrace, each a more convenient location for shipping gold to the Bosporan metalworkers. Adrienne explained that the mysterious whereabouts of Scythian gold deposits were of keen interest to the Greeks.

Justin's description of the aftermath of Philip's battle with King Atheas of the Danubian Scythians includes a rather revealing statement:

> Though the Scythians were superior in courage and numbers, they were defeated by the subtlety of Philip. Some 20,000 young men and women were taken, and a vast number of cattle, but *no gold or silver*. This was the first proof they had of the *poverty of Scythia*.

It seems that while the Scythians had their own gold deposits, they didn't mint them into a currency, or exploit them commercially for export in final artistic form. But Macedon clearly did.

Despite the inconclusive evidence suggested by the archaeometallurgy, I was rapidly coming to the conclusion that the production centre for these ceremonial weapons could, in fact, be close to Vergina. And I couldn't help but sense that the 'nationality' of the Tomb II 'Amazon' was linked to the ethnicity of the gold quiver.

So had Philip returned from the Danube with a captive Scythian concubine, like Theseus of legend who abducted the Amazon Antiope and ferried her back to Athens? Or had the woman, like Medea of Colchis who returned with Jason and his Argonauts, fallen for her captor and willingly been installed at the court of Pella? Neither, I fancied, and I told the Antikas team of my theory that the Tomb II Amazon might be Macedonian-born, like the quiver itself.

Laura was understandably sceptical and questioned why a Scythian-style weapon would have ended up in Tomb II if it did not belong to Philip II's Scythian wife. She pertinently pointed out that the '*gorytos*' was the only example found in Hellenic territory. It was part of an ensemble that included gilded greaves and a silver-gilded iron 'gorget' or throat protector, otherwise known as a 'pectoral'. If we recall Philip's shattered collarbone sustained when fighting the Illyrians, we have some notion of how important this type of upper armour was, explaining why an iron-reinforced pectoral was found in the main chamber too. Laura further believed there were other Scythian indicators in the antechamber of Tomb II: the decorative ivory figures on the remains of the antechamber couch depicted horses and an archer, with horses also featuring on the woman's pectoral.

The couch, a '*kline*' to the Greeks, was fashioned out of wood, with ivory, gold and glass decoration on each side, and may have been purely funerary, or a piece of furniture that had featured in the owner's household. The antechamber example has been reconstructed at the Vergina Museum, where the display cabinet currently reads: 'In the two deep friezes on the long sides there were scenes of Greeks fighting barbarians.' Men and horses are depicted in vigorous poses, including one man kneeling, supposedly an archer, but I could see no obvious barbarian dress. The reconstruction at Vergina is incomplete due to the many lost pieces, so what the gap-ridden puzzle presents may lie in the eye of the beholder, and in this case, the hand of the conservator who pieced the fallen puzzle together.

As a riposte, I pointed out to Laura that the woman's gilded upper-chest-and-throat protector, the pectoral, is said to be 'Thracian' in design, and so the same question could be asked of its origins: what was a Thracian relic doing in Tomb II if it did not belong to Philip's Thracian wife Meda, as the Vergina Museum curators believe? The ceremonial pectoral would have been worn to complement a breastplate or cuirass, traces of which were found. But I soon discovered that these items have only been dubbed 'Thracian' because most examples – though in silver and not gold – were found in modern Bulgaria, which covers much of ancient Thrace, where other artefacts were clearly Greek.[37] There is additional evidence that Thracian tombs, like those in Scythia, were built by Greek masons, with overlapping design themes. As one commentator noted: 'Greek craftsmen were actively participating in the creation of local elite culture.'[38]

In a paper written in 1985, the now senior lecturer of archaeology and classics at Liverpool University suggested that the pectorals and other 'Thracian' tomb finds also date to the same era as the gilded quivers.[39] The design, she added, may have been influenced by the military reforms of Philip II or Alexander when Macedon annexed Thrace, while the horseman we can see depicts Heracles the 'huntsman',

Artist's rendering of the reconstructed inlaid couch at the Vergina Archaeological Museum.

the imagery associated with the Argead royal house. Upon reading this, I ventured, once again, that the origin of the pectorals was a local Macedonian workshop.

I tried to arrange my placeholders of logic and pull this information together into a coherent explanation or two. The simplest looked like this: a local Macedonian craftsman, who made precious objects for both a domestic and export trade that was capitalizing on the new contact with the Scythian world, gave a gold quiver to his king to ingratiate himself at the court, possibly to obtain royal manufacturing contracts. The Roman historian Livy described the metal workshops at Pella, which had produced items of gold, silver and bronze since the reign of Archelaus at the end of the fifth century BC.[40] Bronze arrowheads and lead missiles inscribed with Philip's name, along with the blades of the spears and pikes of his infantry, were all made locally, as was coinage churned out from state mints.[41]

My second explanation was just as straightforward: the Macedonian king might have purchased the locally made ceremonial weapons and armour for a wife or daughter, either as a coming-of-age present or as a wedding gift. If the woman had distinguished herself in battle, the choice of weapons over jewellery is explained. This brings us to the exquisite diadem also found in antechamber of Tomb II, 'the most beautiful piece of jewellery to have come down to us from the ancient world', in Andronikos' opinion. Apart from an austere 'Illyrian-type' broach, this was the only feminine finery found. But diadems were not found in any Scythian female graves.

Eminent scholars such as Nicholas Hammond, besides Theo and Laura, understandably believed that the Tomb II female could be Philip's Scythian bride or concubine, the hypothetical daughter of King Atheas. It was a logical theory which unified the woman with the Scythian bow-and-arrow quiver. But the growing evidence I saw for the domestic production of the very artefact that pointed to that tribal identification, left the door open for other contenders. So I set out to argue their case.

Chapter 15

Warrior Father, Warrior Daughter and the Bactrian

> A good decision is based on knowledge,
> not numbers.
> —Plato

Eugene Borza once insightfully explained that when attempting to unravel the 'true' character of Alexander the Great, a historian needs to deal with three incarnations of the Macedonian king: the 'mythological-romanticized', the 'historical' character and Alexander 'the man'. But there were now several possible incarnations for the Tomb II 'Amazon': there was either Philip II's late wife Meda – which remained the name backed by the Archaeological Museum of Vergina – or a daughter of King Atheas of the Danubian Scythians, an identification favoured by the Antikas team and supported by the Scythian bow-and-arrow quiver. I had introduced a third possibility in 2015, but I now believed there ought to be a fourth candidate on the table, one which has been curiously absent from papers over the past three years since the age of the enigmatic warrioress had been revised upwards.

Theo and Laura's five-year-long study of the bones provided more accurate age profiling for both Tomb II occupants: the male was aged 45 +/– 4 years at death, and the female 32 +/– 2 years, supported by her previously unseen pubic symphysis joint, a more accurate ageing marker, along with her fused collarbone. Although they had given her the statutory four-year leeway in their paper, they felt the evidence suggested the woman was closer to 30.

When reading their conclusions, I first questioned how these ranges fitted the life expectancy of the day. The study of skeletal remains suggests that longevity averages in ancient Greece were around 43 years for men and an even shorter 34 for women. These average lifespans are something of a reversal of the demographics in today's society, where female life expectancy at age 83 is three years longer than that of a male at 79.[1]

Considering the lifestyle markers and wounds found on the Tomb II bones, the short life expectancy is not surprising, but there was another significant factor that impacted female mortality rate: childbirth. In the ancient world, girls married young and were expected to produce offspring when hardly physically mature. The inscriptions on the tombstones in the Aegae necropolis confirm these were predominantly female graves, probably stemming from a high fatality rate giving birth.[2] The treatises ascribed to the medical school of Hippocrates titled *On the Seventh Month Baby* and *On the Eighth Month Baby* hint at the ubiquity of premature delivery.

In the case of men, war culled many young, and yet Philip was still planning his ambitious invasion of the Persian Empire in his mid-40s. We read of Alexander's veteran crack infantry brigade, the Silver Shields, fighting well into their 60s, when they played a pivotal role in the early years of the Successor Wars. Antipater, the tenacious regent who served both Philip and Alexander, was still in office and campaigning through his 70s, as were the dynasts Ptolemy, Seleucus and Lysimachus, who never lost the zeal they first forged with Alexander fifty years before. The Roman satirist Lucian authored a book titled *The Long Lived* and listed a number of eminent philosophers and politicians from this era who made it into their 80s, 90s and even to the venerated age of 104.

The royalty, their court nobles and the barons of Macedon would have faced less hazardous physical labour, days of battle and hunting aside, and even then, they would have been protected by bodyguards. They had access to physicians, a varied diet and were less exposed to famine than the peasant population. Overall, however, the ancient immune system must have been far more resilient to disease and infection in the absence of refrigeration, sanitized water, waste extraction and antibiotics. Their skeletal remains still show the signs of arthritis, tuberculosis and pleurisy alongside other debilitating conditions; the ancients simply had to function and cope with acute illnesses and disabilities we can cure or alleviate today.

The Tomb II female would have been considered 'mature', and the only remaining contender from Philip's *named* wives who might fit this age was his probable sixth, Meda, daughter of the Thracian king, Cothelas, thought to have married Philip II some three to six years before his death; hence her name plaque at Vergina. But if the youth of Philip's other wives at wedlock is any indicator, Meda may well have been younger than 30 when he died.[3] Her name was never mentioned at Philip's funeral, nor in a ritual suicide, whether voluntary to honour her king or 'required' by Alexander and/or Olympias, who was demonstrably in no mood to give any of the then-surviving wives a state burial in a sumptuously large tomb antechamber at Aegae at Philip's death.

Meda was, in fact, only ever mentioned once in ancient texts, appearing in a list of Philip's spouses in the pages of the Greek antiquarian Athenaeus, who was regurgitating an older now-lost source, though how faithfully is questionable.[4] Philip's unremarkable political marriage to the Thracian Meda resulted in no children we know of, and she remains an obscure character without any of the martial exploits that would have qualified her for burial as a weaponized 'Amazon'.[5] Nowhere is the existence of Getae female cavalry units mentioned or women horseback archers in Thrace, so Meda is not an obvious fit for the golden Scythian quiver or, in fact, any other weapon found in the chamber.

The idea of a Scythian princess, first voiced by Nicholas Hammond in 1978 and endorsed by the Antikas team, is an elegant solution which, nevertheless, presents similar problems, not least the fact that her very existence was never mentioned. Tellingly, the conjectured Scythian princess did not feature in the political bargaining of her father, King Atheas, who had to resort to 'adopting' Philip to form an alliance, when offering a daughter in marriage would have been simpler and with clear precedent at Philip's polygamous court. It has been proposed that a daughter was captured after Atheas' defeat, when Philip attempted to herd 20,000 young men and women, cattle and horses, back to Macedon. But that outcome appears doubtful when analyzing Justin's text:

> as Philip was returning from Scythia, the Triballi met him, and refused to allow him a passage, unless they received a share of the spoil. Hence arose a dispute, and afterwards a battle, in which Philip received so severe a wound through the thigh, that his horse was killed by it; and while it was generally supposed that he was dead, the booty was lost. Thus, the Scythian spoil, as if attended with a curse, had almost proved fatal to the Macedonians.[6]

Clearly the captives were lost on the march back to Macedon, Philip was nearly killed along with his impaled horse and he was limping thereafter. Justin was also quite specific in relating that no gold or silver booty was captured.

The idea that either Meda or a Scythian wife would have participated in ritualized suicide or funeral pyre 'suttee' is also open to question, and there is no evidence that Scythians or Thracians resorted to cremation.[7] Herodotus' references to the ritual killings by the Thracians and 'tribes north of Crestonia' referred to voluntary strangulation or the slitting of the throat of the women vying to be inhumed with their husbands. In the case of the Scythians, they didn't specifically choose a wife, although texts do mention concubines, alongside butlers, cooks and grooms being throttled and thrown in the burial pit with the king's carefully prepared corpse.[8] But would a captured Scythian concubine have been honoured in Tomb II in such a way?

Neither is there evidence of a funeral pyre above the antechamber of Tomb II, where the woman was interred. Images from Andronikos' excavations show that what was initially thought to be an altar or a random pile of bricks containing cremation remains, was found only above the main chamber. This suggests a nearby lone cremation of the male.

Andronikos' basic contention that Tombs I, II and III in the Great Tumulus date to broadly 350–310 BC, judging from the burnt sherds found around them and the artefacts within, was generally accepted by scholars in the papers they launched into the 'battle of the bones'.[9] None of the competing arguments suggested Tomb II was built earlier than the reign of Philip II, quite the opposite, in fact. And as Hammond pointed out in 1991, the discovery of the blade of a Macedonian pike known as the 'sarissa', a weapon which was 'invented' by Philip II or introduced by him at least, must date the tomb to his reign or later.[10]

Yet the tomb's two-part construction, pyre remains above the main chamber and the different condition and colour of the male and female bones, each point to a separate or later funeral for the antechamber woman, as does her absence from the texts describing Philip's funeral ceremony.[11] Although Meda and a Scythian bride remain possible candidates, there are compelling reasons to consider the 'Amazon' in a very different light.

The Half-Illyrian Assassin

The Antikas team identified 'riding markers' on the woman's spine, and she was eventually buried as a warrior, a notable status in life that ought to be mentioned somewhere in ancient texts. Years before she died, her left leg was injured, possibly in battle, and yet when she was cremated her bones were not handled with the due care of a royal burial. Her skeleton is far from complete – only one side of her collarbone was collected, for example – and her bones look to have been hastily gathered as they were still covered in funerary ash.

In 2015, I first argued that this combined evidence supported a case for Cynnane, Philip's warlike daughter by his Illyrian wife Audata, a theory which actually reconciles many of the opposing arguments in the 'battle of the bones'. Nevertheless, I was full of apprehension when I first voiced it to Theo face-to-face in December that year when he was visiting his son in Kent. He listened to my points with a respectful silence before thrusting back at me vigorously with a measured counter-argument, like any good anthropological hoplite defending his terrain.

Theo's proverbial 'spear' was potentially lethal to my theory: Cynnane had been discounted on the basis of her age. But this conformed to the 'standard model' of events and the associated assumptions: Cynnane was born to Philip's very first wife Audata, whom he married in 359 BC, so she was birthed soon after. Moreover, Cynnane was old enough to have accompanied her father to war against the Illyrians in 344 BC, when she must have been at least 14 or 15 years old. This may have been the battle in which Philip's collarbone was shattered.[12] So when Cynnane arrived in Asia with her daughter Adea in late 323 or 322 BC following

Alexander's death, she would have been 36 or 37 years old, too old to be the Tomb II warrioress.

It was in the *Stratagems of War* by Polyaenus, a reportedly Macedonian author who wrote in the Roman era, that an account of Cynnane's journey to Asia appears:

> But Cynnane crossed the Strymon [River] forcing her way in the face of Antipater, who disputed her passage over it. She then passed the Hellespont, to meet the Macedonian army, and Alcetas [Perdiccas' younger brother] with a powerful force advanced to give her battle. The Macedonians at first paused at the sight of Philip's daughter, and the sister of Alexander; but after reproaching Alcetas with ingratitude, undaunted at the number of his forces, and his formidable preparations for battle, she bravely advanced to fight against him. She resolved upon a glorious death, rather than, stripped of her dominions, accept a private life, unworthy of the daughter of Philip.

Cynnane cannot have made contact with Perdiccas' brother Alcetas until the end of 323 BC, at the very earliest. Alexander had died in Babylon in June that year and news took time to travel, even along the network of Royal Roads established by the Achaemenid kings with their lookout posts and relay stations every 12 to 17 miles. Although messages transmitted by crier or signal fires from the heart of the Persian Empire could reach the coastal cities in days, people could not. So 322 BC is perhaps more credible for her confrontation with Alcetas.[13]

Theo had also questioned whether Cynnane would have been given the respect of a cremation by either Perdiccas or his brother, who was responsible for her death. Moreover, I already knew that I was contending with the fact that Cynnane's daughter was in her mid-teens when she crossed to Asia: Adea was of marriageable age when she was presented to the newly crowned King Philip III Arrhidaeus and assumed the royal title 'Adea-Eurydice', and the teenager might have been as young as 17 when inciting Antipater's troops to riot in Syria in 320 BC. It is clear that in the harsh and demanding conditions of the time, the women of the competing Macedonian dynasties had to mature fast or die.

But what had become apparent to me from years of research on Alexander is that a number of the 'fundamental' conclusions historians had arrived at were really no more than delicately poised inverted pyramids: huge corpuses of academic papers, 'cottage industries' in some case, have been constructed around a single tenuous point of evidence found in a questionable source. An unfortunate sentence from Justin, which positioned the city of Aegae at ancient Edessa, is just one example that misled scholars for centuries on the identity of Vergina.

The source behind the volumes written on Philip's wives stems from the peripatetic philosopher-come-biographer named Satyrus, who alone listed the woman in a single paragraph. This is how it was later transmitted in the text of Athenaeus, written several centuries later, more than 500 years after Philip died:

> Yet Philip always married a new wife with each new war he undertook. 'In the twenty-two years of his reign, at any rate,' as Satyrus says in his *Life* of him, 'he married Audata of Illyria, and had by her a daughter, Cynnane; he also married Phila, a sister of Derdas and Machatas. Wishing to put in a claim to the Thessalian nation as his own besides others, he begot children by two women of Thessaly, one of whom was Nicesipolis of Pherae, who bore to him Thessalonice, while the other was Philinna of Larissa, by whom he became the father of Arrhidaeus. Further, he acquired also the kingdom of the Molossians by marrying Olympias, by whom he had Alexander and Cleopatra. Again, when he subjugated Thrace, there came over to his side Cothelas the Thracian king, who brought with him his daughter Meda and a large dowry. By marrying her also he thus brought home a second wife after Olympias. After all these women he married Cleopatra, with whom he had fallen in love, the sister of Hippostratus and niece of Attalus; and by bringing her home to supplant Olympias, he threw the entire course of his life into utter confusion.'[14]

Commentators have challenged the reliability of Satyrus, who was certainly not contemporary and wrote some years after Philip's reign, possibly in the following century, using earlier now-lost sources. The surviving fragments of his work suggest he was a gossip-monger and sensationalist, which is not an uncommon assessment of the authors of the day. In another fragment of Satyrus' work he seems to have inserted two otherwise unknown kings in the line of Argead rulers.[15] But Athenaeus, who preserved the above extract, was himself also far from reliable when absorbing earlier sources.[16] As a result, the order of Philip's first four marriages made 'in connection with war', all allegedly falling between 359 and 356 BC, is suspicious if we compare the birthplaces of these women to the location of the conflicts supposedly resolved by the wedlock.[17]

Satyrus believed Philip reigned for twenty-two years, but we read in Diodorus' texts that he sat on the throne for twenty-three or twenty-four years, with Justin mentioning twenty-five. In which case, Philip's kingship commenced between 361 and 358 BC, knowing as we do from unambiguous references to Alexander's accession that Philip died in 336 BC.[18] One possible cause of confusion is the uncertainty surrounding Philip's first years in power and whether he initially acted as guardian, so in effect 'regent', for his young nephew Amyntas Perdicca, who some considered the rightful heir, or whether Philip formally took the kingship from the outset in 359 BC, which is the commonly cited year.[19]

Additionally, Athenian and Macedonian calendars did not synchronize, providing more latitude for error. So there are several floating regnal years in which Philip married and produced his first offspring. The slippage is not unique and can be found in the immediate post-Alexander period when scholars still debate whether events conform to 'high' or 'low' chronologies, a year or two apart.[20]

In Athenaeus' regurgitation of Satyrus' text, the marriage order is only implied and may well be wrong. It is widely accepted that Philip's marriage to Cynnane's mother, Audata, sealed a so-called 'great peace' with Illyria in 359 BC following victory over the Illyrian king Bardylis, who was logically Audata's relative. But the wedding could have taken place later, and the campaign itself may have been in 358 BC if we consider the chain of events that lead to it. Upon taking command of the realm, Philip first had to send ambassadors to Athens and await a reply, subdue the Paeonian tribe to his north and then consider diplomatic approaches to Bardylis before planning an eventual attack. Diodorus' account of these events presents a schedule that would have taken most heads of state two campaigning seasons, not to mention the training of his new army.[21]

The question of when children were born to Philip is further pushed out of focus by historians who unnecessarily link the timing of their births to the order of their mothers' marriages, as if to suggest Philip bedded and impregnated his wives in 'series' and not in 'parallel'.[22] Scholars attempting to defend Philip's conjugal honour even argue for 'marital monogamy'; the other named women, they propose, were simply political mistresses of necessity. Yet the status of their offspring in the dynastic struggles that followed argues otherwise: they were far from 'bastards' seeking legitimacy.

The clear polygamy at Philip's court, with potentially four or five brides taken in his first few years in power, but with year-round military campaigning in between, meant that the king consummated his marriages as he pleased and when he could. The output of children from his twenty-three-year reign was far from prolific, which may say something for his limited leisure time with each.

Satyrus' rundown of wives provides one pertinent example to undermine the notion that children were born in strict 'wedding order': Philip's marriage to Nicesipolis is mentioned before Olympias', which took place in 357 BC, we believe. But Nicesipolis' daughter, Thessalonice, was still a 'ward' of Olympias at the siege of Pydna in 316 BC, some forty-one years later. And she was still sufficiently young when extracted from the siege to give Cassander three sons in the following years. So Thessalonice must have been born well after her mother arrived at Philip's court. Some scholars simply assume that Nicesipolis was wedded as late as 346 BC, a decade after Olympias, in which case Satyrus' marriage order is totally wrong.[23]

For similar reasons, Cynnane may have been born several years later than assumed by the 'standard model'. There is no evidence that she was the oldest of Philip's children, moreover, pregnancies frequently miscarried. If Audata gave birth in 355 BC, only three years after her assumed arrival at court, Cynnane would have been just 32 or 33 when she died in Asia in 323/322 BC. And that falls squarely into the revised ageing of the Tomb II 'Amazon'.

Polyaenus detailed Cynnane's martial exploits in her teenage years: she campaigned with Philip against the Illyrians and killed their queen in single combat. But, as already pointed out by Professor Waldemar Heckel of the University of Calgary, an eminent expert on the 'who's who' of the period, 'there is no reason to equate every skirmish with the Illyrians with the famous battle of 344/3!'[24] Bloody annual engagements extended through the next ten years during the reigns of new Illyrian kings to 335 BC, when Alexander had to deal with one of Bardylis' sons; the 'great peace' sealed by Audata's marriage had obviously collapsed.[25]

There are further clues to suggest Philip's Illyrian campaigns were waged later than commonly assumed, and Cynnane could have been present at any one of them. Diodorus mentions that another of Philip's jilted male lovers named Pausanias sacrificed himself in battle against an Illyrian king named Pleurias, an episode which took place not long before Philip's assassination at Aegae, we may suppose from the context.[26] Moreover, in Polyaenus' extract, Cynnane's eventual marriage to Amyntas Perdicca is positioned immediately after her warrior exploits in Illyria, suggesting her participation in the campaign took place rather late in Philip's reign.[27]

But if Polyaenus' *Stratagems* is accurate as far as her career is concerned, Cynnane's feats must have been legendary, even in her own lifetime:

> Cynnane, the daughter of Philip was famous for her military knowledge; she commanded armies, and in the field charged at the head of them. In an engagement with the Illyrians, she herself slew their queen with a fatal blow to the throat; and she defeated the Illyrian army with great slaughter. She married Amyntas, son of Perdiccas; and, losing him soon after, never would take a second husband. By Amyntas she had an only daughter named Eurydice to whom she gave a military education, and instructed her in the science of war.[28]

The ancient sources for this period are riddled with unfathomable idiosyncrasies and conflicting testimony, and there are no eyewitness accounts from which we might separate wheat from chaff, so what historians are left with are the accumulated romanticized, metamorphosized and somewhat hypothesized episodes in the careers of Philip and Alexander viewed through a very murky prism. It is difficult to imagine, for example, that Cynnane slew the Illyrian queen in hand-to-hand combat, when bodyguards would have surrounded any royalty present. It certainly sounds heroic in the style of the *Iliad* duels, but they rarely occurred in pitched battles of the time.

Far more credible is the ritual execution of a captured Illyrian royal. Perhaps Cynnane slit her throat in front of the troops, an outcome that might have ended a family vendetta harking back to her mother Audata. Philip had himself been an Illyrian hostage when his father was on the throne, and he 'inherited' his father's squabble, Diodorus reported.[29] Court propaganda would have done the rest, and what better gift for Philip to give to his daughter than a locally manufactured golden Scythian bow and quiver, the quintessential marks of an 'Amazon' in the making.

The Huntress, Atalanta

Philip paired Cynnane in marriage with his own guardianed nephew, Amyntas Perdicca, which was something of a consolation prize for the youth whose throne he usurped. Due to this recognition, many called for Amyntas to take the crown at Philip's death, leaving Alexander no option but to have his cousin and rival executed.

Having learnt a thing or two from his father's diplomacy, Alexander exploited the availability of his now-widowed half-sister by offering Cynnane to his new ally, King Langarus of the Agrianians, one of the tribes immediately north of Macedon's unstable border. We can only speculate what degree of resentment Cynnane felt for Alexander. But a wedding gift made to her at either of these marriages could explain how Cynnane came into possession of the sumptuous diadem found with her bones. After Langarus' untimely death, and with Alexander campaigning in Asia, Cynnane had to raise her equally pugnacious daughter, Adea, alone, but she was said to be reluctant to wed again.[30]

In this respect, Cynnane appears to have considered herself something of an 'Atalanta', the virgin huntress of Greek mythology who was famously loath to marry. The sister of Alexander's former second-in-command, Perdiccas, was also named Atalanta, which might suggest the legendary huntress was an icon for Macedonian female nobility. Atalanta appears in boar-hunting scenes on ancient Greek pottery, where she is outfitted as a Scythian, no less, in a geometric-patterned belted tunic, pointed hat and high boots, with a bow-and-arrow quiver slung on her hip in Scythian style.[31] Atalanta took an oath of virginity sworn to Artemis the goddess of the hunt, who was similarly depicted in hunting boots with a quiver. Could the golden Scythian '*gorytos*' have been a symbol of Cynnane's association with these iconic warlike women?

We hear nothing more about Cynnane, except that she was 'training her daughter in the arts of war', until some fourteen years later when she impetuously journeyed to Asia with Adea, defying both Antipater in Macedon and the far-from-unanimously liked Perdiccas. Theo had understandably raised the issue of whether Perdiccas would have given Cynnane due funeral rites. But he was not present when she was killed by his brother near Ephesus, a good distance from his headquarters in either Babylon or Syria.[32]

Perdiccas' men were furious at seeing Philip's daughter killed; the veterans among them may have even seen Cynnane in action in the Illyrians wars. Judging from the reaction of the troops, and surely on Adea's insistence, an immediate 'respectful' but quick cremation was the only solution for Cynnane's body in the heat of Anatolia. Similar honorary pyres for enemy generals are recorded after battle in the Successor Wars a few years on, after which their cremated remains were returned to their families.[33]

Yannis pondered whether her bones were broken into the smaller pieces we see today so that they could be kept in a portable container for the journey, or whether the journey itself led to further fragmenting and even some powdering of the remains. Adea would have ferried her mother's bones back to Macedon two years or so later when accompanied by Antipater and the 'kings' in late 320 BC. But with the highly suspicious Antipater still in office in the state capital to late 319 BC, and with a Polyperchon-Olympias united front in Pella soon after he died, Adea may not have been able to provide her mother with a regal ceremony at the burial grounds of Aegae.

Cassander managed to wrest control of Macedon from Olympias and Polyperchon by 316 BC. He was an astute politician who then set about sweetening the bitter political stage, having just executed them both along with Alexander's son. We read how, with much ceremony, Cassander interred Cynnane's bones at Aegae, where he reburied Adea and Arrhidaeus and even held funeral games. This highly choreographed show of posthumous reverence to Philip's line was Cassander's self-serving declaration of his own kingship in the making. But nowhere in the surviving texts does it specifically state that Cynnane was buried with her daughter and son-in-law, or even at the same time, although some commentators on the tombs have assumed just that.[34] Diodorus' wording reads:

> After this, already conducting himself as a king in administering the affairs of the realm, he buried Eurydice and Philip, the queen and king, and also Cynnane, whom Alcetas had slain, in Aegae as was the royal custom.[35]

Athanaeus' wording on the issue is similarly vague.[36]

Cynnane was never married to a throned king, unlike her daughter Adea, who was wedded to the halfwit King Philip III Arrhidaeus and so would have merited burial in the so-called cluster of the queens. Moreover, Cassander's financial position in 316/315 BC must have been dire: little of Alexander's Asian campaign wealth appears to have made it back to Antipater's militarily active regency, and Cassander had now been at war with Polyperchon for almost three years. Yet a cost-effective solution may have been at hand: the still-unfinished antechamber of Tomb II. In which case, Cynnane's remains ended up in the tomb of her father along with the weapons and armour that recalled her 'warrior' life.

Cassander could have expediently commissioned the vivid hunting scene above the entrance to recall the 'heroic' hunting exploits of Philip, Alexander and his notable bodyguards, some of whom were now Cassander's allies and brothers-in-law via marriages to his sisters. In which case, Cassander was appeasing not just the local nobles, but the powerful successors overseas whose ongoing cooperation was vital.

This remains an '*in extremis*' scenario and Chrysoula Paliadeli reminded me that the soil covering Tomb II did not betray a two-stage burial of the two chambers, plus the artefacts found in the modest votive fires in that soil found in 1977 (including fish plates, salt cellars and cups without handles) looked to date from 340–330 BC, not later. She also pointed out that the provenance of the frieze better fits the instructions of Alexander himself at his father's death, and these were all pertinent observations.

But none precluded a later burial of Cynnane: the rough brickwork either side of the entrance and extending above the frieze permits the notion that soil did cover the whole structure relatively soon after the Tomb II male was cremated. Thus, later ceremonial fires were possibly made by veterans on top of the mound, where artefacts dating to 340–330 BC were consigned to the flames in continued reverence to the national hero below.[37] What they had dedicated were most likely valued heirlooms from the king's reign.

We may also recall that Cassander *did* commission a painting of the Battle of Issus, from which he was absent, by the painter Philoxenus of Eretria; Cassander was not averse to gracing his halls with imagery that recalled the great days of the Argead house into which he was to marry.[38] But when the frieze was completed and just how long delayed after the closure of the main chamber, is unknown. We should recall that stone-floored passageways to tomb entrances – and the '*dromos*' leading to Tomb II – suggest the final resting places of notable kings had been sites of frequent public veneration for some years before the tombs were finally buried under a completed tumulus.

In this radical reinterpretation of Aegae burials, Cassander reunited Philip II with his revered warrior daughter. Once he had achieved his publicity goals, Cassander set about marking the end of an era by symbolically raising the first modest 20-metre-wide tumulus over Tombs I and II; the old royal line was proverbially buried for good. Cassander next established his own part-Argead dynasty through Philip's daughter Thessalonice, and he founded his own eponymous city, Cassandreia, on the coast to the south, most likely with the aim of it becoming the nation's new capital.

Reconciliation in the Battle of the Bones

The well-structured arguments swept up by Eugene Borza should be factored into the 'Cynnane model'. He and others had tenaciously argued that certain weapons and armour found in the main chamber could have once belonged to Alexander the Great. When Alexander's body finally left Babylon, his arms and insignia travelled with him, but the funeral bier was intercepted by Ptolemy's men near Damascus and redirected to Egypt, legitimately or otherwise depending upon the interpretation of Alexander's true wishes.[39] Perdiccas invaded Egypt but was killed on the banks of the Nile; thereafter, exchanges were made between Ptolemy and the generals, who then travelled north to meet up with Antipater in Syria. The aged regent escorted the royals – Adea, Arrhidaeus and the young Alexander IV – back to Macedon, and the entourage could have included a set of Alexander's funerary weapons, either those from the bier or, more likely, those given to Arrhidaeus at Babylon.

If Cassander did place Cynnane's cremated bones in the antechamber of Tomb II, it is not impossible that he had the doors to the main chamber opened (a rather straightforward task according to Costas Zambas who has studied many Macedonian tombs) to place Alexander's helmet and shield beside the bones of his father. It is worth recalling that three pairs of bronze greaves, two ornate swords and six iron spearheads were found in the room, with evidence that a further shield was burned in the pyre debris on the roof.[40] But just how likely is it that the entrance to Tomb II was still accessible to Cassander?

Plagiarizing Plato

It is worth taking a look at Plato's much-debated description of the ideal tomb in his equally idyllic state described in his *Laws*, which was published sometime in the final years before his death in 347 BC, a decade or so before Philip's death:

> The tomb shall be made of porous [spongy] stone, of which the strength is unaffected by age; it shall be vaulted, longer than it is wide, containing stone couches set parallel to one another, and shall be mounded over with soil in a circle ... One end [of the tumulus] shall be left free for those [later] being interred without need of [another] tumulus.[41]

If they were following Platonic convention, the builders of a family-cluster tumulus would have either left the tomb entrances clear or stopped short of completing the 'circle' of the burial mound so that new tombs could be inserted. This is resonant of the smaller tumulus Andronikos found covering Tombs I and II, with Tomb III possibly incorporated later. Other later-dated tombs in family clusters in the adjacent cemetery were discovered with masonry roads to their entrances, suggestive that the construction remained open for a time, presumably to be reused.[42]

The wall of bricks either side of the entrance of Tomb II obviously acted as a retaining wall to hold back soil until the antechamber was completed, and possibly even after, so that dedication could be made outside the entrance. Scholars like Andronikos, who once believed Philip's final wife Cleopatra was interred in Tomb II, must also have concurred that the entrance remained accessible, for she was killed by Olympias some months after Philip's funeral. The stable ground-level soil either side of the tomb would not have put undue pressure on the well-constructed brick wall which was plaster white on the inner side to form an attractive finish to the yard they created at the bottom of the '*dromos*' in front of the entrance. The right side had collapsed, suggesting it stood for some time; certainly some drainage and regular maintenance would have been required if the wall kept the doors and frieze visible for some twenty years.

The camp supporting Arrhidaeus and Adea as the Tomb II occupants argued that this section of Plato's *Laws* was architectural plagiarism. He simply emulated what he, or his pupil Euphraeus, had witnessed in tomb design when based at the Pellan court in the reign of Perdiccas III, Philip's older brother, over whom Euphraeus exerted significant philosophical influence; and it was he who convinced Perdiccas to give Philip his first regional governorship.[43] Plato could, in fact, have simply taken his 'tumulus-extending' advice from Achilles' instructions in the *Iliad*.[44]

But might we assume just the opposite? Philip may well have first incorporated Plato's instructions – transported to him in Pella by Euphraeus – when he built the 'Tomb of Eurydice' his mother, dated to 344/343 BC, which does, in fact, exhibit features of tomb design in transition: although it is a barrel-vaulted structure, 'it is encased in ashlar blocks as if it were a cist tomb' – possibly to deter robbers in the troubled times – observed Professor Olga Palagia, the well-respected professor of classical archaeology in Athens.[45] Even the art on the walls of Tomb I, embodying the Three Fates dressed in white, is resonant of Plato's earlier treatize *Republic*, suggesting the Platonic circle had already influenced the Macedonian court.[46]

Supporting this transition phase idea is the design of the 'Philippeion', the circular family building erected by Philip at Olympia after the Battle of Chaeronea in 338 BC. This contained nine Corinthian columns which were purely decorative in function, similar to those seen on the façades of later Macedonian-styled tombs.[47] Barrel-vaulted tomb design appeared in Macedon just a few years after Plato's *Laws* had been written, so the correlation, either way, is too strong to discount.

The Mystery of Tomb IV

Another fundamental question remained: if Adea-Eurydice merited burial in the cluster of the queens, and if Cynnane was interred in the antechamber of Tomb II, where did Cassander lay Philip III Arrhidaeus to rest? The rarely discussed Tomb IV has been discounted, largely because of the presence of a coin from the reign of Antigonus II Gonatas. But the coin was found in debris of the funeral pyre which was sitting in the upper soil of the tomb infill; it could have been dropped there when Antigonus raised the Great Tumulus over all the tombs decades later. Evidence suggests a funeral may have taken place on the once-vaulted roof of Tomb IV which, according to the museum display plaque, belonged to a male.

Not much remains of Tomb IV, apart from the foundation stones and the 'free-standing' columns from the temple-like façade of this clearly further-evolved Macedonian tomb, whose design suggests this was possibly the deepest and grandest of them all, despite its single chamber.[48] It sits close to the beginning of the '*dromos*' or walkway that descended to the entrance of Tomb II, so the occupant was being linked to the former kings. Some scholars have proposed that Tomb IV was built for Antigonus Gonatas himself, but if that is true, its destruction post-dated the Gallic looting and suggests a second 'invasion' of the cemetery took place, one never documented before the Roman destruction following victory at Pydna.

So could Tomb IV have actually been built by Cassander to hold the remains of Philip III Arrhidaeus? To Andronikos it was clear that a still-standing tomb of this proportion would not have been fully buried by the Great Tumulus, but its foundations clearly were. No one half-buries a tomb, so this is clearly indicative that it had already fallen before the great mound was raised.

As far as the dating of the Great Tumulus itself, which finally covered all the tombs, Nicholas Hammond first proposed that it was raised in the brief tenure of a reunited Macedon by Alexander the Great's former bodyguard, Lysimachus, which commenced in 286 BC.[49] But the more widely accepted theory, supported by the broken tombstones in its soil dating down to 275 BC, still favours tumulus construction by Antigonus II Gonatas soon before Pyrrhus' Galatae looted Aegae.[50] If the Great Tumulus had been raised after they raped the old capital, and bearing in mind that they did discover Tomb I, the Celts would have surely unearthed Tomb II, which sat beside it in the same original modest tumulus.

In our private correspondence, Yannis Maniatis recounted his first meeting with Manolis Andronikos in the excavation pit at Vergina soon after the tombs were discovered, when he happened to be analyzing the marble samples from the locale. Later that evening, in the little village taverna where the archaeological team congregated, Andronikos first explained his Great Tumulus theory: knowing that Alexander had wished to build a great monument for his father, Antigonus II Gonatas raised the mound and respectfully placed the broken tombstones from the adjacent looted cemetery face-down in the infill, as that was exactly how they were found.

Chronological uncertainty still surrounds the nearby above-ground '*heroon*' or cenotaph. Although much of the foundation of the shrine remains, there is no trace of the stones from the walls or the slabs from the roof. This conundrum has not been widely discussed, as tomb robbers don't hang around to pull down sturdy structures; they enter quickly and discreetly, and depart with their booty just as fast. Moreover, the remaining blocks forming the shrine, and also those from Tomb IV, suggest they would have been massive and could not have been readily carted away, even by gold-entranced Celts who cared nothing for the wrath of the Greek gods watching on.

Professor Bartsiokas proposed that the original Gallic looters had removed stones from the shrine's north wall to build an underground tunnel through the floor to the roof of Tomb I.[51] But this does not explain the disappearance of the remaining limestone blocks. Although the village dwellers of modern Vergina used much of the city ruins to build new homes when they settled in the 1920s, the Great Tumulus hid the structures until 1977, when they were discovered in already-raped and mutilated form.

A sentence in the *Greek Alexander Romance* mentions that after burying his father with all due ceremony, Alexander 'founded a temple above his tomb'.[52] The *Romance* is a collection of fables, but each was fashioned out of historical episodes that took place before or on campaign. Potentially supporting the construction of a shrine at Philip's death is an extract from the equally questionable Justin, who claimed that Alexander's mother Olympias 'burnt the body of [Philip's] assassin when it had been taken down, upon the remains of her husband, and made him a tomb in the same place. She also required that yearly sacrifices should be performed to the assassin's manes.'[53] If Justin's statement contains any truth, Olympias was indeed paying tribute to Philip's killer, but the shrines could, of course, be one and the same as they are linked to the one event: Philip's murder after the wedding of his daughter Cleopatra.

An ancient tremor of the scale of the Great Thessalonica quake of June 1978 could have toppled the shrine, perhaps the same seismic event that shattered the marble entrance door of Tomb III, and maybe in those turbulent years, when Macedon was under invasion, the stones from *both* looted structures, which sat outside the original smaller mound covering Tombs I and II, were reused in less-prominent nearby tombs. It is also tempting to speculate that the Romans may have destroyed the more easily accessible buildings. But if they had found periphery riches, their ingenuity and the manpower at their disposal would surely have mined out the whole of the tumulus, along with Tombs II and III.

Clearly, the innards of the Great Tumulus had been bitten into on more than one occasion. Laura and I frequently discussed the looting at Aegae and I had posed the question of why the pillaging only commenced with the era of the roving Galatae. The hundreds of older tumuli scattered across the ancient necropolis broadcast wealth below; they had been visible for centuries and could have been pillaged generations before. I could only imagine that the necropolis of the old state capital was constantly guarded through the centuries until Macedon's borders broke. The survival of Tombs II and III was nothing short of a miracle.

The Grave of the Undocumented Daughter

As a closing note to the tragic but still-murky opera performed by Cassander and his successors at the burial grounds of Aegae, we should consider a remarkable recent find at the nearby town of Veria. In a partially excavated Hellenistic cemetery lay a tombstone positioned before a rock-cut chamber, and carved on the relief is rare wording identifying the occupant:

> Know that beneath me is the tomb of Adea. Terrible Hades seized her after an illness while she was still a virgin, not ready for marriage. She died, leaving in great distress and everlasting mourning her mother Cynnane, who bore her, and her father Cassander.[54]

These are strikingly familiar names. This is the only other Cynnane mentioned in Macedonian history, and both women apparently named their girls Adea. Could they have been related?

Olga Palagia has conjectured that Cassander married a second and otherwise-undocumented daughter of Cynnane who was conceived with Amyntas Perdicca, though there is the possibility that Langarus was the father. Palagia hypothesized that this second daughter was named Cynnane after her mother, and then married to Cassander in her teens, with their subsequent daughter from this union named Adea after her aunt.

If Professor Palagia is correct, there was a branch of Argead royals residing at Veria, some 10km from Aegae as the crow flies. Cassander's 'uncomfortably late' 'first' marriage to Thessalonice when he was in his mid-to-late 30s then becomes less of a mystery, as well as the reverence he showed when reburying Adea-Eurydice and Cynnane at Aegae; they would have been his in-laws.[55] That, in turn, would also explain why the warlike Adea teamed up with Cassander, her brother-in-law, against the family's arch-enemy Olympias.

In Alexander's absence, the Macedonian regent Antipater would have had every reason to marry Cassander, his oldest surviving son, to a granddaughter of Philip II and into the Argead line. The early death of this second Cynnane and their

Warrior Father, Warrior Daughter and the Bactrian 237

The image found on the tombstone at Veria. In the background are Adea's belongings – a mirror, fan, straw hat and jewellery box – which appear suspended as if on the wall of a tomb. The taller woman appears to be holding a sceptre. (*Veria, Archaeological Museum 160. Photo: Olga Palagia*) daughter, before Cassander controlled the state, would account for their burial at Veria, not Aegae, and help to explain why they never featured in surviving texts. Cassander's early career is completely passed over by the sources until his emergence at Babylon shortly before Alexander's death in 323 BC. It follows that the oldest of Cassander's subsequent sons, who briefly held the throne of a divided nation with the name King Philip IV, might, in fact, have been born to this undocumented first wife rather than Thessalonice.

Professor Palagia's hypothesis is enticing and illustrates how little we know about the twists and turns of this generation of king and queen-making at the court of Pella, and of their subsequent demises in the soil of Macedon. As for my own recreation of events, like the nametag on display in the archaeological museum at Vergina, and the never-mentioned Scythian daughter of King Atheas, it remains a hypothesis of deductive reasoning, nothing more. But proposing Cynnane as the 'Amazon' maintains the possibility that the hunting scene was painted after Alexander's campaigns in Asia, and it leaves the door open for the presence of the artefacts of Alexander himself. The style of the burials of Philip's son, daughter and granddaughter, complete with funeral games, may indeed recall Cassander's 'legendary knowledge of Homer', dovetailed with Alexander's earlier heroic funeral rites for Philip himself.[56]

But an additional woman needed to be discussed now that the Antikas team established that the Tomb II female was aged 32 +/– 2 years at death: Alexander's wife, Rhoxane, 'Little Star' in her own language. The logic for including her in the Tomb II shortlist is relatively simple: although her funeral is undocumented, her age fits the Antikas prognosis and many leading scholars accept that the adolescent 'prince' interred in the adjacent Tomb III is Rhoxane's son, King Alexander IV.

A Case for the Little Star

In late 328 BC, some three years after the epic battle at Gaugamela in northern Mesopotamia where the Achaemenid regime of Darius III was finally toppled, Alexander was campaigning in Bactria and Sogdia, two of the so-called 'upper satrapies' of the north-eastern Persian Empire. Alexander first saw Rhoxane dancing among thirty 'maidens' at the court of a noble whose surrender her father had just brokered.[57] Despite reports that Alexander was transfixed by Rhoxane's beauty, second only to that of Darius' wife and unmarried daughters; the marriage was a sensible political manoeuvre, in the style of Philip.[58] Alexander would marry at least two more Asian princesses in his bid for authentic royal status and acceptance across the Persian Empire, a diplomacy that did not endear him to his conservative Macedonian infantrymen.

Rhoxane's father, Oxyartes, was a Bactrian noble with clear influence in the region, and Alexander confirmed him as a governor of one the eastern provinces.[59]

Warrior Father, Warrior Daughter and the Bactrian 239

The marriage was obviously orchestrated to quell any local uprisings, which, according to the calculations of one modern historian, left 100,000 insurgents dead beside 7,000 Macedonians, after numerous sieges and reversals of fortune.[60] When the Macedonian war machine advanced from Egypt into the heart of the Persian Empire, Alexander cited revenge as his mantra: it was unifying, uncomplicated, profitable and legitimate. In contrast, his campaigns through 329/328 BC were bogged down by guerrilla warfare, mountain skirmishes and harsh winter weather in regions where occupation led to a smoldering resentment. A 20,000-strong 'peacekeeping' force had to keep the upper satrapies from revolting again.[61]

Rhoxane joined Alexander's entourage before the bloody campaigning in India, where she may have lost a first child; she fell pregnant again just before the army's return to Babylon in 323 BC. She and her newborn barely emerged unscathed from the succession crisis at Alexander's death, and she was acutely aware of the danger from her rivals. A unique snippet from Plutarch informs us that Rhoxane, in league with Perdiccas, summoned another of Alexander's Persian wives to Babylon, whereupon they murdered her and her sister, once married to Alexander closest companion Hephaestion, and disposed of their bodies down a well.[62]

Following Perdiccas' death in Egypt, Rhoxane and her son were eventually shepherded back to Macedon by Antipater, and they fell into Cassander's hands in 316 BC. As Diodorus described the situation:

> Cassander had determined to do away with Alexander's son and the son's mother, Rhoxane, so that there might be no successor to the kingdom; but for the present, since he wished to observe what the common people would say about the slaying of Olympias and since he had no news of Antigonus' success, he placed Rhoxane and the child [Alexander IV] in custody, transferring them to the citadel of Amphipolis, in command of which he placed Glaucias, one of his most trusted henchmen. Also, he took away the pages who, according to custom, were being brought up as companions of the boy, and he ordered that he should no longer have royal treatment but only such as was proper for any ordinary person of private station.[63]

The writing was on the wall. Sometime between the short-lived accord between Alexander's warring successors from 311–309 BC, Cassander had his henchman poison Rhoxane and the boy; their bodies were to be concealed and Glaucias was to disclose to no one else what had been done.[64] Rhoxane was of 'marriageable age', possibly as young as 14 when Alexander met her in late 328 BC, so she would have been between 31 and 33 years old when she was executed, while their son, who had been crowned King Alexander IV at Babylon, would have been aged 12–14.

Xirotiris had estimated the Tomb III adolescent to have been 13–16-years-old, and Musgrave's 1990 analysis of the bones suggested a male with a dental age of 12–14, though he favoured the lower end of the range. This ruled out Heracles, Alexander's older son, who was believed to be 17 or 18 when Cassander convinced Polyperchon to execute him a few years on.[65] Musgrave noted the 'paucity of bones' from Tomb III and described their colour as 'dirty grey to brown', and some were black from poor burning with pyre debris attached.[66] They have all the hallmarks of a quick and irreverent, secret cremation.

A number of problems come with the identification of Rhoxane with the Tomb II warrioress, but none are insurmountable, and one of them spills over to her son, if he was interred in Tomb III. The first is the date of both burials. Cassander could not have 'celebrated' his crime by housing Rhoxane and Alexander IV in grand barrel-vaulted tombs, as his instructions to his henchman were to secretly bury the bodies 'lest their violent deaths come to light if a funeral were held'.[67] Cassander ruled Macedon until 297 BC, and the next few years saw the brief and troubled reigns of his three sons, when Macedon was divided. After 294 BC, Demetrius the Besieger, Alexander's aged bodyguard Lysimachus and then Demetrius' son, Antigonus II Gonatas, came to the throne. These were kings who might have given Alexander's wife and son due funeral rites, not necessarily for altruistic reasons, but to suggest their roles as legitimate successors and to highlight the collateral damage of the Cassander era.

Although the burials of Rhoxane and her son fail to appear in any surviving texts, the upheavals of the Hellenistic period meant that for almost seventy years after the Battle of Ipsus in Phrygia in 301 BC – the so-called 'Battle of Kings' where Alexander's own generals faced off – there is no surviving coherent account of any substance except Justin's severely précised pages. The 'numerous historians … whom kings had engaged to recount their exploits have fallen into oblivion', Polybius mourned almost 2,250 years ago when trying to piece together the evidence.[68] And with them went the tales of the kings who cremated, exhumed and reburied the former kings of Macedon at Aegae.

If Tomb III was built or sealed sometime after 294 BC, it would tie in with Andronikos' belief that the original modest tumulus that covered Tombs I and II was 'disturbed' sometime after to accommodate it.[69] But could the antechamber of Tomb II have remained incomplete or empty from Philip II's death in 336 BC to the post-Cassander era, some 42 years later? Although this seems highly unlikely, there is one further intriguing piece of evidence that argues for Rhoxane's case.

Scythian Donatives at Athens

As confirmed by an ancient inscription at Athens, sometime between 320 and 317 BC, but most likely when Olympias was in control of Macedon and the son of her supporter Polyperchon was campaigning in southern Greece in 318/317 BC, Rhoxane made dedications to Athena 'Polias', the goddess 'of the state', at the Parthenon. Polyperchon's son had both of the kings with him on campaign for safekeeping, and probably Rhoxane as well, and he also dedicated armour to the goddess, which appears on the same inventory list.

Among the items Rhoxane deposited were a gold '*rhyton*' and gold '*peritrachelidia*'.[70] A '*rhyton*' is a conical drinking horn, but the only examples found in precious metals come from Eurasia and Scythia. According to Strabo's description, '*peritrachelia*', perhaps Egyptian in origin, are crescent-shaped pieces of neck jewellery worn by barbarian women, whose design resembled the slim pectoral or gorget, the defensive upper-chest armour that soldiers fastened around the neck. Alexander himself wore an iron '*peritrachelion*' inset with precious stone at the Battle of Gaugamela.[71]

The decorative gold '*peritrachelidia*' Rhoxane donated at the Acropolis were the type of feminine adornments found in a Scythian tomb in the Crimea and another in the Ukrainian Steppe, one of them discovered with a coin issued by Alexander the Great. The two examples in existence were, once again, 'most probably products of the same workshop' and the manufacturing style was 'Greek', commented Dr Petros Themelis, an expert on Macedonian metalworking who had once worked under Manolis Andronikos. He further stated: 'Rhyta and other rare vessels and jewellery of gold … must have existed in the Macedonian royal court during the period that followed Alexander the Great's campaign to Asia.'[72]

Rhoxane was from Bactria or perhaps Sogdia, an uncertainty stemming from the conflicting texts surrounding place names and events in the upper-province campaigns. Both were regions that bordered the Scythian cultural world, which may have been less nomadic than legend suggests: Scythians allegedly told Alexander that their existence was epitomized by 'a yoke of oxen, a plough, an arrow, a spear and a cup'. After giving him a dressing-down for trying to 'subjugate the whole human race' and 'coveting things beyond his reach', they joined forces with the local rebels to oppose the Macedonians until their chieftains were all but exterminated.[73]

If Rhoxane dedicated at the Parthenon the type of gold objects which have only otherwise been found in the Scythian world, though 'Greek' in their style of manufacture, then surely it is possible that the Scythian-styled gold bow-and-arrow quiver belonged to her as well. They were not inconceivably gifts Alexander bestowed on his exotic wife, recognizing her status but also her unique ethnicity in the Macedonian-controlled world.

I explained this chain of reasoning to Laura, who understandably challenged why Rhoxane would be interred in the tomb of Philip II, and not in Tomb III with her son. I had proffered Rhoxane's name in the spirit of historical discussion by a process of elimination, and not from a personal conviction of her presence,

Achaemenid fluted silver *rhyton* with partial gilding from the fifth/fourth century BC. (*Alamy.com*)

so I had no perfect answer. But I proferred one nonetheless: perhaps, I conjectured, whoever retrieved her cremated bones from wherever Cassander's henchman buried them – whether Lysimachus, Demetrius or his son Antigonus – saw more political value in building Alexander's son his very own tomb; he was 'part-Alexander the Great', after all. Rhoxane, on the other hand, was fully Asiatic, which perhaps precluded her from the cluster of the queens, as maybe did Alexander's own absence from Aegae.

To enable Theo, Laura and Yannis to travel any further in the quest for tomb identities, permission for DNA, carbon dating and isotope testing of the bones from all three Great Tumulus tombs now needed to be granted. Only through these forensic processes might the team establish where these royals had once lived in early life, broadly when they were interred and their interfamily blood ties.

The genealogical geometry was clear, and I attempted to articulate it with the help of Konstantina Drosou and her genetics expertise: if the Tomb III adolescent and the Tomb II 'Amazon' shared identical mitochondrial DNA, there would be a strong case for Alexander IV and Rhoxane, especially so if their 'haplotyping' (the collection of variants, such as nucleotide changes and mutations, in a genome) suggested Asian origins. If 'autosomal markers' (DNA variants inherited from both parents, found within the chromosomes) suggest the 'Amazon' is related to the

Gold *peritrachelidion* or pectoral discovered in 1971 in a kurgan at Tolstaya Mogila in the Ukrainian Steppe, thought to be of Greek workmanship. (*Museum of Historical Treasures, Kiev. Alamy.com*)

Tomb II male next door, there would be grounds for concluding she was, indeed, Philip II's daughter Cynnane.[74] However, those who still believe that Tomb II post-dated Philip II may argue a thought-provoking alternative: Cassander interred Arrhidaeus there with his warlike half-sister Cynnane, while Adea was buried with ceremony in the cluster of the queens.

If no genetic relationships were observed, the doors remain open for Meda and a Scythian princess. Isotope testing of her skeletal remains could help establish the geographical region she was raised in.

If the same forensics could be eventually extended to the full complement of bones from Tomb I, including those still in storage in Thrace, the oldest skeletal remains could be identified, logically those of the original occupant. If the bones were those of a mature male who shared the same Y-chromosome with the man in Tomb II, they are likely the remains of Amyntas III, the father of Philip II, assuming the carbon dating correlated to his reign. Their DNA, in turn, could reveal any family blood ties to the 'prince' and the 'Amazon'.[75]

The possibilities for future forensics seemed exciting, daunting and long overdue in light of the last forty years of unending controversy. If Professor Andronikos were alive to witness them, he would surely relive that 'feeling of both hope and dread'.

Chapter 16

Preparing to Gene-Tag the Royals

> Nothing exists except atoms and empty space; everything else is just opinion.
> —Democritus

Since DNA 'fingerprinting' was developed in 1984, and first used for a court conviction in 1988, significant scientific advances have dramatically reduced the size of the genetic material required to achieve results. Researchers are also now better equipped to eliminate foreign contaminants from the authentic 'endogenous' DNA and they can pinpoint 'lifestyle' markers that provide clues to habitat. With next-generation rapid sequencing technology – a fast process for determining the unique line up of nucleotides DNA – analysis is set to provide deeper profiling to reveal markers present in our genome that can reveal a breadth of information about our ancestry.

Talking Genes, Carbon and Stable Isotopes

The search for ancient DNA, known as 'paleogenetics' and likened to 'archaeology of the blood', is proving even more enlightening. A decade ago, one study appeared to prove Herodotus more reliable than his historic reputation: the results appeared to confirm that the Etruscans *did* arrive in Italy from Lydia in Anatolia around 1200 BC, just as the historian claimed. The Etruscan language has only partly been deciphered. Unlike its neighbours, it has no Indo-European roots, supporting the theory that they were migrating refugees from a non-indigenous civilization and one that we could associate with the fall of Troy.[1]

A similar groundbreaking study took place in 2015 with the first ancient-genome project to sequence the DNA of more than 100 individuals from ancient graves, which was able to chart a massive Bronze-Age migration from the steppes of Russia and Ukraine. The report stated: 'Early Bronze Age men from the vast grasslands of the Eurasian steppe swept into Europe on horseback about 5,000 years ago – and may have left their women behind. This male-dominated migration may have persisted for several generations, sending men into the arms of European women who interbred with them, leaving a lasting impact on the genomes of living Europeans.'[2] The migrating 'Yamnaya', as they are known, appear to have comprised ten men to every woman; they arrived with knowledge of metallurgy and animal husbandry, and possibly the mysterious ancestral tongue we call 'proto Indo-European'.[3]

In June 2017, various journals reported on DNA extracted from mummified corpses in Egypt, with the conclusion that the pharaohs were more European in origin than the country's current inhabitants, perhaps finally explaining the ancient depictions of fair-haired and blue-eyed Libyans from the period, including a pharaoh's daughter.[4] The successful extraction of DNA was a surprising forensic feat because palaeogenetecists had previously assumed that the hot climate and the dampness of Egyptian tombs, along with the chemicals and minerals used in mummification, would have degraded DNA beyond any viable stage.

Archaeology underwent an earlier revolution when accurate dating of relics was first made possible by C14 radioactive carbon isotope testing developed in the late 1940s. The theory was elegantly simple but remained notoriously difficult to apply: the atmosphere is constantly producing 'radiocarbon', and during its life a plant or animal is exchanging carbon with its surroundings, so it will have the same proportion of the C14 isotope as the atmosphere. When the plant or animal dies, no further C14 is acquired, and what was absorbed in life undergoes radioactive decay at a known and calculable rate. The older a sample, the less C14 it will contain, with 50 per cent decaying in 5,730 years, its natural 'half-life'.

A number of factors initially raised questions over the accuracy of the dating method, such as the assumption that atmospheric production of C14 had remained stable over the millennia; water flowing over rocks to the oceans and ice-age melt water might have affected isotope levels, along with volcanic activity. Although recalibrating the data against objects datable by other means – annual growth rings in sub-fossilized trees, for example – has helped factor out these 'instabilities', sometimes common sense still had to be overlaid on results.

Yannis, who established the very first radiocarbon dating laboratory in Greece, once pointed out to an archaeologist who was basing his dating conclusions on the C14 results from a wooden relic in a grave, that the method would not date the tomb, but rather the age of the tree from which the artefact was made! Wood may have been cut from a 50-year-old trunk, whose planks were reused over many years before being fashioned into the tomb furniture, and if the wood had been reduced to charcoal, it is almost impossible to tell whether it came from inner or outer tree rings, which would have formed in growth decades apart. This is known as the 'old wood' effect.

Alongside C14 dating, isotope signatures of bones and even tooth enamel can provide tell-tale signs of a person's geographic origin: as plants and animals are eaten, minerals from the soil enter the body and its unique composition can identify a location and potentially even a water source. Population migrations have been plotted this way.

Isotope testing has already commenced on the skull of a male found decades ago in Italy in the fallout from Mount Vesuvius, which erupted in AD 79, covering Pompeii and Herculaneum. The working theory was intriguing: the remains of this nobleman in his 50s, found by the beach adorned with gold jewellery and an ornate short sword of the equestrian class, may be Pliny the Elder, the Roman naturalist and admiral. Pliny, who hailed from Como in Italy's north, was 56 when he perished, commanding the local fleet on the day the volcano erupted. His son recorded Pliny's attempt to rescue the victims.

The newspaper article announcing the Italian study neatly worded the hopeful outcome: Italian scientists are just a 'test tube away' from the possible identification.[5] Isotope testing will try to determine if the deceased had lived in the Como region, and then the morphology of the skull, in a Prag-Neave-Musgrave-type reconstruction, will be compared with a surviving bust of Pliny.

Another recent investigation particularly relevant to the Vergina tomb debate concerned a Swedish Viking grave dating to the tenth century AD. Bones of a warrior were found scattered among weapons and horse skeletons, and DNA analysis discovered two X chromosomes, confirming the soldier was female. This was the first hard evidence that the 'shield maidens' of Scandinavian folklore truly existed. Isotope testing showed that she travelled extensively, perhaps due to the Viking seasonal plundering, while some commentators interpret the presence of a gaming board as her role as a military strategist among men.

These new advances in forensics boded well for the bones of Macedon, where the challenge was not just tomb humidity, the cremation of bones at high temperatures and bones covered in soil infill, but also the analysis of skeletal remains that had been found completely submerged in water.

Fate Throws a Lifeline

Towards the end of 2015, soon after the results of the six-year-long study of Tomb II bones had been published, Dr Katerina Lagos, the professor of History at California State University in Sacramento and director of the Hellenic Studies Program, organized a presentation for Theo. He had met Katerina through Professor Carol Thomas some years earlier when her parents owned a well-known restaurant in the university district of Seattle, close to the University of Washington. Soon after giving the lecture, Theo was offered a $15,000 grant to continue the Vergina research, the first formal funding since the 6,000 euros received from the Aristotle University back in 2010.

In a strange twist of fate, the decade of delays since Yannis and Theo had first requested further forensics suddenly became fortuitous: the discovery of the skeletal remains from Tomb I in the basement at Vergina in July 2014 came just before a planned visit by experts to identify the most promising bones from Tombs II and III for DNA, radiocarbon dating and isotope testing. The Tomb I remains could now be included.

Heading the proposed project, Chrysoula Paliadeli had persisted with their application for multidisciplinary forensics which included the Tomb I remains. The Ministry of Culture finally referred their case to the Central Archaeological Council. The team, with Yannis and Konstantina Drosou, an expert in evolutionary biology and biotechnology working with the collaboration of the University of Manchester, appeared in person to plead their case with a carefully prepared power-point presentation.[6]

Permissions for the various analyses were finally granted on 12 April 2016, two years after the original application, but sadly, only for the Tomb I bones, which had been sitting in earth infill for 2,300 years. The permit also included skeletal remains found in an even less benign environment: in 2008, important cremated bones were recovered in a gold vessel full of water and in two additional vessels from a grave close to the ancient 'agora', or market place, of Aegae. The ministry's conditions seemed clear: if you can isolate DNA as well as collagen for C14 and isotope testing from these cremated bone samples, you might then be given a permit for the bones from Tombs II and III.

The problem of accessing ancient human remains was well summed up by an article in the science journal *Nature* titled 'Stop Hoarding Ancient Bones': 'the quest to chronicle the past using DNA from ancient humans and animals has become a cut-throat "game of bones", in which a handful of genetics laboratories are hoarding precious samples.' DNA extraction involves milling small bone fragments of 37cm into powder, so only the few most likely to yield results are selected.[7] Apparently, scientists have been calling for more careful stewardship of DNA-rich specimens to ensure that they remain available for multiple research teams to study. Teeth and the petrous bones of the inner ear are especially rich in genetic material, and laboratories compete for powdered samples. The petrous bone was chosen by the Antikas team from the remains of the babies found in Tomb I.

The terms of the Great Tumulus permits seemed rather unprogressive. If DNA could not be isolated from the cremated agora remains, why should the cremated Tombs II and III 'prime candidates' be refused analysis? Moreover, they are the most likely samples to be identified with historic individuals, considering that Tomb I became a dumping ground for corpses, like the several-times-opened grave discovered in 1987 at Finikas near Thessalonica. Nevertheless, the submerged agora bones, found at Vergina in 2008 in an unmarked grave, presented an intriguing possibility in the quest for the family of Alexander the Great.

Heracles: Alexander's Forgotten Son

The mysterious burial site found in 2008 lay close to the ancient market place of Aegae in the proximity of the sanctuary of Eucleia, which was commissioned by Alexander's grandmother Eurydice. It measured some 8 × 10 metres in total and had been back-filled with earth. There were no burial markers or tombstones. Inside the first grave lay a large bronze cylindrical vessel with vertical handles attached by heart-shaped leaves; on top sat a slightly conical lid with ornamental handle. When it was lifted, a gold cylindrical vase, or '*pyxis*', was revealed inside, also with a lid. The vase was found to be full of water, mud and organic material, but was crowned by a gold oak wreath.[8] In the muddy water lay the cremated bones of an adolescent male, along with evidence of a gold-and-purple fabric.

The following year, in the same burial area but 5 metres further south, separate containers were unearthed, one of them a unique silver Panathenaic amphora ornamented with gold. Beside it lay a silver water pourer constructed in two parts like the 'hydria' found in Tomb III. These containers housed the cremated remains of a child aged 3–7 years and an adult, their genders undetermined. Gold discs, possibly from a diadem, and a further gold olive wreath pointed to the presence of royalty. It fell to Professor Chrysoula Paliadeli and her assistant, Athanasia Kyriakou, to start probing into the mystery. They immediately contacted Yannis and an experienced conservator, who performed a painstaking micro-excavation of the *pyxis* to separate bones from the intense network of roots that had penetrated the barrel over time.[9]

What was clear from the exceptional quality of the first wreath, similar to the examples found in Tombs II and III, was the importance of this male teenager, who was no older than 17 when he died. Ceramic fragments in the grave suggest this was probably from the late fourth century BC, soon after Alexander's reign. What was also apparent from this unmarked grave was that it had been *deliberately* hidden. The secret burial of a teenage 'royal' presented another almost unique set of circumstances that might be linked to Alexander's oldest son.[10]

The tale of Heracles, born to Alexander's part-Asiatic mistress Barsine, is rather tragic when viewed from any angle. Barsine was said to be the daughter of a half-Rhodian woman and Artabazus, a Persian governor with Achaemenid royal blood who had been given sanctuary in Macedon by Philip II when Alexander was a boy. But despite Barsine's regal lineage, the accounts we have infer that Alexander declined to marry her, leaving Heracles little chance of being recognized as his heir. Ignored by all the historical sources until after Alexander's death, the boy became another exploited pawn in the Successor Wars.

Heracles was rejected by the assembly at Babylon and grew up in obscurity, probably as an unofficial hostage of Antigonus the One-Eyed in Pergamum in

Above: the bronze cylindrical vessel. Below: the gold pyxis inside with the submerged gold oak wreath in the state it was discovered. (*Aristotle University of Thessaloniki – Vergina Excavation Archive*)

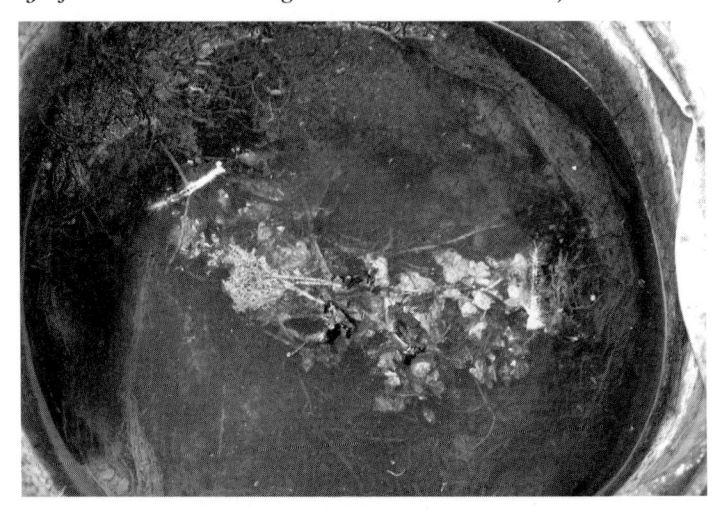

Anatolia. In 310/309 BC, when the boy was around 17, the desperate Polyperchon, who was by now allied with Antigonus, presented Heracles to the Macedonians to undermine Cassander, who had been de facto ruler of the state since executing Olympias and Alexander IV in 315 BC. The Macedonians are said to have 'regarded the restoration of the king without disfavour', which we might interpret as their rejection of Cassander's usurpation of power.[11] We know nothing about Heracles' appearance, his personality or his upbringing during those intervening years; some scholars even suggest the boy being introduced by Polyperchon was a pretender and not Alexander's offspring at all.[12]

The persuasive Cassander convinced the gullible Polyperchon to execute the prince; as his reward, Polyperchon would receive land grants and a new military post in the Peloponnese. In Justin's words, Cassander 'sent secret orders that he [Heracles] should be put to death together with his mother Barsine, and that their bodies should be privately buried in the earth lest the murder should be betrayed by a regular funeral'. In other words, they followed the plight of Rhoxane and her son.[13] What does remain clear is the importance Cassander placed on ending the boy's bid for the throne.[14]

Polyperchon was obviously desperate to cling on to some form of power in the fast-changing post-Alexander world, but he had been previously loyal to Olympias and the infant King Alexander IV. If some fealty tinged with regret extended to Alexander's remaining son, then it is conceivable that he covertly cremated and buried Heracles at Aegae as close to the family tombs as he dared, and with the apparel of royalty. Traces of fire at the site suggest due rites of passage were performed, and the location of the graves, inside the city's fortified walls and not in the external cemetery, is a further mark of respect.[15]

In November 2014, Dr Athanasia Kyriakou, the point person at Aristotle University during the Antikas team study, published an article on the agora burial site which focused on the construction of the partly submerged gold oak wreath. When the workmanship was compared with the Tomb II and III examples, it was apparent that each of them, three of only five fourth-century gold wreaths ever discovered in Macedon, belonged, once again, 'to the same artistic tradition and possibly the same place of production'; another wreath found near Amphipolis is included in the list.[16] A skilled single goldsmith might have been responsible for their manufacture using gold from the same deposits, though the extremely high purity of the ore made any isotope testing difficult, with the aforementioned caveats on the accuracy of this approach.[17]

Just as intriguing was the substance Yannis analyzed on the inside of the conical lid of the bronze barrel containing the *pyxis*: a thick black line appeared to have been painted with a crude brush on the inner concave side in a material that looked like tar. Infrared spectroscopy revealed this was not the abundant pine pitch of the era, but bitumen or asphalt from a petroleum source. This was the kind of combustible ingredient in what later became known as 'Greek fire' in the Byzantine era. Its forerunner was an early form of flame thrower, as described by Thucydides to assault a city in the Peloponnesian War; the highly combustible liquid was propelled through an iron pipe by bellows blowing over a cauldron containing coals, sulphur or 'brimstone' and pitch.[18]

Yannis concluded that because there are very few locations in Greece where this material could be found, it is most logical to assume an Iran-Iraq connection, where it was widely reported in ancient texts, and thus it originated in ancient Persia and was brought to Macedon as a result of Alexander's campaign. Bitumen was used across Mesopotamia and in the mortar of the famous walls and gates of Babylon, and was perhaps imported to Macedon to be used in the ever-developing siege technology of Philip and Alexander. For Yannis the symbolism was clear: the adolescent in the burial had ties to the East!

The possibility that Heracles had been found was tantalizing, but only DNA profiling of all the individuals found in the cluster of Philip II could provide additional proof of a family blood tie to these agora remains. If the adult found adjacent proved to be female and had the same mitochondrial DNA as his, we would have grounds for claiming Barsine had been found. But there were insufficient bones to estimate the age of the adult from skeletal evidence alone. This was unfortunate because I had already argued that Barsine was a granddaughter, not daughter, of Artabazus, who was already well advanced in age when Alexander encountered him in Asia.[19]

New applications were made in 2009, 2012 and 2014 by Chrysoula, Yannis and a team for multi-disciplinary forensics to further examine the agora finds but, alas, no funding was approved at that stage. The mystery of the hidden teenage 'royal' remained.

Tomb I: The Bone Repository

On 5 April 2017, Laura was finally able to prepare specimens from the Tomb I bones found in the Vergina Laboratory for their overseas journey to various chosen laboratories. They would travel first to Yannis at the National Centre for Scientific Research Demokritos in Athens, and then on to the Institute of Biotechnology at the University of Manchester for DNA testing under the auspices of Konstantina Drosou. The Macedonian royalty were destined to journey as far post mortem as they had travelled in life.

The remainder of the Tomb I bones, those which had sat for two decades or more in the office occupied by Nikolaos Xirotiris and then Antonis Bartsiokas, were yet to leave the Komotini Archaeological Ephorate in Thrace, even though a delivery request to the Archaeological Service had been tendered the year before by Chrysoula Paliadeli and Yannis. The remains of the teenager from the ancient agora were still housed at the Archaeological Museum of Thessalonica, and Yannis journeyed north to collect them in person.

On 27 April, Laura met Yannis in Athens to finally decide which specific samples would be used in the forensics, and Konstantina flew in from the UK to chaperone the selected fragments back to Manchester. A decision also had to be made on which bones to hold back for future testing, when new technologies might be available that would beggar belief today, just as DNA sampling and spectral analysis would have been incomprehensible to Léon Heuzey and his team in 1855, or to Heinrich Schliemann when digging at Mycenae, Tiryns and Troy. This was a big day for the project; after some forty years of controversy that had divided an academic community, the bones would soon be travelling to their 'final solutions'.

One of the best sources of DNA are unburned and intact teeth which can often be found at the edge of funeral pyres; when gums 'boil', teeth can literally pop out some distance and manage to avoid the highest temperatures. Although tooth roots are often intact for DNA extraction, the crowns are usually absent, frustrating ageing efforts. Both unburned and burned teeth were found in the remains of the pyre found on top of Tomb II, as well as in the gold chest, and some roots remained in the jawbone. Intact teeth were also found in Tomb I, but not at the agora burial.[20]

So the pressure was now on Konstantina. With a post-doctorate in biomolecular archaeology, she had six years of experience in both fieldwork and laboratory disciplines in Greece, Romania, the UK and at the Roman necropolis at Sanisera on Menorca. Her first Bronze-Age site experience was memorable: at what is commonly referred to on the island of Samos as the 'Tomb of Ajax', the cousin of Achilles, she found herself working for a manipulative archaeologist who never paid her. When corresponding with Konstantina, she admitted to me that this experience led her to assume there would be no other kind of archaeologist other than that, and she was happily surprised to revise her opinion after she met Theo, Laura and the archaeological team in 2014: 'The first thing I noticed was how passionate they are; I hope I will still have that enthusiasm when I reach their age!'

Konstantina is also an expert in ancient Greek mythology and philosophy, but she knew from the age of 10 that her future lay in tombs after reading of the find of Tutankhamun in the Valley of the Kings. Since then, she was fascinated about the prospects for ancient DNA testing and was sure this would be the future of archaeology. She was right, though she never anticipated she would be involved in a project of this import.

Konstantina and I had first exchanged emails in March 2017, when I was able to question her on the prospects of isolating DNA from cremated remains. Her reply was professionally cautious: she explained that it is largely sample-specific and there are too many variables involved to predict the chance of success before the actual analysis. In cremated bones, DNA can survive up to 800°C, but the length of the cremation plays a major role as well, and there are only estimated models. As a reference point, I knew that modern commercial funeral kilns are set between 700 and 1,000°C with a 60–90-minute cycle time; that, followed by milling after burning, turns everything to fine ash. I also knew from the academic papers on experimental cremations with various woods that in extreme circumstances funeral pyres can become hotter than 800°C. Clearly, isolating DNA from the ancient cremated bones of Aegae would be a challenge.[21]

'Theo the Thracian'

Anyone who had come into contact with the skeletal remains from Vergina had to undergo DNA testing themselves, so that their unique signatures could be isolated and identified to rule out contamination. On 16 March 2017, Theo and Laura sent their personal swabs to Konstantina, who was in the process of contacting all anthropologists or archaeologists who had previously handled the Vergina bones, including tracking down a conservator who had worked with the remains from the agora and who now lived in Nigeria with her diplomat husband.[22] The team provided Konstantina informed consent and permission for their 'haplotyping' and for the discussion that followed.

Laura's results from mitochondrial DNA were predictable: as a redhead with Scottish, Irish, Danish and Swedish ancestors, her maternal family roots lay with the Mesolithic hunter-gatherers of south-western Europe, a genetic marker that dominates today in the populations of Scandinavia and the Basque country. Yannis found that his maternal ancestors descended from a haplogroup that constitutes less than 2 per cent of the modern Greek population; it is traceable back to early farmers and stock breeders who migrated from the East, with a last genetic mutation taking place in the Early Bronze Age in the Caucasus region. They went on to populate what is now Finland, the Central Slavic countries and Germany.

Just as unanticipated was Theo's maternal grouping, which came from southern Central Europe. To soften the blow for a proud Greek raised in the heartland of ancient Macedon, Laura labelled him as he might have been known in the ancient world: a 'Thracian'. This was somewhat ironic, as it was the Thracians who were often depicted by the Greeks as 'red-haired' in vase paintings.[23] But the results better tied in with his family roots in Constantinople, the westernmost part of Thrace, which covered much of modern Bulgaria.

If the Argead kings of Macedon were truly of Argive descent and Dorian stock, their warlords, brought into the aristocracy as Philip expanded the state, were of clans indigenous to the rugged regions of Upper Macedonia. What had added colour to the genetic kaleidoscope of Macedon was Philip's method of expanding the state: he imported captives and conquered tribes onto the fringes of the realm to populate and work the land, and of course serve in his growing professional army. Rather than creating a diffuse national identity, Philip's policy seems to have stirred the new residents into adding the ethnonym 'Makedon' to their names in a new spirit of nationalism as battles were won.

Philip's tribal integration is further evidenced by a speech Alexander gave to his mutinous troops at the city of Opis on the banks of the Tigris just a year before he died. To counter the rising sedition, Alexander reminded his infantrymen: 'Philip took you in when you were a collection of impoverished nomads ... dressed in skins and herding a few sheep on the mountains ... he brought you down ... into the plains' and 'made you city dwellers ... with the benefits of law and a civilized way of life.'[24] So while the Greeks may have grudgingly acquiesced to the notion that the kings of Macedon were of Hellenic Argive descent, it is unlikely they viewed the general populace as anything but barbarians.

Theo's genetic make-up is beyond dispute or opinion, despite any cultural loyalties, affiliations or desired heroic lineages he may covet. Konstantina cautioned me that DNA knows no nations, no race and certainly no modern borders; from it we cannot deduce specific modern ethnicity and should not push political agendas. Theo's ancestors may have first entered Thrace and then the cultural sphere of Macedon in any one of the legendary cultural upheavals, the tribal migrations of prehistory or even Philip's conquests in the nation's bordering lands. As one modern evolutionary biologist put it: 'DNA neither cares nor knows. DNA just is. And we dance to its music.'[25]

Theo the Hippologist

Theo has many scholarly titles, including archaeozoologist, but at heart he remains a 'horse man' and a lover of anything equine; 'horses carry my soul' is his favourite phrase, extracted from an ancient poem by Parmenides.[26] In the foreword to his 2004 book on equestrian races at the ancient Olympics, Theo made a topical dedication to Laura, 'who has suffered with patience for fifteen years, the endless absences and insomnias of a horse vet, and bent affectionately over the graves of heroes, riders and horses in order to help resolve the mystery of the Greek pathos for the art of equitation'.[27]

Theo reminded me that the name Philip, 'Philippos' to the Greeks, was derived from the Greek '*philos*' and '*hippos*', thus a 'friend' or 'lover' of the 'horse'. A member of the Hellenic Equestrian Association and former founder-president of the Hellenic Pony Club, as well as a regular judge and vet at international equestrian competitions, Theo is the first person any scientific body approaches if ancient horse bones are excavated. He is the 'father of modern hippology' in Greece, no less.

Herodotus claimed there were once 'fish-eating' horses in Macedon. For some, this was almost as unbelievable as the mythical 'flesh-eating' mares of the

Theo preparing a rare Archaic Period horse skeleton found at Sindos.

Thracian King Diomedes, those Heracles had to tame during his Eight Labours and the very horses from which Alexander's stallion Bucephalus was said to be descended. But sure enough, in 2004, Theo and Laura reported on their examination of a recently exhumed horse carcass; over 20 per cent of its diet had been marine, probably ground fishmeal, so abundant was marine life close to the shores of the Thermaic Gulf. I wondered if Philip fed this protein-rich food to his racehorses competing at Olympia; he won victory wreaths in 356 BC, the year of Alexander's birth, as well as in 352 BC and 342 BC.[28]

In order to die 'a happy man', Theo would like archaeologists to find the grave of Bucephalus. It would be located in the Punjab region of Pakistan, where the stallion died either from wounds or old age following the Battle at the Hydaspes River when Alexander was entering India. He nostalgically founded a city, Bucephala, in the steed's honour. Unfortunately, the course of the river has changed dramatically in the past two millennia and one of the most famous horses of all time still lies in an unmarked burial site.

The story of Bucephalus, 'Ox-Head', commenced when Alexander was a youth. A Thessalian horse dealer named Philonicus was attempting to sell the stallion to Philip. Watching on with growing frustration at the various attempts to mount the unruly steed, Alexander begged his father to dispense with the 'useless fools' and let him try to master the horse.[29] Philip questioned whether his son could manage the beast any better and asked what the price of his impertinence might be if he failed. Alexander retorted: 'I will pay for the horse myself.'

Noting it was scared of its own shadow, Alexander turned Bucephalus into the sun, stroked the fear out of him, jumped upon his back at a run and spurred Bucephalus into a gallop, to the cheers of the onlookers. 'Alexander, Macedon is too small for you, you will need to find yourself a worthy kingdom,' came Philip's alleged praise, which, with the benefit of hindsight, housed something of a veiled warning; Alexander would be exiled for his ambition a few years later.

According to Arrian, Bucephalus' name derived from '*bous kephale*', 'ox head' in ancient Greek, either for an ox-shaped white star on his black forehead or a similarly shaped branding mark of the Thessalian breeder who sold the horse to Philip for the enormous sum of 13 talents, equivalent to 338kg of silver or US $180,000 at 2019 value.[30]

Alexander's colourful first encounter with Bucephalus was uniquely preserved by Plutarch, who cited a suspicious folio of state correspondence elsewhere as sources for his biographies, much of which made its way into the fable-rich *Greek Alexander Romance*. So the episode's historicity must be open to question, as it resonates of Homeric parallels in which the heroes of the *Iliad* were epitheted 'breakers' or 'tamers' of horses, a necessary rite of passage in becoming a true warrior. It also parallels the myth of Bellerophon mounting the wild winged Pegasus.

Horses were, nonetheless, an integral part of the Macedonian army and Alexander would undoubtedly have read Xenophon's treatise on the skills every cavalry officer needed. The distances travelled by Alexander's cavalry on campaign were staggering, while the ever-more dissatisfied and mutinous Macedonian infantry marched on foot to the regions beyond the Indus. Theo had his own view on the perfect mount for extended campaigning: 'If Philip and Alexander, who rode something like 25,000 and 45,000 kilometres in their respective campaigns, used diagonal trotters, their rumps would be minced meat! It seems apparent to me that they must have ridden Greek lateral movers.' Theo's equine curiosity was now probing at the genetic level.

Horses, humans and almost all mammals walk or trot 'diagonally'. We instinctively move the left hand and right foot at the same time, just as horses move the forward left and hind right leg in sync, and vice versa when changing step. Aristotle first commented on the phenomenon, and then Pliny the Elder in Roman times.[31] The result is a bouncing ride, especially at the trot.

Backing-up Theo's hypothesis was the recent discovery of a genetic mutation which has significant benefits to the horse and rider alike. Referred to as 'gaiters' or 'pacers', though Theo prefers the term 'lateral movers', horses with the mutation move the front and hind legs on the same side together, and, as a result, much faster. This configuration makes for a more comfortable ride and results in fewer injuries to the horse: 'you can drink a cup of coffee on a lateral mover,' Theo claimed.

Taking this contention forward, the wielding of spears and the hurling of javelins by cavalry, and also hunting on horseback in an age without saddles or stirrups, must have been easier on this genetic strain. Riders sat on animal skin shabraques or lined cloths, and to control the horse they relied on reins attached to the sidebars of snaffle-bits and harsher spiked rollers, along with prick-spurs attached to boots. Pulling off wheeling tactics and keeping in tight formation was critical for survival, as were well-trained horses responsive to the rider's commands. Experienced cavalry officers on good mounts were invaluable to an army and more highly remunerated than their infantry counterparts, perhaps by a factor of three.[32]

Theo proposed that the Macedonian cavalry horses *were* most likely lateral movers for exactly these reasons, and he believed the breed was identifiable well before Alexander's day. The vases, coins, statues and other artefacts we have from the period depicting the mythical Pegasus and other celebrated horses victorious at the Greek games, frequently show them in a 'gaiting' stride, not trotting.

Between 2012 and 2016, Theo had DNA samples from 262 ancient horse skeletons found across mainland Greece and Crete analyzed by Dr Gus Cothran at the Animal Genetics Laboratory at Texas A&M University. In August 2017, Dr Cothran and a team of specialists from the US, Sweden, Spain, Iran and Japan published their finds. The results were remarkable: more than 80 per cent bore the gait gene, but Theo felt he still needed 'more skeletons to confirm the ancient DNA theory, so no one throws tomatoes at my theory'.[33]

In a wider study of DNA from 382 horses from seventy-two breeds, researchers managed to isolate the gene 'which has a major impact on gaitedness', now labelled 'DMRT3'. They concluded that the mutation took place 'recently' in horse evolution, either just before their human domestication or, more likely, just after, some 5,000–6,000 years ago. The report corroborated Theo's thoughts: although the exact geographic origin of the mutation could not be ascertained, it is thought that it could have spread widely via the military exploits of Alexander the Great. Furthermore, the Romans, and their use of Greek horses, could have helped spread the mutation throughout Europe and the Middle East. Theo's once controversial equine theory had finally taken root.

Once more, I recalled Justin's reporting on Philip II's troubled Scythian campaign that '20,000 fine mares were sent into Macedonia to raise a breed', although all the booty was lost when the Macedonians were attacked on their return.[34] Pliny gave insight into why female horses were chosen: 'The Scythians prefer mares for purposes of war, because they can pass urine without breaking their gallop.' That notion is undermined by Scythian and Sarmatian iconography in which stallions are depicted, though Herodotus reported that they castrated their horses to make them more tractable.[35]

Following in the footsteps of his father, Alexander is said to have sent 5,000 Scythian horses of Central Asian stock back to Macedon, a huge undertaking when considering the distance and pasturing required along the way. Moreover, the Hellespont or Bosphorus had to be crossed on barges, a reversal of his outbound feat when he invaded Asia with a similar number of cavalry mounts. It must have been a spectacular horse drive to have taken part in.

Adrienne Mayor at Stanford University researched the breeds as part of her quest for the Amazons: besides the short, robust and rugged Mongolian-type of horse found with their owners in Scythian graves, skeletons suggest they may have ridden the forerunners of the shimmering-coated and blue-eyed Akhal Teke horses from what is today Turkmenistan and the Ferghana Valley. These latter are 'tall and elegant with high-set necks, long legs and visible tendons, and relatively small hooves'. Both types are depicted in ancient Greek art.[36]

Adrienne followed with a description of the speed, power and beauty of these 'Golden Horses' whose ancestors were coveted by emperors, kings and adventurers from China to Macedon, including Genghis Khan and Marco Polo. Their descendants, the svelte Akhal Tekes, the 'greyhounds of the horse world', have a 'floating stride', otherwise described as a 'soft gait that seems to float over the ground'.

Recent DNA studies confirm Akhal Tekes are one of the earliest domesticated breeds of horse, with much of the research under the auspices of an international collaboration titled 'The Equine Genetic Diversity Consortium' (EGDC). Akhal Tekes, like Persian Arabs, are known for their endurance and chosen for distance travel, and their forerunners may have been one of the stock of choice for the Scythians. Although they don't exhibit the 'gait-keeper' gene, as it is commonly called, their smooth stride reinforces Theo's appreciation of the quality of the mount the Macedonians must have required. There are only some 3,500 pedigreed Akhal Teke horses remaining today, and a programme is underway to accelerate their breeding.

Adrienne reminded me that Bucephalus was said to kneel for Alexander to mount him more easily, unlike any other Macedonian horse.[37] 'It was well-known that Scythian horses knelt to allow riders to mount, a lifesaver for unhorsed riders holding their weapons in the heat of battle on the steppes. This has led some to speculate that Bucephalus may have actually been of Scythian stock, or perhaps trained by a Scythian groom if not,' she added.[38] It is unlikely that horses from eastern Eurasia had been imported into Macedon before Alexander's campaigns in the region, but more local mares from northern Thrace or the Scythian Danube could have been. 'If only we could locate the fine grave holding the bones of the noble Bucephalus in the ruins of his namesake town founded by Alexander in Afghanistan!' Adrienne opined. I could see why she and Theo had maintained an enthusiastic dialogue since 2008.

Image from a frieze of figures on an amphora found in a Chertomylk kurgan depicting a Scythian training a horse to kneel for the rider to mount.

Theo the 'Impatient'

On 19 May 2017, just as the first Vergina bones were beginning their voyages to laboratories around the world, Theo suffered a major stroke at the age of 77. A large embolism had formed in the middle cerebral artery at the right side of his brain and he suddenly collapsed, fortunately when Laura was at home. Theo was rushed to a local hospital, where surgeons took advice from the medical team in Thessalonica, but he lost the use of the left side of his body. Laura and I conference-called frequently in the days that followed when the prognosis was uncertain.

Ironically, after all the time the Antikas team had dedicated to studying cremations at Vergina, Theo had to sign a document enabling his body to be burned, should he pass away. The Greek Orthodox Church does not permit cremation of those who were baptized, and there are still no crematoriums in Greece, despite EU law requiring them. As a result, many Greeks have to travel to Bulgaria or Germany to cremate loved ones. The church does, however, permit 'disinterment', the digging up of a buried corpse once a three-year lease is up on a cemetery grave.

Laura reminded me that medical staff make the worst patients; 'impatients' she calls them, and this applied to Theo, a former military doctor. For the first two weeks he received intense treatment at the 424 Military Hospital, and was then transferred to a rehabilitation centre on the outskirts of Thessalonica. Laura began driving the three-hour round trip four times a week to visit. Theo's long-term memory was still shaky, but his immediate thought processes seemed intact, sufficiently so that he recommended laser therapy for his recovery.

Back in 1986, Theo had penned a pioneering paper on the therapeutic effects of 'soft laser treatment' on horses, which accelerated the healing of wounds, and now he wanted the benefits himself. One of Theo's human trials had been memorable. In 2000, Jim Stansfield, the chief photographer of *National Geographic*, visited Theo and Laura when they lived on the foothills of Mount Olympus. The magazine was running a Millennium article on Alexander the Great and it needed images of a Thessalian stallion that resembled Bucephalus.

Theo found a suitable horse, and one early morning Anemos, as the stallion was named, was filmed galloping across a wheat field. While Jim was able to capture another black stallion rearing up into the perfect dramatic pose, which was 'very Bucephalus of the horse' Theo recalls telling him, a recurring back problem was aggravated after days of carrying heavy photographic equipment across the hilly terrain. Theo managed to treat Jim with laser therapy, and had him proverbially 'back in the saddle' in no time and snapping away with his camera.

I finally conferenced with Theo in his hospital bed on 16 July 2017. 'I am being taken care of, but I am longing for a glass of wine,' he told me. 'David, come down to see me and we will make new libations to all Pierian Muses with double-distilled tsipouro!' I listened and laughed as Theo indulged himself in ancient quotes, quips and his longing for the local pomace brandy. It was clear he was on the mend, mentally at least.

An ancient Greek expression reminds us that: 'There is no evil devoid of good'. Sure enough, the Antikas team determined that nothing was going to be wasted by the recent setback. Laura was able to collate the X-rays of Theo's spine for future research; his age and lifestyle provided a useful benchmark, particularly his time in the saddle which was shared by many ancient nobles. Among the tell-tale signs for regular horse riding are changes to the spine; photographs of Theo's could now be compared to ancient skeletons and hopefully be of use to anthropologists.

Throughout the summer of 2017, Theo continued his therapy. He was soon beating Laura at Scrabble, but he still had issues with his short-term memory, could not walk unassisted and his concentration span was short. Nevertheless, they felt some progress had finally been made on all other fronts. Dr Margarita Gleba had been given the go-head by Chrysoula Paliadeli to study the textile stains on the bones of the Tomb II male, Yannis Maniatis was awaiting the C14 results from Tomb I and the agora bones, and Konstantina Drosou was preparing to undertake the DNA analysis on them. In the words of the Italian publication reporting on the possible remains of Pliny, the 'royal' bones from the first Vergina tomb might just be a 'test tube away' from being given names.

Chapter 17

The Little Summer of Saint Demetrius

> Wait for the wisest of all counsellors, time.
> —Pericles

In early October 2017, I flew into the new international airport at Kalamata in the southern Peloponnese which is overlooked by Mount Taygetos, whose northern hills and slopes were once the hunting ground of the Spartans. This was the first part of an overdue personal odyssey I planned to start in Messenia, one of the poorest parts of Greece in modern times and yet one of the richest in antiquity. The region is now famous for its large and meaty aromatic olives, best enjoyed with a hard spicy sheep's cheese known as 'sfela'.

I determined to visit the Mycenaean-era remains of what is known as 'Nestor's Palace' and the ancient stadium at Olympia, where I would self-indulgently watch dawn spread its 'rosy fingers', to use Homer's colourful description of the birth of each sunrise. Sure enough, the shadows cast by the Hill of Cronus slowly receded to where the treasuries of each participating city-state once stood above the holy precinct. To the north, and still shrouded in the smoke-blue haze of the waking day, lies the 600ft-long stadium, the distance Heracles is said to have run without taking a breath.

Still standing majestically dominant before the archway into the arena are the base and columns of the Philippeion, erected as a 'political statement of Philip's dominance over Greece', I heard one Greek tourist guide declare. Philip had the wall of the sacred precinct diverted to house his circular 'propaganda' which, I also noted, remains conspicuously absent of any description which might guide the passers-by.

'Many are the sights to be seen, and many the wonders to be heard; but on nothing does god bestow more care than on the Eleusinian Rites and the Olympic Games,' wrote Pausanias when making his pilgrimage though the region.[1] War was put on hold in Greece for the sacred festival that marked the athletics and equine races, despite the fact that the nearby cites of Elis and Pisa had battled for centuries for control of the archaic site. When Pisa finally capitulated, the city was destroyed and its stones were used to build the great Olympian Temple of Zeus, which would become one of the Seven Wonders of the ancient world.

The Philippeion, Olympia, today. (*Author photo*)

Thucydides, Socrates, Plato, Aristotle and Demosthenes all visited Olympia whilst writing themselves into history; before them, Herodotus had given readings of his *Histories* to the crowd as wreaths of wild olives were being placed on the victors' heads, one of them, allegedly, belonged to a Macedonian king. Perhaps they recited and orated at the renowned '*heptaechoes*' portico, where the acoustics guaranteed seven reverberations around the grove where Ptolemy Philadelphus once made a dedication to remind Greece where true power and wealth resided.

Across the Dancing Floor of Ares

I drove across the hills and shadowed valleys of the once Sparta-policed Lacedaemon, and I journeyed north up the knuckled spine of Greece. Departing the Peloponnese on a tight schedule, I first entered the once-mighty Mycenaean city of Argos and walked through the Argive amphitheatre, which is now encroached upon by modern housing.

In the second century AD, when Pausanias produced his *Guide to Greece*, the metropolis was already more Roman-looking in construction. Argos once boasted twenty-nine tombs of legendary mortals and heroes associated with the city, including that of Homer's Lycymnius, an Argive warrior killed by Heracles' son Tlepolemus. It was upon his tomb that Pyrrhus of Epirus is said to have collapsed in his war against Antigonus II Gonatas, after his famed elephants had fallen and blocked his escape through the main city gate.[2]

When marching to war in his distinctive goat-horned helmet, Pyrrhus was likened to the mighty Alexander: 'The other kings, they said, represented Alexander with their purple robes, their bodyguards, the inclination of their necks, and their louder tones in conversation; but Pyrrhus, and Pyrrhus alone, in arms and action.'[3] He was decapitated at Argos and given funeral rites with a cremation by Antigonus, but neither his nor any of the twenty-nine graves have ever been found.

I swung out of the city and headed north by the easternmost route through Livadia and Orchomenus, where Mycenaean-era tombs are still being unearthed, adding to the 4,000 Bronze Age graves discovered over the past 150 years.[4] I followed the road south-west to the oracle at Delphi, with its impossibly beautiful location where mountains hang over a precipitous gorge. Legend claims that Apollo shook the ground in contempt at the approach of the Celtic Gauls when they plundered its sacred grove; rocks came crashing down in the thick of a lightning storm and hail pelted the invaders. Ancient Greek heroes even rose from the dead and appeared before the marauders.

Over 100,000lb of gold and 110,000lb of silver were said to have been lifted from the Delphic precinct, possibly including the self-dedicated gold statue of Alexander I, a haul that underpinned the story of the famed 'gold of Tolosa' that was allegedly rediscovered by the Romans in a sacred Celtic lake in 106 BC.[5]

The winding journey up the mountain pass was peaceful and the ancient heroes appeared to be sleeping. But the atmosphere of the sanctuary at Delphi, where the Greeks believed Heaven and Earth truly met, was still haunting. I introduced myself to the remains of the monument to Craterus, who was Alexander's foremost general by the end of the Asian campaign and whose stone niche overlooking the Temple of Apollo was over 15 metres long and 6 metres wide; a hunting scene once depicted him assisting Alexander spear a lion.[6]

Leaving the sanctuary back-dropped by its steep hillside theatre and higher hidden stadium where Philip had presided over the Pythian Games in 346 BC, I struck inland east and then north, with Mount Parnassus and its rugged range on my right, into the hairpin bends of the hills of Kallidromo and through Mendenitsa. The route winds through the ranges that separate Attica from Boeotia, the 'dancing floor of Ares' as it was known because of the innumerable major battles waged on the plains and dedicated to the god of war. The mountains and narrow gorges that backbone central Greece and so thoroughly separated communities with their limited cultivable land, explains the emergence of the fiercely independent city-states that failed to unite except in times of invasion; more often than not, they were engaged in fratricidal war.

Late in the afternoon, I arrived at Thermopylae, the most famous 'defensive gate' in the history of the western world, whose hot baths were tourist attractions even in ancient times. Over the past 2,500 years the sea has receded, making it difficult to imagine the tight terrain that bottled up vast enemy numbers, a

Laura Wynn-Antikas and author in front of the remains of the monument to Craterus at Delphi.

former topography you can still experience, for example, at the village of Kamena Vourla 10km south-east along the coast. Despite the neon signs and the broad-laned highway that threads its way past modern tourist plaques of Thermopylae, it retains something of its hallowed reputation, bordered by almost sheer mountains sides.

When I spied the rubble that looked as if it were debris of the so-called defensive 'Phocian Wall' spanning the narrow defile, I imagined not the 300 Spartans with their 4,200 allies and enslaved helots who defied Xerxes for three days in 480 BC, but the desperate Greek coalition blocking the Galatae under Brennus in 279 BC. Looking behind me to the south, I could picture them streaming through the hidden track above, while panic-stricken Greek ships looked on and rescued any stranded soldiers they could.

The most fervent of the Galatae fought naked for their gods that day, and their trumpets blasted harsh tones that amplified the tumult of war. Greek ships sitting off the coastal marshland bombarded the invaders' flanks while Greek hoplites maintained their tight phalanx formation despite repeated wild Celtic charges. The kinsman of the bravest Athenian erected a memorial with a shield dedicated to 'Zeus of Freedom' at Thermopylae, but it had been lifted by the Roman dictator Sulla and ferried back to Italy by the time Pausanias visited the pass.

Today, the battle with the Celts has been subordinated to a suitably laconic epitaph to the better-known Spartan heroes which marks the burial ground at the foot of the Kolonos Hill where they fell. Hundreds of arrowheads were excavated from the very spot as a testament to their last stand against, the tourist plate reminded me, 1,700,000 Persians in Herodotus' reckoning; modern scholars suggest they totalled 100,000–150,000. The lines of the lyric poet Simonides, who lived through the Persian Wars, softy cried: 'Oh stranger, tell the Lacedaemonians that we lie here, obedient to their words.' The original tomb of the Spartan king Leonidas, which was once topped by a lion to guard the pass, has long since disappeared.

I departed Thermopylae as shadows from the rugged peaks were leaning towards the sea, and headed towards Lamia in Thessaly, where Alexander's regent Antipater was besieged by Greeks soon after his death. To the east lay the Pelion Mountains and Mount Othrys, where the lost city of Phthia still lies hidden and facing down the dramatic gulf and south across to Euboea. Phthia was famous as the residence of Achilles and his father, and even earlier still, King Hellen of the eponymous race.[7]

The route from Lamia took me north-west to the shrine of Dodona in Epirus. Here, following an earlier battle, Pyrrhus had donated the round shields of Antigonus' fallen Macedonians with a dedication that once read:

> This metal destroyed Asia rich in gold,
> this metal made slaves out of Greeks,
> this metal is lying fatherless
> by the pillars of Zeus of water-streams,
> the spoil of proud-voiced Macedon.[8]

It was late in the evening when I finally departed the forest grove foliated in heavy tranquillity, so I detoured to Dium and spent the night in a small family hotel where Theo and Laura had held their wedding reception a decade ago. My balcony stared up the Olympian slopes to the west and at the archaeological museum in front; the ruins of the sanctuary of Zeus lay nearby. Established by Macedon's King Archelaus I, Dium had witnessed army purification rituals by Philip II and then Alexander on the eve of his crossing to Asia to take on the Persian Empire when he had Athens by the throat. Bronze statues of the thirty-four elite Companion Cavalry who died fighting Darius' army at the Battle of the Granicus River near Troy once stood in its grove.[9] The iron tethers where animals were shackled and slaughtered can still be seen in the rocks laying before the sacrificial altar, which is backdropped by the theatre, field and sacred lake where Alexander erected his tent of the 100 couches.

Destroyed and rebuilt by subsequent kings, and only unearthed in 1806, Dium had been explored by Léon Heuzey in 1855 and then again in 1861 in his quest for the forgotten city of kings. Today the ruins are slowly being subsumed by forest, fig trees and spreading brooks that carry wash from the adjacent mountains. Even the tourist paths appear to be losing the battle with the encroaching scrub. It remains an uplifting location, graced with the sanctuaries of Dionysus, Demeter and the later ruins of the Hellenistic and Roman theatres, baths and the shrine of Asclepius and Isis. Each confirmed the perennial importance of this marshy and verdant valley in the foothills of the gods where Orpheus is said to have been buried.[10]

On a fine but chilly morning, I skirted around the northern side of Mount Olympus and closed in on ancient Pydna. 'Shining Olympus' was still snow-covered and gleaming to my left; its summit, said Homer's *Odyssey*, was 'stormless' and basked in cloudless 'ether', the pure upper air. The description ignores the frequent squalls and tempests that rage about its peaks, when the gods are obviously infighting or angry at the race of men below. The ancient inhabitants of the region had wisely barred themselves from climbing the mountain to check on the state of affairs above.

Pressing Issues at Pydna

I arrived in Makrygialos in the early afternoon and was greeted by Laura at the entrance to their grove. Theo was enjoying a rare day home from the rehabilitation centre to attend the crushing of olives, an annual event attended by all the local smallholders whose crops had been carried to a stone mill in the fields above the town. Lambs and goats were roasting on spits, and ouzo and retsina were splashing eager glasses along with sweet red Romeiko wine from the island of Lemnos, bottled just weeks before.

The pressing had been a success, and unlike the brownish juice emerging from their neighbours' crops, Theo and Laura's extra virgin olive oil was pale green and rendered even more 'extra' by the lower-yielding unripe olives plucked from the branches; the result was 'agourelaio', early harvest oil. Higher in antioxidants and polyphenols and pleasantly astringent, agourelaio is much prized, so I was impressed when a 5-litre can was put aside for me.

That evening we invested ourselves once again in the glow of their olive-wood fire. As for the ongoing forensic testing of the Great Tumulus bones, this point marked, as Laura put it, the 'end of the beginning of the next round'. There was an air of expectation and it was now simply a matter of waiting for results.

Considering everything I had learned about their research over the past eight years, I couldn't help questioning them on both the unexpected scale and the emotional cost of their extended work. I asked the inevitable question: if they knew then what they now know, would they have taken it on with almost no formal funding, and with the pitfalls and barriers along the way?

All learning has an emotional base, Theo reminded me, proudly quoting Plato. I could see his mind churning over an answer that was as thought-provoking as the question: 'Thank the Olympian Gods we did not know!' It was the wisest possible reply.

Laura added that they had been emotionally involved from the start: 'Vergina – Aegae – is the holy grail of excavation sites; how could we refuse?'

It reminded me of the parable of the stonecutters once more. What the dedicated curiosity of the team Chrysoula Paliadeli had assembled had done was not to analyze bones, or identify composite materials while attempting to isolate strands of DNA, they had started rebuilding episodes from a momentous past in vivid forensic 3D; a CSI 'crime-scene investigation' worthy of a television series.

The $15,000 donation from America was all but spent, principally on the carbon dating Yannis Maniatis had organized at the laboratory in Germany. Fortunately, the tenacity of Konstantina meant the DNA tests fell under the auspices of the University of Manchester at no cost to the project. I asked Theo and Laura what they would do next if a larger research budget was available, and soon realized it would be no 'Spartan' laconic reply.

Now that they had established that the Tomb II antechamber weapons and armour belonged to the 'Amazon', Laura wanted the artefacts to be re-examined for further identity clues. She also voiced her hope that a new generation of archaeologists, perhaps those trained on-site at Vergina each summer, would take up the gauntlet; those still unscarred by the 'battle of the bones'. With the wisdom of all her years working on Vergina excavations, Professor Paliadeli had already voiced her own hope and a caution on this front:

> It is a question of time and patience until future generations of historians and archaeologists are able to deal with all the findings, both current and future, in a cool, detached manner and approach on ancient Macedonians and the culture in an unprejudiced way. Until then one must question the intentions of all those who, beneath the dubious protection of a 'given objectivity', claim that they support scientific truth.[11]

Theo wanted the Tomb I bones to undergo a definitive study, one beyond the cursory looks given by Musgrave and Xirotiris in whose office they sat for years, where Bartsiokas later found them. Of course, to do that, the bones we found in 'forgotten' storage at Vergina need reuniting with the fragments still in Thrace. It has been almost a year since their removal was requested. Theo added that someone needs to start a database for the bones of the 'prince' in Tomb III.

The organic material from Tombs II and III still needed analysis, as well as more oral histories from all the excavators to determine where all this was found. Theo explained that the remains of leather could confirm the animal from which it was skinned, domestic or foreign, and he reminded me that Andronikos had found a feather from a large bird on the antechamber larnax. Wood fragments in the tomb can also be analyzed for the tree source and its age, and Theo pointed out that the remains of leather from the lining of greaves might still contain specks of epidermis, the skin of the wearer, for DNA extraction.

Laura recalled that Chrysoula Paliadeli had always wanted to create a website at the Aristotle University detailing the Vergina remains, human and otherwise, in which the bones would undergo 3-D imaging to make future studies easier and to guard against the loss of visual detail through further bone degradation. Towards the end of the Tomb II project in late 2014, Laura had found a useful 3-D imaging course offered jointly by the University of Glasgow and Glasgow School of Art.[12] Once she was familiar with the discipline, Laura would be able to undertake the work on the Vergina bones herself. She was offered a full scholarship to cover the $15,000 tuition fees, but when she crunched the numbers for accommodation and living expenses, the course was simply impossible to commit to.

'Don't forget DNA testing of the two unburned teeth found in the funeral pyre on the roof of Tomb II. Who the heck do they belong to?' Laura added in animated style. I *had* forgotten the two unburned teeth, a canine and a molar, which are intact with crowns and roots, and so prime candidates for DNA preservation and for the ageing of their owners. Did they belong to the killer's accomplices who were executed by Alexander 'at the tumulus of his father'?[13] Andronikos had found two skeletons above the tomb and neither had been given any funeral rites; if they were Heromenes and Arrhabaeus, the accused co-conspirators, their common heritage might finally be revealed.[14]

'More horses!' sang Theo like one of the ancient rhapsodes reciting the *Iliad* before a village campfire. Although there are plenty of horse skeletons from the graves of Vergina and the other ancient cities of Macedon, some predating the Trojan War, a bigger DNA database is needed to find out which breeds the Macedonians rode and if any Asian stock had made its way to Europe. There was a horse tooth found in the remains of Tomb IV; its radio carbon dating could help date the tomb itself.

Discussions broadened to the shortfalls of archaeology in Greece. Laura proposed a programme to educate museum curators on the options they have when exhibiting human remains, especially where preserving chemicals and consolidants are being used and skeletal reconstructions attempted. She was venting her frustration with the glue, vinyl, the 'souvlaki sticks' that held them together, and at the anthropologists' annotations in ink found written on some of the bones.

Laura also wanted a new law passed so that only anthropologists could remove bones from newly discovered tombs.

But above all, we all wished for ongoing DNA, C14 and stable isotope testing on the remains from Tombs II and III. I hoped that the bones found at Amphipolis could be included. If the 60-plus-year-old woman is related to the adolescent in Tomb III, we would have some reason to name her 'Olympias'. Back in 2015, the Greek government earmarked 236,000 euros for a two-year anthropological study to include 1,000 bone fragments from graves close to the Casta Hill site for comparison with tomb skeletons. But the permit expired in summer 2017 before any forensics took place.[15] Work came to a standstill at Amphipolis, although the Greek minister for Culture and Sports more recently announced that the tomb would be open to the public within three years, now that 2.8 million euros of new funding had been secured.[16]

We each felt that the latest-generation forensic disciplines should be extended to *all* skeletal remains in northern Greece that appeared to belong to nobility. This could establish not only their family relationships, but the very origins of the race, which might exorcise, or endorse, some ghosts from the founding myths of Macedon.

As well as the necropolis of Vergina, there are the 1,004 graves at Archontiko near Pella, which bear witness to a rich warrior society dating back to the late Iron Age; so far, only 5 per cent of the graves have been studied.[17] Alongside these are remains from the tombs at Agios Athanasios and Derveni, where artefacts suggest the same workshop as those in Tomb II.[18] Twenty-six skeletons in extraordinary condition have also been recovered from Iron Age tombs located between Vergina and Veria at which Laura had already worked for two years. At Pydna there are still thousands of bones that have never been studied. I had heard that private landowners are reticent to dig down on their own terrains as unearthed graves prevent development of the site, and they face stiff fines if they fail to report an antiquity and potentially imprisonment if finds are exploited.

On a Pydna plot a stone's throw from Theo and Laura's house, sits a field cradling Macedonian-styled stone tombs, one of which yielded a fine gold myrtle wreath. A hastily thrown up and now-rusting corrugated iron roof on a flimsy-looking wooden frame stands over the excavation as an ugly testament to the ubiquity of local finds. Laura and I had climbed around the structure and thrust our cameras through the chicken wire. I wondered what the ancient Macedonians would make of our architectural advancement, and what modern farmers think of these beautiful tombs which exceed any memorial they might expect today.

Just to the south sits a tomb at Sevasti dated by the excavator to 320 BC. Its impressive jug or 'krater', with its spearheads and symposium cups, suggests a high-status returning soldier of Alexander the Great. In eighty-or-so plundered tombs at Finikas, coins dating to the reign of Amyntas III were retrieved.[19]

272 *Unearthing the Family of Alexander the Great*

Protective corrugated structures over tombs at Kitros and the outskirts of Makrygialos, ancient Pydna, housing Macedonian-style Tombs. (*Author photos*)

Unfortunately, modern construction and the foundations of a new Carrefour superstore have ruled out further study of the ancient settlement to which they belong. Many 'finds' in northern Greece are, in fact, 'rescue excavations', hurriedly undertaken in the face of modern development which unceremoniously cements them over, often without sufficient time for archaeologists to analyze the graves. The completion of excavations of the prehistoric cemetery at Vergina was necessitated by a new road which passed right through it to link Veria with Vergina and the adjacent villages.[20]

I recalled Eugene Borza's pessimistic summation of excavations in Northern Greece published some years before:

> The future of Macedonian studies is problematic. Archaeological investigation is inherently slow and expensive in both excavation and publication. Greek scholars are pressed financially, overworked by heavy teaching obligations at their universities, frustrated by short excavation and study seasons, and burdened by the expense of publication. Excavators who have no university affiliations, but work for the Archaeological Service ... are subject to the vagaries of the national budget and to the competition among dozens of sites for limited financial resources.

Borza continued with a poignant personal note: 'I myself was present one morning in Pella in 1985 when the director of the excavation there received a phone call from Athens announcing that her funds for continuing had suddenly been axed. She excused herself from our conversation to dismiss the workmen.'[21]

Theo and Laura were stoical when relating current events at Vergina on that November evening, a discussion weighted down by melancholy despite the forward steps. They reminded me that a brand-new museum is nearing completion on 140 hectares of land to the west of the town. Substantially financed by the European Regional Development Fund, which contributed over 4.5 million euros to the second phase of construction, the new 'polycentric' museum will house exhibitions, archaeological parks and an interactive visitor centre. Originally due to be completed in 2016, it is now hoped that its doors will open sometime in 2020. A further 1 million euros is being invested in redevelopment of the palace and necropolis areas.[22]

Dr Angeliki Kottaridi, who now sits on the Museum Policy Board of the Ministry of Culture, drew up the master plan for development at Vergina and must take much of the credit for securing the European grant. She now oversees sixteen other projects with a total budget of 32 million euros that finds its way to museums, monuments and archaeological sites in the region of Emathia. Sadly, not a cent of the money is allocated to any further analysis of the Great Tumulus bones.

As far as I was concerned, the bones were the heart of Vergina and the key to unlocking the mysteries of the royal tombs, underpinning a tourist trade that sees a constant stream of buses disembarking curious passengers in the car park by the Great Tumulus. But excavations had always been divided between the jurisdictions of the Ephorate of Emathia, under the auspices of Dr Kottaridi, and the archaeological work sponsored by the Aristotle University, headed by Professor Chrysoula Paliadeli. The university has a new building, The Interdisciplinary Centre for Archaeological Studies 'Manolis Andronikos', which sits adjacent to the current museum where summer courses on archaeology are held, but the laboratory where Theo and Laura were shunted around for six years falls under the authority of the Ephorate.

We wound up our discussion when the embers of the fire were burning low. I was due to fly to London early the next day and wondered if another national strike was planned. It would have been an outcome that no longer overly concerned me; by now I knew the routes that would bypass the motorway closures, along the valleys in which King Perseus fled Pydna and where Caranus once marched his emigrating city in search of his prophesised land. I could flank the plains where Philip drilled his pikemen to such devastating effect, through the fields where Alexander had perfected his cavalry flying wedges.

We emptied the carafe of wine reflecting on Alexander's untimely death in Babylon, which ended his almost thirteen-year meteoric reign. I had summed him up as an 'elusive equation':

> A calculable axiom of Aristotle's empirical and categorising present, and an indefinable irrational number from the Homeric past. He was a mythopoeic conqueror who at once lived by the tenets of the strategically sound and the proportionally outrageous; a tribal leader recalling heroic deeds, and a mortal seeking apotheosis through his progression from Macedonian king, to Greek hegemon, pharaoh of Egypt and the Persian king of kings.[23]

Alexander would surely be vexed and not a little frustrated that not more post-mortem activity was taking place around his corpse, unless he had anticipated the words of the sapient Roman, Cato the Younger: 'After I'm dead I'd rather have people ask why I have no monument than why I have one.'[24]

Many historians would argue that Alexander didn't deserve a tomb at all. Few monuments had been built during his campaigning, when no new permanent bridges or road network is documented. His 'Alexandrias' were more often than not Asiatic settlements refounded; they appear little more than mud brick forts and a market, or a forced amalgamation of smaller settlements into a larger hastily walled town. Through his campaign decade much had been destroyed. This did not represent a true attempt at architectural permanency, or a city that might last another 10,000 years like the sturdy 'Cyclopean' walls of Mycenae or the mighty columns that porticoed the Sanctuary of Apollo at Delphi.[25]

Alexander's infrastructure was simply redolent of military occupation and the flotsam and jetsam of campaign necessity. The statement that he was essentially 'a destroyer, not a creator' epitomizes the view of many historians, old and new, and it was surely the opinion of the anti-Macedonian Demosthenes, and perhaps even Alexander's teacher, Aristotle, as a rift between them is said to have formed in the final campaign years.[26] What the sober mentor thought of his pupil's demands that Athens provide him with divine honours, we can only speculate. Demosthenes' sarcastic reply became immortalized instead: 'Let Alexander be the son not only of Zeus but also of Poseidon if he so wishes.'[27]

The closely timed deaths of Demosthenes, Aristotle and Alexander, each within the years 323–322 BC, has been termed 'one of the most marvellously significant synchronisms in the history of civilization', marking as it did the end of the productive period of genius in Greece. It also heralded in an age when anecdote and fable gradually usurped the truth, which is why unravelling Alexander over dinner became such a popular pastime over the centuries.[28] He remains, as one scholar observed, a 'bottle that can be filled with any wine'.[29]

When our own wine carafe emptied, I pointed out to Theo and Laura that we had been 'drinking like barbarians': the Greeks had coined the phrase 'to drink in the Scythian fashion' because the unruly tribes from the north liked to imbibe their ferments neat, whereas the Greeks traditionally diluted or 'cut' their wine with water. The Persians, however, had a more judicious use for alcohol:

> If an important decision is to be made, they [the Persians] discuss the question when they are drunk, and the following day the master of the house where the discussion was held submits their decision for reconsideration when they are sober. If they still approve it, it is adopted; if not, it is abandoned. Conversely, any decision they make when they are sober, it is reconsidered afterwards when they are drunk.

True to Herodotus and Persian custom, I vowed to review the contemplations of our evening the following day in London.

At 7 am on a sunlit morning, I quietly drove out of the olive grove that wrapped itself around Theo and Laura's house on my way to the airport at Thessalonica, the city founded by Cassander who merged twenty-six smaller towns into a metropolis he named after his 'captured' wife, Thessalonice, 2,300 years ago. The day was tranquil; this was the 'The Little Summer of Saint Demetrius' in Greece, as the latter half of October is known, and true to tradition, the weather had been fine and calm, almost devoid of wind. Fishing boats were beached upon the shore of an unrippled sea in Makrygialos, and the shadow of Mount Olympus stood kind and cloudless.

Yet I could not avoid the premonition that this was just the proverbial calm before yet another anthropological storm. I predicted that when the first forensic results from the various laboratories arrived at Vergina and its tomb of the thirteenth god, the Olympian deities would witness the hubris of man once more.

Postscript

> There is only one way to avoid criticism:
> Do nothing,
> Say nothing,
> And be nothing.
> —Aristotle

In the academic world, convention requires material scientists, archaeologists and biotechnologists like Yannis Maniatis, Konstantina Drosou and Margarita Gleba to present their finds in academic publications specific to their disciplines before announcing them to a wider audience. This was certainly true of the anthropological work by the Antikas team and it remains so for the pending forensics on the Great Tumulus bones.

However, ahead of publication, I was made privy to the very first results from the radiocarbon dating of the initial batch of bones from Tomb I. Taken together, they are nothing short of remarkable: they help answer outstanding questions and they pose many more. Ancient Aegae had clearly been witness to more upheavals than the pages of the surviving texts let on. The dating is conclusive proof that Tomb I could not have housed Philip II, and the results further weaken the argument that Arrhidaeus was entombed in Tomb II.

A follow-on book is planned with the aim of revealing what has been found. But to complete this complex picture, Greece's Ministry of Culture and the associated governmental departments need to provide permits for the next stage of DNA, radiocarbon and stable isotope testing on the bones from Tombs II and III to allow Laura, Yannis and their team to complete what they have started.

At the time of completing this manuscript, in early November 2017, the Tomb I bones in storage at the Archaeological Ephorate in Thrace had still not been delivered to Vergina to be included in the already-authorized tests. And, sadly, no further funding is planned or allocated for further study of the royal bones that are the true magic of Vergina.

The author, Yannis Maniatis and Laura Wynn-Antikas in the Archaeometry Laboratory at the National Centre for Scientific Research Demokritos in Athens.

Notes

Reference Notes

The reference notes provided are as brief as practically possible, to act as a guide to both ancient and modern commentary on the Vergina tomb excavations, rather than an exhaustive list of reading materials on any particular episode. As for the history behind the campaigns of Philip and Alexander, there exists a whole corpus of modern studies based on various interpretations of the episodes reported by non-eyewitness accounts. Readers are encouraged to undertake their own research and form their own opinions, as the histories we have of the era are more often than not contradictory. And despite the thousands of academic papers dedicated to the age of Alexander, there is much more to be said if the 'standard model' is challenged.[1]

Chapter 1: The day of archangels

1. Andronikos (1984) p.67 for the lack of funds.
2. Andronikos-Fotiadis (1978) p.4 for the original 1962/63 digs.
3. Andronikos (1978) p.3 for the similarity of the red soil with the cemetery and Drougou dating sherds.
4. Andronikos-Fotiadis (1978) p.3 for the first finds.
5. Andronikos (1984) p.219 for the fifty looted tombs.
6. Andronikos (1984) p.69 for the keystone explanation.
7. Andronikos (1984) p.73 for the replacing of the keystone.
8. Andronikos (1984) pp.70, 218 for the 'single solemn announcement'.
9. Andronikos (1984) p.218 for Rhomaios' guidance.

Chapter 2: A Meeting of Controversies

1. Thucydides 1.61.2; the failed Athenian attempt to take the city took place in 432 BC.
2. 'Heretical', quoting Drougou-Paliadeli (2005) p.47.
3. Useful discussions of the collapse of the Bronze Age and Dark Age that followed in Thomas-Conant (1999) and Robbins (2001).

280 *Unearthing the Family of Alexander the Great*

4. Quoting Richard Janko 2013 conference in Michigan for the population drop. Robbins (2001) p.139 ff for the clues back to plague and the *Iliad* although this was linked to the Greek encampment at Troy, which may, nevertheless, have been synonymous with a wider pestilence in Greece.
5. The script we refer to as 'Linear B' was developed for an earlier unknown language and largely restricted to bureaucratic records of Crete and then Mycenaean Greece. The Homeric epics were probably first put into writing when Greece adopted the Phoenician alphabet around 800 BC.

Chapter 3: How a Kingdom May Rise and Fall and Vanish

1. Homer, *Odyssey* 4.238–39.
2. Herodotus 8.137–39 for the significant other founding legend.
3. Justin 7.1.7–12. Other versions in Pausanias 9.40–8–9, and Diodorus 17 for fragments of references for the turmoil at Argos. Plutarch *Alexander* 2.1 for the genealogy from Caranus to Alexander. Thucydides 2.100.2 gives a run-down of the early kings, and Eusebius and Livy also related the myth. Grant (2017) p.7 ff for discussion of the founding legends.
4. Webster Wilde (2000) p.18 for the history of the Delphic shrine. It is theorized she may have been speaking in a pre-Hellenic tongue; Graves (1955) Introduction.
5. Pliny 10.33, Justin 7.1.1 and Strabo 7.11.1 report that Macedon was once named Emathia; discussed in Carney (2015) p.110.
6. Hesiod *W D* lines 109–201 for the ages of men.
7. Herodotus 7.73 for the Phrygians of 'Bryges'.
8. Justin 7.1 ff. Herodotus 8.138.1 for Midas' rose gardens.
9. Diodorus 7.16.1 for the oracle which was actually given at Delphi to Perdiccas in another version of the founding story.
10. Thucydides 2.99.2–3 for the conquest of the region by Alexander I in the alternative founding myth.
11. Herodotus books 3–6 is the principal source for the rise of Darius I.
12. Herodotus 8.137 and Justin 7.1–2 give an Argead list of kings, in which Alexander I was the seventh, descended from Perdiccas who founded the Argead dynasty. The kings Coenos and Tyrimmas came before Perdiccas in other texts, notably Satyrus *FGrHist* 631F1. See Grant (2017) p.10 ff for other lineage traditions.
13. Herodotus 5.105.
14. Herodotus 6.105–06.
15. Herodotus 6.106 ff for the build-up to battle at Marathon.
16. Epigram from one of the tombs of the Athenians.

17. Herodotus 7.33–34 for the pontoons and 8.109–10 for Themistocles' warning; Green (1998) p.75 for discussion of the Macedonian contractor.
18. Green (1998) p.58 ff for discussions of the invading numbers. Herodotus 8.126 ff for the build-up to the final battle, 7.127 for the Echedorus River failing to meet the Persian needs.
19. Herodotus 5.18–21 and 8.136.
20. Green (1998) p.248 ff for discussion of numbers at Plataea. Modern calculations suggest anything from 70,000–120,000 Persians, where Herodotus 9.32 claimed 300,000. Herodotus 9.31.5 for the Macedonian presence.
21. Roisman-Worthington (2010) p.130 for the possible origins of the clan name 'Argead'.
22. Herodotus 9.45, Plutarch *Aristides* 15.2.3 for Alexander's assistance to the Greeks; discussed in Green (1998) pp.258–59.
23. Herodotus 9.70 stated 43,000 survived and only 3,000 in their camp.
24. According to Demosthenes *Aristocrates* 13.24 and *On Organization* 23.200, but Perdiccas not Alexander I mentioned as ruling Macedon at the time after Plataea, an error; see Sprawski (2013) p.55. The 50,000 were depleted in battle on the plain before 10,000 were allegedly slaughtered in their camp; hence the estimate of 35,000. The Greek element would have defected thereafter.
25. Aristotle *Athenian Constitution* 15.2, Herodotus 5.94, scholia on Thucydides 1.57.2, see Themelis (2017) p.6. Herodotus 8.136 for '*eurgetes*' and '*proxenos*'; Dio Chrysostom 25 for the title 'Philhellene'.
26. Thucydides 2.100.2 for Archelaus' infrastructure.
27. See Borza (1995) p.37ff for the timber resources; Theophrastus *On Plants* 5.2.1 for a contemporary statement on its importance. Thucydides 2.100 ff for the reign of Archelaus.
28. Justin 7.5.
29. For Philip's career, the most coherent sources are Justin 7.5 ff and Diodorus 16.1–95.
30. Justin 7.4.5 names the half-brothers and his stepmother; 8.3.10–11 for Philip attacking Olynthus for them.
31. Athenaeus 13.557b–e preserves a fragment of Satyrus' *Life of Philip* who stated he married 'kata polemon', generally translated as 'after a war' though 'in connection to a war' might be preferable; Carney (2000) pp.52–54.
32. Diodorus 16.3.1–2 for Philip's reorganization of the army.
33. Principal sources for the battle at Chaeronea are Diodorus 16.85.2–16.86.4, Polyaenus 4.2.2, Justin 9.3.4–9.3.11, Plutarch *Alexander* 9.2 and Plutarch *Moralia* 177e–f.
34. Plutarch *Alexander* 3.8, Justin 12.16.6. Quoting Hammond (1994) p.137 for the 'first land empire' in Europe.

35. Carney (2000) p.62 and Grant (2017) p.14 for Olympias' heritage.
36. Diodorus 16.91–92.
37. Diodorus 16.8.3 ff for the development of gold mines; those at Mt Pangaeum were mentioned by Strabo, Herodotus, Theophrastus and Pliny whose claim the Phoenician Cadmus had first developed.
38. Fredericksmeyer (1979) for Philips being worshipped by Athens. Quoting Osborne on 'captive ally' from Palagia-Tracy (2003) p.74. Diodorus 16.91 ff for the fullest details of the build-up to Philip's assassination.
39. Borza (1995) p.47 for a discussion on land reclamation.
40. Diodorus 16.92. 1–4 for portents of assassination; 16.92.5 for the thirteenth statue.
41. Diodorus 16.95-96, Justin 9.7–9.8. Full sources in Carney (2000) p.66.
42. The formal title of 'queen' discussed in Carney (2000) pp.32–33.
43. Justin 7.2.4–6.
44. Plutarch *Alexander* 10.4 for suspicion falling on Alexander and Justin 9.8.1–14 for Olympias' role.
45. Plutarch *Alexander* 11.1–6, Arrian 1.1–6 for the campaigns in the north. Arrian 1.7–9, Diodorus 17.8.2–17.14.4, Plutarch *Alexander* 11.6–13.5, Justin 11.3.6–11.4–8 for the campaign against Athens and Thebes.
46. Diodorus 17.4.1–17.4.2, Justin 11.3.1–2 for Alexander's establishing his right to succeed his father as head of the League of Corinth.
47. Plutarch *Alexander* 14.6–7, Diodorus 17.93.4, Pausanias 8.7.6.
48. Diodorus 17.16.3–4 for the festival at Dium.
49. Diodorus 17.17.3–5 for troop numbers crossing to Asia. Following the Loeb Classical Library edition, (1963), 17.17.4 footnote 4: Diodorus is our only source for the detailed troop list of Alexander. Justin 11.6.2 gave 32,000 foot and 4,500 cavalry; Plutarch *Alexander* 15.1 cited 30,000–43,000 foot and 4,000–5,000 horse; Arrian 1.11.3 stated 'not much more than' 30,000 foot and 5,000 horse. Plutarch *Moralia* 327d–e claimed Aristobulus stated 30,000 foot and 4,000 horse, Ptolemy 30,000 foot and 5,000 horse, and Anaximenes 43,000 foot and 5,500 horsemen. Diodorus 17.17.2, Justin 11.5.10 for the spear.
50. Clear examples of Alexander's diplomacy in coastal Anatolia in Arrian 1.17–29 discussed in Grant (2017) p.29 ff. For the battle at the River Granicus, Arrian 1.13–16, Diodorus 17.19–21, Plutarch *Alexander* 16, Justin 11.6.8–11.13. For the Battle of Issus, Arrian 2.8–11, Curtius 3.9–11, Diodorus 17.33–34, Plutarch *Alexander* 20.5–11, Justin 11.9.1–11.10.
51. Arrian 2.16.1–2.24.5, Curtius 2.2–4, Diodorus 17.40.2–17.46.5, Plutarch *Alexander* 24–25, Justin 11.10.10–11.14, Polyaenus 4.3.3–4.3.4, 4.13 for events at Tyre.
52. Following the battle at Issus, the Macedonians had received envoys from the freshly defeated Darius III, the 'antagonist to Alexander's genius',

who reportedly spoke some Greek; with them came, reportedly, the offer of a huge ransom for the return of the Great King's captured family and possibly a concession to divide the Persian Empire at the Halys River or Euphrates – sources conflict: there may have been as many as three separate offers. For Darius' peace offerings and Alexander's rejection, see Curtius 4.11.1–14, Arrian 2.25.1, Plutarch 29.7–9 and Diodorus 17.54; discussed in Grant (2017) p.38.

53. Arrian 3.11–15, Curtius 4.13–16, Diodorus 17.57–61, Plutarch *Alexander* 31.6–33.11, Justin 11.13.1–11.14, Polyaenus 4.3.6, 17 for the battle at Gaugamela.
54. Arrian 3.6.3–3.182, Curtius 5.1.17–5.7.11, Diodorus 17.64.3–17.72.6, Justin 11.14.7–12, Plutarch *Alexander* 35.8 to events at Persepolis.
55. Arrian 5.25.1–5.29.1, Curtius 9.2.1–9.3.19, Diodorus 17.93.2–17.95.2, Plutarch *Alexander* 63, Metz Epitome 68–69, Justin 12.8.9–12.17 for the episode at the Hydaspes River. Plutarch *Alexander* 66.4 for the suspiciously high number of fighting men; see Grant (2017) p.59 and footnote 400 for discussion of the numbers.
56. Arrian 6.6–11, Curtius 9.4.15–9.5.21, Diodorus 17.98–99, Justin 12.9.1–12.10.1, Plutarch *Alexander* 63, Plutarch *Moralia* 327b, 341c, 343d–e, 344c–d for Alexander near death in Mallia.
57. Arrian 6.24.4, 6.25.3.
58. Plutarch *Alexander* 68.
59. Arrian 7.4.4–7.48, Diodorus 17.107.6, Plutarch *Alexander* 70, Plutarch *Eumenes* 1.6–7, Athenaeus 12.538b–539b, Aelian 8.7 for the Susa weddings.
60. Plutarch *Alexander* 73–75, Diodorus 17.112.1–17.116.7, Arrian 7.16.5–7.24.4, Justin 12.13.1–6 for the pre-death portents.
61. Grant (2017) chapter 9 for events at Babylon; the principal source is Curtius book 10.
62. Heckel (2006) p.54 for the uncertainty of his birth date.
63. Curtius 10.5.7–10.10.20, Justin 13.1–4, Diodorus 18.2–4, Arrian *Events After Alexander*, Photius Codex 82 for events at Babylon after Alexander's death.
64. Plutarch *Demetrius* 3.5. Diodorus 21 for the Battle of Ipsus; alluded to in Justin 15. Diodorus 20.53.1–4, Justin 15.2–3 for the declaration of kinships.
65. 'Labyrinthine' quoting Bagnall-Derow (2004) p.101.
66. Pausanias 10.20.4 for the height of the Celts. Pausanias 10.19.9 stated 152,000 infantrymen and 20,400 cavalrymen, Diodorus 22.9.1 stated 150,000 infantry and 10,000 cavalry, and Justin 24.6 stated 150,000 infantry and 15,000 cavalry were under Brennus' command.
67. Arrian 1.4.7–8.

284   *Unearthing the Family of Alexander the Great*

68. Diodorus 22.3 ff for the sacrifices.
69. Pausanias 1.4. ff for the battle at Thermopylae and 1.4.1–2 for Greece's exhaustion.
70. For the Gallic attack on Delphi conflict, Justin 24.7–8 and Pausanias 10.23.1–14 claimed the Gauls were defeated at Delphi.
71. Pausanias 1.11.1 for Pyrrhus' ancestry. He had briefly held the western portion of Macedon for four years from 288 BC when he had wrested control from Antigonus' father, Demetrius the Besieger. Plutarch *Pyrrhus* for his career and Diodorus 22.8 ff.
72. Pausanias 1.12.5 for his costly battles at sea off Sicily; Diodorus 22.6.1 ff for the expression.
73. Quoting Plutarch *Pyrrhus* 26.6; Diodorus 12.12 claims Pyrrhus was reviled but did nothing as he needed the Celts.
74. Andronikos (1984) p.86 for the wall shelf, discussed in Bartsiokas-Carney (2007–2008) p.16.
75. Polybius 2.41.
76. Known as the 'Chremonidean War', this conflict is thought to have taken place between 267–261 BC. It is poorly documented at Pausanias 1.7.3, 3.6.4–6 and Justin 26.2.
77. Following and quoting Grant (2017) pp.384–85.
78. Plutarch *Aemilius* 16–23, Livy 44.33 ff for the campaign at Pydna. The exact site of Pydna has not yet been discovered; Diodorus 18.49.2 claimed it was moved inland *ca*. 410 BC but Olympias' attempt to escape her siege by ship (Diodorus 19.50.4, Polyaenus 4.11.3) suggests it was re-established back on the coast, possibly close to modern Makrygialos.
79. Livy 30.33 (though Polybius 15.11 does not) even claimed a Macedonian phalanx fought in Hannibal's ranks at Zama.
80. Polybius 7.10.7–12 for his own exile. Livy 33.4.4 for the phalanx numbers at Pydna; Lee-Whittaker-Wrightson (2015) p.89 for discussion.
81. Livy 45.29 for the closure of mines. Cicero *De Officiis* book 2 (Expediency) 22 and Plutarch *Aemilius* 38.1 for the consequences. Here 'for all time to come' meant until Cicero's own day. Polybius 30.15 reported seventy Epirote towns were sacked and 150,000 people were sold into slavery. Grant (2017) p.155 ff for an account of the battle and its aftermath.
82. Pausanias 7.8.5.
83. Roisman-Worthington (2010) p.546 ff for the moveable borders of Macedon.
84. Roisman-Worthington (2010) p.569 for the earthquake and p.567 for the plaques; p.557 for Slavic incursions.
85. Here referring to the internal dividing door of Tomb III and the main chamber of Tomb II.

Chapter 4: A Phoenix Rises from the Ashes

1. Attributed to him, perhaps spuriously and with some degree of poetic licence in wording.
2. Andronikos (1984) p.17.
3. Quoting Drougou-Paliadeli (2005) p.59.
4. From Drougou-Paliadeli (2005); the inscription mentioned a 'propylon' derived from the ancient 'propylaion' or entrance building that resided before a gate.
5. Translation from Drougou-Paliadeli (2005) p.56. Andronikos (1984) p.17 for the 'Romioi'.
6. Following Borza (1995) pp.12–15.
7. Borza (1995) p.48 for malaria in the region.
8. Andronikos (1984) p.55 for the epigram.
9. Petsas first visited Pella in 1953; Petsas (1963) p.15.

Chapter 5: The Scientist's Elation and the Desecrator's Guilt

1. Discussion of the city proportions and citadel in Thomas-Conant (2005) p.24 ff.
2. Ceram (1951) p.32 ff; p.36 for the 'onion' analogy.
3. Ceram (1951) p.37 for the date at Troy.
4. Quoting him from Drougou-Paliadeli (2005) p.73.
5. Hatzopoulos-Loukopoulos (1980) p.192 for the 1951 commencement.
6. Andronikos (1984) pp.56–58 for the first excavation of the Great Tumulus; nineteen funerary monuments were found. Quoting Drougou-Paliadeli (2005) p.202.
7. Saatsoglou-Paliadeli *Palace* p.202 and p.101 for its dimensions. Andronikos (1984) p.38 for Heuzey's quote.
8. Andronikos (1984) p.2 for the destruction of the acropolis; p.44 for the robber trenches.
9. Andronikos (1984) pp.55–62; for 'jumping-off point' see Drougou-Paliadeli (2005) p.155.
10. Andronikos (1984) pp.24–25 for the tumuli sizes, dating and multiple graves.
11. Quoting Drews (1988) p.xi for 'magnificent obscurity' and p.9 for the Israelite comparison.
12. Hatzopoulos-Loukopoulos (1980) p.204, 206.
13. Satsoglou-Paliadeli *The Case of Vergina* p.692 for the 67 grave markers.
14. Andronikos (1984) p.64 for the first finds.
15. Andronikos (1978) Preliminary, p.14.
16. Andronikos (1978) Preliminary, p.14 for the positioning of the *heroon* and p.18 for the 4-metre height of the original mound; Andronikos (1984) p.65 for it standing outside the smaller tumulus.

17. Hammond (1991) p.74 for the sources of the hero worship of Amyntas and Philip II.
18. Quoting Andronikos (1984) p.86 and Carney (1992) p.91 ff for the comb.
19. Quoting Andronikos (1978) Preliminary, p.14.
20. Following the description in Andronikos (1978) Preliminary, p.16; Andronikos (1984) p.88 for Zeus' thunderbolt.
21. Andronikos (1984) and see Pliny 35.108–109 for the statement that Nicomachus painted this theme, and with 'speed'.
22. Following the description of Franks (2012) p.11; Andronikos (1984) p.88 for the 'not of this world' paintings and p.90 for the comparison with da Vinci.
23. Borza-Palagia p.87 for 'illusionist'.
24. Drougou-Paliadeli (2005) p.164 for the artists, following the analyses in Andronikos (1984) who mentioned stylistic and iconographic affinities with the Naples Mosaic, which copies a lost painting depicting Alexander fighting Darius, and which is generally attributed to Philoxenus of Eretria, who remains a candidate for the hunting frieze; see p.118.
25. Quoting Andronikos (1984) p.70.
26. Andronikos-Fotiadis (1978) p.8 for the sceptre and p.3 for the sponge.
27. Andronikos (1984) p.72 for the organic matter.
28. Andronikos (1984) pp.128–31 for the likenesses.
29. Quoting Andronikos (1984) p.71.
30. Borza-Palagia (2007) p.86 for tomb design.
31. Andronikos (1984) p.73 for the solitary moment outside the tomb.
32. Andronikos (1984) p.220 and Andronikos (1978) Preliminary p.30 for the stucco thickness..
33. Andronikos (1981) pp.170–71 for his post-cremation dumping of remains on the roof and Andronikos (1984) p.221 for his revised opinion of the altar. L Wynn, for one, pointed to the lack of a nearby pyre as a case for a cremation on the roof.
34. Andronikos (1981) p.171 for 'immediate' burials and (1984) pp.227–28 for the circumstances behind the 'special haste'. Kyriakou (2015) p.275 for the oak and Zeus. In Hesiod's *Theogonea* the origins of tribal Greece and Macedonia started with Deucalion who bore a son, Hellen, from whom the 'Hellenes' were derived. He in turn bore three sons who became the founders of eponymous tribes: Aeolus, Dorus and Xuthus who bore Ion and (according to other writers) Achaeus. By Zeus, Deucalion's daughter, Thyla, produced two sons, Magnes and Macedon who 'rejoiced in horses'; Magnes journeyed south into Thessaly and Macedon remained in the region of Mount Olympus and Pieria, the heartland of what was once Emathia, the 'prehistoric name for the cradle of the Macedonian kingdom'. A fragment of the *Makedonika* of Marsyas of Pella (broadly contemporary with Alexander) informs us

that it was the two sons of Macedon, Amathus and Pieria, who became the eponymous founders of these two regions; see Grant (2017) p.6 ff.
35. Andronikos (1984) p.220.
36. Musgrave (1990) p.291 ff for the revised ageing to 12–14. Andronikos (1984) p.220 for the Tomb II pyre.
37. Xirotiris-Langenscheidt (1981) pp.156–57 for warnings on sex determination of an adolescent; 13–16 years was established from the teeth and skeletal maturation. N. Hammond and P. Green advanced the view the adolescent was Alexander IV; Andronikos (1984) p.231 was less convinced.
38. Kottaridi Aigai (2011) p.106 for confirmation of the lack of pyre remains above Tomb III.
39. Andronikos (1984) p.97 for the inverted comma hesitation and (1980) p.169.
40. Andronikos (1978) p.3 for the sherds and Andronikos (1984) pp.221–22, 226 for the tomb dating; p.22 for the Corinthian-style lamp dated to 350–325 BC.
41. Quoting from the official website of the Polycentric Museum of Aegae; Andronikos (1984) p.97 for the 'great haste' of the funeral.
42. *Iliad* 24.788 ff.
43. Andronikos (1984) p.219 for his admission of using self-perpetuating arguments.
44. Andronikos (1984) p.231.
45. Andronikos (1984) p.223 for the *gorytos* dating argument.
46. Andronikos (1984) p.83 for the uniqueness of the columns.
47. Dimacopoulos (1995) p.10 for the finds in Tomb IV; Drougou-Paliadeli (2005) p.181 for a carved ivory head and the clay figurines.
48. Andronikos (1984) p.223 for 'speaking stones'; Andronikos (1984) p.82 for the five skeletons.
49. Quoting Carney (2015) p.97.
50. Hammond (1978) p.333; *Iliad* 23.245 ff.
51. Discussed in Chrysostomou (2012) p.505, Drews (1988) pp.202–04, Thomas-Conant (1999) p.20; Thucydides 1.12.3 for linking the Return of the Heraclidae with the Dorian invasion in 1104 BC, eight years after Eratosthenes' date for the fall of Troy in 1184 BC; Herodotus cited a date of 1250 BC. Many other dates have been proposed for the fall of Troy; see Grant (2017) p.217.
52. Carney (2015) p.113 referring to her 1996 article *Were the tombs under the Great Tumulus at Vergina Royal?*
53. See Paliadeli (2014) p.697 ff for more detail of the Eucleia find.
54. See discussion of the patronymic at Andronikos (1984) pp.50–51.
55. McGurdy (1935) p.17 for the sources of Eurydice's rumoured Illyrian heritage; Strabo 7.326, Plutarch *Moralia* 14, for example; she may have been from the royal Lyncestian house.

56. Plutarch *On the Education of Children* 20; discussed in McGurdy (1932) p.20 with translation. Drougou-Paliadeli (2005) pp.251, 255 for the association of the female head. A further inscription of Eurydice was found on the base of a column used in a Christian basilica at Palatitsia; p.255.
57. Saatsoglou-Paliadeli (1999) p.354 for Heracles Patroos and Drougou-Paliadeli (2005) p.74; it was found in 1969 in the 'tholos' or circular colonnaded room.
58. Andronikos (1984) p.11 for his early tasks.
59. Quoting Andronikos (1984) p.70 and Andronikos (1978) Preliminary, p.30.

Chapter 6: Of Scythians and Amazons

1. Arctinos *Aethiopis*, Fr. 2; also see the scholiast on Homer, *Iliad* 24.804 which links the final lines of the *Iliad* to the follow-on *Aethiopis*.
2. Lucian, *Toxaris: A Dialogue on Friendship*.
3. Andronikos-Fotiadis (1978) p.11.
4. Tsigarida (2010) pp.313–14 for the significance of myrtle.
5. Andronikos (1984) p.178; p.179 for the jewellery.
6. Andronikos (1984) pp.178–79, 189 for attributing the greaves to the main chamber male; 100 for the sealing of the door.
7. Andronikos (1984) p.184.
8. Aeschylus *Prometheus Bound* 410–415, translation by V. Vellacott from Hardwick (1990) p.18.
9. Hardwick (1990) p.19 for Isocrates' *Panegyric*.
10. Mayor (2014) p.182 for Scythian mounts trained to kneel; p.188 for dogs and birds of prey; p.191 ff for trousers; p.32 for the dolls.
11. See Grant (2017) p.256 for discussion; also, Cohen (2010) plate III for Amazonomachy at Pella. Leaf (1892) for the theory that the *Iliad* and *Odyssey* were Ionian productions.
12. Drews (1988) p.37 for the observation on literature and language.
13. Quoting Drews (1988) p.197 for 'patchwork of light and darkness'. Herodotus 8.137–139 for the significant other founding legend.
14. Herodotus 7.152 and echoed again at 2.123 and 4.5. See discussions in Grant (2017) p.231 and Hansen (2017) pp.421–22.
15. Webster Wild (2016) pp.12–13 and Mayor (2014) pp.87–88 for the etymology of 'Amazon'.
16. Herodotus 4.110 ff. Possibly modern Therme; see Webster Wilde (2016) p.108; Mayor (2014) p.250 for the route.
17. Webster Wilde (2016) p.58 for the advent of the Sarmatians; Mayor (2014) p.235 for the etymology. *Airs, Waters, Places*, a treatize ascribed to Hippocrates, described the Sarmatian tradition; Mayor (2014) p.86.
18. Mayor (2014) p.157 ff for the treatment of their children.

19. Following Guliaev (2003) p.114.
20. Plutarch *Theseus* 26.2–27.1.4, Hellanicus FGrH 323 and F 17c; see discussion in Silver (2018) p.101.
21. Pausanias 1.2.1.
22. Discussed in Webster Wilde (2016) pp.10–11 and p.19 for the meaning of Melanippe.
23. For Pindar see Pausanias 7.2.7. Discussed in Webster Wilde: p.18 ff for the worship of Artemis; p.82 for Pindar, and p.41 for Justin's alternative Amazon origins; p.85 for the armed priestesses.
24. Strabo 11.6.2–11.11.8, Pliny 6.19.50 for the Greek generalization; discussed in Mayor (2014) p.35. Herodotus 4.12 for traces of Cimmerian culture.
25. Herodotus 4.64.
26. Tillisch (2004) p.5 for probable ethnicities. Curtius 7.8.23 for the Greeks ridiculing the desert regions.
27. Herodotus 4.5 ff.
28. Herodotus 4.3 ff, translation by Aubrey de Selincourt, Penguin edition (1954); Mayor (2014) p.218 ff for viper venom and blood oaths.
29. Tillisch (2004) p.103 for the muscular right arms.
30. Guliaev (2003) p.115. Webster Wilde (2016) p.55 for the 25 per cent overall and p.63 for the single earring; more details in Mayor (2014) pp.64–65 and p.73 for new DNA tests.
31. Mayor (2014) p.69 for a description of typical jewellery.
32. Curtius 7.8.10; compare to Arrian 3.27.4–5 referring to the Ariaspians; see Grant (2017) p.305.
33. Herodotus 4.17 and 4.108 ff for examples of the Graeco-Scythian tribes; 4.76 for Anacharsis heritage, Diogenes Laertius *Anacharsis* for other traditions and epithets.
34. Boardman (1999) p.28 ff for the foundation of Miletus.
35. See Mayor (2014) p.236. The 2011 discovery reported at http://www.reginaldgibbons.northwestern.edu/2011/03/25/who-still-speaks-ancient-greek/
36. Herodotus 4.17, 4.21, 4.102 for the mixed tribes.
37. Plutarch *Alexander* 46.1–3 for Thalestris' meeting with Alexander; also, Curtius 6.5.24–32, Justin 12.4.5–7, Diodorus 17.77.1–3. Justin provided an alternative name, Minithyha.
38. Arrian 7.13.2, 7.13.6.
39. Quoting Quintus of Smyrna *The Fall of Troy*, cited in Mayor (2014) p.17.
40. Quoting Mayor (2014) p.171 for 'equaliser'.
41. Mayor (2014) p.336 for women gladiators; pp.339–50 for the Mithridatic Wars.
42. Mayor (2014) p.74 for the height of the Saka-Scythian tribes; p.82 for the regiments at Hadrian's Wall.

290   Unearthing the Family of Alexander the Great

43. Plutarch *Demetrius* 19.6.
44. Herodotus 4.73–75.
45. Mayor (2014) p.147 ff for hemp and intoxicants.
46. Grant (2017) for the treatment of Herodotus; quoting Momigliano (1966) p.133.
47. Pausanias 1.23.9.

Chapter 7: The First War of Women

1. Diodorus 16.95.2–4; extracted from Borza (1999) p.65.
2. Quoting Fredericksmeyer (1990) p.305; see discussion in Grant (2017) p.112.
3. Philip was operating under the auspices of the Amphyctionic Council in the Third Sacred War against the Phocian defilers of Apollo's sanctuary and was eventually given Phocis' two seats on the council. The Macedonian hegemon was now representing the justice of thirteen Greek peoples and under the blessing of a god, a cause possibly aided by Theopompus' publishing of *On the Funds Plundered from Delphi*. Diodorus 16.35, Justin 8.2.3–5 for Philip leading a coalition of Macedonians, Thessalians and Thebans wreathed like gods. This was the so-called Battle of the Crocus Field in Thessaly in 353/352 BC; discussed in Grant (2017) pp.111–12.
4. For Leuctra see Plutarch *Pelopidas* 22–23, Xenophon *Hellenica* book 4.2 ff, 6.4.12 ff, Diodorus 15.52–56.
5. Lee-Whittaker-Wrightson (2015) p.60 for the shock troops and reserves.
6. Xenophon *Memorabilia*; discussed in Hanson (1989) p.3 ff.
7. Curtius 4.13.4 for Parmenio and his tactical ability.
8. Polyaenus 4.2.10 for the 300-stade forced marches of Philip and Frontinus 4.1.6 for the rations; Heckel-Jones (2006) p.12 for discussion. Frontinus 4.1.6 for the waggonless army; discussion in Gabriel (2010) pp.85–86. Frontinus 4.2.4 and Aelian 14.48 for flogging and execution; Roisman-Worthington (2010) p.451 for discussion. Davis (1914) p.78 for the hoplite loads and Grant (2017) p.118.
9. Roisman-Worthington (2010) p.451 for the cavalry wedge sources.
10. Diodorus 16.3.1.ff, 16.4, 16.4.3, 16.35.4 ff, 16.74.5, 16.85.5 and 17.7 for the ever-increasing numbers in Philip's army; discussed in Hatzopoulos-Loukopoulos (1980) p.40.
11. Translation from the inscription still surviving in Athens; Grant (2017) p.24.
12. Here the so-called Tomb of Flowers and the Judgement Tomb have been unearthed; these were obviously burial places of court nobles and possibly one of Alexander's most prominent bodyguards. It is speculated that Peucestas

of Mieza, the 'eighth' bodyguard by 323 BC, was buried in the Tomb of Judgement.
13. Aristotle *Politics* 11253a 15–19 *Poetics* 1448b 5–9.
14. See discussions in Grant (2017) p.429 ff.
15. Quoting Hatzopoulos for 'first among equals' from Palagia-Tracy (2003) p.409.
16. Theopompus F224 see Hatzopoulos-Loukopoulos (1980) p.42.
17. Mnesimachus *Philip* from Athenaeus 10.421b; author's translation.
18. Pausanias 8.7.5.
19. Athenaeus 10.421b for Xenophon likening the banquets to 'workshops of war'.
20. Quoting Fredericksmeyer (1981) p.334 on 'harem for political purposes'.
21. 'Fifth' conforming to Satyrus' list at Athenaeus 8.557c–e.
22. See discussion in Carney (2000) p.25. Plutarch *Moralia* 401a–b for Olympias' other names, corroborated by Justin 9.7.13. Palagia (2018) p.23 ff for the throne argument. However, the heroes of old were said to occupy thrones in Greek drama.
23. Plutarch *Alexander* 77.7–8.
24. Plutarch *Alexander* 9.6–11, Athenaeus 13.557d, Justin 9.7.3–4.
25. Diodorus 16.93.7 for Attalus' prominence at court and Curtius 8.8.7 for Alexander's distrust and lack of forgiveness for Attalus' comment that Cleopatra may produce a 'legitimate' heir to the throne; Plutarch *Alexander* 9.7–9, Satyrus fr.5, *Romance* 1.21.1, Justin 9.7.3 for the banquet at which Attalus insulted Alexander. Plutarch *Alexander* 9.4–11 for events that led to the flight of Alexander and Olympias.
26. Homer *Iliad* 1.121–129; following the observation by Carney *Polygamy* (1992) p.176.
27. Plutarch *Alexander* 10.1–2 for the Pixodarus affair.
28. Justin 9.7.10–13 alleged that Olympias put a gold crown on the crucified Pausanias after she returned from Epirus, scattering his ashes on Philip's grave and providing him with a tomb of his own. Hatzopoulos (2017) p.3 ff for discussion of the historicity of these events.
29. Pausanias 8.7.7 stated the baby was a son. Justin 9.7.12 for the alternative death; Diodorus 17.2.3 for the girl being born just days before Philip's death.
30. Plutarch *Alexander* 4 for Alexander's anger. Arrian 3.6.5 uniquely stated Cleopatra had been renamed 'Eurydice'.
31. Euripides *Medea* 288; mentioned at Plutarch *Alexander* 10.6.
32. For Cleopatra's execution and children Plutarch *Alexander* 10.8, Pausanias 8.7.7, Justin 9.7 and 11.2 for Caranus. Athenaeus 13.557e for the name of her daughter, Europa.

33. Carney (2000) pp.57–58 for Audata's heritage; see Athenaeus 13.557b–c, Arrian *Events After Alexander* 1.22.
34. Polyaenus 8.60.
35. Plutarch *Moralia* 327c–d. Arrian *Events After Alexander* 1.22 for her child by Amyntas.
36. Arrian 1.5.4–5; Athenaeus 13.560 f.
37. Curtius 10.5.7–10.10.20, Justin 13.1–4, Diodorus 18.2–4, Arrian *Events After Alexander*, 1.22–24, for events at Babylon after Alexander's death.
38. Roxane was Bactrian or Sogdian; the campaign and siege of the so-called Rock of Sogdia, the Rock of Sisimithres (Chorienes) and the Rock of Ariamazes are confused; see Heckel (2006) pp.241–42 and 187 for identifications and Heckel (1987) p.114 for discussion.
39. Discussed in Grant (2017) p.441 ff; also see Curtius chapter 10, Justin 13.1–3, Arrian *Events After Alexander* and Photius.
40. Curtius 10.5 ff for the infighting at Babylon and Arrian *Events After Alexander* 1.1 ff.
41. Plutarch *Moralia* 337d–e.
42. Discussed at length in Grant (2017) chapter 9.
43. Arrian *Events After Alexander* 1.22, Polyaenus 8.60 for Cynnane's crossing to Asia.
44. Quoting Bosworth (1993) p.425 for 'Amazon and an idiot' and following Heckel (1978) p.157 for the first Macedonian queen in a generation.
45. Justin 13.6.4, Diodorus 18.23.1–18.25.6, Arrian *Events After Alexander* 1.21, 1.26 for Perdicca's marriage negotiations.
46. Polyaenus 8.60, Arrian *Events After Alexander* 1.22.2–4 for Adea's rabble rousing. Palagia (2008) p.195 for the meaning of Hadeia.
47. Diodorus 18.49.1–3, Plutarch *Phocion* 31.1, *Heidelberg Epitome* 1.4.
48. Diodorus 19.11.9 for Antipater deathbed utterance.
49. Arrian 7.12.5–6 and Curtius 10.4.3 for the correspondence from Olympias and Antipater and Alexander's quip about his mother. Plutarch *Alexander* 39.13 for the tears.
50. Arrian *Events After Alexander* 1.38, Diodorus 18.39.7. See Justin 14.5, Diodorus 18.75 for Adea appointing Cassander regent.
51. Diodorus 18.49.4, Pausanias 1.11.3, Plutarch *Alexander* 68.4–5, Justin 12.14.3, Arrian 7.12.6–7.
52. Grant (2017) p.729 for Cleopatra's suitors during this period.
53. Diodorus 19.11.8–9.
54. See Grant (2017) p.370 ff for poisons in the ancient world, with full discussion of Alexander's last will and testament and p.325 for the *Book of Death*.
55. Quoting from Athenaeus 13.560 f, also Aelian 13.36, Diodorus 19.11.1–8, Justin 14.5.1–10.

56. Diodorus 19.11.3–5 and Aelian 13.36, Justin 14.5.10.
57. Webster Wilde (2016) p.64 for the Bulgarian finds.
58. Hardwick (1990) p.15 for Priam's wording.
59. Following the idea of J. Walsh in *Antipater and Early Hellenistic Literature*; Cicero *De Officiis* and Plutarch suggested a corpus of letters on statesmanship written by Antipater.
60. Diodorus 19.35.1 ff, Justin 14.6 ff.
61. Diodorus 19.36.2 ff, Justin 14.6 ff; Polyaenus 4.11.3 for the bungled escape attempt. Pausanias 9.7.2 for the stoning of Olympias.
62. Discussed in Grant (2017) p.517. Diodorus 19.49–52 for Olympias' end and quoting from the Loeb Classical Library edition (1947) and from Justin 14.6, translation by Rev. J.S. Watson (1853). Justin 14.6.1–13, Polyaenus 4.11.3 for further detail. Diodorus 17.118.2 for her corpse remaining unburied.
63. Diodorus 19.52.1, 19.61.2, Pausanias 8.7.7, Justin 14.6.13.
64. McGurdy (1935) p.1 for the regent role; pp.6–8 for the title of 'queen'.
65. Quoting from Bury-Barber-Bevan-Tarn (1923) p.11.
66. Aeschines in his speech *The False Legation* paints a picture of a woman who acted for the wellbeing of her children; McGurdy (1935) p.19. Justin 7.4.7 and 7.5.8 saw the opposite in her. Also discussed in Carney (2000) p.43 ff. Discussed in Grant (2017) p.765.
67. Diodorus 19.59.3–5 for Phila's wisdom and qualities.
68. Discussed in Grant (2017) p.728; Diodorus 19.59.4 reported that Antipater valued Phila's wisdom and consulted her on policy; she was charged with the defence of Cyprus late in Demetrius' reign, Diodorus 19.67.1, and she acted as a diplomat for Demetrius to Cassander, Plutarch *Demetrius* 32.4. For Cratesipolis' actions at Sicyon, see Diodorus 19.67 and 20.37, Polyaenus 8, Plutarch *Demetrius* 9. The roles of Phila, Cratesipolis, Cynnane and Olympias are discussed in Carney (1995) p.389. Diodorus 19.16.4–5 for Stratonice's role in the sixteen-month siege that saw Docimus and Attalus finally captured, probably in Pisidia, though the location is not stated.
69. Discussed in Grant (2017) pp.131–32.

Chapter 8: The Battle of the Bones

1. Xirotiris-Fotiadis p.144 for the positioning of the bones in the larnax.
2. Xirotiris-Langenscheidt (1981) pp.142–43.
3. Hammond (1978) p.335
4. Xirotiris-Langenscheidt (1981) p.142 ff and p.148 for facial gracility of nobility and p.154 for the muscles.
5. Xirotiris-Langenscheidt p.144 for the positioning of the bones in the larnax and p.154 for the comparison with the female bones. Antikas-Wynn-Antikas

(2016) p.9 for bone colour at different temperatures: 200–300C (brownish), 550–600C (greyish), over 650C (white).
6. Andronikos (1984) p.228 for the ages.
7. Xirotiris-Langenscheidt p.143 and p.145 for shrinkage discussion. Musgrave (1990) p.279 for 'skeletally mature' discussion; p.156 for the height estimation.
8. Audata was old enough for marriage in 359/358 BC and so at least aged 39 when Philip died. Phila is thought to have been born soon after 375 BC and would have been aged 39; Arrhidaeus was older than Alexander, so at least 21 when Philip died, so Philinna must have been at least 37, if not older; Heckel (2006) pp.207–08; p.179 for Nicesipolis' death after childbirth. Meda probably married Philip in 342 BC, see Heckel (2006) p.158.
9. Carney (2015) pp.94–95 for a correlating process of elimination. Justin 7.4.8 for 'an advanced age'; also see Isocrates *To Philip* 106–08 for the 'long and happy life' of Amyntas.
10. Diodorus 15.60.3 for the one-year reign of Alexander II, other sources suggest two years. Diodorus 16.2.10 for a description of the rout. Polyaenus 4.10.1 for the Illyrians taking no prisoners.
11. The Roman emperor Septimus Severus had the tomb locked according to Cassius Dio 7513.2 but Caracalla, who saw himself as a reincarnation of Alexander, allegedly saw the tomb in AD 215; see Grant (2017) p.290 footnote 145.
12. As an example, Andronikos (1984) p.119.
13. 'Tug of war' following Nevett (2017) p.274. Carney (1992) p.1 for 'obsessive', quoted in McLeod (2014) p.1.
14. Carney (2000) p.68 for the background to Meda.
15. Hammond (1978) p.336, drawing from Justin 9.2.1–6.
16. Justin 9.11.15. When Philip was attacked by Thracian Triballi, it remains unclear whether any women or horses of similar number returned to Macedon; Justin's text suggests not.
17. Hammond (1978) p.335 and (1991) p.77. This draws from Herodotus 5.5 in which the ritual suicide, or murder, of the favourite wife of the king is described. See Herodotus 4.71.4 and 5.5 for the Thracian tradition and for tribes north of Crestonia. Diodorus 19.34.1–6 for a further example of suttee.
18. Herodotus 4.104–105, 4.111–9, 4.125, 4.48; Strabo 7.3.2–5, 11.14, 14.12.3–4 for the mixed traditions; discussed in Mayor (2014) pp.96–98; p.98 for the common language in Pontus; p.104 ff for tattoos. For the meaning of tattoos see Herodotus 5.6 and Tsiafakis (2015) p.96 ff. Tattooing denoted noble birth.
19. Justin 11.2.1, Arrian 1.25.2 for the naming of the accomplices executed 'at the tumulus of Philip'.
20. Diodorus 19.34.1–6 for Ceteus' funeral and the cremation of his wife.

21. Demosthenes *Philippic* 1.40. He was alluding to the reactive boxing style of barbarian boxers who are always one step behind their opponents' moves and strategy, and here equating it to Athens' amateurish opposition to Philip II of Macedonia. 119.8 for the comment on slaves; see Mahaffy (1896) p.2. *Oration* 11.22 for Philip punishing his body for the sake of power; see Riginos (1994) p.104.
22. Demosthenes *On the Crown* 67; see Plutarch *Moralia* 177f for the collarbone, Justin 7.6.14 for the lost eye and 9.3.2 for the thigh wound. There are however additional sources that reported these injuries; see full discussion and list in Riginos (1994) p.116.
23. Plutarch *Moralia* 331b and 739b. Also see corroborating statements from Clement of Alexandria *Protrepticus* 4.54.5 in Fredericksmeyer (1979) pp.39–40. Full list of sources in Riginos (1994).
24. Justin 9.3.2.
25. Hatzopoulos (2008) p.93 for a list of supporters of the 'Philip II camp'.
26. Following Hatzopoulos (2008) p.94 for the wording surrounding the antagonism between Petsas and Andronikos.
27. Professor Demetrius Kanatsoulis. See Hatzopoulos (2008) p.94 for a summary of their opinion.
28. Following the commentary of Hatzopoulos (2008) p.94. Quoting the Minister of Macedonia-Thrace who presented Andronikos with the Great Cross of the Order of the Phoenix; see Roisman-Worthington (2010) p.588.
29. Athenaeus 14.620b. Cited in Adams (1980) and also in Lehmann (1982) p.441.
30. Boyd (1978); more in Lehmann (1980) p.528.
31. Grant (2017) pp.5–6 for Alexander's appearance; further details in Stewart (1993) pp.341–50 and Carney-Ogden (2010) p.13.
32. Pausanias 5.20.9. See Andronikos-Fotiadis (1978) pp.7–9 for the ivory likenesses. Andronikos (1984) pp.126, 130, 230 and Adams (1980) p.69 for the scarring Andronikos thought he saw in the sightless right eye. Plutarch *Moralia* 335b and Plutarch *Alexander* 4.2 for Alexander's glance and neck tilt.
33. Justin 11.1.4. Ovid and Propertius used a similar phrase.
34. Andronikos (1984) pp.164 and 166–67 for the torch.
35. Andronikos (1980) p.168 ff.
36. Andronikos (1984) p.226 for the club of Heracles and lion reliefs.
37. See throne arguments in Palagia (2018) p.23 ff.
38. Andronikos (1984) p.229.
39. Palagia (2017) and pp.415–16 for the dating of sherds and Palagia (2018) p.28 for the location of the sherds above the tomb and position of the bones.
40. Hammond (1991) pp.70–71 for the tomb of Eurydice and its dating; Palagia (2017) p.415 for Eurydice's date of death.
41. Andronikos (1984) pp.165–66.

42. Plantzos (2017) p.69 for discussion. The archaeologist was Antonis Zois.
43. Andronikos (1987) p.3.
44. Using the terminology of Hammond (1991) p.72.
45. Andronikos (1987) p.6, from Seneca *Epistle* 90.32, quoting Posidonius; Andronikos (1984) pp.223–24 for the flat roof observation.
46. Plato *Epinomis* 987d. Boardman (1999) p.104 ff for Ionian masons in Persia. Saatsoglou-Paliadeli *The Case of Vergina* p.697 for the openness of Greeks in assimilating aspects of foreign civilizations.
47. Borza (1987) p.111 ff for Alexander's panoply.
48. Quoting Rose-Körpe (2016) p.373. Arrian 1.110.7–8, Plutarch *Alexander* 15.7, Diodorus 17.17.6–7, 17.18.1 for Alexander's antics at Ilium.
49. Quoting Rose-Körpe (2016) p.375 for Xerxes' visit.
50. *Iliad* 18.
51. Arrian 6.9.3 for the sacred shield of Troy.
52. Franks (2012) p.31 for the examples of hunting scenes in Asia.
53. Andronikos (1978) Preliminary, p.18 for the restorers nearby and p.19 for their survival.
54. The historians were A.M.P. Giallombardo and B. Tripodi; see Hatzopoulos (2008) p.95 for details of their paper.
55. *Iliad* 2.105–107.
56. The sceptre was originally mentioned in Andronikos-Fotiadis (1978) p.8. A full report of the 'sceptre incident' in Borza-Palagia (2007) p.110.
57. Diodorus 18.26.4–18.27.1.
58. Borza (1999) p.73.
59. For example, no iron helmets were found among the forty-four helmets recovered from graves at the Archontiko cemetery near Pella which is thought to be the ancient Macedonian city of Tyrissa; see Chrysostomou (2012) p.511.
60. Borza-Palagia (2007) pp.111–12. Andronikos (1984) p.144.
61. Andronikos (1978) Preliminary, p.34 for Athena on the helmet.
62. Plutarch *Alexander* 32.9.
63. Pliny 35.110 for the identification with a fresco by Philoxenus of Eretria.
64. Curtius 3.11.24–3.13.3, Arrian 2.15.1, Athenaeus 607 ff for the treasures seized after battle at Issus. Plutarch *Alexander* 21.5 ff for the separation of the captive women. In contrast, Diodorus 17.77.7 and Justin 12.3.11–12 claimed Alexander added concubines to his retinue.
65. Grant (2017) p.28 ff for Alexander's financial position and policy in Anatolia; p.30 for the haul. Also Bellinger (1963) p.29 ff for discussion of Alexander's finances.
66. Plutarch *Alexander* 21.6 for Darius' height: 'the tallest man in the Persian Empire'.

67. Plutarch *Alexander* 8.2, Arrian 1.11.5 and 15.7–9 for the date of the Granicus battle.
68. Plutarch *Alexander* 32.5 for a description of the helmet worn at Gaugamela.
69. Arrian 1.16.2–3 and Plutarch *Alexander* 16.12–15; Arrian 1.14.4 suggested there was a similar number ('little less') of mercenaries to the Persian cavalry stated at 20,000, and that all died bar 2,000 prisoners; 1.16.2. The Macedonians allegedly lost only eighty-five cavalrymen and thirty infantrymen (less according to Aristobulus, so claimed Plutarch). Modern interpretations suggest more like 5,000 mercenaries were present; discussion in Parke (1933) p.180, Green (1974) p.179 and in detail pp.499–500.
70. Curtius 10.6.4 and 10.7.13; Borza-Palagia (2007) p.117 for discussion.
71. Borza (1987); see commentary in Hatzopoulos (2008) p.98.
72. Hammond (1989) p.221 for the plumes on the helmet; discussed in Franks (2012) p.121.
73. Diodorus 19.15.3 for Eumenes on the insignia. They also appear earlier at Diodorus 18.60–63, Curtius 10.6.4, 10.7.13, Diodorus 18.60–63, Plutarch *Eumenes* 13.3, Nepos *Eumenes* 7.2, Polyaenus 4.8.2.
74. Homer *Iliad* 1.245.
75. Quoting Paspalas (2000) p.531. Williams-Ogden (1994) p.47 for earlier eastern influences.
76. See discussion in Grant (2017) p.764.
77. Polybius 31.29.3; translation from Franks (2012) p.79.
78. As noted by Chrysoula Paliadeli in her 2004 monograph on the frieze; see Saatsoglou-Paliadeli (2004).
79. Herodotus 5.21, Athenaeus 6.256c–d for Bubares and Xenophon *Hellenica* 4.1.33 for Artabazus' game reserve; discussed in Franks (2012) pp.81–82.
80. Quoting from and discussed in Grant (2017) p.21.
81. Themelis-Touratsouglou (1997) p.217 for Persian weights and measures.
82. Arrian 4.13.1.
83. Herodotus 7.125–126. Also, evidence could be argued from Pliny, Aristotle, Xenophon and Aelian; see Hatzopoulos (2008) p.103 footnote 51; see Franks (2012) p.39 for sources mentioning lions in Macedon. Xenophon *On Hunting* 11.1 for the wild animals on Olympus; discussed in Franks (2012) p.99.
84. Pausanias 9.40.8. Franks (2012) p.40 for the coins of Amyntas III.
85. For more on the boar-hunt symbolism see Saatsoglou-Paliadeli (2004).
86. Following terminology of Kyriakou (2015) p.252. Palagia (2017) p.413 for the lion association.
87. Borza-Palagia (2007) disputes that Plato's *Laws* 947 D was referring to 'vaulted' tombs but rather a 'scissors' vault long known in Greece. The artefact providing the dating was a Panathenaic amphora bearing the name 'Lykiskos', an archon at Athens in 344/343 BC.

298 *Unearthing the Family of Alexander the Great*

88. Summary of these arguments in Lehmann (1982) pp.438–42.
89. See Calder (1981) p.334 and Lehmann (1982) pp.437–38 for the diadem discussion.
90. Following Burstein (1980) p.146 for the diadem descriptions. Argument reiterated in Fredericksmeyer (1980) p.332 and (1983) p.99 ff.
91. Franks (2012) p.121.
92. Fredericksmeyer (1990).
93. 'In haste' quoting Musgrave (1991) p.7.
94. Pliny 124 for the work of the surgeon, Critobulus; discussed in Prag-Neave (1997) p.73.
95. Quoting from Prag-Neave (1997) p.62.
96. Prag-Neave (1997) p.63.
97. Prag-Musgrave-Neave (1984) p.77 for the unbiased reconstruction. Also, Prag-Neave (1997) p.64 for 'completely open minds' about the identity of the skull being reconstructed.
98. Prag-Neave (1997) p.63 for the asymmetries; p.64 for the surgeon's observation.
99. Prag-Musgrave-Neave (1984) p.68. Xirotiris-Langenscheidt (1981) p.154.
100. Quoting Prag-Neave (1997) p.64.
101. Prag-Neave (1997) p.68 for the admission they completed the modelling from known likenesses; p.76 for the anticlimax of version two; p.77 for following ancient portraits of his nose.
102. *The Falsification of Macedonian History, Ancient Jewish Sources and Testimony on Macedonia* by N.K. Martis, Athens (1984).
103. See www.historyofmacedonia.org for arguments from the FYROM.
104. Roisman-Worthington (2010) p.572 ff for the national identity debate and the new repiblic.
105. Dimacopoulos (1995) p.14 ff for the construction plans for the archaeological museum.
106. Paliadeli (1993) pp.122–47; see commentary in Hatzopoulos (2008) p.95, p.101 and p.108 for the kausia. See Kingsley (1991) for arguments; the argument dates back to A.M.P. Giallombardo in 1991; Hatzopoulos (2008) p.100 for details.
107. Roisman-Worthington (2010) pp.87 and 343–44 for Yauna. Takabara means 'wearing shields on their heads'. The epithet possibly refers to the shield-shaped flat hat, the 'kausia'; discussed in Grant (2017) p.23. Kingsley (1981) for arguments that it originated with the chitrali. Paliadeli (2003) p.1 ff for the various sources and arguments.
108. Paliadeli (1993) p.142.
109. Roisman-Worthington (2010) p.584 ff for the Hunza and Kalasha.

110. Faklaris (1994); discussed in Hatzopoulos (2008) p.101. D. Kanatsoulis, Professor of ancient history at the University of Thessalonica and Greek archaeologist Photius Petsas had challenged the Aegae identification back in 1977; see Hatzopoulos (2008) p.94.
111. See Hall (2014) p.105 for Hammond's sources, including Justin 7.1, Theophrastus *On Winds* 27, Claudius Ptolemy 3.13.39, Diodorus 16.3.5–6. Also discussed in Carney (2015) p.110 ff.
112. See Hall (2014) p.105. Faklaris was following Diodorus 7.16 and Herodotus 8.138.2–3.
113. Carney (2015) p.109 ff, which includes her 1996 article titled 'Were the Tombs under the Great Tumulus at Vergina Royal?' Andronikos (1984) p.59 for Papazoglou's contribution. Also see Petsas (1963) p.169 for the geographical confusion. In fact, as far back as 1975, Professor Fanoula Papazoglou of Belgrade University had demonstrated that Justin's age-old identification of Aegae with Edessa was a mistake.
114. Dr Kottaridi is Head of Department of Museums, Exhibitions and Educational Programmes for the 17th Ephorate of Prehistoric and Classical Antiquities of Emathia, of which, since 2010, she is director. As an example of the 'official line' on the identifications see Kottaridi *Aigai* (2011); quoting Borza's review of that title on amazon.com.
115. Hatzopoulos (2008) p.102 for these counter-arguments. Carney (2015) p.116 for the contents of the Derveni tombs A and III. The historians were P.G. Themelis and J.P. Touratsouglou. Hatzopoulos (2008) p.112 for Stella Drougou's argument published in 2005. Quoting Hatzopoulos on 'first among equals' in Palagia-Tracy (2003) p.409.
116. Carney (2015) p.114 for the uncertainty of the Argead star and following Carney's wording p.117 on distinguishing the royal dead. Sixteen-point stars decorated the larnax found at Agios Athanasios, for example.
117. Palagia (2017) p.414. Andronikos (1984) p.225 for his contention that a shrine by a tomb was unique. Kyriakou (2016) pp.143–53 for discussion of the Stenomakri Tumulus at Vergina.
118. Rose-Körpe (2016) p.375.
119. Borza (1987); see commentary in Hatzopoulos (2008) p.98; also, Satsoglou-Paliadeli *The Case of Vergina* p.691 for his inadequate archaeological knowledge.
120. Borza-Palagia (2007) p.84 footnote 18 for a summary of the moratorium. Quoting Hatzopoulos (2008) p.102.
121. A detailed description of Zambas' hypothesis was published in Zambas (1999) pp.561–63. For a comparative drawing of the Macedonian tomb at Lefkadia, together with Tomb II at Vergina and two other Macedonian tombs

see Zambas (2016) p.530, fig. 2. Hatzopoulos (2008) p.102 also highlighted Zampas' challenge to Andronikos on tomb construction.
122. Theodore Antikas personal correspondence with C. Paliadeli dated 1 May 2005. He argued the left tibia, which Bartsiokas did exhibit by photo, is an internal bone surrounded by muscle so would show less pyre effects.
123. Palagia (2000); summed up in Hatzopoulos (2008) p.104. For Cassander's presence in Babylon, Plutarch *Moralia* 180f, Plutarch *Alexander* 74.2–6.
124. Borza-Palagia (2007) p.118.
125. Borza (19991) p.73.
126. Quoting M.B. Hatzopoulos *La Macédoine: Géographie, historique, Langue, Cultes et croyances, Institutions* (Travaux 2) De Boccard (2006) p.93, as translated in Briant (1974) p.167.
127. Hatzopoulos' report, from which this quote is extracted, appeared in *Tekmeria*, Volume 9 (2008) pp.91–118, and is provided in full in Antikas-Wynn-Antikas (2014) Introduction.
128. Hatzopoulos (2008) p.112.
129. S.I. Rotroff has argued in early 1984 for the dating of the salt-cellars; see Hatzopoulos (2008) p.98.
130. Hatzopoulos (2008) p.111 for the salt-cellars.
131. Hatzopoulos (2008) pp.109–10 and Borza *Tombs* (1987).
132. Following the historiographical definition of Carr (1987) pp.29–30.
133. An adage credited to both Voltaire and André Gide: *Croyez ceux qui cherchent la vérité, doutez de ceux qui la trouvent.*
134. Quoting Bartsiokas (2000) p.513.
135. Musgrave-Prag-Neave-Lane Fox-White (2010) p.5. Bartsiokas-Carney (2007–2008).
136. Musgrave-Prag-Neave-Lane Fox-White (2010) section 5.
137. A good summary of these arguments can be found in Hall (2014) p.109. Hatzopoulos (2008) p.116 for discussion of Greek attitude to the dead body. Franks (2012) p.124 for the observation on the crown.
138. Bartsiokas (2000) p.513.
139. Hatzopoulos (2008) p.104.

Chapter 9: Bones Don't Lie!

1. Drougou-Paliadeli (2005): *Vergina: The Land and its History*, Militos Editions and Troia Editions; the co-author was Dr Stella Drougou, her colleague from the original excavations day with Manolis Andronikos.
2. In 2006/2007, an application was submitted, with Chrysoula Paliadeli, for a new proposal under the 4th European Structural Programme for Greece entitled 'Systematic and multidisciplinary investigation and digital documentation of

the skeletal material from the royal tombs of Vergina'. Yannis would coordinate all the scientific elements which included: 1) Anthropological investigation (morphometric analysis and statistical treatment, determination of biological age and gender, palaeopathological examination, anatomic and forensic examination); 2) Physicochemical analysis: DNA to determine gender and kinship, paleodiet investigation with isotopes, spectroscopic investigation for determining the temperature of cremation and comparison between the cremated bones of the different individuals, microscopic (optical and SEM) examination and mapping of the cracks in the bones and foreign material depositions, investigation, analysis and characterization of materials in the remains of the cremation pyres; 3) 3D imaging and archiving to be undertaken by a private company which Yannis had found and appointed to do this task. The anthropological team participating in that proposal was led by Professor Theodore Pitsios from the Anthropological Museum of Athens University. For the DNA analysis Yannis had secured the collaboration of Professor Terry Brown from the Institute of Biotechnology of Manchester and the rest of the analysis would be undertaken by Yannis' laboratory and team. This was not funded.
3. In 2008, the team wrote, with Chrysoula Paliadeli, a new proposal jointly coordinated by the University Excavations of Vergina and the National Centre for Scientific Research Demokritos in Athens. The same teams were involved plus the Laboratory of Photogrammetry and Remote Sensing of Aristotle University (Professor Petros Patias) who would now to do the 3D imaging. Yannis had again secured the participation of Terry Brown of Manchester for the DNA and Douglas Ubelaker for forensic examination and both were in that proposal. Not funded.
4. Livy 31.34.8.
5. Borza (1999) p.5. Also discussed in Satsoglou-Paliadeli *The Case of Vergina* p.692. As notable examples, we know that either Alexander's regent Antipater, or perhaps an Antipater of Magnesia, wrote a historical work titled *On the Deeds of King Perdiccas in Illyria*; there once existed a book on Alexander the Great by a Philip of Pella, and fifteen fragments survive of a domestic history by Theagenes.
6. The IT role was filled by Alexander Tourtas, an expert in underwater archaeology.
7. Kyriakou (2014) p.251.
8. Quoting Hughes (2011) p.58
9. Antikas- Wynn-Antikas (2015), Results.
10. Summarized in Andronikos (1984) p.227.
11. Sagan (1995): *The Demon Haunted World: Science as a Candle in the Dark*, Random House, p.213

12. Xirotiris-Langenscheidt (1981) p.158.
13. Plutarch *Demosthenes* 20.2 for the shield motto.
14. Riginos (1994) p.106 for a list of the sources.
15. The paper was titled 'Perimortem Weapon Trauma to the Thoracic Vertebrae of a 2nd Century BCE Adult Male Skeleton from Central Macedonia, Northern Greece', T. Antikas, L. Wynn-Antikas, J. Naylor, L. Stefani, *Journal of Palaeopathology*, 16 (2004) pp.69–78.
16. Lee-Whittaker-Wrightson (2015) p.34 for details of the torsion-powered devices.
17. Diodorus 16.34.5.
18. The eye wound can be found in Demosthenes *On the Crown* 18.67, Justin 7.6.14, Diodorus 16.34.5; Plutarch *Alexander* 3.2 for the oracle that predicted it; Riginos (1994) p.106 ff for more sources, which variously claim the project was an arrow, javelin or catapult bolt.
19. Riginos (1994) p.106 for discussion of the tortoise sheds and their use.
20. Marsyas of Pella's account via Didymus *On Demosthenes* 12.43–50, corroborating Theopompus' version.
21. Pliny 124 for the surgeon's work.
22. An image of such an arrowhead can be found in Hatzopoulos-Loukopoulos (1980) p.64.
23. The developing art of rhetoric discussed in Grant (2017) p.28 ff; Suetonius *Julius Caesar* 56.2, drawing from Cicero *Brutus* 262, for Cicero's likening rhetoric to curling irons; the analogy repeated in Quintilian 2.5.12, 5.12.18–120. Riginos (1994) p.108 ff for the legends attached to the incident.
24. Antikas-Wynn-Antikas (2015) *Results*.
25. L. Scheuer and S. Black (2004) *The Juvenile Skeleton* Elsevier, Academic Press, Amsterdam.
26. See Antikas-Wynn-Antikas (2015) *The female in the antechamber*.
27. Herodotus 1.94 for Etruscan origins.
28. Grant (2017) p.251 for discussion.
29. Theopompus *Histories* 115, *FGrHist* F204 =Athenaeus 517d–518a, for Etruscan women. Several features of his description appear in Plato's *Republic* 73 and Xenophon's description of Sparta, the *Constitution of the Lacedaemonians* 1.2–10. Mayor (2014) p.124 for Etruscan Amazon art.
30. Quoting Adams (1980) p.68 on personal signature. Andronikos (1984) p.189 for his reservations.
31. See discussion in Hall (2014); the wound was described by Didymus Chalkenteros in his commentary on Demosthenes' *On the Crown*. Plutarch *Moralia* 739b for additional uncertainty. Justin 9.3.2 for the thigh wound. Adams (1980) p.70 for Philip's leg wounds and Riginos (1994) p.116 ff for the upper leg or thigh.

32. Hippocrates, vol. III, The Loeb Classical Library, T.E. Page (ed.), translation by Dr E.T. Withington, Harvard University Press (1928).
33. Grant (2017) pp.383–84.
34. Justin's preface discussed in Grant (2017) p.299.
35. Following the observations in Rose (2003) p.43.
36. Following the argument in Garland (2010) p.2. Davis (1914) pp.42–43 for the exposure of children.
37. Quoting Bothmer (1952) p.19.
38. Kottaridi (2011) pp.103, 142; see Palagia (2017) p.411 for discussion.
39. 'Hasty' was Musgrave's own admission reiterated by Bartsiokas-Carney (2007–2008) p.17.
40. Bartsiokas-Carney (2007–2008) p.15 and p.18 footnotes 13 and 15 for commentary on the Tomb I tomb-robber theory. Robin Lane-Fox mentioned the theory in his 1980 book *The Search for Alexander*.
41. Quoting Drougou-Paliadeli (2005) p.197.
42. Quoting Carney (2015) pp.92–93.
43. Musgrave (1990) p.291 for the colour and condition of the bones.
44. Musgrave (1990) p.293.

Chapter 10: Orphic Masks and Burial Rituals

1. Homer *Odyssey* 8.578–580.
2. Following Cotterill (1915) p.44.
3. See Collins (2008) for full discussion of magic in the ancient Greek world, Introduction p.xiii. References to Thessaly from Ovid's Metamorphoses book 5, *Ino and Athamas*, line 444. Hades was later referred to as Plouton (the Roman Pluto) and Hades came to denote the place, rather than the person who ruled the underworld. Lucan *De Bello civili* book 6 has a son of Pompey consulting a witch on the outcome of the forthcoming battle against Caesar.
4. Graves (1955) p.140 for the mythology of werewolves.
5. Collins (2008) Introduction p.xiii for discussion of 'On the Sacred Disease' from the Hippocratic corpus and p.53 for the commercial centre of witchcraft, following Aristophanes' Clouds. For magnetic stones and Thales of Miletus see Collins (2008) pp.8–9 and p.46 for the Athenian court for inanimate objects.
6. Pausanias 1.32.3–4 recounted the haunting of Marathon and Plataea.
7. Aelian 13.3; translation in Hansen (2017) pp.182–83.
8. Quoting Andronikos (1984) p.70 and Andronikos (1978) Preliminary, p.30. He later reflected that the 'scientist's elation' effectively overwhelmed the guilt. Graves (1955) p.122 for the subterranean claims by Hades.

9. Dr Maniatis completed his MSc and PhD in England on the use of Scanning Electron Microscopy for characterization and technology of ancient ceramics and other archaeological materials.
10. Faklaris' paper appeared in *The Archaeological Works of Macedon and Thrace*, 3 (1989) p.30. The Egyptologist was Mr Boufidi. Faklaris confusingly mentions 1200 BC as the Twelfth Dynasty.
11. Diodorus 16.93.1 for the white cloak.
12. Diodorus 16.93.1 for the white cloak. Aelian 8.15.
13. Kyriakou (2015) p.276 and Fredericksmeyer (1979) p.51 for the inscription to Zeus Philippios and p.58 for Isocrates' letter, *Epistle* 3.5.
14. Antikas (2003) p.145 for the Sindos horses.
15. Chrysostomou (2012) p.503 for the golden death masks.
16. See arguments in Despini (2009).
17. Kyriakou (2015) p.251 and p.275 for the connection to Zeus.
18. Quoting Ceram (1951) p.37.
19. *Iliad* 23.1 ff; 'manslaughtering' following the translation of Richmond Lattimore.
20. Homer *Iliad* 23.163 ff for the pyre arrangements; translation by R. Lattimore, University of Chicago Press (1951).
21. Quoting Antikas (2003) p.149.
22. Homer *Iliad* 23.259–261.
23. Homer *Iliad* 23.241 for the bones at the centre of the pyre.
24. Quoting Antikas-Wynn-Antikas (2015), pp.3, 4; Pliny 19.4, 36.21.
25. Vitruvius *On Architecture* 8.6.10–11 warned of the dangers of lead; Pliny 34, 54.175–178.
26. Strabo 10.1 mentions 'Karystian stone … which is combed like wool'; also mentioned in Plutarch *De Oraculorum Defectus*. Theophrastus *On Stones* 2.17 mentions what is thought to be asbestos though some believe this was lignite.
27. *Iliad* 24.67 for 'the clothing of the gods'.
28. Sherwood Fox (1915) pp.xvi–xvii.
29. Following Kevin Clinton, *Myth and Cult: The Iconography of the Eleusinian Mysteries*, Stockholm, Svenska Institutet i Athen (1992). In the case of the closed gold larnax holding the female bones, it is highly unlikely to have come from an alabaster object.
30. Quoting Arvaniti-Maniatis-Wynn-Antikas-Antikas (2016) Conclusions.
31. The male and female observations in Arvaniti-Maniatis-Wynn-Antikas-Antikas (2016) 2, Conclusions.
32. Schliemann (1880) pp.214, 295, 337.
33. Davis (1914) p.63 for the white cloaks of Argos.
34. Green (1974) p.6 for 'sub-Homeric' enclave.

35. Kottaridi (1999) 1, p.114 ff for evidence of inhumation and cremation. Lee-Whittaker-Wrightson (2015) p.17 for the comparison with burial practices in Greece.
36. Diodorus 17.2.1.
37. Musgrave (1990) p.6 for his earlier risky proposition. Prag-Neave (1997) p.63 and Musgrave (1991) p.276 for the 'oven'.
38. Themelis-Touratsoglou (1997) provides further examples of tombs with cremation remains on the roof and evidence of the pyres nearby.
39. Based on an image from *The Tombs of Derveni*, Themelis and Touratsouglou (1997).
40. Andronikos (1978) Preliminary, p.28 for the dimensions of the pyre remains.
41. Hatzopoulos (2017) p.6 for translation of the Oxyrhynchus Papyri VX 1798.
42. Justin 11.2.1 for the executions at the tomb pyre and specifically a 'tumulus'; Hatzopoulos (2017) p.8 for the weapons, following Hammond.
43. Drougou-Paliadeli (2005) p.164 for evidence of the pathway.
44. Kyriakou (2015) p.267 for the Derveni wreath.
45. Hatzopoulos (2017) p.7 for the Armenian text.
46. Andronikos (1984) p.179 and p.226 for the additional shield.
47. In 2011, during the cataloguing process, Laura voiced the importance of this small bone in the scheme of things, but there was little support for her curiosity to enable her to fathom deeper, and the stray finger bone could not be located.
48. Personal communication between C. Zambas and Y. Maniatis.
49. Tsiafakis (2015) p.98 ff for the linen wrappers.
50. *Iliad* 24.31, 24.664, 24.784 and *Odyssey* 24.63 for Hector's eleven-day delay before Achilles promised safe passage to the Trojans to collect his corpse for burning on the tenth day inside the citadel of Troy. *Odyssey* 24.63 for Achilles' seventeen-day delay; compare to Herodotus' term for mummification. *Odyssey* 23.170 and 24.68 for jars of honey laid with the ashes of the dead. Ambrosia is mentioned as a preservative at 14.171, 16.670, 19.39; discussed in Willcock (1976) p.63.
51. Tolman-Scoggin (1903) p.110 footnote 42 for evidence of embalming at Mycenae.
52. Cotterill (1915) p.66. Herodotus 4.71 ff for the Scythian practices. *Odyssey* 11.25–30 for the sweet wine.
53. Quoting Ovid's *Metamorphoses* book 5, *Ino and Athamas*, line 444.
54. Hansen (1999) p.7 for the jury duty stipend. Davis (1914) p.69 for unskilled labour pay.
55. Williams-Ogden (1994) p.31 for slave prices. Grant (2017) p.132 for discussion of relative values of the obol.

306   *Unearthing the Family of Alexander the Great*

56. Lucian *On Funerals* 10.
57. From the *Suda*, translation in Hansen (2017) pp.138–39.
58. See Palagia (2008) p.201 for the possible depiction of such a scroll, quoting Palagia on 'passport'.
59. Discussed in Grant (2017) p.502.
60. Following Cotterill (1915) p.45.
61. Gill (2008) p.342 ff.
62. Hatzopoulos-Loukopoulos (1980) p.57 for the gold/silver relative values.
63. Troxell (1997) p.86 ff, Bellinger p.7 ff.
64. For example, Gill (2008) p.344.
65. Troxell (1997) p.86.
66. Troxell (1997) p.86 ff and p.93 ff, Bellinger (1963) p.6 ff.

Chapter 11: Entering the Chthonic Debate

1. Yannis' speech was titled 'Investigation of an Unusual Composite Material from the Larnax of Tomb II, Main Chamber, at the Great Tumulus at Vergina'.
2. The summary paper Yannis presented was Maniatis-Arvaniti-Antikas-Wynn-Antikas-Orsini-Ribechini-Colombini (2014).
3. The book is titled *From Citadel to City State: The Transformation of Greece, 1200–700 B.C.E.*
4. Thomas (2007), besides many other books on ancient Greece.
5. It has been suggested the city was founded as Hedonoi after a local Thracian tribe, but as Xerxes symbolically sacrificed nine girls and nine boys there on his way to Greece (Herodotus 7.114), its name by then represented 'nine-ways'.
6. Maniatis-Malamidou-Koukouli-Chryssanthaki-Facorellis (2010).
7. Plantzos (2017) p.65 ff for details of the announcement and the politicking that followed.
8. One is a historian, another specializes in animal bones, the other is a geologist and the last studies fossils from pre-history, Neanderthals for example.
9. Bartsiokas-Carney (2007–2008) p.16; from Faklaris (1978), the excavation report. Drougou excavated the upper section of the tomb in late 1977 but not the final lower levels. Her October 1977 log does not provide details of the depth of upper-level bones finds.
10. Bartsiokas-Carney (2007–2008) pp.16–17. The paper suggests the bones were moved by tomb robbers and placed above the soil coming through the roof.
11. The femur and tibia; thighbone and shinbone.
12. Bartsiokas-Arsuaga-Santos-Algaba-Gómez-Olivencia (2015), Significance.
13. Curtius 7.8.8.
14. Arrian 2.12.6–8, Curtius 3.12, 15–17, Justin 11.9.12, Diodorus 17.11.4.2 (implied at 17.114–134 also) for Alexander's reply. The Persian Queen

Mother Sisygambis mistook Hephaestion for Alexander on account of his height. Plutarch *Alexander* 21.6 for Darius' height: 'the tallest man in the Persian Empire', thus kings were supposed to be so.
15. Xirotiris' statement appeared in the *Kathimerini* newspaper, 28 July 2015, under the heading 'The struggle for the tomb of Philip brings revelations'. The article stated: 'The box in the workshop of The Democritus University Thrace, where, as Mr. Bartsiokas mentioned in the "K", he found the skeletal material of the tomb I, contained only the baby's skull. Based on this, Mr. Xirotiris argues that "the femur with a tibia comes from anthropological material from another excavation of the country gathered in the laboratory from various archaeological sites of the country (Crete, Epirus, Chalcidice, etc.)."'
16. Pausanias 10.20.4 for the height of the Celts.

Chapter 12: Finding Material Witnesses

1. Paliadeli had written a monograph in 2004 stating the hunt might depict real historical persons; Hatzopoulos (2008) p.114 for discussion. See Saatsoglou-Paliadeli (2004).
2. Grant (2017) p.485 for the numbers of bodyguards.
3. Pausanias 1.6.2.
4. Andronikos (1984) p.126 for Philip's hooked nose, in Andronikos' opinion.
5. Saatsoglou-Paliadeli (2004) pp.145–47, figs. 14, 26 pls.15a, 27b. Also Drougou-Paliadeli (2005) p.268.
6. Andronikos (1984) pp.109–10.
7. Athenaeus 12.539d.
8. Aristotle *Prior Analytics* 2.27
9. Aristotle *The History of Animals*, discussed in Lloyds (1999) p.23 ff. For Aristotle's own appearance, Diogenes Laertius *Lives of Eminent Philosophers, On Aristotle* 5.1.
10. Franks (2012) pp.4, 18, 78 for the sacred nature of the grove and p.86 for its antiquity; p.94 for the mythological elements.
11. Plato's view in his *Laws* 7.824a discussed in Franks (2012) pp.18, 60, 97; p.99 for Heracles 'kynagidas'.
12. Plutarch *Alexander* 40–41, translation from the Loeb Classical Library edition (1919).
13. Athenaeus 1.18a.
14. The historians were A.M.P. Giallombardo and B. Tripodi discussed in Hatzopoulos (2008) p.100.
15. *Iliad* 23.173–74, Theodore Antikas, personal correspondence with Chrysoula Paliadeli 1 May 2005.

16. Quoting Antikas (2003) p.150.
17. Xenophon *On Hunting* 1.1–2, discussed in Hansen (2017) p.364.
18. See Ma (2011) pp.526, 530, 535 for the huntsmen.
19. This elite group included Perdiccas, Leonnatus, Seleucus, Ptolemy, Lysimachus, Peithon and Aristonus plus a notable recent eighth, Peucestas, who saved Alexander with the 'shield from Troy' in India. As many as fourteen names have been associated with the position of 'somatophylax' of bodyguard in the campaign accounts; some died, and one was executed, whilst others were retired (those originally appointed by Philip II) or they simply faded out of the story. After Hephaestion's death, a vacancy presented itself and Peucestas was already absent in the East; possibly an established royal hypaspist (or a hyperaspisantes, a shield carrier), Peucestas had become an 'eighth' addition to a fellowship traditionally seven in number. Peucestas had been appointed governor of Persis and the bodyguard role was only bestowed on those operating in the king's immediate presence (as the title suggests). In which case – and perhaps alongside a recently promoted Seleucus – Eumenes was being cited in his place, an elevation that might have come with the acquisition of Perdiccas' hipparchy; from Grant (2017) pp.486–87.
20. Andronikos (1984) p.220.
21. The bones were analyzed by Theo and Laura and the conclusion appeared in a 2015 paper titled *Examination of the Cremated Remains of a Woman and her Fetus from the Macedonian tomb at Agios Athanasios, Greece*, an unpublished report submitted to the Director of the Archaeological Museum of Thessaloniki.
22. Tsimbidou-Avloniti (2002) p.94. She is now retired, having served for many years as Head of the Department of Archaeological Studies, Monuments and Research at the 16th Ephorate of Antiquities of Thessaloniki, Greece (now renamed as Ephorate of Antiquities of the District (Perifereia) of Thessaloniki).
23. Aelian 3.32 for Alexander's playing and Plutarch *Pericles* 1.5 for Philip's derogatory remark.
24. Tsimbidou-Avloniti *Tombs* (2015) p.5 for the unique nature of female lyre playing.
25. Diodorus 19.59.3–5 for Phila's qualities.
26. Nicanor and Iollas; Diodorus 19.11.8.
27. Tsimbidou-Avloniti *Tombs* (2015) pp5–6 for the eight armed men watching on; p.7 for the iron greaves and cuirass.
28. Plutarch *Demetrius* 36; discussed in Palagia (2017) p.423.
29. Quoting Carney (1992) p.98.
30. A full description of the Agios Athanasios excavation can be found in 'Excavating a painted Macedonian tomb near Thessaloniki. An astonishing

discovery', Maria Tsimbidou-Avloniti, featured in *Studies in Classical Archaeology I*, *Excavating Classical Culture, Recent Archaeological discoveries in Greece*, BAR International Series 1031 (2002), p.91 ff. This has now been published in the *acta* of the annual archaeologists' meeting named *To Archaiologiko Ergo in Macedonia and Thrace*, ΑΕΜΘ 26, 2012 (2017), 283–90, with an English summary.
31. Tsimbidou-Avloniti (2002) p.92 for the Agios Athanasios cloth.
32. Andronikos (1984) p.191 ff for the fabric description.
33. Aeschylus *Agamemnon* for his walking on a purple garment and his *Oresteia for the Furies*; discussed in Jenkins (1985) pp.116–18; pp.125–26 for the significance of gold and purple. For the Knossos inscription see Spantidaki (2016) p.14.
34. Herm (1975) p.25 for the self-identification as Canaanites and pp.52–63 for the Amorite-Canaanite migrations that saw the cities settled. Herodotus 1.1 ff stated that Phoenicians carried off Io, daughter of the king of Argos. In retaliation, the Greeks abducted Europa from Tyre and so Paris stole Helen from Sparta.
35. Tyrian purple fetched its weight in silver at Colophon in Asia Minor, according to Theopompus cited in Athenaeus 12.526.
36. Plutarch *Alexander* 36.2–4.
37. Homer *Odyssey* 24.73 ff. See Andronikos (1978) Preliminary, p.42 for the treatment of Hector's bones and Andronikos (1984) p.170. Also *Iliad* 24.788 ff.
38. For the cloth analysis see Drougou (1987) and Drougou (2018).
39. Moraitou (2007) pp.5–9 for the analysis.
40. Onesicritus' sighting of cotton in Strabo 15.1.63–65.
41. Strabo 2.1.9, 15.1.28.
42. Cotton is mentioned by Herodotus at 3.107 and 7.65.
43. Curtius 5.2.18.
44. Spantidaki (2016) p.16 for flax and wool imports.
45. Herodotus 5.88 for linen chitons; discussed in Jenkins (1985) p.120. Spantidaki (2016) p.16 for possible papyrus sails and pp.21–22 for fishing nets.
46. Gleba (2012) p.45 ff; p.47 for vinegar.
47. Moraitou (2007) p.9.
48. Quoting Spantidaki (2016) p.19; p.232 ff for the Trachones fabric 23.
49. Quoting Margariti (2010), Abstract.
50. Personal correspondence between 5 and 12 September 2017.
51. Michel-McGovern (1987) pp.135–43 for the processing of purple dye.
52. The paper confirming the papyrus was found in 1978 and removed in 1990 is Andronikos-Drougou, Faklaris-Saatsoglou-Paliadeli-Kottaridi (1990) p.170.
53. Andronikos-Fotiadis (1978) p.8

310 *Unearthing the Family of Alexander the Great*

54. Janko (2008) p.1.
55. Palagia (2008) p.201 for the gold tablets with Orphic texts. Pausanias 9.30.7 for Orpheus' grave.
56. Janko (2017) p.1 and footnote 3.
57. Janko (2017) p.2 ff.
58. Janko (2017) p.7 ff.
59. Palagia (2008) p.197 for the hanging possessions.

Chapter 13: Afterlife in Amphipolis

1. Lucian *How to Write History* 40–41; see Grant (2017) p.388 for its context.
2. The tale is recounted in Phlegon of Tralles *Book of Marvels* 2.1, and Proclus *Commentary on Plato's Republic* 2.115; see translations in Hansen (2017) pp.113–17.
3. Carney (2000) p.59 for the lineage of Machatas, brother of Philip's wife Phila. He was possibly the father of Alexander's wayward treasurer, Harpalus.
4. Tsimbidou-Avloniti *Tombs* (2015) p.2 for the handshake symbolism and p.3 for griffins.
5. Quoting Palagia *Gods* (2016) p.95.
6. David (1914) p.25 ff for marriage and courting and p.27 for the line from Xenophon *Economics* 7 ff. David (1914) p.21 for the layout of the typical Athenian house.
7. Jenkins (1985) p.111 for the wedding ceremony.
8. Plato *Republic* 5.455c, discussed in Hawley-Levick (1995) p.29 and p.131 quoting Hawley.
9. Silver (2018) p.60 for the significance of the grasping of the wrist.
10. Euripides *Medea* 230–248, translation by D.Kovacs. The lines above from Sophocles.
11. Silver (2018) pp.1–11 for a summary of the slave-wife institution.
12. See discussion in Hawley-Levick (1995) p.75 ff and Webster Wilde (2000) p.16 ff. David (2014) p.27 for the quince and fertility.
13. Arrian 1.11.1 and Diodorus 17.16 for worship of the Muses.
14. Carney (2000) pp.62–63 for Olympias' renaming; also discussed in McGurdy (1932) pp.23–27.
15. Graves (1955) pp.10, 17 for the consumption of laurel leaves, otherwise known as bay leaves.
16. Plutarch *Alexander* 2.4. Marinatos (1970) p.49 for other snake cults. Graves (1955) p.28 for the symbolism of snakes.
17. Quoting Drougou-Paliadeli (2005) p.137; images on pp.136, 143; p.223 for the representation of the goddess.
18. Plutarch *Alexander* 3.1.

Notes   311

19. Diodorus 16.2.3 for Philip's Pythagorean training.
20. The soul-drawing wand was described by Clearchus in *On Sleep* in Proclus *Commentary on Plato's Republic* 2.122; Hansen (2017) pp.140–41 for translation. For Aristeas see Pliny the Elder 7.174; for Empedocles see Diogenes Laertius 8.77 and Athenaeus 8.365e. Cotterill (1915) p.44 for snakes.
21. See Grant (2017) p.252 for Ephorbus and sources. For Empedocles see Diodorus 10.6.1–3; translation in Hansen (2017) pp.135–36.
22. Following the argument in Williams-Ogden (1994) p.39.
23. Cohen (2010) p.187 ff.
24. Cohen (2010) p.195. She is Professor of Art History at Dartmouth College.
25. Following the description given in Rhomiopoulou (1997) p.21.
26. Palagia (2019) p.27 for the this not-fully unearthed 'Tomb of Eurydice'.
27. Fredericksmeyer (1979) p.50 for Philip's worship at Amphipolis.
28. See Oikonomides (1982) and Carney (2006) p.104 ff for detail of Olympias' tomb.
29. The lion may well have been positioned closer to the sea and Strymon River; it was moved in the twentieth century by foreign excavating teams, and marble from the Casta Hill surround or '*peribolos*' had been used to dam the river at some time in antiquity and replaced by the lion monument, confusing recent excavators.
30. Arrian 7.14.4, Plutarch *Alexander* 72.3 for the execution of the doctor; Plutarch *Alexander* 72 for Alexander's sacrifice to the shades of Hephaestion and 'blood-soaked hunt'. Plutarch *Pelopidas* 34.2 for the shearing of horses and mules, Arrian 7.14.5 for the references to the temple of Asclepius in Ecbatana.
31. Mavrojannis (2016) p.657; Diodorus 18.4.1–3 for the cancelled so-called 'last plans' of Alexander.
32. Diodorus 17.115.1 ff for the tearing down of 10 furlongs of the city walls and description of the structure. Plutarch *Alexander* 72.1–3, Arrian 7.14.7, 7.23.6 for Hephaestion's elevation. Arrian claimed the oracle permitted 'hero' only. Mavrojannis (2016) pp–659–60 for the fleet and return of Hephaestion's body.
33. Mavrojannis (2016) p.657. Grant (2017) p.777 for Hephaestion's cavalry regiment.
34. Diodorus 16.93–95, Justin 9.6–7.
35. For Alexander's intimacy with Bagoas the eunuch, see the 'Vulgate' tradition of Curtius 6.5.23, 10.1.26, 10.1.22–38, also Plutarch *Alexander* 67.7–8, Athenaeus 13.603a–b.
36. Discussed in Grant (2017) pp.777–78.
37. Cassius Dio 80.18.1–3.
38. Pausanias 1.7.1 claimed Ptolemy II Philadelphus brought the body from Memphis to Alexandria; see Grant (2017) pp.462–64 for discussion. The slip

312 Unearthing the Family of Alexander the Great

      of the tongue was recorded in Plutarch *Alexander* 27, though this is hardly likely. 'Hypostaseis' is a substance in which a god could exist in different forms. Strabo 17.1.43 indicated Callisthenes stated the oracle's reply confirmed Alexander as the son of Zeus. Diodorus 1.28.1–4 for the journeying of Belus and Danaus from Egypt.

39. Following Grant (2017) p.17.
40. Lucian *Dialogues of the Dead* 12, translation from Lucian, *Complete Works*, Delphi Classics (2016), p.xiv.
41. Grant (2017) p.462 for further detail.
42. Following Palagia (2016) p.384.
43. Souvaltzi (2002) p.20.
44. Arrian 3.3.6 for snakes; he also stated Aristobulus claimed they were guided by two ravens; Strabo 17.1.43 for crows; Grant (2017) p.343 for discussion.
45. Quoting Bosworth (1988) *From Arrian to Alexander* p.203.
46. The inscription was recorded by Arrian 6.29.5–8 and with minor variations by Plutarch *Alexander* 69.3 and Strabo 15.3.7.
47. Discussed in Grant (2017) p.434 ff.

Chapter 14: The Queen's Gold and the King's Craftsmen

1. Quoting from Williams-Ogden (1994) p.10.
2. Gold from the 121 graves in the cemetery of Sindos near Thessalonica falls into this category.
3. Andronikos (1984) p.177 termed them 'hoops'.
4. Andronikos (1984) p.186 for seventy-four arrowheads; p.187 for the alloy.
5. Mayor (2014) p.85 for the 'floating anchor' technique and p.212 for construction of a bow.
6. Herodotus 4.3 ff for the use of whips against slaves in revolt.
7. For display, the rings had been arranged with the widest at the centre of the five, to conform to what was considered the shape of a bow. But if two of the rings were moved, the gradually tapering shape emerges.
8. The 'sagaris' was allegedly invented by the Amazon queen Penthesilea; Mayor (2014) p.220 ff and Pliny 7.56.201.
9. Herodotus 4.5 and 4.20 for the Royal Scythians.
10. Image from Derevyanko-Molodin (2016) p.341.
11. Bivar (1972) p.285 ff
12. Wilde (1999) pp.46–47
13. Wilde (1999) p.48 for the 10–12-year-old in chain-mail. Mayor (2014) p.68 for the wear to the fingers.

14. Olga Novoseltceva and Svetlana Pankova.
15. Mayor (2014) p.111 for the tattoos photographed by Dr Pankova.
16. Williams-Ogden (1994) pp.14–15 for trace elements and impurities, quoting Keyser-Clark (2001) p.105 on 'diagnostic fingerprint', though here referring to electrum.
17. Dr Despina Ignatiadou, private correspondence dated 5 December 2017.
18. Herodotus 3.63, 6.46–47, 7.12; Thucydides 1.100.2; Strabo 7.331.
19. In the annual publication of the Archaeological Excavations of Macedonia and Thrace.
20. The testing methods described in Vavelidis-Christophides-Melfos (1997) p.84 ff.
21. Williams-Ogden (1994) p.124 for the political unit. Tsetskhladze (1998) p.55 ff and quoting p.66 for Greek construction of Scythian and Thracian tombs and 'Hellenised'.
22. Treister (1996) p.212 ff for discussion of Panticapaeum metalworking.
23. Green (1996) p.15 for the blockade of the Mediterranean.
24. Green (1996) for Sicilian and Adriatic wheat import routes.
25. Demosthenes *Against Leptines* 20.31 stated that half of the 800,000 '*medimnoi*' of corn came from the Bosporan kingdom. Williams-Ogden (1994) p.122 for the change of name to Euxine Sea.
26. Shcheglov-Katz (1991) p.102
27. Andronikos (1984) p.181.
28. Treister (2008) p.21 for the identical *gorytos* template.
29. Quoting Professor Paul Keyser, who was introduced to us by Adrienne Mayor.
30. Keyser-Clark (2001) p.106 for the addition of copper to electrum, p.110 for hardening with copper.
31. Keyser-Clark (2001) p.114 for 'wet' chemical analysis; p.113 for subatomic beams.
32. Keyser-Clark (2001) p.108 for 'surface enrichment'.
33. Williams-Ogden (1994) p.178 for the gold Alexander stater found in the region.
34. Plutarch *Alexander* 25.6–8, Pliny 12.62, Plutarch *Moralia* 179e–f.
35. Drougou (2018) p.87 ff for the Hermitage link and local production close to Vergina.
36. Private communications with the Hermitage in April and May 2017.
37. Andronikos (1984) p.189 for silver Thracian examples.
38. Tsetskhladze (1998) p.55 ff for the similarity and Greek influences and quoting p.77.
39. Dr Zofia Archibald.
40. Livy 45.33.5–8.
41. Themelis (2017) pp.7–8 on local metalworking.

Chapter 15: Warrior Father, Warrior Daughter and the Bactrian

1. Angel (1947) pp.18–24.
2. Andronikos (1984) p.26 for the predominance of female graves.
3. See Tronson (1984) p.116 ff for 339/338 BC; Heckel (2006) p.158 favours 342 BC. Olympias, Cleopatra and Phila are all thought to have been teenagers when Philip married them; the age of other wives is more speculative. See Antikas-Wynn-Antikas (2015) *Discussion* for discussion of Meda's age.
4. Athenaeus 8.557c–e.
5. See Tronson (1984) p.116 ff for 339/338 BC; Heckel (2006) p.158 favours 342 BC.
6. Justin 9.3.
7. Hammond (1991) p.77 for his suggestion of ritual suicide.
8. See Herodotus 4.71.4 and 5.5 for the Thracian tradition and for tribes north of Crestonia.
9. Andronikos (1978) p.3 for the sherds and Andronikos (1984) pp.221–22 for the tombs dating.
10. Hammond (1991) p.76. We have no proof that the sarissa was first introduced by Philip but it was never mentioned before his reign.
11. Andronikos (1978) p.28 for the dimensions of the pyre covering the 'back' portion of the tomb, i.e. the main chamber only.
12. Riginos (1994) pp.105, 115 for the linking of this injury to Philip's battle with Illyrians.
13. Arrian *Events after Alexander* 1.23, Polyaenus 8.60 for Cynnane's death.
14. Athenaeus 8.557c–f. Translation from The Loeb Classical Library (1937).
15. Satyrus proposed the kings Coenos and Tyrimmas came before Perdiccas in other texts; Satyrus *FGrHist* 631F1.
16. Satyrus was epitomizing 'Lives' (we don't know when he wrote, before 250 BC but possibly much earlier as a 'peripatetic' pupil). We don't know, in fact, if the citations we have in Athenaeus or Diogenes Laertius were from Satyrus direct or taken through Heraclides Lembus who epitomized Satyrus' *Lives* (in the reign of Ptolemy VI Philomotor).
17. Tronson (1984) pp.116–26 for discussion of Satyrus' list and the order of marriages and Carney (2000) p.55.
18. Justin 9.8.1, Diodorus 16.1.3, 16.95.1, 17.1.1.
19. Justin 7.5.9–10 claimed he acted as guardian.
20. Satyrus stated 22 years, Athenaeus 557C, which conflicts with Justin 7.5.9–10 (who stated Philip acted as guardian) and Diodorus 16.1–3, via Diyllus, stated 24 years. The scholiast to Aeschines 3.51 suggests 359 BC (archonship of Callidemus in the first year of the 105th Olympiad, thus 359 BC). Heckel (2006) p.211 for the calendar explanation.

21. Diodorus 16.4.1 ff.
22. Borza (1990) p.207 ff for the problem of children born in quick succession.
23. Heckel (2006) p.179 for the late marriage dating.
24. Polyaenus 8.60. Heckel (1987) p.119.
25. Mahaffy (1896) p.119 for the dates of the campaigns.
26. Diodorus 16.93.6.
27. After Bardylis and then Grabos and Pleuratus I, there was hostility by certain Illyrian tribes under Glaucias and Cleitus right up to Alexander's accession and 335 BC. Heckel (1987) p.119 for his comment and Polyaenus.
28. Polyaenus 8.60; adapted from the translation by R. Shepherd (1793).
29. Diodorus 16.69.7 for the 'inherited squabble'.
30. Polyaenus 8.60 for Cynnane's reluctance to marry again.
31. Mayor (2014) p.4 for Atalanta's dress.
32. See Grant (2017) p.722 ff for discussion of Syrian headquarters.
33. Nepos *Eumenes* 13, Plutarch *Eumenes* 19.1–2; upon Eumenes' death his ashes were returned to his wife, children and mother. For Craterus' death see Plutarch *Eumenes* 7.13, Arrian *Events After Alexander* 26, Nepos *Eumenes* 4.4, Diodorus 19.44.2, 19.59.3. Arrian *Events After Alexander* 1.23 confirmed Alcetas' troops were indignant at Cynnane's death.
34. Diodorus 19.52.5, Athenaeus 4.155a for the burials. Burstein (1982) p.148 disagrees and sees the translation corrected as 'with' Cynnane, thus altogether.
35. Diodorus 19.52.2
36. Athenaeus 4.155a (from Diyllus).
37. Andronikos (1984) p.64 for detail of the offering fires.
38. According to Pliny the Elder 35.110.
39. Diodorus 18.26.4. See Grant (2017) for discussion of the legitimacy of Ptolemy's action and Alexander's original succession instructions.
40. Andronikos (1984) p.140 ff.
41. Plato *Laws* 947 D, translation from Hammond (1991) p.73.
42. Drougou-Paliadeli (2005) p.202 for the Bella tomb with a masonry road to its entrance for this purpose.
43. Athenaeus 11.509d–e and 11.506e; see discussion of where the governorship might have been in King (2018) p.71.
44. *Iliad* 23.245 ff.
45. Hammond (1991) p.73 for Euphraeus visiting Macedon around 360 BC at the court of Perdiccas III. Palagia (2017) p.415 for the tomb's construction style and Palagia (2018) p.27 for the observation on tomb robbers.
46. Plato *Republic* 617c.
47. Palagia *Argeads*, p.152 for the Corinthian columns and Philippeion.
48. 'Temple-like' from the Vergina display panel.

316 *Unearthing the Family of Alexander the Great*

49. Hammond (1978) p.334 for the dating.
50. Chronology of the Great Tumulus discussed in Carney (2015) p.97.
51. Bartsiokas-Carney (2007–2008) p.16.
52. See discussion in Andronikos (1984) pp.65, 228.
53. Justin 9.7.11.
54. Translation from Palagia (2008) p.195.
55. Palagia (2008) p.204 ff.
56. For Cassander's 'legendary knowledge of Homer' see Athenaeus 14.620b. Cited in Adams (1980), also in Lehman (1982) p.441.
57. Curtius for his go-between role. Compare to Arrian 4.21.6, Plutarch *Alexander* 58.3–4, Strabo 11.11.4.
58. Curtius 3.12.21–23 for Barsine's descriptions and Arrian 4.19 for similar descriptions of both Roxane and Darius' wife.
59. Arrian 6.15.3, Curtius 9.8.9–10 for his continued governorship
60. Holt (2005) p.107.
61. Bosworth (1988) p.238 for the defence force. Grant (2017) p.51 for discussion.
62. Plutarch *Alexander* 77.6; see Grant (2017) p.457.
63. Diodorus 19.52.4–5.
64. Quoting Diodorus 19.105.1–2; also Justin 15.2.2–5, Pausanias 9.7.2.
65. Musgrave (1990) p.280 ff. Grant (2017) p.733 ff for Heracles' fate and ageing.
66. Musgrave (1990) p.291 for colour.
67. Justin 15.2.3.
68. Polybius 8.10.11.
69. Andronikos (1984) pp.221–24 for their dating.
70. Diodorus 18.68.2 for the presence of the kings with Alexander.
71. Plutarch *Alexander* 32.9 for the peritrachelion of gold with insets of precious stones.
72. Themelis (2017) p.9 and Palagia-Tracy (2016) pp.166–68.
73. Curtius 7.8.17 for the oxen and plough as sign of domestication; 7.9.9 for battle with the Scythians; 7.8.12 ff for their complaints to Alexander.
74. Genetically, this would be challenging, because tests for autosomal markers would be needed, instead of uniparental markers.
75. Father and son would share the same Y-chromosome, because this is inherited almost exclusively from the paternal line. The Y-chromosome recombines with its X counterpart for about 10 per cent. The remaining 90 per cent of the Y-chromosome is the non-recombining part (NRY) which is able to identify paternal bonds. Therefore, the prince would have the same NRY with Amyntas III and Philip II. In the case of the Amazon, if she was the daughter of Philip II, she would share 50 per cent of autosomal DNA.

Chapter 16: Preparing to Gene-Tag the Royals

1. Grant (2017) p.251 for discussion.
2. Quoting from http://www.sciencemag.org/news/2017/02/thousands-horsemen-may-have-swept-bronze-age-europe-transforming-local-population.
3. Curiously, a high percentage of them were lactose intolerant: https://phys.org/news/2015-06-ancient-dna-reveals-europeans-skin.html.
4. Robbins (2001) p.167 for the fair-haired and blue-eyed Libyans.
5. The article on the skull thought to be Pliny the Elder can be found at http://www.haaretz.com/archaeology/1.809751.
6. Dr Terry Brown had given his blessing for Konstantina, his PhD student, to work on the bones at Manchester at no cost to the project. Terry had been a keynote speaker at the 2014 International Symposium of Archaeometry in Los Angeles; Yannis is the Chairman of the Standing Committee.
7. Quoting from the article at www.nature.com/news/stop-hoarding-ancient-bones-plead-archaeologists-1.22445.
8. Following Kyriakou (2014) p.256.
9. The conservator was Vanessa Papageorgiou. The osteoarchaeologist of the Aristotle University examined the bones and determined the age of the adolescent at 15–17 years.
10. Her paper appeared in 2011 referenced Saatsoglou-Paliadeli (2011).
11. Diodorus 20.20.1–2 and 20.28.1.
12. Grant (2017) p.733 ff.
13. Justin had a habit of confusing mothers and children, so Barsine may, or may not, have shared Heracles' fate; Heckel (2006) p.18 (Alexander IV) and p.242 for the confusion (ref. Rhoxane).
14. Justin 15.2.3, Diodorus 20.28, Pausanias 9.7.2 for Heracles' death.
15. Kyriakou (2014) p.277 for the traces of fire and p.278 for the location's significance.
16. Kyriakou (2015) p.251, p.258 ff. See D. Williams in Palagia-Tracy (2003) p.233 for the wreath from Tzagezi near Amphipolis.
17. A parallel study came to a similar conclusion on the style of craftsmanship of the myrtle wreaths found in tombs across the Greek world: of the eight gold or gilded examples discovered in Macedon, five were from the same workshop, including that of 'Amazon' found in Tomb II, which closely resembles a wreath discovered in a grave at Pydna; see Tsigardia (2010) pp.305–12. Bettina Tsigarida is Director of the Museum and Ephorate of Pella. The blue enamel found on four of them, a unifying though restrained example of colour known as 'polychromy', dates them to the mid-to-late fourth century BC; the even bolder use of inset gemstones in others fashioned later is linked

318   Unearthing the Family of Alexander the Great

to Alexander's opening trade routes with the East. Williams-Ogden (1994) p.16 for polychromy and its development.
18. Thucydides 4.1001.
19. Grant (2017) pp.733–43.
20. In the gold chest burned teeth were found.
21. For example, the experimental studies of Shipman-Foster-Schoeninger (1984) p.308; also in *The Analysis of Burned Human Remains*, C.W. Schmidt and S.A. Symes (eds) 2nd Edition (2015).
22. The conservator was Vanessa Papageorgiou who had worked on the agora bones.
23. Mayor (2014) p.97 for red-haired Thracians.
24. Arrian 7.9.2–3.
25. Richard Dawkins, *River out of Eden, A Darwinian View of Life*, p.133.
26. The phrase is found on the Derveni Papyrus.
27. Antikas (2009) p.5.
28. The Olympic victories listed by Theodore Antikas in private correspondence to Chrysoula Paliadeli 1 May 2005. The fish-eating horse article of 2004 was titled 'Pathological Finds in Human and horse Skeletons from Recent Excavations at Sindos and Polykastro'; also mentioned in Antikas (2003) p.145.
29. Plutarch *Alexander* 6–7.
30. Arrian 5.19.4–6. Theo remains unconvinced by Arrian's explanation and reminded me that '*Phi*' and '*Beta*' were interchangeable in the ancient alphabet; what could then have been a 'B' not 'P' might actually have simply stood for 'cattle-branded', the generic meaning of '*bous*' (thus B), and it was this that gave rise to his name.
31. Aristotle *On the Movement of Animals*. For Pliny see Cothran (2010) p.8.
32. Roisman-Worthington (2010) p.465 for the military pay comparison.
33. The study is titled *Greek Horse DNA Statistics: January 2012–December 2016* by T.G. Antikas.
34. Justin 9.2.
35. Pliny 8.66. Herodotus 7.4.8.
36. Mayor (2014) p.179.
37. Arrian 4.13.1.
38. Personal correspondence on 11 September 2017.

Chapter 17: The Little Summer of Saint Demetrius

1. Pausanias 5.10.1.
2. Plutarch *Pyrrhus* 34 for Pyrrhus' death in Argos and Pausanias 2.22.8–2.25.8 for the Homeric story attached to the tomb of Lycymnius. He was the illegitimate son of Electryon, the son of Perseus and Andromeda.

3. Plutarch *Pyrrhus* 5.3–7. Pyrrhus always wore a helmet with goat horns protruding.
4. Detail of the Orchomenus tomb at http://www.archaeology.wiki/blog/2017/09/12/a-significant-archaeological-discovery-was-made-near-orchomenos-of-boeotia/.
5. Herodotus 8.121 for the statue of Alexander I; the Gold of Tolosa (Toulouse) discussed in Grant (2017) p.784, and footnote 71; Strabo 4.1 provided detail for Roman tradition of the fabled 15,000-talent 'aurum Tolosanum', the cursed gold of Tolosa looted from Delphi.
6. Plutarch *Alexander* 40.5 reported that a hunting scene in which Alexander fought a lion was represented on Craterus' monument at Delphi. Also, Pliny 34.64 for the monument; Borza-Palagia (2007) p.97 for its significance and pp.90–103 for lion hunts and their representation; pp.101–202 for Craterus' monument and dedication. Curtius 8.1.11–18, 8.1.14–18, 8.6.7, 8.8.3, Arrian 4.13–14, Plutarch *Alexander* 55 for additional hunting incidents involving Alexander. See discussion and measurements in Stewart (1993) p.270 and descriptions on p.390.
7. In legend Deucalion and Pyrrha were the sole survivors of the Great Flood and they made their way to Thessaly. Their son Hellen, king of Phthia in Thessaly, gave birth to Aeolus and Dorus and Achaeus and Ion through his grandsons; they founded the races of the Aeolians, Dorians, Achaeans and Ionians.
8. Pausanias 1.13.2.
9. Plutarch *Alexander* 16.15–17, Arrian 1.16.4–5, Pliny 34.64, Justin 11.6.12–13; Stewart (1993) pp.388–90 for all sources and translations.
10. Pausanias 9.30.1 for Orpheus' burial.
11. Satsoglou-Paliadeli *The Case of Vergina* p.698.
12. The course was titled 'Medical Visualization and Human Anatomy'.
13. Justin 11.2.1.
14. Arrian 1.25.1–2, Justin 11.2.1 for the names of the assassins; Heckel (2006) p.5, Aeropus, for the possible identification with the disgraced commander, their father.
15. For the budget see the article at: http://www.ekathimerini.com/226923/article/ekathimerini/life/amphipolis-archaeological-study-misses-out-on-funding.
16. Made of 1.5 million euros from Central Macedonian regional authority and 1.3 million euros from the European Union regional development programme.
17. A summary of the tombs and excavations at Archontiko can be found at http://www.ekathimerini.com/131106/article/ekathimerini/life/archontiko-dig-bears-witness-to-rich-warrior-society.
18. Derveni tombs discussed in Carney (2015) p.116. Themelis-Touratsouglou (1997) p.146 and p.204 for summaries of the similarities between the

Derveni tombs and Vergina Tomb II. Chrysostomou (2012) for the Archontiko finds. Tsimbidou-Avloniti (2002) p.92 for the female bones found in a silver larnax at Agios Athanasios.
19. The excavator was M Bessios.
20. Drougou-Paliadeli (2005) p.73 for the rescue excavation.
21. Borza (1999) p.78.
22. Source, the official Aegae website at https://www.aigai.gr/en/news/espa.
23. Grant (2017) p.708.
24. Borza (1999) p.77 for 'aberration'.
25. Strabo 8.6.11, Pausanias 2.7, 7.3 related the legend that Perseus, the legendary founder of Mycenae, employed the giant Cyclops to construct Mycenae's city walls; see Thomas-Conant (1999) p.5.
26. Grant (2017) p.75 ff. Quoting Schliemann in Ceram (1951) p.34 for the 10,000 years.
27. Hyperides *Demosthenes* 31.
28. Following Grant (2017) p.80 and quoting Gudeman *Greeks* (1894) p.57.
29. Grant (2017) p.71 for the quote from A. Heuss.

Reference Note

1. Grant (2017) for a full discussion of the 'standard model', particularly relating to Alexander's death and the Successor Wars that followed.

Bibliography

A multitude of books distracts the mind.
—Socrates

Ancient Bibliography

The English titles of ancient works are often the result of a very liberal translation process, so here they have been referred to by the popular names.

Aelian: *Historical Miscellany*
Arrian: *The Campaign of Alexander*
Arrian *Successors*: *Events after Alexander*
Athenaeus: *The Dinner Philosophers*
Cassius Dio: *Roman History*
Curtius: *History of Alexander the Great*
Diodorus: *Library of World History*
Diogenes Laertius: *Lives and Opinions of Eminent Philosophers*
Frontinus: *Military Stratagems*
Herodotus: *The Histories*
Hesiod: *Theogony*
Hesiod W D: *Works and Days*
Homer: *Iliad*; *Odyssey*
Justin: *Epitome of the Philippic History of Pompeius Trogus*
Livy: *The Early History of Rome*
Nepos: *Eumenes*; *Lives of Eminent Commanders*
Pausanias: *Guide to Ancient Greece*
Photius: Photius' précis of Dexippus' epitome of Arrian's *Events After Alexander*

Pliny the Elder: *Natural History*
Plutarch: *Alexander: The Life of Alexander* from his *Parallel Lives*, Codex 82
Plutarch: *Eumenes: The Life of Eumenes*
Plutarch: *Pelopidas: Life of Pelopidas*
Plutarch: *Phocion: Life of Phocion*
Polyaenus: *Stratagems of War*
Polybius: *Histories*
Quintilian: *Institutes of Oratory*
Strabo: *Geography*
Thucydides: *History of The Peloponnesian War*
Xenophon: *History of Greece*; *On Horsemanship*; *The Education of Cyrus*

Modern Bibliography

For clarity, only the publication being referred to in the book is italicised, though usual convention would be to include in italics the journal or publication in which the article appeared.

W.L. Adams, '*The Royal Macedonian Tomb at Vergina: An Historical Interpretation*', The Ancient World 3 (1980), pp.67–72.

M. Andronikos, *Vergina: the Royal Graves in the Great Tumulus*, Athens Annals of Archaeology 10 (1977), pp.59–60.

M. Andronikos, *The Royal Graves of Vergina* (Athens, 1978).

M. Andronikos, *The Royal Tombs at Vergina and the Problems of the Dead*, Athens Annals of Archaeology 13 (1980), pp.168–78.

M. Andronikos, *Vergina, The Royal Tombs* (Ekdotike Athenon, 1984).

M. Andronikos, *Some Reflections of the Macedonian Tombs*, The Annual of the British School at Athens, volume 82 (1987), pp.1–16.

M. Andronikos and M. Fotiadis, *The Royal Tomb of Philip II: An unlooted Macedonian grave at Vergina*, Archaeology 31, number 5 (September/October 1978), pp.33–41.

Andronikos-Drougou, Faklaris-Saatsoglou-Paliadeli-Kottaridi, *Excavation of Vergina*, Proceedings of the Athens Archaeological Society (1990), pp.170–83

J.L. Angel, *The Length of life in Ancient Greece*, Journal of Gerontology, volume 2, number 1 (January 1947), pp.18–24

T.G. Antikas, *Horses and Heroes in the Tomb of Philip II*, Minerva, volume 1, 13.1 (2002), pp.46–49.

T.G. Antikas, *The Honor to be Buried with Horses from Mycenaean Nemea to Macedonian Vergina*, Les Équidés Dans Le Monde Méditerrranéen Antique,

Actes du colloque organisé par l'École française d'Athènes (26–28 November 2003).

T.G. Antikas, *Olympica Hippica: Horses, Men and Women in the Ancient Olympics* (Euandros, 2004).

T.G. Antikas, *Bucephalas, Common Burials of Horses and Heroes in Antiquity*, Ichor Journal 55 (2005), pp.86–97.

T.G. Antikas and L.K. Wynn-Antikas, *New finds from the cremains in Tomb II at Aegae point to Philip II and a Scythian Princess*, International Journal of Osteoarchaeology (online 2015).

T.G. Antikas and L.K. Wynn-Antikas, *A Re-examination of the Cremains from the Unlooted Macedonian Tomb 'B' at Pella, Greece*, unpublished report submitted to the Director of the Archaeological Museum of Pella (2016).

T. Arvaniti, Y. Maniatis, L. Wynn-Antikas and T.G. Antikas, *Study of Gypsum Detected on Ancient Cremated Bones in Greece: An Unknown Funerary Custom of Natural Mineralisation* (Aristotle University of Thessalonica, 2016).

T. Arvaniti, Y. Maniatis, L. Wynn-Antikas and T.G. Antikas, *Investigation of Materials Deposited on Cremated Bones of Royal and high Status Macedonian Burials: Revealing Ancient Unknown Funerary Customs?* (Aristotle University of Thessalonica, 2016).

R.S. Bagnall and P. Derow (eds), *The Hellenistic Period, Historical Sources in Translation* (Blackwell, 2004).

B. Barr-Sharrar, *Vergina Tomb II: Dating the Objects*, The Ancient World 22, number 2 (1991), pp.11–15.

A. Bartsiokas, *The Eye Injury of King Philip II and the Skeletal Evidence from the Royal Tomb II at Vergina*, Science 288 (2000), pp.511–14.

A. Bartsiokas and E. Carney, *The Royal Skeletal remains from Tomb I at Vergina*, Deltos Journal of the History of Hellenic Medicine (2007–2008).

A. Bartsiokas, J.-L. Arsuaga, E. Santos, M. Algaba and A. Gómez-Olivencia, *The Lameness of King Philip II and Royal Tomb I at Vergina, Macedonia*, first published in Proceedings of the National Academy of Sciences (June 2015).

A.R. Bellinger, *Essays on the Coinage of Alexander the Great*, Numismatic Studies Issue 11, American Numismatic Society (1963).

A.D.H. Bivar, *Cavalry Equipment and Tactics on the Euphrates Frontier*, Dumbarton Oaks Papers, volume 26 (1972), pp.271–91.

J. Boardman, *The Greeks Overseas, Their Early Colonies and Trade* (Thames and Hudson, 1999 edition).

E.N. Borza, *The Royal Macedonian Tombs and the Paraphernalia of Alexander the Great*, Phoenix 41, number 2 (summer 1987), pp.105–21.

E.N. Borza, *In the Shadow of Olympus, The Emergence of Macedon*, (Princeton University Press, 1990).

E.N. Borza, *Makedonika, Essays by Eugene N. Borza* (Regina Books, 1995).

E.N. Borza, *Before Alexander: Constructing Early Macedonia*, Publications of the Association of Ancient Historians 6 (Regina Books, 1999).

E.N. Borza and O. Palagia, *The Chronology of the Macedonian Royal Tombs at Vergina*, Jahrbuch des *Deutschen Archdologischen Instituts 122* (2007), pp.*81–126*.

A.B. Bosworth, *From Arrian to Alexander: Studies in Historical Interpretation* (Clarendon Press, 1988).

A.B. Bosworth, *Conquest and Empire, The Reign of Alexander The Great* (Cambridge University Press, 1988).

A.B. Bosworth, *Perdiccas and the Kings*, Classical Quarterly 63 (1993), pp.420–27.

A.B. Bosworth and E.J. Baynham, *Alexander the Great in Fact and Fiction* (Oxford University Press, 2000).

B.V. Bothmer, *Ptolemaic Reliefs I. A Granite Block of Philip Arrhidaeus*, Bulletin of the Museum of Fine Arts, volume 50, Number 280 (June 1952), pp.1927.

T. Boyd, *The Arch and the Vault in Greek Architecture*, American Journal of Archaeology, volume 82, number 1 (winter 1978), pp.83–100.

S.M. Burstein, *The Tomb of Philip II and the Succession of Alexander the Great*, Echos due Monde Classique, 26, 2 (1982), pp.141–63.

J.B. Bury, E.A. Barber, Edwyn Bevan and W.W. Tarn, *The Hellenistic Age: Aspects of Hellenistic Civilization* (W.W. Norton and Co., 1923).

W.M. Calder III, *Again the So-Called Tomb of Philip II*, American Journal of Archaeology 85 (1981).

E. Carney, *Tomb I at Vergina and the Meaning of the Great Tumulus as an Historical Monument*, Archaeology News 17 (1992).

E. Carney, *The Politics of Polygamy: Olympias, Alexander and the Murder of Philip*, Historia: Zeitschrift für Alte Geschichte, Bd. 41, H.2 (1992), pp.169–89.

E.D. Carney, *Women and Basileia: Legitimacy and Female Political Action in Macedonia*, The Classical Journal 90, number 4 (1995), pp.367–91.

E.D. Carney, *Women and Monarchy in Macedonia* (University of Oklahoma Press, 2000).

E.D. Carney, *Olympias, Mother of Alexander the Great* (Routledge, 2006).

E.D. Carney, *King and Court in Ancient Macedonia, Rivalry, Treason and Conspiracy* (The Classical Press of Wales, 2015).

E.D. Carney and D. Ogden (eds), *Philip II and Alexander the Great, Father and Son, Lives and Afterlives* (Oxford University Press, 2010).

C.W. Ceram, *Gods, Graves and Scholars, The Story of Archaeology* (Alfred A. Knopf, 1971 edition, Book Club Associates, London).

A. Chrysostomou and P. Chrysostomou, *'The Gold-Wearing' Archaic Macedonians from the Western Cemetery of Archontiko, Pella* (Threpeteria, Studies on Ancient Macedonia, 2012)

A. Cohen, *Art in the Era of Alexander the Great, Paradigms of Manhood and Their Cultural Traditions* (Cambridge University Press, 2010).

D. Collins, *Magic in the Ancient Greek World* (Blackwell Publishing, 2008).
H.B. Cotterill, *Ancient Greece* (1996 edition by Oracle Publishing Ltd).
S. Dalley, *The Mystery of the Hanging Garden of Babylon: an Elusive World Wonder Traced* (Oxford University Press, 2013).
W.S. Davis, *A Day in Old Athens* (IndyPublish.com, 1914).
A. Despini, *Gold Funerary Masks*, Vereinigung der Freunde Antiker Kunst, 52 Jahrg (2009), pp.20–65.
J.E. Dimacopoulos, *A Shelter in the Style of a Tumulus; Vergina, an Underground Archaeological Site and Museum in the style of a Crypt* (Ministry of Culture Archaeological Receipts Fund, 1995).
R. Drews, *The Coming of the Greeks, Indo-European Conquests in the Aegean and the Near East* (Princeton University Press, 1988).
S. Drougou, *The Vergina Fabric, First Observations*, AMITOS, Honorary Volume for Professor Manolis Andronikos, Aristotle University of Thessaloniki (December 1987), pp.303–16.
S. Drougou, *The Gold-Threaded Textile of Vergina-Aigai*, B Oezen-Kleine (ed.), Festschrift fuer Heide Froning (Istanbul, 2018), pp.81–92.
S. Drougou and C. Paliadeli, *Vergina: The Land and its History* (Militos Editions and Troia Editions, 2005).
P. Faklaris, *Aegae: Determining the Site of the First Capital of the Macedonians*, American Journal of Archaeology 98, number 4 (1994), pp.609–16.
H.M. Franks, *Hunters, Heroes, Kings: The Frieze of Tomb II at Vergina* (The American School of Classical Studies at Athens, 2012).
E.A. Fredericksmeyer, *Divine Honors for Philip II*, Translations of the American Philological Association (1974) volume 109 (1979), pp.39–61.
E.A. Fredericksmeyer, *Again, the So-Called Tomb of Philip II*, American Journal of Archaeology, 85 (1980), pp.330–34.
E.A. Fredericksmeyer, *Once More the Diadem and Barrel-Vault at Vergina*, American Journal of Archaeology, 87 (1983), pp.99–102.
E.A. Fredericksmeyer, *Alexander and Philip: Emulation and Resentment*, Classical Journal 85, number 4 (April–May 1990), pp.300–15.
R.A. Gabriel, *Philip II of Macedonia, Greater than Alexander* (Potomac Books Inc, 2010).
R. Garland, *The Eye of the Beholder, Deformity and Disability in the Graeco-Roman world*, second edition (Bristol Classics, 2010).
D.W.J. Gill, *Inscribed Silver Plate from Tomb II at Vergina, Chronological Implications*, The American School of Classical Studies at Athens, Hespera 77 (2008), pp.335–58.
M. Gleba, '*Linen Clad Etruscan Soldiers*' in Wearing the Cloak, Dressing the Soldier in Roman Times (Oxbow, 2012).
D. Grant, *In Search of the Lost Testament of Alexander the Great* (Matador Press, 2017).

R. Graves, *The Greek Myths, Complete Edition* (Penguin, 1955; 1992 edition).
P. Green, *The Greco-Persian Wars* (University of California Press, 1998).
P.M. Green, *Alexander of Macedon, 356–323 BC: A Historical Biography* (University of California Press, 1974; 1991 edition).
A. Gudeman, *Literary Fraud Amongst the Greeks*, in Classical Studies in Honour of Henry Drisler (Macmillan, 1894), pp.52–74.
V.I. Guliaev, Amazons in Scythia: *New Finds at the Middle Don, Southern Russia*, World Archaeology, volume 23, Number 1 (2003), The Social Commemoration of Warfare, pp.112–25.
J.M. Hall, *Artefact and Artifice, Classical Archaeology and the Ancient Historian* (University of Chicago Press, 2014).
N.G.L. Hammond, *Philip's Tomb in Historical Context*, Greek, Roman and Byzantine Studies 19, number 4 (1978), pp.331–50.
N.G.L. Hammond, *Arms and the King: The Insignia of Alexander the Great*, Phoenix 43, number 3 (autumn 1989), pp.217.24.
N.G.L. Hammond, *The Royal Tombs at Vergina: Evolution and Identities*, The Annual of the British School at Athens, volume 86 (1991), pp.69–82.
N.G.L. Hammond, *Philip of Macedon* (Duckworth, 1994; 2002 edition).
M.H. Hansen, *The Athenian Democracy in the Age of Demosthenes, Structure, Principles and Ideology* (University of Oklahoma Press, 1999).
W. Hansen, *The Book of Greek and Roman Folktales, Legends and Myths* (Princeton University Press, 2017).
V.D. Hanson, *The Western Way of War, Infantry Battle in Classical Greece* (Oxford University Press, 1989).
L Hardwick, *Ancient Amazons – Heroes, Outsiders or Women?*, Greece and Rome, Second Series, volume 37, number 1 (April 1990), pp.14–36.
M.B. Hatzopoulos, *Macedonian Institutions under the Kings 1, A Historical and Epigraphic Study*, Meletemata 22 (1996).
M.B. Hatzopoulos, *The Burial of the Dead (at Vergina) or the Unending Controversy on the Identity of the Occupants of Tomb II*, TEKMHPIA 9 (2008), pp.91–118.
M.B. Hatzopoulos and L.D. Loukopoulos (eds), *Philip of Macedon* (Ekdotike Athenon S.A., 1980).
R. Hawley and B. Levick (eds), *Women in Antiquity, New Assessments* (Routledge, 1995).
W. Heckel, *Kleopatra or Eurydike?*, Phoenix 32, number 2 (1978), pp.155–58.
W. Heckel, *Fifty-Two Anonymae in the History of Alexander*, Historia: Zeitschrift für Alte Geschichte, Bd. 36, H. 1 (1st Qtr, 1987).
W. Heckel, *Who's Who in the Age of Alexander the Great* (Blackwell Publishing, 2006).
W. Heckel and R. Jones, *Macedonian Warrior: Alexander's elite infantryman* (Osprey Publishing, 2006).

G. Herm, *The Phoenicians, The Purple Empire of the Ancient World* (William Morrow and Company, 1975).
F.L. Holt, *Into the Land of Bones, Alexander the Great in Afghanistan* (University of California Press, 2005).
J. Hornblower, *Hieronymus of Cardia* (Oxford University Press, 1981).
S. Hughes, *CT Scanning in Archaeology*, Computed Tomography – Special Applications, Dr Luca Saba (ed.), InTech (2011).
R. Janko, *Reconstructing (again) the Opening of the Derveni Papyrus*, Zeitschrift für Papyrologie und Epigraphik 166 (2008), pp.37–51, online version accessed at http://ancphil.lsa.umich.edu/-/downloads/faculty/janko/reconstructing-again-derveni.pdf.
R. Janko, *Papyri from the Great Tumulus at Vergina, Macedonia* (Zeitschrift für Papyrologie und Epigraphik, 2017).
I.D. Jenkins, *The Ambiguity of Greek Textiles*, Arethusa (1985), 18, 2.
P. Keyser and D.D. Clark, *Analyzing and Interpreting the Metallurgy of Early Electrum Coins*, in Hacksilder to Coingae: New Insights into the Monetary History of the Near East and Greece, numismatic Studies number 24 (The American numismatic Society of New York, 2001).
C. King, *Ancient Macedonia* (Routledge, 2018).
B.M. Kingsley, *The Cap that Survived Alexander*, American Journal of Archaeology 85 (1981), pp.39–46.
B.M. Kingsley, *Alexander's 'Kausia' and Macedonian Tradition*, Classical Antiquity, volume 10, number 1 (April 1991), pp.59–76.
A. Kottaridi, *Macedonian Burial Customs and the Funeral of Alexander the Great*, International Congress, Alexander the Great: From Macedonia to the Oikoumene, Veria 27–31.5.1998 (1999).
A. Kottaridi, *Vasilikes pires sti Nekropoli ton Aigon*, Ancient Macedonia VI, International Symposium I. Thessaloniki: Institute for Balkan Studies (1999), pp.631–42.
A. Kottaridi, *Queens, priestesses and high priestesses: the role of women at the Macedonian Court*, in Heracles to Alexander the Great. Treasure from the Royal Capital of Macedon, a Hellenic Kingdom in the Age of Democracy, exhibition catalogue, Ashmolean Museum, Oxford (2011), pp.93–125.
A. Kottaridi, *A Tour through the Museum of the Royal Tombs of Aigai* (Kapon Editions, 2011).
A. Kyriakou, *Exceptional Burials at the Sanctuary of Eukleia at Aegae (Vergina): The Gold Oak Wreath*, The Annual British School at Athens, 109 (2014), pp. 251–85.
A. Kyriakou, *The History of a Fourth Century BC Tumulus at Aigai/Vergina. Definitions and Space and Time*, in Tumulus as Sema, Space Politics, Culture and Religion in the First Millennium BC (Walter de Gruvter GmbH, 2016).
R. Lane Fox, *Alexander the Great* (Penguin, 1973; 1986 edition).

W. Leaf, *A Companion to the Iliad* (Forgotten Books, 1892; 2018 edition).

G. Lee, H. Whittaker and G. Wrightson (eds), *Ancient Warfare: Introducing Current Research, Volume 1* (Cambridge Scholars Publishing, 2015).

P.W. Lehmann, *The So-Called Tomb of Philip II: A Different Interpretation*, American Journal of Archaeology, volume 84 (1980), pp.527–31.

G.E.R. Lloyd, *Science, Folklore and Ideology, Studies in the Life-Sciences in Ancient Greece* (Bristol Classical Press, 1999).

J. Ma, *Court, King and Power in Antigonid Macedonia*, in Brill's Companion to Ancient Macedonia (Brill, 2011).

J.P. Mahaffy, *Greek Life and Thought, From the Death of Alexander to the Roman Conquest* (Macmillan and Co, 1896).

Y. Maniatis, T. Arvaniti, T.G. Antikas, L. Wynn-Antikas, S. Orsini, E. Ribechini and M.P. Colombini, *Investigation of an Unusual Composite Material Found in the Larnax with Cremated Bones in Royal Tomb II at Vergina*, first presented at the ISA Conference at the Getty Villa and UCLA (2014).

Y. Maniatis, D. Malamidou, H. Koukouli-Chrussanthaki and Y. Facorellis, *Radiocarbon Dating of the Amphipolis Bridge in Northern Greece, Maintained and Functioned for 2,500 Years,* Radiocarbon volume 52, number 1 (2010), pp.41–63.

S.P. Marinatos, *Mycenaean Elements within the Royal Houses of Macedonia*, in Ancient Macedonia, Papers Read at the First International Symposium held in Thessaloniki, 26–29 August 1968, Institute for Balkan Studies (1970), pp.45–52.

C. Margariti, S. Protopapas and V. Orphanou, *Recent Analyses of the Excavated Textile Fibre Fund from Grave 35 HTR73, Kerameikos Cemetery, Athens, Greece*, Journal of Archaeological Science 28 (2011), pp.522–27.

T. Mavrojannis, *The 'Great Tumulus' at Amphipolis, Remarks on its Chronology in Comparison to the Debate for 'Deification' of Hephaestion*, Vestigia, Miscellenea di studi storico-religioso in onore di Filippo Coarelli nel suo 80° anniversario (Franz Steiner Verlag, 2016), pp.645–62.

A. Mayor, *The Amazons, Lives and Legends of Warrior Women Across the Ancient World* (Princeton University Press, 2014).

G.H. McGurdy, *Hellenistic Queens, A Study of Woman-Power in Macedonia, Seleucid Syria, and Ptolemaic Egypt* (Ares Publishers, 1932).

R.H. Michel and P. McGovern, *The Chemical Processing of Royal Purple Dye: Ancient Descriptions and Elucidated by Modern Science*, Archaeomaterials 1 (2) (1987), pp.135–43.

A.D. Momigliano, *Studies in Historiography* (Harper Torchbooks, 1966).

J. Musgrave, *The Skull of Philip II of Macedon*, Current Topics in Oral Biology, proceedings of a meeting held in the Department of Physiology, The Medical School, University of Bristol, UK, on 4 and 5 July 1985 to mark the retirement of Professor Declan J. Anderson, Professor of Oral Biology, University of Bristol (1984).

J. Musgrave, *Dust and Damn'd Oblivion: A Study of Cremation in Ancient Greece*, The Annual of the British School at Athens, volume 85 (1990), pp.271–99.

J. Musgrave, *The Human Remains from Vergina Tombs I, II and III: An Overview*, The Ancient World (1991), pp.3–9.

J.H. Musgrave, A.J.N.W. Prag, R. Neave and R. Lane Fox, *The Occupants of Tomb II at Vergina. Why Arrhidaios and Eurydice must be excluded*, International Journal of Medical Science 7, number 6 (2010), pp.1–15.

L. Nevett, *Theoretical Approaches to the Archaeology of Ancient Greece, Manipulating Material Culture* (University of Michigan Press, 2017).

A.L.N. Oikonomides, *The Epigram on the Tomb of Olympias at Pydna*, Ancient World 5 (1982), pp.9–16.

O. Palagia, *Hephaestion's Pyre and the Royal Hunt of Alexander*, in Alexander the Great in Fact and Fiction (Oxford University Press, 2000), pp.167–206.

O. Palagia, *The Grave Relief of Adea, Daughter of Cassander and Cynnana*, in Macedonian Legacies: Studies in Ancient Macedonian History and Culture in Honor of Eugene N. Borza, edited by Timothy Howe and Jeanne Reames (Regina Press, 2008), pp.195–214.

O. Palagia, *Grave Markers, Tombs, and Tomb Paintings, 400–30 BCE*, in A Companion to Greek Architecture (John Willey and Sons, Inc., 2016).

O. Palagia, *Visualising the Gods in Macedonia: from Philip II to Perseus*, Pharus 22 (1) (2016), pp.73–98.

O. Palagia, *The Argeads: Archaeological Evidence*, in The History of the Argeads, New Perspectives (Harrassowitz Verlag, 2017).

O Palagia, *The Royal Court in Ancient Macedon: The Evidence for Royal Tombs*, in Hellenistic Court: The Monarchic Power and Elite Society from Alexander to Cleopatra (The Classical Press of Wales, 2017).

O. Palagia, *Alexander the Great, the Royal throne and the funerary thrones of Macedonia*, Karanos 1 (2018), pp.23–24.

O. Palagia and S.V. Tracy (eds), *The Macedonians in Athens*, 322–229 BC (Oxbow Books, 2003).

C. Paliadeli, *Aspects of Ancient Macedonian Costume*, JHS 113 (1993), pp.122–47.

H.W. Parke, *Greek Mercenary Soldiers* (Ares Publishers, 1933).

S.A. Paspalas, *On Persian-Type Furniture in Macedonia: The Recognition and Transmission of Forms*, American Journal of Archaeology, volume 103, number 3 (July 2000), pp.531–60.

P.M. Petsas, *A Few Examples of Epigraphy from Pella*, Balkan Studies 4 (1963), pp.157–70.

D. Plantzos, *Amphipolitics: Archaeological Performance and Government in Greece under the Crisis*, in Greece in Crisis: The Cultural Politics of Austerity (I.B. Tauris, 2017).

A.J.N.W. Prag, J.H. Musgrave and R.A.H. Neave, *The Skull from Tomb II at Vergina: King Philip II of Macedon*, Journal of Hellenic Studies 104 (1984), pp.60–78.

J. Prag and R. Neave, *Making Faces: Using Forensic and Archaeological Evidence* (The British Museum Press, 1997).
K. Rhomiopoulou, *Lefkadia, Ancient Mieza* (Ministry of Culture Archaeological Receipts Fund, 1997; 2000 edition).
A.S. Riginos, *The Wounding of Philip II of Macedon: Fact and Fabrication*, Journal of Hellenic Studies cxiv (1994), pp.103–19.
M. Robbins, *Collapse of the Bronze Age, The Story of Greece, Troy, Israel, Egypt and the People of the Sea* (Authors Choice Press, 2001).
J. Roisman and I. Worthington (eds), *A Companion to Ancient Macedonia* (Wiley-Blackwell, 2010).
C.B. Rose and R. Körpe, *The Tumuli of Troy and the Troad*, in Tumulus as Sema, Space Politics, Culture and Religion in the First Millennium BC (Walter de Gruyter GmbH, 2016).
M.L. Rose, *The Staff of Oedipus, Transforming disability in Ancient Greece* (University of Michigan Press, 2003).
C. Saatsoglou-Paliadeli, *In the Shadow of History: The Emergence of Archaeology*, The Annual of the British School at Athens, Volume 94 (1999), pp.353–67.
C. Saatsoglou-Paliadeli, *The Palace of Vergina-Aegae and its Surroundings*, in The Royal Palace Institution in the First Millennium BC, Regional Development and Cultural Interchange Between East and West, Monographs of the Danish Institute at Athens, volume 4 (2001).
C. Saatsoglou-Paliadeli, Chr. (2004). Βεργίλα. Ο Σάθος ηοσ Φηιίππoσ. Ζ Τοητογραθία κε ηο Κολήγη, Αζήλα: Βηβιηοζήθε ηες ελ Αζήλαης Αρταηοιογηθής Δηαηρείας 231.
C. Saatsoglou-Paliadeli, *The Royal Presence in the Agora of Aegae*, featured in Heracles to Alexander the Great, Treasures from the Royal Capital of Macedon, a Hellenic Kingdom of the Age of Democracy (Ashmolean Museum, University of Oxford, 2011).
C. Saatsoglou-Paliadeli, *Ancient Macedonia in the Light of Recent Archaeological Evidence. The Case of Vergina*, Aureus, volume dedicated to Professor Evangelos K. Chrysos (November 2014).
H. Schliemann, *Ithaka, der Peloponnes und Troja* (Commissions-Verlag Von Giesecke & Devrient, 1869).
H. Schliemann, *Mycenae and Tiryns* (Charles Scribner's Sons, 1880).
L. Souvaltzi, *The Tomb of Alexander the Great at the Siwa Oasis* (Editions Georgiadis, 2002).
W. Sherwood Fox, *A Problem of Cults and Agriculture*, in Proceedings of the Forty-Seventh Annual Meeting of the American School of Philological Association Held at Princeton, N.J. (December 1915). Also in the July and November Meetings of the Philological Association of the Pacific Coast Held Respectively

at Berkeley and San Francisco, California (1915), volume 46, John Hopkins University Press.

P. Shipman, G. Foster and M. Schoeninger, *Burnt Bones and Teeth: an Experimental Study of Color, Morphology, Crystal Structure and Shrinkage*, Journal of Archaeological Science 11 (1984), pp.307–25.

M. Silver, *Slave-Wives, Single Women and 'Bastards' in the Ancient Greek World, Law and Economic Perspectives* (Oxbow Books, 2018).

A.H. Sommerstein and I.C. Torrance, *Oaths and Swearing in Ancient Greece* (De Gruter, 2007).

S. Spantidaki, *Textile Production in Classical Athens* (Oxbow Books, 2016).

S. Sprawski, *When did Alexander I of Macedon get his Cognomen 'Philhellen'?*, Przegel ad Humanistyczny 2 (2013).

A. Stewart, *Faces of Power, Alexander's Image and Hellenistic Politics* (University of California Press, 1993).

R. Stoneman, *The Greek Alexander Romance* (Penguin, 1991).

W.W. Tarn, *Heracles Son of Barsine*, Journal of Hellenic Studies 41 (1921), pp.18–28.

P.G. Themelis and Y.P. Touratsouglou, *The Tomb of Derveni* (TAP, 1997).

P.G. Themelis, *Macedonian Metalworking*, published online March 2017 at https://issuu.com/sonjcemarceva/docs/macedonian_metalworking_-_petros_g.

C.G. Thomas, *Alexander the Great in his World* (Blackwell Publishing, 2007).

C. Thomas and C. Conant, *Citadel to City-State, The Transformation of Greece, 1200–700 B.C.E* (Indian University Press, 1999).

C. Thomas and C. Conant, *The Trojan War* (Greenwood Press, 2005).

S. Tillisch, *Scythians is a Name Given to them by the Greeks*, Masters of Philosophy thesis, Copenhagen (2004), Academia.edu.

H.C. Tolman and G.C. Scoggin, *Mycenaean Troy, The Mycenaean Age and the Homeric Poems* (New York Book Company, 1903).

M.Y. Treister, *The Role of Metals in Ancient Greek History* (Brill, 1996).

M.Y. Treister, *Masters and Workshops of the Jewellery and Toreutics from Fourth-Century Scythian Burial Mounds*, in Scythians and Greeks (Exeter University Press, 1999; 2005 edition).

M.Y. Treister, *Bronze and Silver Greek, Macedonian and Etruscan Vessels in Scythia* (2005), presented at the XVII International Congress of Classical Archaeology, Meetings between Cultures in the Ancient Mediterranean, Rome, 22–26 September 2008, Session: Tracia and Dacia.

H.A. Troxell, *Studies in the Macedonian Coinage of Alexander the Great*, Numismatic Studies Issue 21 (1997), American Numismatic Society.

G.R. Tsetskhladze, *Who Built the Scythian and Thracian Royal Tombs*, Oxford Journal of Archaeology 17 (1) (1998).

D. Tsiafakis, *Thracian Tattoos*, Bodies in Transition, Dissolving the Boundaries of Embodied Knowledge, Morphomata, Volume 23 (2015).

B. Tsigarida, *A New Gold Myrtle Wreath from Central Macedonia in the Collection of the Archaeological Museum of Thessaloniki*, The Annual of the British School at Athens, volume 105 (2010), pp.305–15.

M. Tsimbidou-Avoliniti, *Excavating a painted Macedonian tomb near Thessaloniki. An Astonishing discovery*, in Excavating Classical Greece, Recent archaeological discoveries in Greece, Studies in Classical Archaeology 1, BAR International Series 1031 (2002). The most thorough publication of the find can be found in Μ. Τσιμπίδου-Αυλωνίτη, Μακεδονικοί τάφοι στον Φοίνικα και στον Άγιο Αθανάσιο Θεσσαλονίκης. Συμβολή στη μελέτη της εικονογραφίας των ταφικών μνημείων της Μακεδονίας (with summaries in English and Italian, ΤΑΠΑ, Αθήνα 2005).

M. Tsimbidou-Avoliniti, *The Macedonian tombs at Phoinikas and Aghios Athanassios (Thessaloniki/Greece): Two astonishing funerary monuments of the 4th c. BC* (2015), from a May 2013 lecture at the University of Nanterre, France, as part of the NARNIA project training course: Interior Decoration in the Eastern Mediterranean during Hellenistic and Roman Times. Mosaics, Paintings, Iconography, Materials, Techniques and Conservation.

M. Vavelidis, G. Christophides and V. Melfos, *Ancient Gold Mines near Krenides in Philippoi Area (Macedonia, N. Greece)*, conference paper (1997).

P.A. Veleni, *Macedonia-Thessaloniki, from the exhibits of the Archaeological Museum* (Archaeological Receipts Fund Publications Department, 2009; 2013 edition).

L. Webster Wilde, *The Amazons, Women Warriors in Myth and History* (Robinson Press, 2016).

M.M. Willcock, *A Companion to the Iliad, based on the translation of Richmond Lattimore* (The University of Chicago Press, 1976).

D. Williams and J. Ogden, *Greek Gold, Jewelry of the Classical World* (Harry N Abrams Inc. Publishers, 1994).

N.I. Xirotiris and F. Langenscheidt, *The Cremations from the Royal Macedonian Tombs of Verigina*, Archaiologiki Ephemeris (1981), pp.142–60.

C. Zambas, *Restoration of the retaining wall of the Tomb of Philip B*, in 'Archaeological excavations in Macedonia and Thrace', AEMTH 13, 1999, pp.553–65.

C. Zambas, *Observations on the Design and Construction of the Macedonian Tombs*, in Costas Zambas, Vassilis Lambrinoudakis, Evangelia Simantoni-Bournia, Aenne Ohnesorg (eds.), ΑΡΧΙΤΕΚΤΩΝ, Honorary Volume For Professor Manolis Korres (Melissa Publishing House, Athens, 2016, pp.527–41.)

Index

The Index relates to names appearing in the main chapter text only, not images, footnotes or bibliography.

Abduction of Persephone, 50, 194, 197–8
Achaeans, 9
Acheron, river, 157
Achilles, 18, 23, 30, 59, 72, 83, 104, 107, 148–50, 156, 178, 183, 197, 233, 253, 267
Acropolis, Athens, 14, 37, 106, 241
Acrostics, 190
Achaemenids, 12, 22, 72, 97, 108, 183, 204, 225, 238, 249
Adams, Winthrop Lindsay, 99, 137
Adea Eurydice, 86–91, 94–9, 107, 110–12, 118, 166–7, 169, 197, 224–5, 228–36, 244
Adriatic, 23, 32–3, 35, 212
Aeacids, 198
Aegae, vii, 7–8, 12, 18–20, 29–45, 57–60, 70, 83, 90, 94, 97–100, 106, 113–16, 132, 144–5, 150, 152, 158–61, 165, 170, 181, 186–7, 195–204, 222, 225, 228–43, 248–54, 269, 277
Aegean Sea, 12–13, 19, 39, 44, 108, 113, 187
Aegina, 158
Aegisthos, 104
Aemilius Paulus, 32–3, 125, 199
Aenea, 116, 151
Aeolians, 9

Aeropus, 85
Aeschylus, 9, 64, 65
Agis of Sparta, 217
Afghanistan, 114, 259
Agamemnon, 22, 83, 104, 147–8, 182
Agios Athanasios, 116, 151, 179–82, 194, 271
Agora, 248, 251–4, 261
Akhal Teke, 259
Albania, Albanians, 5, 38, 81, 113
Alcetas, 225, 230
Alexander I, 13–15, 47, 59, 73, 80, 108–109, 198, 265
Alexander II, 17, 78, 94
Alexander III, 'the Great':
  accession, vii, 18–22, 83–5, 117, 226
  Amazons/Scythians, 72–4, 216
  appearance, 99, 100, 168, 173, 175, 177–8
  armour and insignia 103–107, 109–11, 116, 119, 167, 181, 232, 238
  attitude to Persians, 24, 26, 105, 168, 184
  birth, 18, 256
  character, 221, 274
  conquest of Persia, vii, 8, 18–24, 33, 52, 73, 83, 88, 97, 99, 103–108, 114, 137, 168, 173, 182–6, 193, 199–202, 225, 231, 238, 239–43, 252, 255–9, 275

cult of, 106–108, 201
currency, 108, 159–60, 241
death, vii, 9, 24–6, 28, 85, 88, 97, 106–108, 118, 138, 170, 179–80, 199, 201–204, 225, 229, 231, 238, 274–5
funeral bier, 24–6, 87, 94–5, 103–104, 201–203, 232
generalship, 274
in legend, 88, 155, 235, 25
lineage, 18, 23–4, 56, 80–1, 83, 201–202
military reforms, 8, 20–2, 30, 52, 218, 257, 274
reign, vii, 6, 9, 57, 85, 116
religion, 22–4, 275
sexuality, 199
wives and sons, 24–6, 57, 85–6, 88–90, 115, 164, 175, 190, 230, 238–44, 249–52
Alexander IV, 57, 86–9, 115, 142, 175, 230, 232, 238–40, 243, 251
Alexander V, 181
Alexander Molossus, 18, 83
Alexander Romance, *see* Greek Alexander Romance
Alexandria, 26, 34, 137, 201–203, 274
Alexandria Eschate, 186
  Alexandrias, across Asia, 274
Alexeev, Andrey, 210, 216–17
Agrianians, 85, 229
Amastris, 66
Amazon, river, 74
Amazons, 63–84, 86–91, 103, 134–8, 151, 162, 191, 204, 206, 209–12, 217, 221–4, 229, 238, 259
  Amazonomachy, 103, 155
    Tomb II 'Amazon', 63, 84, 91, 126, 134–5, 138, 162, 191, 204, 209–10, 212, 217, 221–4, 228–9, 238, 243–4, 269

Ambrosia, Nectar of the Gods, 156
Amphipolis, 89, 129, 160, 164, 188, 193, 198–9, 201, 239, 251, 271
  Lion of Amphipolis, 199
Amyntas I, 12–13, 15
Amyntas III, 15, 17, 48, 60, 94, 109, 195, 198, 202, 244, 271
Amyntas Perdicca, 84–5, 197, 226, 228–9, 236
Anacharsis, 70
Anatolia, 12, 18, 20, 22, 26, 28, 32, 34, 39, 43–4, 83, 88, 91, 106–107, 135, 140, 143, 160, 186, 213, 230, 245, 251
  see also Asia Minor
Andronikos, 1–3, 8, 44, 45, 47–50, 52–61, 63–4, 74, 84, 91, 93–126, 136, 140, 144, 150, 153–5, 159, 161, 169, 173, 175, 179, 182, 188, 190, 192–3, 197–8, 204–206, 214, 219, 223–4, 233–4, 240–1, 244, 270, 274
Anemos, 261
Angel, John Lawrence, 129
Anteas, 175
Antigonus the One-Eyed, 26, 29–30, 87–8, 91, 107, 239, 249, 251
Antigonus II Gonatas, 29–32, 58, 73, 180–42, 144, 151–2, 157, 160–2, 166, 169–73, 178, 183, 187–90, 198, 206, 210–12, 216–17, 220–1, 224–5, 230, 243, 247–8, 253–61, 267–75
Antiope, 67, 217
Antipater, Antipatrids, 29, 85–8, 91, 107, 178, 180–1, 217, 222, 225, 230–2, 236, 239, 267
Antisthenes, 123
Aphrodite, 63, 151
Apollo, 11, 83, 143, 178, 265
  Sanctuary of, Delphi, 29, 77, 196, 265, 275

Arabia, Arabs, 24, 34, 259
Arados, 182
Arbela, *see* Gaugamela
Archaic Period, 9, 20, 38, 47, 152, 156, 164, 178, 189, 263
Archangels, 1–2, 50
Archaeological Museum of Thessalonica, 2, 52, 110–11, 114, 120, 142, 162, 169, 253
Archaeological Museum of Veria, 44, 127
Archelaus I, 15–16, 32, 60, 195, 219, 267
Archers, archery, 14, 64, 66, 70, 137–8, 209–11, 218, 223
Archers' rings, 209–11
Archontiko, 148, 271
Ares, 17, 63, 66, 264–5
Argeads, 14–17, 26, 29, 59, 70, 84, 90–1, 94, 101, 104, 113, 116, 138, 148, 160, 178, 181, 204, 219, 226, 231, 236, 254
 see also Temenids
Argos, Argives, 11, 14–15, 31, 34, 59, 65, 80, 102, 109, 148, 152, 160, 254–5, 264–5
Aristides, 50
Aristonus, 201
Aristophanes, 138
Aristotle, 1, 28, 58, 60, 80, 115, 132, 150, 177, 189, 217, 257, 264, 274–5, 277
Aristotle University of Thessalonica, 39, 45, 56, 98, 114, 125, 161, 212, 247, 251, 270, 274
Armenia, Armenians, 34, 66, 155
Arrian, 72–3, 108, 216, 257
Arrhidaeus, 26, 82–92, 94–112, 117–20, 132, 140, 166–9, 175, 184, 190, 197, 225–6, 230, 232–4, 244, 277
 see also Philip III Arrhidaeus
Artabazus, 108, 249, 252

Artaxerxes III, 18
Artemis, 59, 67, 178, 229
Artemisium, 14–15
ARTEX Hellenic Centre for Research and Conservation of Archaeological Texts, 186
Arvaniti, Theodora, 151
Asbestos, 150–1
Asclepius, 199, 268
Asia Minor, 35, 125
 see also Anatolia
Assembly of Macedones, 24, 80, 85–9, 106–107, 193, 199, 249
Assyria, Assyrian, 74
Aster, 134
Atalanta, huntress, 229
Atalanta, sister of Perdiccas, 229
Atheas, 96, 98, 165, 217, 220–1, 223, 238
Athena, Athena Polias, 105, 241
Athenaeus, 88, 175, 178, 180, 222, 226–7
Athens, Athenian, 12–15, 17–22, 28, 37–8, 67, 70, 72, 78, 86–8, 91, 97–100, 103, 106, 113, 119, 124, 138, 143–7, 151, 157, 186, 189, 194, 199, 212, 217, 227, 233, 240, 253, 267, 273, 275
Atreaus, 104
Atropates, 72
Attalus, baron, 58, 83–4, 201, 226
Attica, 39, 47, 119, 145, 186, 265
 Attic War of legend, 64
Audata, 84, 94, 224, 226–9
Axes, 106, 149, 175, 206
 see also sagaris
Avaroslavs, 34
Avenue of Sphinxes, 202
Axius, river, 179

Babylon, vii, 9, 22–6, 43, 85–8, 94, 104, 106–107, 118, 138, 144, 173, 197,

199, 201, 225, 230, 232, 238–9, 249, 252, 274
Bactria, Bactrians, 26, 85, 221, 238–41
  Graeco-Bactrian Kingdoms, 186
Bakalakis, Georgios, 41
Balkans, 8, 18, 20, 28, 37, 39, 77, 113, 125, 159
  Balkan Wars, 38
Banquet, *see* symposium
Barbarians, 12, 15, 64, 70–1, 80, 85, 97, 125, 202, 218, 241, 255, 275
Barbes, 39
Bardylis, 84, 227–8
Barsine, mistress of Alexander III, 96, 249, 251–2
Bartsiokas, Antonis, 117–21, 131–2, 139–40, 166–9, 235, 252, 269
Battle of Kings, *see* Ipsus
Bellerophon, 257
Bel Marduk, 144
Berytos, 182
Bible, 43, 189
Bitumen, 24, 251–2
Black Sea, 16, 66, 68, 70, 74, 212–13, 216
Boar hunt, 109, 177–8, 229
  boar tusk helmets, 11
Bodrum, 73, 156, 204
  see Halicarnassus
Bodyguards, 19, 24, 26, 80–1, 85–6, 104, 108, 118, 134, 173, 175, 179–80, 201, 222, 229, 231, 234, 240, 265
Boeotia, Boeotians, 13, 39, 132, 265
Book of the Dead, 43, 146, 202
Borza, Eugene, 103–10, 114–19, 125, 167, 221, 232, 273
Bosporus, Kingdom of, 16, 71, 212–13, 216
  see also Crimea
Bottiaea, 115

Boyd, Thomas, 99, 103
Brahmins, 23
Brennus, 266
Briant, Pierre, 110
Bristol University, 7, 110–11
British Museum, 145, 188, 202, 210
Bronze Age, 9, 12, 146, 148, 150, 156, 245, 253, 265
  Early Bronze Age, 245, 254
  Late Bronze Age, 43, 152, 160
Bubares, 108
Bucephalus, 256–61
Budini, 71
Bulgaria, Bulgarians, 38–9, 89, 113, 218, 254, 260
Bunarbashi, 44
Burstein, Stanley, 98
Byblos, 182
Byzantine Empire, 34, 37
  Byzantine period, 38, 104, 126, 252
Byzantium, 34

C14 (radiocarbon dating), 124, 164, 187, 243, 244–8, 261, 269–71, 277
Cadiz, 183
Calcium, 146
California State University, 98, 247
Callipidae, 71
Cambyses, 203
Camels, 108–109
Canaanites, *see* Phoenicians
Caranus, 11–12, 38, 44, 56, 59, 109, 274
Caria, 67, 70, 83, 140, 157, 186
Carney, Elizabeth, 115, 120, 141, 171
Carter, Howard, 43, 127
Carthage, Carthaginians, 30, 32–3, 125, 183, 212
Cartonnage, 145–6
Cascade Mountains, 124
Caspian Sea, 23, 68, 72

Cassander, 26, 29, 87–90, 94, 99, 104–10, 118, 120, 142, 164, 175, 178–81, 190–1, 198, 201, 227, 230–40, 243–4, 251, 275
Cassandreia, 231
Cassius Dio, 201
Casta Hill Tomb, Amphipolis, 129, 164, 194, 198, 201, 271
CT (computed tomography scans), 127, 155
Catapults, 81, 133, 157
Cato the Younger, 274
Caucasus, 73, 254
Cavalry, Macedonian 8, 17, 22, 24, 30, 33, 78–80, 85–6, 107, 148, 173, 177, 179, 199, 257–8, 274
Celtic, 28
   Getae, 223
   Greek, 78, 257
   Roman, 73
   Sassanid, 209
   Scythian, 209, 259
   Thessalian, 257, 261
Celts, Celtic Gauls, Galatae, 19, 28–32, 45, 144, 169, 199, 234, 235, 265–7
Central Archaeological Council, 102, 248
Cerberus, 157
Ceteus, 97
Chaeronea, battle of, 17–18, 26, 32, 79, 81, 98–9, 132, 146, 169, 199, 233
Chalastra, 148, 179
Chalcidice, 17, 212
Chaldeans, 24
   see also Magi
Charles V of Spain, 74
Charon, 143, 157, 178
Chersonesus, 213
Chertomylk, 209–13, 216
China, country, 259

Christians, Christianity, 34, 37
Chryselephantine, 154–5
Cicero, 5, 33, 134
Cilician Gates, 105
Cimmerians, 68, 206
Classic Age of Greece, 9, 11, 37, 39, 60, 72, 115, 119, 144, 162, 197, 210, 233
Cleitus, Black, 106
Clemson University, 115
Cleopatra, daughter of Philip II, 18, 87–8, 91, 100, 197, 226, 235
Cleopatra, last wife of Philip II, 58, 63, 83–4, 89, 91, 111–12, 120, 140, 166–7, 226, 233
Cloaks, capes, 19, 146, 152, 173, 182, 186
Cluster of Philip II, see also Tombs I, II, III
Coinage, currency, 15, 17–18, 30, 58–9, 81, 106, 109, 116, 133, 140, 157–60, 175, 179, 183, 214, 216–19, 234, 241, 258, 271
Colchis, 64, 74, 209, 217
Colorado State University, 135
Common Peace, 79
Common Assembly, see Assembly of Macedones
Como, 247
Companion Cavalry, see cavalry
Companions, of kings, 20, 80, 104, 168, 173, 177, 199, 239
Concubines, 23, 81, 96, 105, 165, 175, 217, 220, 223
Constantinople, 34, 123, 254
Corinth, Corinthian, 11, 18, 20, 22, 79, 233
Cornwall, tin mines, 183
Cothelas, 96, 222, 226
Cothran, Gus, 258
Cotton, 39, 183–7

Couches, 19, 35, 54, 58, 83, 129, 154, 179, 190–1, 218, 232, 267
Craterus, general, 87, 91, 177, 180, 265
Craterus, husband of Philinnion, 193
Cratesipolis, 91
Cremation, of Philip II, 20, 112, 167
   Agios Athanasios, 179
   Agora, 248–9, 251
   archaic practices 148–9, 151–7, 240, 247
   Casta Hill, 198–9
   Derveni, 116, 129, 153
   extracting DNA, 253–4
   dry boned, 117–18, 120, 131
   green/flesh-boned, 117–18, 120, 131
   in Homer/Troy, 52, 103, 149, 152, 183
   law in Greece, 260
   Mycenae, 156
   Scythian/Thracian, 223
   Tomb I, 140, 198
   Tomb II main chamber, 8, 55–6, 93–4, 112, 117–18, 120, 129, 131, 148, 150, 153, 156, 167, 170, 223, 231, 248
   Tomb II antechamber, 93–4, 151, 191, 224–5, 230, 232, 248
   Tomb III, 57, 142, 240, 243, 248
   Tomb IV, 58
   Tomb of Eurydice, 102
   with huntite/gypsum, 146, 151
Crenides, 79
Crestonia, 223
Crete, Cretans, 81, 146, 182, 187, 258
Chthonic gods, 143, 157, 159, 192, 196
Curses, curse tablets, 143, 223
Curtius Rufus, 70, 168, 184, 186, 216
Cybele, 68
Cyclops, 134, 275
Cynoscephalae, 32–3

Cynnane, 84–9, 94, 197, 224–32, 234, 236, 238, 244
Cyrene, 91
Cyrus the Great, 72, 109, 203–204, 209
Dacia, 34
Damascus, 105, 232
Danaans, 148
Danube, river, 20, 28, 70, 96, 97, 138, 201, 217, 259
Dardanelles, 13, 33, 39, 43
Dardania, 34
Darius I, 12–13, 18, 68, 108, 183, 212
Darius III, 20–3, 97, 105–106, 168, 183–4, 201, 238, 267
Darics, 18
   see also coinage
Dark Age of Greece, 9, 65, 108, 148, 152
Daumet, Pierre, 38
Deformities, lameness, 138
   female antechamber woman's, 135–8
   Philip II's, 98, 136, 223
Delphi, 11, 15, 18, 22, 29, 77, 177, 196, 265, 275
Demeter, 50, 143, 195, 197–8, 268
Demetrius the Besieger, 29, 73, 91, 175, 180–1, 240, 243
Democritus, philosopher, 103, 245
Democritus University, Thrace, 93, 111, 117, 139–40, 166
Demosthenes, 77, 97, 102, 117, 132, 134, 264, 275
Derdas, 226
Derveni, tombs, 110, 116, 129, 151, 153, 155, 188, 271
   Derveni Krater, 188, 212
   Derveni Papyrus, 188
Deucalion, 74
Diadems, 52, 55, 63, 86, 101, 103–104, 107, 109–10, 114, 219, 229, 249
Dimacopoulos J.E., 113

Diodorus, 77, 97, 104, 115, 133, 138, 146, 153, 226–30, 239
Diomedes, Thracian king, 256
Dionysius of Syracuse, 133
Dionysus, 23, 88, 195–6, 268
　Dionysus Zagreus, 151
Dium, 22, 123, 170, 267, 268
Diviners, divination, 18, 32, 154
DNA, *see* genes
Dnieper, river, 209
Dodona, 267
Don, river, 67, 138
　see also Tanais, river
Dorians, Doric, 9, 19, 50, 59, 87, 99, 186, 254
Drachmas, 32, 102, 157, 159
　see also coinage
Dromos, dromoi, 50, 56, 231, 233–4
Drougou, Stella, 1–2, 116, 140
Duris of Samos, 88, 134

Earthquakes, 34–5, 56, 139
Echedorus, river, 12–13
Edessa, 38, 44, 225
Egypt, Egyptian, 16, 22, 26, 28, 30–1, 34, 37, 43, 57, 87, 94, 107, 146, 164, 175, 186, 199, 201–202, 204, 212, 232, 239, 241, 246
　art, 139
　Egyptology 146
　hieroglyphs, 43
　mummies, 111, 127, 145–6, 156, 246
　papyrus, 154, 189
　pharaohs 146, 156, 202, 246, 274
　scarabs, 145, 146
El Dorado, 74
Electrum, alloy, 205, 216
Elephants, 23, 30, 33, 86, 89, 184, 264
Eleusinian Mysteries, 63, 188, 195, 263
Elysian Fields, 149, 151, 157
Elis, 263

Emathia, 11–12, 39, 167, 273–4
Empedocles, 196
Ennea-Hodoi, 164
　see also Amphipolis
Epeius, 74
Ephesus, 67–8, 143, 230
Ephorate of Emathia, 167, 274
Ephorbus, 196
Epilepsy, 96, 143
Epirus, Epirotes, 5, 18, 20, 30, 34, 81, 83, 88, 91, 123, 140, 157, 196–8, 264, 267
Eretria, 13, 105, 231
Ethiopia, 24
Etruscan, Etruscans, 135–6, 210, 212, 245
Euboea, Euboeans, 108, 150, 267
Eucleia, 59
　cult of, 195
　Sanctuary of, 60, 249
Eumenes of Cardia, 107
Euphraeus, 233
Euphranor, 81
Euphrates, river, 22, 24
Euripides, 80, 84, 161, 195
Europa, 120
European Regional Development Fund, 102, 273
Eurydice, mother of Philip II, 17, 59–60, 84, 91, 102, 109, 175, 195, 233, 249
　as a royal title, 84, 87
　as a common name, 91
Eurydice, daughter of Sirrhas, 59
Euxine Pontus, Euxine Sea, 39, 213

Faklaris, Panayiotis, 114–16, 145–6, 166–7
Farming, crops, 19, 143, 184, 186, 254, 271
Fergana Valley, 186

Finikas, 194, 248, 271
First World War, 39
Fortuna, 137
Fox, Sherwood, 151
France, Diane, 135
Franks, Hallie, 110, 177
Fredricksmeyer, Ernst, 110
FTIR (infrared spectroscopy), 145, 251
Funeral pyres, *see* cremations
Furies, 182

Gaia, 79
Gaiters, *see* lateral movers
Galatae, *see* Celts
Galatia, 32
Gallic Celts, *see* Celts
Ganges, river, 23
Gaugamela, 22, 97, 105, 106, 238, 241
Gelani, 71
Genes, genetics, gene testing, DNA, 65, 70, 124, 142, 171, 187, 243–8, 252–61, 269–71, 277
Genghis Khan, 259
Georgia, 74, 209
German, Germany, 44, 145, 148, 210, 214, 254, 260, 269
German Archaeological Institute, Berlin, 214
Getae, 96, 223
Getty Museum, 161
Giza, 204
Glasgow School of Art, 270
Glaucias, 239
Gleba, Margarita, 183, 187, 261, 277
Gold, Vergina/Greek artefacts, 15, 30, 35, 44, 50, 52–8, 60, 64–8, 84, 93, 96, 100–107, 120, 125, 129, 131, 137, 147–50, 154–5, 158, 179, 182–3, 187–90, 193, 199, 202, 204, 205–19, 223, 229, 241, 248–3, 265, 267, 271
assaying, 216
currency, 18, 79, 140, 158–60
extraction, 74, 205, 213–16
locations, 5, 12, 79, 211–19, 241, 247
Persian, 17–18, 85, 267
plating, 137
provenance of, 205 212–16
purity, 205, 212–16
Gold of Tolosa, 265
Gorget, *see* pectoral
Gorytos, 54, 58, 64, 70, 205, 211, 213–15, 218, 229
Goths, 34
Graeco-Bactrian Kingdoms, 186
Granicus, river, 22, 106, 267
Great Flood, 74
Great Migration, 70
tribal migrations, 9, 47, 68, 245, 247, 255
Great Tumulus, 1–2, 8, 29–32, 35, 45, 47–51, 56–9, 90, 101–103, 111–16, 124, 130, 154, 157–8, 161, 173, 181, 187–90, 224, 231–6, 240, 243, 248, 268, 270, 273–7
Greaves, 52, 54, 136–8, 181, 218, 232, 270
Greek Alexander Romance, 155, 235, 257
Greek city-states, 9, 14, 17, 64, 265
Greek Civil War, modern, 29, 39
Greek elections, modern, 2, 98
Greek war for independence, 37–40
Greek fire, 252
Greek Orthodox Church, 2, 260
Green, Peter, 98, 142
Griffins, 164, 194
Gyges, 158
Gypsum, 151

Hades, 50, 144, 149, 154, 197, 198, 236
Hadrian, Hadrian's Wall, 73
Haliacmon, river, gorge, 5, 12, 39, 115, 145, 212
Halicarnassus, 73, 156, 204
Hamadan, 199
Hamburg University, 210
Hammond, Nicholas, 7–8, 39, 45, 59, 60, 74, 93–4, 96, 108, 114, 129, 142, 220–4, 234
Hannibal, 32–3
Harrapan civilization, 184
Hatzopoulos, Miltiades, 117, 119, 121
Hecate, 143
Hecatombid Dynasty, 156
Heckel, Waldemar, 228
Hector, 58, 63, 103, 148, 156
Helen of Troy, 148
Helios, 79
Hellanicus, 67
Hellas, Hellenes, Hellenic, ancient, 12, 14–15, 17, 24, 38, 145, 159, 186, 212, 218, 236, 255
  Hellenic League, Pan-Hellenic Games, 15
Hellen, legendary king, 267
Hellenic Equestrian Association, 255
Hellenic Pony Club, 255
Hellenistic Era, 9, 60, 186, 190–1, 240, 268
Hellespont, 12, 22, 43, 66, 83, 137, 225, 259
Hemp, 13, 73, 186
Hephaestion, 11, 168, 175, 177, 199, 239
Heptaechoes, 264
Hera, 102
Heraean Games, Argos, 102
Heracles, hero, 15, 17, 23–4, 56, 58–9, 66–8, 72, 81, 86, 101, 256, 263–4
  Heracles the huntsman 177, 218
  Heracles Patroos, 60

Heracles, son of Alexander III, 86, 240, 249–52
Heraclion, 146
Heraclitus of Ephesus, 43
Herculaneum, 247
Hermes, 50, 143, 157
Hermione, Peloponnese, 183
Hermitage Museum, 210, 213, 216–17
Herodotus, 65–74, 96, 109, 115, 156, 158, 183–5, 196, 206, 212, 223, 243, 255, 258, 264, 267, 275
Heroic Age, 65
Heroon, Great Tumulus shrine, 30, 47–9, 58, 101, 116, 198, 235
Hesiod, 12
Hetairas, 194
Heuzey, Léon, 37–8, 45, 115, 140, 164, 253, 268
Hierapolis, 145
Hieroglyphs, 43
Hill of Cronus, 263
Hindu Kush, 23, 114
Hippo, 67
Hippocrates, 137, 222
Hippolyta, 66–7
Hippostratus, 226
Hissarlik, 44, 148
  see also Troy
Hitler, 39
Hittites, 12
Holy Land, 35
Homer, Homeric Age, epics, 9, 20, 31, 35, 39, 43–4, 52, 56–9, 63–5, 80, 89–91, 99, 103–104, 109, 143, 148–60, 178, 182–3, 186, 188–9, 195, 197, 199, 229, 233, 238, 257, 263–4, 268, 270
  Homeric hymns, 188, 195, 197
  Iliad, 9, 20, 35, 43, 52, 58–9, 64–5, 89–90, 99, 103–104, 148, 150,

156, 178, 182, 186, 189, 229, 233, 257, 270
Odyssey, 11, 59, 65, 99, 182–3, 268
Homeridai, 65
Hoplite, weapons, warfare, 11, 13–14, 20, 33, 78, 266
Horses, horsemanship, ancient, 33, 50, 56, 58, 64–74, 79, 98, 108, 118, 128, 138, 148–50, 154–5, 175, 178–9, 188, 206, 211, 218, 223, 245, 247, 255–61, 270
   equine genetics, 128, 138, 245, 247, 255–61, 270
   hunting scene friese, Tomb II, 2, 50, 56, 104, 108–109, 114, 118, 173–9, 231, 238
Huntite, 144–8
Hydaspes, river, 23, 256
Hyrcania, 72
Huns, 34
Hunza, 114

Ilium, *see* Troy
Illyria, Illyrians, 17–18, 21, 32–4, 47, 54, 60, 79, 83–5, 88–9, 94, 218–19, 224–30
Illyricum, 34
Iollas, 88, 90, 180
Immortals, Persian crack regiment, 14, 29
India, 23, 33, 97, 106, 184–6, 201, 239, 256
Indian Ocean, 23
Indo-Europeans, 245–6
Indus river, Valley, 23, 125, 184, 257
Interdisciplinary Centre for Archaeological Studies, 274
Ionians, 9, 103, 114, 186, 213
Ionian League, 12
Ipsus, 26, 29, 240

Iron Age, 12, 126, 155, 161, 271
   Early Iron Age, 45, 152
Isis, 268
Isocrates, 64, 146–7
Isotope testing, 145, 158, 187, 214, 243, 244–8, 251, 271, 277
Israel, Israelites, 47
Issus, battle of, 22, 105–106, 231
Italy, 30–3, 136, 183, 187, 212, 245, 247, 267

Janko, Richard, 187–91
Jason, Golden Fleece, Argonauts, 74, 217
Justin, 11, 38, 44, 83–4, 98–100, 137–8, 154, 167, 217, 223–6, 235, 240, 251, 258

Kalamata, 263
Kalasha, 114
Kallidromo, 265
Kamena Vourla, 266
Kapodistrian University of Athens, 118
Karagodeuaskhsh, 214
Karamanlis, Konstantine, 3, 98
Karystos, 150
Katsifas, Christos, 142, 214
Kausia, 109, 114–15, 173, 180
Kazakhstan, 68
Kerameikos, 186
Kerch, 212
Keyser, Paul, 214–16
Kherson, *see* Chersonesus
Killgrove, Kristine, 166
Kitros, 6–9
Kline, *see* couches
Knossos, 182
Koine Greek, 190
Komotoni, Komotini Archaeological Ephorate, 166
Kolonos Hill, 267

Kopanos, 115
Kore, *see* Persephone
Kotridis, Kostas, 127
Kottaridi, Angelika, 115, 139, 161, 167, 273–4
Koutles, 39
Kozani Basin, 145
Kyane, 50
Kyriakou, Athanasia, 125, 249, 251
Kurgans, 70, 210, 214

Lagos, Katerina, 247
Lagus, 175
Lake Maeotis, 66
    see also Sea of Azov
Lameness, *see* deformities
Lamian War, 87
Lane Fox, Robin, 98, 108, 120, 140
Langarus, 85, 229, 236
Langenscheidt, Franziska, 93–8, 111–12, 117, 132–5
Laomedon, court companion, 201
Laomedon, legendary king, 68
Larissa, Thessaly, 94, 181, 226
Larnax, gold funerary chest, 52–9, 62, 93, 101–102, 129, 131, 148, 150, 155, 157, 179, 182, 253, 270
Lateral movers, 257–8
Latin, Latins, 11, 30, 47, 70, 150, 170, 189
Lavrion, 145, 212
Lead, lead poisoning, 143, 145, 150, 187, 215–16, 219
League of Corinth, 18, 20, 22, 79
Lebanon, 182
Lefantzis, Michaelis, 129
Lefkadia, 115, 117
    see also Mieza
Lehman, Phyllis Williams, 99, 110, 117
Lemnos, 268
Leonnatus, 175

Leuctra, battle of, 78
Leochares, 99, 177
Leonardo da Vinci, 50
Leonidas, Sparta King, 29, 267
Leonidas, tutor to Alexander, 216
Lete, 111
Leuca, 151
Libyans, 246
Linen, 12, 147, 156, 183, 186–7
Lions, lion hunt, 17, 101, 108–10, 154, 175, 177, 194, 199, 265, 267
Lisippa, 67
Litochoro, 123
Livadi, 6
Livadia, 265
Liverpool University, 218
Livy, 33, 124, 219
Louvre, 38, 175
Lucian, 63, 157–8, 202, 222
Lyceum, 189
Lycia, Lycians, 135
Lycymnius, 264
Lysimachus, 26, 28, 222, 234, 240, 243
Lysimachea, 29
Lysippus, 81, 177

Macedon,
    cantons, 5, 30, 81, 113–5
    dress, 19, 109, 114–15, 146, 152, 173, 180, 186
    extent of empire, 23–4
    founding myths, 11–12, 65
    geographical importance, 33–4, 39
    Language, 9, 47, 190
    life expectancy, 221–2
    Modern Macedonia, FYROM, 37–41, 113–14, 164
    religion, 18–24, 65, 101, 116, 143, 151–9, 193, 196
    rise and fall of, vii, 7–9, 11–35, 41

role of women, 20, 63, 64, 81–92, 102, 137, 180, 188, 194–5, 197
tomb design, 2, 38, 50, 53, 55, 99–109, 117, 154, 156, 179, 204, 232–4, 240
Machatas, 60, 193, 226
Machates, 193
Magi, 24
  see also Chaldeans
Magnesia, 34
Magnesium 146
Makran desert, 23
Makrygialos, *see* Pydna
Malaria, 5, 23, 38–9, 41, 44, 137
Marathon, 13, 68, 194, 212
Marco Polo, 259
Mardonius, 12, 14–15
Massagetae, 209
Masks, 143–8, 160–1
Mausolus, 156, 204
Meda, 96, 115, 218, 221–6, 244
Medea of Colchis, 217
Medes, *see* Persians
Media, 72
Melanippe, 67
Meliki, 6
Memphis, Egypt, 26, 94, 202
Mendenitsa, 265
Menelaus, 196
Mercenaries, 22, 28, 30, 33, 78, 86, 106, 140, 158, 160
Mesolithic, hunter gatherers, 254
Mesopotamia, 22, 97, 238, 252
Metaxas, Ioannis, 112
Methone, 111, 134, 196
Metropolitan Museum of Art, New York, 214
Midas, Gardens of, 12, 115
Mieza, 80, 115
Miletus, 70

Ministry of Culture, 124, 140, 151, 166–7, 248, 273, 277
Minoan, Minoans, 146, 196
Mithridatic Wars, 73
Moesia, 34
Molossia, Molossians, 18, 81, 83, 196–8, 226
  see also Epirus
Mongolia, Mongols, 68, 259
Moraitou, Georgianna, 184–7
Mount Bermion, 12, 115
Mount Ida, 44
Mount Olympus, 12, 22, 44, 109, 123, 146, 261, 268, 276
Mount Othrys, 267
Mount Paikon, 45
Mount Pangaeum, 79
Mount Parnassus, 265
Mount Taygetos, 263
Mount Troodos, 150
Mount Vesuvius, 247
Murex, *see* Tyrian Purple
Murgab Plain, 203
Muses, 60, 195
  Pierian, 261
Museum of Byzantine Culture, 161
Musgrave, Jonathan, 110–12, 117, 120, 127, 131, 134–5, 139–42, 153, 167–9, 240, 247, 269
Mycenae, Mycenaean civilization, 9, 11, 39, 43, 65, 74, 91, 104, 146–8, 152, 156, 186, 196, 253, 263–5, 275
Myrmidons, 148

Naousa, 115
Napoleon, Napoleonic Wars, 37
Napoleon III, 38
Naqsh-e Rustam, 204
National Archaeological Museum of Athens, 184, 212

National Centre for Scientific Research Demokritas, 124, 252
National Geographic, 261
National and Kapodistrian University of Athens, 118
Naucratis, 146
Navarino Bay, Battle of, 37
Naxos, 13
Nearchus, 86, 201
Neave, Richard, 111, 112, 120, 134, 153, 247
Nebuchadnezzar, 24
Nectanebo II, 202
Nectar of the Gods, 156
Nemea, Neman Games, 109
Neokastro, 6
Neoptolemus, tragic actor, 19
Nestor's Palace, 263
New York Times, 98
New York University, 110, 177
Nicesipolis, 82, 90, 94, 139, 226–7
Nicomachus of Thebes, 50, 197
Nile river, delta, 26, 87, 94, 146, 202, 212, 232
Nineveh, 43
Noah's Ark, 74

Obols, 157–9
 see also coinage
Odysseus, 124
Olbia, 213
Old Testament, 43
Olmstead, Albert Ten Eyck, 41
Olympian gods, 2, 19, 143, 146, 151, 159, 269, 276
Olympias, 18–20, 81–91, 94, 96, 107, 111, 118, 132, 155, 157, 178, 180, 195–201, 222–40, 251, 271
Olympic Games, 9, 15, 81, 102, 195, 263
Onesicritus, 184, 193
Oracles, 22

Orchomenus, 265
Orpheus, Orphism, 143, 148, 151, 160, 188, 196–7, 268
Ossuary urns, 31, 52, 58, 131, 151, 155, 157
 see also larnax
Ottoman Empire, Ottoman Turks, 37, 38
Oxford University, 45
Oxyartes, 238

Pacers, see lateral movers
Paeonia, Paeonians, 113, 227
Pakistan, 114, 184, 256
Palagia, Olga, 118, 181, 233, 236–8
Palatitsia, 6, 38, 104, 116
Paleodemology, 129
Paliadeli, Chrysoula, 1, 50, 114, 116, 124–5, 129, 140, 161, 173, 175, 178, 231, 248–9, 252, 261, 269–70, 274
Paliampela, 6
Panegyris, 83
Panticapaeum, 212
Parmenides, 255
Parmenio, 78
Parthians, 186, 209
Parthenon, 65, 100, 241
Papyrus, vii, 13, 154, 187–91
Pasargadae, 203
Pases, 157–8
Patroclus, 59, 104, 148–54, 178, 183
Pausanias, travelographer, 29, 67, 74, 81, 109, 169, 263–4, 267
Pausanias of Orestis, bodyguard-assassin, 19, 83–4, 132, 201
Pausanias, jilted lover of Philip II, 228
Pectoral, 54, 103, 218–19, 241
Peleus, 197
Pella, 16, 30–1, 33, 41, 45, 60, 65, 78, 80–1, 85–9, 101, 108, 116, 125–6, 148, 151, 160, 170, 175, 178–9,

188, 193, 195–6, 199, 215, 217, 219, 230, 233, 238, 271, 273
Pelion Mountains, 267
Peloponnese, 7, 9, 11, 31, 37, 59, 85, 89, 146, 183, 251, 263–4
Peloponnesian War, 5, 15, 90, 164, 252
Pelops, 104
Penelope, 124
Pennsylvania State University, 103
Penthesilea, 70, 72
Perdiccas I, 20
Perdiccas II, 15
Perdiccas III, 17, 84, 94, 228, 233
Perdiccas, bodyguard, 26, 85–7, 107, 175, 199, 225, 229–30, 232, 239
Pergamum, 249
Pericles, 203, 263
Peristeri, Katerina, 164, 199
Peritrachelia, Peritrachelidia, Peritrachelidion, 241
Persephone, 50, 102, 143, 194–8
Persepolis, 22–3, 97, 204
Perseus, hero, 24
Perseus, Macedonian king, 32–3, 124, 274
Persians, Persian Empire, Great Kings, vii, 8–9, 12–24, 26, 28–9, 52, 64–5, 68, 72–3, 77, 80–6, 97, 103–108, 114, 144, 147, 159, 168, 184, 186, 201, 203, 206, 212, 216–17, 222, 225, 238–9, 249, 252, 259, 267, 274–5
Petasos, 114
Petsas, Photius, 41, 98
Peucestas, 104
Phalangites, 17, 32–3, 52, 78, 79, 132, 219, 224, 274
  see sarissa
Phalanx, 14, 32–3, 78–80, 266
Phateli tribe, 214
Pheidippides, 13

Phila, daughter of Antipater, 91, 180, 181
Phila of Elimea, 94, 193, 226
Philinna, 82, 94, 226
Philinnion, 193, 198
Philip II:
  appearance, 52, 100, 111, 168, 175, 177, 179
  as hostage; court, 19, 32, 74, 80–2, 102, 183, 193, 223, 227, 254
  birth; accession, 17, 85, 94, 103
  bodyguards; plans to invade Persia, 64, 83, 140, 147, 159–60, 201, 222
  character, 77–83, 97
  cult of, 48, 198
  currency, 18, 59, 81, 159, 160, 179
  death, vii, 19–20, 56, 58, 83–4, 89, 94, 97–104, 109–12, 117–20, 130, 132, 146, 153–7, 167, 184, 191, 201, 222, 226–8, 232–5, 238, 240
  diplomacy, 9, 77–83, 97, 227, 229, 238, 254
  divine/divination, 18–19, 48, 99, 146–7, 154, 198, 263
  extent of empire, 18, 113, 254–5
  facial reconstruction, 111–12, 117, 120
  finances, 19, 31, 85
  generalship, 17–18, 77–83, 97, 132–4, 164, 199, 217–19, 227, 133–4, 252–5, 274
  in legend, 32
  lineage, 80, 105
  military reforms, 8, 17–19, 32, 52, 78–82, 218, 224, 252–5, 274
  reign/era, 44, 94, 96, 116, 119, 152, 178, 190–1, 197, 212–13, 224–8
  relationship with Alexander, 18, 77, 83, 180, 256–7

religion, 18–19, 22, 77, 78,
    146–7, 267
Scythians, 96–8, 132, 165, 166,
    217–24, 229, 238, 258
sexuality; armour and insignia,
    101–105
wounds, 97–100, 111–12, 120,
    132–7, 168–9, 196, 218, 223–4
Philip III Arrhidaeus, 26, 82, 83–7,
    89–99, 101, 104, 105–12, 117–20,
    132, 140, 166–9, 175, 184, 190,
    197, 225–6, 230–4, 244
Philip IV, 238
Philip V, 32
Philippeion, Olympia, 99, 233, 263
Philippics, 18
    see also coinage
Philonicus, 256
Philotas, 177
Philoxenus of Eretria, 105, 231
Phocian Wall, 266
Phoenicia, Phoenicians, 22, 103, 146,
    182–3, 187
Phrygia, Phrygians, 12, 45, 68, 74, 105,
    108, 135, 145, 240
Pieria, hills/mountains 5–6, 8, 35, 38,
    115, 261
Pike, pikemen, see sarissa
Pillars of Hercules, 183
Pindar, 15, 22, 67
Pindarus Mountains, 88
Piraeus, 14
Pisa, Peloponnese, 263
Pisa University, 145
Pixodarus, 83, 140
Plataea, 13–15, 108, 144, 194, 212
Plato, Platonic, Platonism, 20, 103,
    109, 177, 180, 194, 221, 232–3,
    264, 269
Pleurias, 22
Pleurisy, 128, 222

Pliny the Elder, 50, 150, 186, 189, 205,
    247, 257–8, 261
Plutarch, 26, 30, 45, 60, 73, 82, 84–6,
    98, 105–107, 177–83, 196, 199,
    239, 257
Pluto, 102, 143, 151, 197
Pnyx, 97
Poisons, poisoning, 23, 64, 72, 88, 97,
    150, 156, 239
Polyaenus, 225, 228
Polybius, 31, 33, 108, 124, 240
Polyperchon, 87–91, 107, 230–1,
    240–1, 251
Pompeii, House of the Faun, 105, 127,
    213, 247
Pompey the Great, 73
Pontus, 39, 45, 70, 73
Porus, 23, 106
Portents, 24, 143, 203
Poseidon, 79, 143, 275
Poseidippus of Pella, 170
Prag, John, 111–12, 120, 134,
    153, 247
Priam, 43–4, 72, 89, 148
Priene, 109
Primogeniture, 17, 82
Princeton University, 151
Prophesies, 11, 20, 22, 274
Psammetichus, pharaoh, 146
Phthia, 267
Ptolemy I Soter, bodyguard, 26,
    28–31, 34, 85, 87, 94, 107, 173,
    175, 202–203, 222, 232
Ptolemy II Philadelphus, 202, 264
Ptolemy the Thunderbolt, 28
Ptolemy IV, 202
Punjab, 106, 256
Pydna, 6–8, 48, 89–90, 108, 129, 170,
    198, 227, 268, 271
    Battle of, 7, 32–3, 124–5, 234, 274
Pyrrha, 74

Pyrrhus of Epirus, 30–3, 140, 198–9, 234, 264–5, 267
Pythagoras, 126, 196
Pythia, 11, 29, 196
Pythian Games, 265

Quiver, *see gorytos*

Reincarnation, 192–4, 196, 198, 201, 204
Renaissance, European, 37
   Macedonian, 34
Rhodes, Rhodians, 13, 175, 249
Rhomaios, Konstantine, 3, 39, 44–5
Rhoxane, 24, 57, 85, 86, 90, 164, 175, 238–43, 251
Rhyton, 241
Rolle, Renate, 210
Rome, Republic, Empire, period, writers, 8, 11, 29–34, 52, 60, 70, 72–3, 77, 84, 88, 94, 124, 132, 135, 136, 150–1, 157, 161, 167, 175, 184, 186–7, 201–202, 219, 222, 225, 247, 253, 257–8, 264–5, 267–8, 274
   invasions, 30–4, 108, 125, 199, 234–5
   Roman army, 30–4, 73, 125, 199, 234, 258
   senate, 32
Romeyka, 70
Roumlouki, Romioi, 38
Royal Roads, Persian, 225
Russia, Russian Steppes, 37, 58, 64, 68, 210, 214, 216–17, 245

Sacred Band, 199
   see also Thebes
Sacred Disease, 143
Sacred Wars, 78
Sagaris, Scythian axe, 206
   see also axes
Saint Demetrius, 263, 275

Saint Tryphon, 8
Saka, *see* Scythians
Salamis, 14, 108
Samaras, Antonis, 164
Samos, 13, 88, 134, 253
Samothrace, 195–6
Sanctuary of Apollo, Delphi, 29, 77, 196, 265, 275
Sanctuary of the Mother of the Gods, 116, 196
Sanisera, 253
Saratov University, 213
Sarcophagus, 52, 54, 202
Sardis, 12, 88
Sarissa, *see* pike, pikemen
Sarmatians, 67, 73, 258
Sassanids, Sassanid Empire, 209
Satyrus, 226–7
Sauromatae, 67
Scarabs, 145–6
Sceptres, 50, 52, 103–107, 188, 190
Schliemann, Heinrich, 39, 43–4, 59, 74, 147–8, 151, 253
Schliemann, Sophie, 148
Scipio, 34
Scythes, son of Heracles, 68
Scythia, Scythians, 54, 58, 63–74, 84–5, 89, 96–8, 132, 138, 156, 162, 165–6, 196, 205–24, 229, 238, 240–1, 244, 258–60, 275
Sea of Azov, 66
   see also Lake Maeotis
Sea Peoples, 9
Second Macedonian War, 32
Second World War, 39, 44, 112
Seleucus, Seleucids, 26, 28, 31–4, 222
Seljuk Sultanate, 35
SEM (scanning electron microscopy), 145–6, 161, 187
Sema, Alexandria, 202–203
Seneca the Younger, 37, 93

Serbia, 39
Seres, 186
Sevasti, 271
Seven Sages of Greece, 70
Seven Wonders of the ancient world, 263
Shinbone, 54, 136–7, 167
Sibyls, 144
Sicily, 30, 133, 196, 212
Sidon, 182
Sigeium, 103
Silk, Silk Road, 129, 186–7
Silver, Vergina/Greek artefacts, 7, 30, 35, 50, 52, 54–60, 105, 142, 147, 159–60, 182, 211, 218–19, 249, 265
   Agios Athanasios, 179
   currency, 32, 79, 157–60, 216, 257
   extraction, 199, 212–16
   Persian, 199
   plating, 216
   provenance of, 199, 212–16
   purity 199, 212–16
   Scythian, 67, 211, 217, 223
   Silver mines/locations, 18, 79, 160, 199, 212, 219
Silver Shields, 107, 222
Simonides, 13, 267
Sindos, 148
Sinope, 213
Sisygambis, 184
Siwa, 199, 201–202
Skagit Valley College, 124
Skopje, 113–14, 164
Skudra, 12
Slavs, Slavic, 112, 164, 254
Smithsonian Museum of Natural History, 124, 129
Socrates, 77, 110, 173, 264
Sogdia, 238, 241
Solomon, king of mines, 74
Solon, 70

Sophocles, 195
Souvaltzi, Liana, 202
Spantidaki, Stella, 186–7
Sparta, Spartans, 13–15, 29, 31, 78, 125, 177, 194, 196, 217, 263, 264–7, 269
Spells, 143
Stanford University, 210, 259
Stansfield, Jim, 261
Staters, 159–60
   see also coinage
Stoics, stoicism, 32
Stone, Oliver, 120
Strabo, 184, 186, 212, 241
Strymon river, 15, 34, 164, 199, 225
Styx river, 157–8
Successors, vii, 9, 34, 104, 138, 231, 239–40
   successor kingdoms, vii, 9, 34, 114, 231, 239
   Successor Wars, 9, 28, 91, 97, 107, 170, 222, 230, 239, 249
Sulla, 267
Superstition, 33, 143–4, 160
Susa, 22, 24, 86, 183–4
Suttee, 97, 223
Symphysis, pubic, 134–5, 221
Symposium, ancient court, 80, 178–81, 271
Syracuse, 133
Syria, 26, 33–4, 87, 105–108, 225, 230, 232

Tanais river, 67
   see also Don river
Tarquinia, 136
Tarsus, medallion, 52
Temenus, Temenids, 11–12, 15, 65, 116
Temple of Athena, Troy, 103
Temple of Nymphs, Mieza, 80
Temple of Zeus, Olympia, 65, 263

Tetradrachms, 160
  see also coinage
Texas A&M University, 258
Textiles, 145, 162, 183–7, 261
Thalestris, 72
Thebes, Thebans, 14, 21, 50, 78, 196, 197
  Theban Sacred Band, 199
Themelis, Petros, 241
Themiscyra, 66
Thermaic Gulf, 5, 37, 256
Thermodon river, 66
Thermopylae, 13, 19, 28–9, 265–7
Theophilus, 105
Theophrastus, 150, 189
Theopompus, 134, 183
Theseus, hero who founded Athens, 67, 72, 217
Thesmophoria, 195
Thessalonica, 3, 5, 39, 56, 123, 139, 148, 161, 170, 194, 210, 235, 248, 260–1, 275
Thessalonice, 90, 94, 226–7, 231, 236, 238, 275
Thessaly, Thessalians, 14, 17, 20, 28, 32, 34, 37, 82, 87, 89, 94, 123, 143, 146, 181, 226, 256–7, 261, 267
Thetis, 197
Third Macedonian War, 33
Three Fates, 50, 197, 233
Thrace, Thracians, 12–14, 18–21, 26, 28–34, 47, 77, 89, 96, 98, 105, 113, 115, 132, 166, 169, 188, 211, 217–18, 222–3, 226, 244, 254–6, 259, 269
Thucydides, 5, 15, 90, 203, 212, 252, 265
Tibia, 136
Tigris, river, 255
Tiryns, 253
Titans, 195

Tito, Josip Broz, 113
Tlepolemus, 264
Tolland Man, 127
Tomb I, 48–50, 57, 99–101, 104, 110–12, 120, 139–41, 166–9, 194, 197–8, 224, 231–5, 240, 244, 247, 252–3, 261, 269, 277
Tomb II, 2, 6, 8, 48–61, 63–74, 84, 89–112, 115–21, 124, 126–39, 144, 148–62, 165–70, 173–84, 187–91, 193, 198, 204–206, 210–15, 217–28, 231–5, 238–40, 243–4, 247, 249, 251, 253, 261, 269–71, 277
Tomb III, 'Prince's Tomb', 56–8, 60, 99, 101, 115, 142, 188, 190–1, 214, 224, 233, 235, 236–43, 248–51, 269–71, 277
Tomb IV, 'Tomb of the Free-Standing Columns', 58, 234–5, 270
Tomb of Ajax, 253
Tomb of Persephone, *see* Tomb I
Tomb/grave robbers, 2, 31, 45, 50, 102, 118, 140–1, 169, 233, 235
Tomyris, 209
Trachones, 186
Trajan, 73
Treaty of Bucharest, 38
Treister, Mikhail, 214
Triballi, 98, 169, 223
Tripod, 11, 52, 102, 109, 150
Troy, Trojan War, Wooden Horse, 11–12, 18, 22–3, 43–4, 59, 65, 72, 74, 83, 91, 103–107, 116, 135, 148–54, 156, 158, 178, 183, 196, 245, 253, 267, 270
Tsimbidou-Avlonitou, Maria, 180–1
Turkey, Turks, Turkic, 35, 37–9, 44–5, 68, 73, 105, 123, 145, 148, 181, 183
Turkmenistan, 259

Tuscany, 136
Tutankhamun, 43, 127, 145, 171, 253
Tyche, 170
Tyre, 22, 182–3
    Siege of, 182
    Tyrian Purple, 145–6, 183
Tzamala, 161
    Wool, 64, 73, 114, 183, 184–7

Ubelaker, Douglas, 124
UCLA, 161
Ukraine, 64, 67, 68, 183, 209–13, 217, 245
Underworld, 20, 102, 126, 143, 149, 151, 157–8, 193–7
University of Calgary, 228
University of Cambridge, 7, 183, 187–8
University of Colorado, 110
University of Glasgow, 270
University of Heidelberg, 145
University of Illinois, 123
University of London, 188
University of Manchester, 111, 248, 252, 269
University of Michigan, 187
University of Paris, 98
University of Utah, 99
University of Washington, 124, 161–2, 247

Valla, 38, 114–15
Valley of the Kings, 43, 127, 253
Vavelidis, Michael, 212, 214
Veil of Lethe, 149
Vergina, *see* Aegae
Vergina Archaeological Museum, 5–6, 8, 102–103, 113–16, 137–9, 144, 184, 191, 205, 211, 218, 222, 234, 238, 273–4
Vergina Star, 52, 54, 101, 113, 116,

Veria, 5, 44, 127, 161, 191, 236, 238, 271, 273
Veterans, of the campaigns, 28, 87, 89, 107, 116, 199, 230–1
Via Egnatia, 33–4, 161
Vienna, 37
Viking, 247

Webster Wilde, Lynn, 209
Wheeler, Sir Mortimer, 121
White, Hugh, 120
Wynn-Antikas, Laura, viii, 6–8, 121, 123–44, 151–62, 169, 171, 173, 175, 183–90, 206, 210–21, 236, 241, 243, 252–6, 260, 261, 266–77
Wreaths, 18–19, 52, 54, 56–8, 63, 78, 81, 101, 116, 125, 131, 148, 154–5, 175, 180, 249–51, 256, 264, 271

Xenophon, 78, 109, 194, 257
Xerxes I, 13–14, 18, 29, 104, 108–109, 144, 212, 266
Xirotiris, Nikolaos, 93–8, 111–12, 117, 132–5, 139–40, 166–9, 240, 252, 269
X-Rays, XRF (X-Ray Fluorescence), 127, 142, 145, 158, 216, 261

Yamnaya, 246
Yugoslavia, 39, 113

Zachos, 98
Zama, 33
Zambas, Costas
Zeus, 44, 50, 56, 68, 79, 81, 143, 170, 195, 197–8, 206, 267, 275
    Zeus-Ammon, 199–202
    Zeus of Freedom, 267
    Zeus Meilichius, 196
    Zeus Philippos, 146
    Zeus of water-streams, 267